AKHENATEN and NEFERTITI

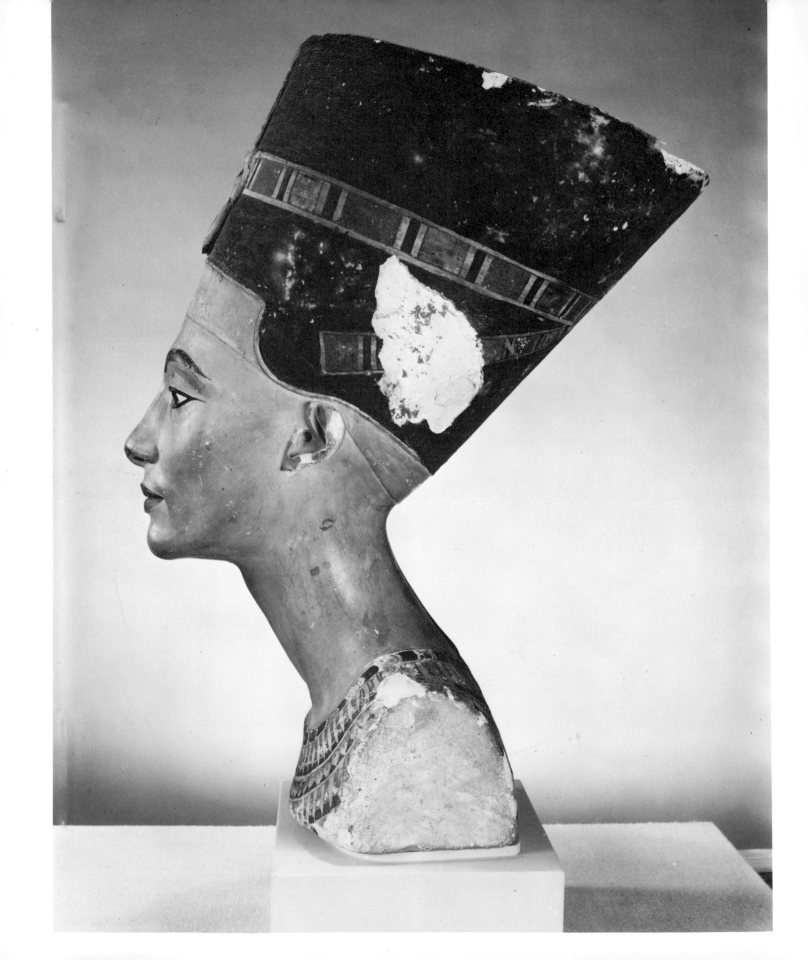

AKHENATEN and NEFERTITI

Cyril Aldred

A Studio Book

The Brooklyn Museum
in Association with
The Viking Press
New York

TITLE PAGE: Fig. 1.   Painted limestone bust of Nefertiti. This celebrated portrait is usually accepted as the studio model prepared by the master sculptor from which lesser craftsmen would fashion their likenesses of the Queen. Excavated by the Deutsche Orient-Gesellschaft in 1912 in the studio of the Chief Sculptor Tuthmose at Tell el Amarna. Late Period. Height 48 cm. Ägyptisches Museum, Berlin (West) 21300.

The Brooklyn Museum in association with The Viking Press, Inc.
First published in 1973 by The Viking Press, Inc.
625 Madison Avenue, New York, N.Y. 10022
Published simultaneously in Canada by
The Macmillan Company of Canada Limited
SBN 670-11139-2
Library of Congress catalog card number: 73-6065
Printed in U.S.A.

CONTENTS

Foreword	7
Preface	9
Introduction: The Amarna Revolution	11
The Historical Outline	16
The Monuments of Akhenaten and Nefertiti	28
The Development of the Amarna Style—The Early Period	48
The Development of the Amarna Style—The Later Phases	58
Iconography	67
The Character of Amarna Art	72
Notes	80
Catalogue	89
Bibliography	224
Concordance I	230
Concordance II	231

SEE PAGE 31

FOREWORD

Indirectly, this book has come into being because on August 7, 1823, the citizens of the Village of Brooklyn established an Apprentices' Library. That library soon became a repository for objects as well as books, and twenty years later it was renamed The Brooklyn Institute, forerunner of The Brooklyn Institute of Arts and Sciences, of which The Brooklyn Museum is a part to this day.

The year 1973 therefore marks the 150th anniversary of the planting of the seed from which the Museum grew to become one of the major art museums of the United States. Among its most important assets is the Department of Egyptian and Classical Art, and that Department was accordingly designated some three years ago by Thomas S. Buechner, then Director of the Museum, to assemble an exhibition of Egyptian art to celebrate a century and a half of growth and achievement on the part of the Institute and its Museum. The subject chosen for the exhibition was the age of Akhenaten—the so-called Amarna Period—and more than three years have gone into its preparation.

For writing a catalogue of this jubilee exhibition the Museum has been fortunate in securing the services of Cyril Aldred, a friend of long standing and one of the few great art historians among Egyptologists of today. Mr. Aldred is a leading authority on the art and archaeology of Dynasty XVIII and is the author of a recent study of King Akhenaten, the most enigmatic ruler of that Dynasty.

The book he has produced for The Brooklyn Museum is more than a mere catalogue. It not only contains meticulous descriptions of about 180 objects gathered in Europe and the United States especially for this exhibition, but it also provides an Introduction that offers a new interpretation of the fateful seventeen years (1378–1362 B.C.) during which Akhenaten and his consort Nefertiti broke with a tradition of one and a half millennia in an endeavor to create a new philosophy of life and a new style of art. Beautifully written and abundantly illustrated, Mr. Aldred's book should serve for years to come as a commentary on one of the most complex and controversial periods of Egyptian art and history.

Bernard V. Bothmer
Curator of Egyptian and Classical Art
February 1973   The Brooklyn Museum

CHRONOLOGY

ARCHAIC PERIOD		MIDDLE KINGDOM	
Dynasties I–II	c. 3100–2686 B.C.	Dynasties XI–XIII	c. 2060–1674 B.C.
OLD KINGDOM		SECOND INTERMEDIATE PERIOD	
Dynasties III–VI	c. 2686–2181 B.C.	Dynasties XIV–XVII	c. 1674–1559 B.C.
FIRST INTERMEDIATE PERIOD		NEW KINGDOM	
Dynasties VII–X	c. 2181–2040 B.C.	Dynasties XVIII–XX	c. 1559–1085 B.C.

DYNASTY XVIII

Ahmose	1559–1531 B.C.
Amenhotep I	1534–1504 B.C.
Tuthmosis I	1514–1502 B.C.
Tuthmosis II	1504–1489 B.C.
Tuthmosis III	1490–1436 B.C.
Hatshepsut	1489–1469 B.C.
Amenhotep II	1444–1412 B.C.
Tuthmosis IV	1414–1405 B.C.
Amenhotep III	1405–1367 B.C.
Amenhotep IV (Akhenaten)	1378–1362 B.C.
Smenkhkare	1366–1363 B.C.
Tutankhaten (Tutankhamen)	1362–1353 B.C.
Ay	1353–1349 B.C.
Haremheb	1349–1319 B.C.

DYNASTY XIX

Ramesses I	1320–1318 B.C.
Sety I	1318–1304 B.C.
Ramesses II	1304–1237 B.C.
six other kings	to 1200 B.C.

DYNASTY XX
1200–1085 B.C.

PREFACE

I owe a great debt of gratitude to the Curator and Staff of the Department of Egyptian and Classical Art in The Brooklyn Museum, including the Wilbour Library of Egyptology, for unstinted help and encouragement at every stage in the preparation of this work, from the marshaling of data of all kinds to the lavish provision of photographs in color and black-and-white especially taken for this study. Whatever merit the book may possess is entirely due to their expert ministrations without which it could never have been started, still less finished. In particular I am under heavy obligation to Elizabeth Riefstahl, Associate Curator Emeritus, whose keen eye and editorial pen have corrected my errors, removed ambiguities, and improved my expression. I am also greatly obliged to Dr. J. Málek of the Griffith Institute, Oxford, for a large number of bibliographical references provided at short notice. And special thanks are due to Dr. Donald Redford of the Akhenaten Temple Project, University Museum, University of Pennsylvania, for permitting me to examine his forthcoming report on the *talatat* uncovered at Karnak.

I must, however, absolve my colleagues in The Brooklyn Museum from all responsibility for the opinions advanced in this work which are my own. If they too feel that they can share some, at least, of my views, I shall feel that my labor has been well rewarded.

C.A.

57399

INTRODUCTION: THE AMARNA REVOLUTION

The personality and ideas of the dishonored Pharaoh Akhenaten, who in the fourteenth century B.C. for little more than a decade turned the deep and powerful flow of ancient Egyptian culture into unfamiliar channels, first aroused the interest of an earlier generation of Egyptologists when they lighted upon the remains of his capital city at present-day Tell el Amarna in Middle Egypt. This site of the township that he built as the "horizon" or seat of the Aten, his own version of the Egyptian sun god, has given its name in modern times to the culture he promoted, from its beginnings in Karnak to its extinction seventeen years later with the death of Akhenaten. Subsequent investigations at Tell el Amarna and elsewhere during the past century have, if anything, increased the curiosity of scholar and layman alike, and from being the most obscure and execrated of all the ancient kings of Egypt, Akhenaten now bids fair to become the most praised of her famous men. For he presents us with a rare, even unique, case of a revolutionary who not only imposed his changes from above, but in the process also promoted a novel style of art that has left us more than its proper quota of masterpieces, including the most publicized work of antiquity in the painted bust of his chief queen, Nefertiti (Fig. 1).

But Akhenaten's principal claim to fame has been his substitution of an abstract and monotheistic religion for the many cults of ancient Egypt. This was the worship of the Aten, a heavenly father and kingly god, manifest in the sunlight. In imposing this doctrine upon his subjects, Akhenaten swept away much of the obscure imagery and esoteric symbolism of the old religion and replaced them by an easily recognizable and immediately attractive iconography centered around the public and domestic activities of the royal family (Figs. 2, 3; Nos. 16, 130). The hymn that was written to the Aten, perhaps by the King himself, with its organic sequence of thought has been likened to Psalm 104, that meditation upon the might and providence of a similarly effulgent god, and has won for him firm partisans among successive generations of historians and students of religion. One of the greatest of his champions has been led to claim him as the world's first idealist and the world's first individual: the most remarkable figure of the ancient world before the Hebrews.[1]

Recent research, more keen and critical, however, has shorn Akhenaten of many of the virtues that were once thought to be his alone among the pharaohs. Scholars no longer tend to see in him the social revolutionary who replaced the old hereditary ruling caste by new men of lowly origins ready to accept his heretical doctrines. Those of his followers whose connections can be traced appear to be the sons of his father's officials, even when they declare in the usual deprecatory fashion that their King had advanced them to their exalted stations from humble beginnings.[2]

Similarly those modern eulogists who see in Akhenaten a pacifist visionary, eager to preach the brotherhood of mankind even among the traditional foes in Syria and Kush and to repress the bellicose claims of his army, have been embarrassed by the discovery of frag-

Fig. 2. Painted limestone stela from a house shrine, showing Akhenaten and Nefertiti seated on stools of state with their eldest daughter, Merytaten, between them, and the next two on their mother's lap. Akhenaten holds out an earring to Merytaten, while Nefertiti places a hand on her head. The play with the trinket is repeated by Maketaten, who dangles an earring for Ankhesenpaaten. The disk of the Aten with its rays bringing life to the nostrils of the King and Queen shines down upon this scene of domestic bliss. Excavated by the Deutsche Orient-Gesellschaft in 1912 outside the boundary wall of a house at Tell el Amarna. Early Period. Height 43.5 cm. Egyptian Museum, Cairo JE 44865.

OPPOSITE PAGE: Fig. 3. Painted limestone stela from a house shrine, showing Amenhotep III and Queen Tiye seated upon thrones before altars heaped with offerings. Opinions differ as to whether this is a posthumous representation of Amenhotep III, carved after Year 8 of the reign of his son, or an icon commemorating the living King made late in the reign of his co-regent. Excavated by the Egypt Exploration Society in 1924 in the house of Panehsy at Tell el Amarna. Late Period. Height 30 cm. British Museum, London 57399.

ments of battle scenes and reliefs showing him in the age-old stance of the conquering king smiting the enemies of Egypt (No. 57). The pacifist interpretation of his foreign policy has also to be abandoned in the face of evidence that there was no wholesale collapse of his northern "empire" during his reign.[3] Nor did he neglect the army in favor of other sections of the community. Soldiers figure prominently in the Amarna reliefs, and of the score or so of favored courtiers who were granted tombs at Tell el Amarna by their grateful King, at least half a dozen were military officers. It is in fact clear from the reforms that had to be introduced by his successors that during the reign of Akhenaten the army had become corrupt through being granted too much power and privilege.[4]

Another change that has been accredited to him is the suppression of a superstitious and reactionary priesthood that continued to act in overt or hidden opposition throughout his reign. Such ideas as a struggle between Church and State, which arose in nineteenth-century Europe and obsessed its contemporary historians, will not stand up to close examination in the world of the Late Bronze Age in the fourteenth century B.C. As so often happens in religious conflict, a mere nuance separated the doctrines of one set of beliefs from those of another. Both the Aten heresy and its great rival the Amun orthodoxy believed in a Supreme Creator, a Sole One, who was hidden or far off. Both were solar cults, but the new religion placed rather more emphasis upon the visible image of godhead in the light that radiated from the sun disk, the Aten.[5] In the milieu of the Late Bronze Age, however, there was no possibility of a secular government; religion and politics were but aspects of the same essential activity. The king was ex officio the high priest of every deity in every temple of the land, the intermediary between man and the gods. Members of the royal family, such as Akhenaten's maternal grandparents and his uncle, held high and lucrative posts in the hierarchy of the important gods Min, Amun, and Re-Atum. The King himself was the Chief Prophet of the Aten (No. 11), and it is probable that the priesthood of his god was drawn from the sacerdotal and lay staffs of the great rival cults, who alone would have had the administrative experience necessary to establish and maintain the new foundations in the major cities of Egypt—places like Heliopolis, Memphis, Akhmim, and Hierakonpolis, besides Thebes and Tell el Amarna itself—where monuments to the Aten have been found.

In his teachings Akhenaten placed great emphasis upon the principle of Maat. "Living in Maat" was one of the epithets he constantly applied to himself, and even the name of his state barge seems to have meant "Appearing in Maat" (No. 114), a name that had already been given to the temple of Amenhotep III at Soleb. The word *maat* was formerly translated as "truth," and the special stress that Akhenaten gave to this term is often held responsible for a realism or truth to nature that many observers have claimed to detect in the style of art which he promoted. The unflattering appearance, often bordering on caricature, in which his artists were usually accustomed to depict him is ascribed to this love of truth, a thesis we shall examine in due course. Here it will suffice to point out that *maat* in Amarna contexts refers to that harmonious, well-regulated cosmic order that was established at the beginning of Creation and that has nothing to do with any abstract standard of veracity.[6]

If many of the innovations that have been accredited to Akhenaten today appear less radical than they once did, it is because they are now seen to have already existed in the subconscious areas of Egyptian thought and required little stimulus to be brought to the surface. For the world of Dynasty XVIII into which Akhenaten was born had suffered drastic changes from the Egypt that had preceded it. The Asiatic occupation of Lower Egypt in the seventeenth century B.C. and the accession of its Hyksos kings to the throne of Egypt had transformed the culture of that land as it had developed during the millennium and a half since the first pharaoh had united the North and the South into one kingdom. The introduction of the horse-drawn chariot from Asia at about the same time had wrought profound changes in the world of the Late Bronze Age all over the Near East. This formidable fighting vehicle in the hands of warriors expert in the management of horses and proficient in the use of new weapons, such as the javelin, composite bow, and heavy bronze sword, scattered to the winds the feudal levies opposed to them as well as the old order that had sustained such outmoded forces. The new warrior society, which is so memorably mirrored in the *Iliad*, spread throughout the Near East, forming a ruling military caste among the petty states of Syria and Palestine. Egypt itself did not escape its impact, and in liberating themselves from Hyksos supremacy the Theban princes who challenged their pretensions adopted all the devices, strategy, and organization of the new order, doubtless incorporating into their armies the Asiatic condottieri they had defeated in the last phases of their struggle. By the time that Ahmose, the first king of Dynasty XVIII, was firmly in the saddle, all vestiges of feudalism had been replaced by a military autocracy which set the pattern of government in Egypt for the rest of its history as an independent state.[7]

In the process the pharaoh lost much of his eminence as a remote god incarnate and became an invincible warlord, the incarnation on the battlefield of warrior gods such as the Asiatic Baal and Reshep or the Egyptian Montu. He is shown in his chariot charging alone into the thick of Egypt's foes like some Homeric hero, while his athletic feats as horseman, archer, or oarsman are vaunted as truly superhuman. After his death his mortuary cult was observed daily in large temples, the walls of which were decorated with records of the great deeds of his lifetime.

His immediate entourage was drawn from his *maryannu*,[8] that military aristocracy which was a cardinal feature of government in all the nations of the Near East. The father of Akhenaten, Amenhotep III, had married the daughter of the commander of his chariot forces, and Akhenaten himself seems to have taken as his chief wife Nefertiti, another member of this same powerful military family, which may well have been a collateral of the royal line.[9] The structure of this new society is seen in the form of salutation that foreign potentates employed in addressing their brother the pharaoh, a salutation they employed to greet not only him but also his wives, his chariots, his horses, and his chief men, usually in that order. Foreign wives and slaves, particularly skilled and lively Asiatics, brought their ideas of this new order of society right into the center of Egyptian government and probably account for the fresh delight in personal greatness and the pride in worldly success that are striking features of the age. Such influences can be traced not only in the wealth and luxury of the court but also in the huge temples with their colossi and obelisks that were raised to the gods by their sons, the pharaohs.

With this military government came a more efficient and centralized form of administration in a chain of command from the pharaoh at the head, ruling through his high officers of state, such as the vizier, chief steward and treasurers, and a hierarchy of lesser officials. Though most of these men were scribes without any army training, and their chief qualifications were an ability to read, write, and reckon, they sustained the logistics of a military state. It was clear that this form of government was highly dependent upon the character of the man at the top. Apart from the pharaoh and his heir, there was no individual or group of men whose jurisdiction extended to the entire kingdom even in a subordinate capacity,[10] and thus there was no power capable of challenging the absolute authority of the king. It is small wonder, therefore, that the Vizier Rekhmire should declare, "Every King of Upper and Lower Egypt is a god by whose guidance men live. He is the father and mother of mankind, alone, without a peer."[11] It was this belief that induced the ruling caste to follow the teaching of Akhenaten enthusiastically, however arbitrary or heretical it might have appeared.

In step with this rationalization of the Egyptian political and economic machinery, there was a radical overhaul of doctrine and belief, particularly in the theology taught at Heliopolis, the headquarters of the influential cult of Re, the sun god, and a traditional center of Egyptian thought. Here dogma had been revised and restated, perhaps as a result of contact with other solar religions in Asia. The old sacred books were drastically re-edited and new compilations introduced, expressing a synthesis of ancient beliefs centered around the conception of a supreme sun god, alone without a peer, like a heavenly pharaoh.

During Dynasty XVIII, therefore, under the leaven of foreign ideas, great developments took place in Egyptian thought, particularly in the spheres of religion, cosmogony, economics, and politics. Not all these changes, however, were immediately reflected in art, where a natural conservatism, inseparable from the practice of age-old crafts, regulated form and content. The successful Theban princes who ushered in the brave new world of Dynasty XVIII tried to give some respectability to their rebellion by reviving the hallowed style of the Middle Kingdom and so created a tradition with sufficient momentum to persist for several reigns. New materials, however, were introduced during this period and gave fuller scope to craftsmen and a challenge to designers. The use of bronze in place of copper became more general, glass made a brilliant appearance, and faience reached heights of technical excellence. Everyday speech began to modify the classical traditions of literature and even to infiltrate the monumental texts. The wine of the new world of the Late Bronze Age was straining the fabric of the old bottles of Egyptian orthodoxy. It is likely that many of the changes introduced almost overnight by Akhenaten would have come about in any case, that he merely acted as a catalyst to a reaction that had been long delayed. Though the failure of his teachings led to a hasty scramble back to the *status quo,* many of his innovations remained as permanent features of pharaonic culture, such as the design of the royal tomb, the vernacular language of the monuments, certain fashions of dress, and several features of architectural sculpture.

THE HISTORICAL OUTLINE

Akhenaten was born sometime about the year 1394 B.C., the second son of King Amenhotep III by his chief wife, Queen Tiye. He was called after his father Amenhotep (Amun-is-content), and himself became known to historians as Amenhotep IV on his accession to the throne. His elder brother, Prince Tuthmosis, by virtue of his position as heir apparent, held the office of High Priest of Ptah, the god of Memphis, the chief city of Egypt, and other important priesthoods besides high army command.[12] But as he never succeeded his father, we must assume that he died prematurely, like so many of the first-born of Egypt, and that Prince Amenhotep then stood in his place as the next in line of succession.

During his father's long reign Egypt reached an acme of power and prosperity. Its sphere of influence stretched from the Fourth Cataract of the Nile in the south to the borders of Syria in the north. The wealth of tropical Africa and of the Orient poured into the treasuries of court and temple[13] and supported the mighty building projects of Amenhotep III at Bubastis, Memphis, Thebes, Elephantine, Soleb, and other large cities of Egypt and Nubia. At few periods in the history of Egyptian culture has so widespread and high a standard of artistic achievement been attained, from the monolithic Colossus of Memnon and its companion flanking the entrance to the great mortuary temple of Amenhotep III at Thebes, to exquisite jewels and miniature statuary prepared for his burial and those of his courtiers. This was a high noon of opulence and luxury stimulated by the tastes of civilized Asia and the Aegean, no less potent in the fifteenth century B.C. than they were in the days of Imperial Rome.

At the court of his father, Prince Amenhotep came under the influence of eminent men of the day, foremost among whom was Amenhotep-son-of-Hapu, noted as a skilled administrator who disposed of the manpower of the country and who, in his old age, was appointed the High Steward of the King's eldest daughter, Queen Sitamun. Even in his own lifetime his King had conferred on him the unprecedented honor of a mortuary temple in the row of such royal monuments at Western Thebes. A thousand years after his death, when he was deified, his wisdom was still treasured, though it is lost to us today, and we cannot say whether or not it had any influence in forming the ideas that the young Prince Amenhotep was developing.

Close relatives of Amenhotep-son-of-Hapu, however, must have had privileged access to the heir apparent; for instance, a cousin of his, also called Amenhotep, as the High Steward in Memphis looked after the King's important affairs in that city and even discharged commissions as far afield as Abydos. This official's half brother Ramose was also in due course to become the Chief Minister of Amenhotep IV in Upper Egypt.

Another and even more prominent family was intimately connected with the royal house. Its doyens were Yuya, the Master of the Horse, and his wife, the high priestess Tuyu, the maternal grandparents of

Prince Amenhotep. Yuya, a man of striking appearance, with long wavy hair, broad face, large aquiline nose, and fleshy lips, apparently came from a line of chariot commanders and may have been a close relative of the mother of Amenhotep III. He was sufficiently influential to have arranged the marriage of his daughter Tiye to Amenhotep III, when that monarch was a mere boy.[14] One of his sons, Anen, the uncle of Prince Amenhotep, held high office in the priesthoods of Amun and Re-Atum and was eminent at the court of his royal brother-in-law. It is almost certain that it was another son, Ay, who followed the family profession of chariot commander and subsequently inherited all Yuya's offices at the court of Amenhotep IV. Ay, in fact, appears to have stood in the same relation to Amenhotep IV as Yuya did to Amenhotep III, since Ay's daughter Nefertiti, like her aunt Tiye before her, married the Pharaoh on his elevation to the throne.[15]

At Memphis, Amenhotep IV must early have come under the influence of the sun cult of nearby Heliopolis, where the worship of Re, chief god of the solar pantheon, had undergone a great development since the end of the Middle Kingdom. The rethinking that the priesthood of Re, the traditional wise men of Egypt, had applied to the ancient doctrines of the solar religion was in the direction of a monotheism that did not exclude the old gods but attempted to assimilate them as names, or aspects, of the one god Re, the force that activated the life of the universe. In this reformed doctrine Re is hailed as the sole god who has made myriads out of himself, all gods having come into being from him.[16] The constant element in the transformation that Re was daily thought to undergo, from a living deity by day to a dead god by night moving to a resurrection at dawn, is the Aten or great disk of the sun. The Aten illuminated the world of the dead as well as the living and brought both to life. There is thus little cause for surprise that in time the appearance was accepted for the reality that lay behind it and that the disk became a sun god in its own right. The Aten appears as early as the reign of Tuthmosis IV, when it is described as a great universal god whose commanding position in the sky entitles it to rule over all that it shines upon. In the reign of Amenhotep III it acquired even greater importance, being attached to the names of the King's barge, his palace, some of the royal children, and perhaps the King himself. The expanded form of the Aten's name, expressing a religious teaching or dogma, and therefore sometimes referred to by scholars as "didactic," may well have been devised during the reign of this King, although it was not yet, as later, enclosed in two cartouches as were the principal names of every pharaoh. At least there seems some evidence to show that a shrine was built to the Aten at Thebes during the time of Amenhotep III.[17] The circumstances were therefore propitious for the young Prince Amenhotep to assimilate these new doctrines, particularly as he appears to have had a palace at Heliopolis.[18] He proved a willing pupil who soon surpassed his teachers in his fervor for the new thought and became the adept to whom revelation was granted, and the instigator of change. From the beginning he followed the worship of the sun god under the didactic name that became his profession of faith, "Re-Herakhty, the living, rejoicing in the horizon in his aspect of the light which is in the disk."[19] In a land where the pharaoh was thought to be the latest incarnation of the creator god, the first ruler of Egypt, the entourage of the young King could follow his divinely inspired teaching, or the interpretation he put upon ancient dogma, without any questioning.

The reign of Amenhotep III had seen a great upsurge in antiquarian interest in the remote past, perhaps as a result of research into the ancient archives. An attempt had been made to identify the tomb of an archaic king at Abydos as the burial place of the god Osiris and to make it a center of pilgrimage. Old records were consulted in order to revive the proper ritual for the first jubilee held by the Pharaoh; and it is perhaps no coincidence that an Early Dynastic slate palette should have been reworked on its reverse during the reign of Amenhotep III.[20] This regard for the remote past had indeed begun earlier, in the reign of Tuthmosis IV, who, upon his accession, had released the Great Sphinx of Giza, an embodiment of Re-Herakhty, from engulfing sands, thus honoring a pledge he had made to the god at a time when it had seemed unlikely that he could ever gain the throne of Egypt.

Perhaps an increase in the power and glory of kingship during the reign of Amenhotep III is thus partly the outcome of intensive study of Egypt's past. The emphasis that Amenhotep IV put upon "living in truth" may indicate that he was reviving the ideas of a much earlier age, when the Pharaoh Djoser of Dynasty III, for example, had been Re and the Egyptians' greatest god. At least it is clear that with the advent of the new King, his courtiers worship him as a sun god, prostrating themselves or bending low in his presence (No. 136), and that he has his own prophet like any deity (No. 11). One modern observer has not hesitated to remark that the King was by no means disinclined to claim a share in the sun god's divinity, and that share sometimes approached complete identity.[21]

Whether this exaltation was the result of antiquarian research or the steady progress to absolute grandeur that had characterized the Dynasty, the reign of Amenhotep IV began quietly enough. At some time in his career, presumably when he reached manhood at about sixteen years of age, he was appointed co-regent of Amenhotep III and his rule began. For this event he was given a chief wife, Nefertiti, and a *harim*. High officials, usually the sons of his father's ministers, were appointed to assist him. A complete trousseau of royal possessions, from crowns and thrones to clothing and jewelry, was provided for him, and his names and titularies were established. He assumed the prenomen Neferkheprure-waenre (Beautiful like the forms of Re, the Unique one of Re) and added the epithet, "Divine Ruler of Thebes," to his nomen, Amenhotep, with for good measure the additional phrase, "Great in His Duration." He twice appears in a relief on the Third Pylon at Karnak (Fig. 4) wearing the Blue Crown of his coronation and standing behind the much larger figure of his father, Amenhotep III, in the state barge.[22]

How long he acted as his father's co-regent is a matter of dispute, some authorities claiming that if there was a co-regency at all, it lasted only a few months, other students, this writer among them, postulating a period of as much as eleven years.[23] With this contro-

Fig. 4. Part of the reliefs on the east face of the northern tower of the Third Pylon of the Great Temple of Amun at Karnak, showing Amenhotep III in the state barge of Amun making an offering to the god within a shrine. He is followed by the smaller figure of another king, almost certainly the co-regent Amenhotep IV, which has been almost completely effaced. The damaged area was concealed beneath a layer of plaster into which the representation of an altar was cut.

versy we shall be only marginally concerned in this study.

His chief queen, Nefertiti, was evidently a woman of nonroyal birth since she lays no claim in her titles to being the daughter or sister of a king, though she is referred to as the royal heiress, who was usually a princess holding rights to the throne that passed to her husband on his marriage to her. There is little doubt that she was the daughter of her husband's Master of Horse, Ay, who is addressed constantly by a title which, in the case of his counterpart Yuya at the Court of Amenhotep III, has been translated as "Father-in-law of the King."[24] Ay was an important official of Amenhotep IV and increased his power and privilege throughout his lifetime until he eventually attained the throne on the extinction of the royal line with the death of Tutankhamen (Fig. 5). There is every reason to believe that he owed such distinction to his membership in a privileged family that was a collateral of the royal house. His daughter, Nefertiti, the cousin of Akhenaten, was a very important Queen. Her name is often associated with that of her husband in monumental inscriptions. She usually appears in a tall blue crown, which somewhat resembles the war crown often worn by her husband (Fig. 1). She alone makes offerings to the Aten on a par with the King, and on one occasion she sits on a royal stool while he is content with a simple one (No. 16). In the earlier years of the reign, at least, she is represented as an eminently desirable woman according to an Oriental standard of attractiveness, and this degree of grace is emphasized by the epithets that are applied to her on the monuments: "Fair of Face, Mistress of Happiness, Endowed with Favors, Great of Love." There seems little doubt that, like her husband, she is to be regarded as a deity, perhaps as a Venus figure (No. 31).

In her retinue her sister Mutnodjme figures prominently, being accompanied by two dwarf attendants and accorded a special order of precedence immediately after the royal children. Of these there were eventually six daughters, all apparently born in the first nine years of the reign. The eldest three, Merytaten, Maketaten, and Ankhesenpaaten, were the most important. The youngest three, Neferneferuatentasherit, Neferneferure, and Sotepenre, occasionally appear, but nothing is known of their fate.

The new co-regent inaugurated his reign by opening quarries at Gebel el Silsila for extracting sandstone for the building of a great temple at Karnak to his god "Re-Herakhty in his aspect of the sunlight which is in the Aten." Laborers from one end of the country to the other were marshaled for the work of cutting and transporting the stone, and his high officials were given the responsibility of directing them. This great building project had hardly got underway when an event occurred which at this distance of time has all the appearance of a revolution. The Aten celebrated a jubilee, presumably on the theory that, being a heavenly king, it could acquire the titulary of a pharaoh, have its long didactic name enclosed in two large cartouches, and like a king undergo the rejuvenation of the *sed* festival or jubilee.[25] This epiphany of the Aten coincides with the appearance of a new symbol. In place of the former representation of the god as Re-Herakhty, a man with the head of a falcon crowned with the disk of the sun encircled by a uraeus, there now bursts upon the scene the Disk itself, encircled by the uraeus with a pendant *ankh* sign and sending forth rays of light, each ending in a hand that receives offerings or embraces the persons of the King and Queen or brings to their nostrils the breath of life in the form of an *ankh* (Nos. 16, 27).

The rayed disk, hitherto an unfamiliar symbol and possibly an elaboration of the hieroglyph for sunshine, appears coincidentally with an entirely new style of art. The royal family, particularly the King, is represented in a fashion (No. 6) that is far removed from the refined traditional style that had been perfected in his father's

Fig. 5. Fragment of limestone carved in sunk relief
with figures of Ay and his wife, Tiy, being presented
with gold collars and other valuable gifts by the royal
family at the Window of Appearances of the Palace.
The fragment was cut out of the reliefs on the north
wall of the tomb of Ay at Tell el Amarna, but happily
was recovered for the Cairo Museum. Middle Period.
Length 43 cm. Egyptian Museum, Cairo 10/11/26/1.

21

reign. This new expressionistic style was hastily adopted by the King's followers, who were depicted as bent double or prostrate in the royal presence, and as having to a lesser extent all the physical deformities of their royal exemplar (Fig. 6).

Apart from the sanctuaries of the Aten at Karnak, buildings for the worship of the Disk were erected at other sites, from Heliopolis in the north to Sesebi in the Sudan, but the King was obsessed with the idea of finding "the place of origin"[26] where the Aten had first manifested itself at the creation of the world and of establishing there a resident city dedicated to his god. Other deities had such seats in the large towns where their worship had long been observed. Only the newcomer, the Aten, had no such habitation. Akhenaten claims to have been directed in his search by his heavenly father, the Aten itself. Under this divine guidance the spot in which the Aten originated turned out to be a huge natural amphitheater about eight miles in diameter lying on the east bank of the Nile almost exactly halfway between Memphis and Thebes. Amenhotep called this place Akhetaten, the Horizon or Seat of the Aten, but it is more commonly known today by the modern composite name of Tell el Amarna (Fig. 7).

The King claimed that when he found the site it belonged to no one, whether god, goddess, prince, princess, or any man; and this may well have been the case, for no traces of earlier occupation have been found there, probably because of the lack of cultivable land in the locality. Akhenaten demarcated the site by hewing three stelae (X, M, and K) in the living rock at the northern and southern extremities.[27] Exactly when this was done is problematic, since the dates in the inscriptions have been destroyed, but Year 4 of the reign has been deduced from internal evidence. The inscriptions on the stelae tell how, on the day of demarcation, the King offered a great oblation to Re-Herakhty before summoning his courtiers and showing them the site, declaring that he proposed to build temples and palaces there and to cut a tomb for himself, Nefertiti, and Merytaten in the eastern hills. He then went on to promise that the tombs of his high officials should also be hewn in the same hills, despite any misgivings they might have at leaving their family burial grounds.

The royal family paid another state visit to the site in regnal Year 6 and set up more stelae giving the precise dimensions of the town and specifying its boundaries. During the years between these visits much of the Central City was laid out, with large estates of the wealthy as well as hovels of the poor, with the Great Palace, which ran along the river front for more than 750 meters, the Great Temple, set within an enormous enclosure, and a smaller temple, the Mansion of the Aten. The South City housed the more important officials and had a *maru,* or viewing temple, which contained the "sunshades" or kiosks dedicated to the daily rejuvenation of the Queen and some of the princesses. All the domestic building was in mud-brick, plastered and painted, but had stone fittings, such as windows, doorways, and lustration slabs. The temples and the offices of the Great Palace were built almost entirely of stone.

The later Boundary Stelae dated to Year 6 show that in that year the King had changed his name from Amenhotep to Akhenaten

Fig. 6. Stela in yellow-brown quartzite with figures of Bek and his wife, Tahery. Bek is represented with the heavy breasts and potbelly of his royal patron and teacher. Acquired in the art market in 1963. Early Period. Height 67 cm. Ägyptisches Museum, Berlin (West) 1/63.

Fig. 7. Plan of Tell el Amarna, from W. Stevenson Smith (Smith 1958). Reprinted with the permission of Penguin Books Ltd.

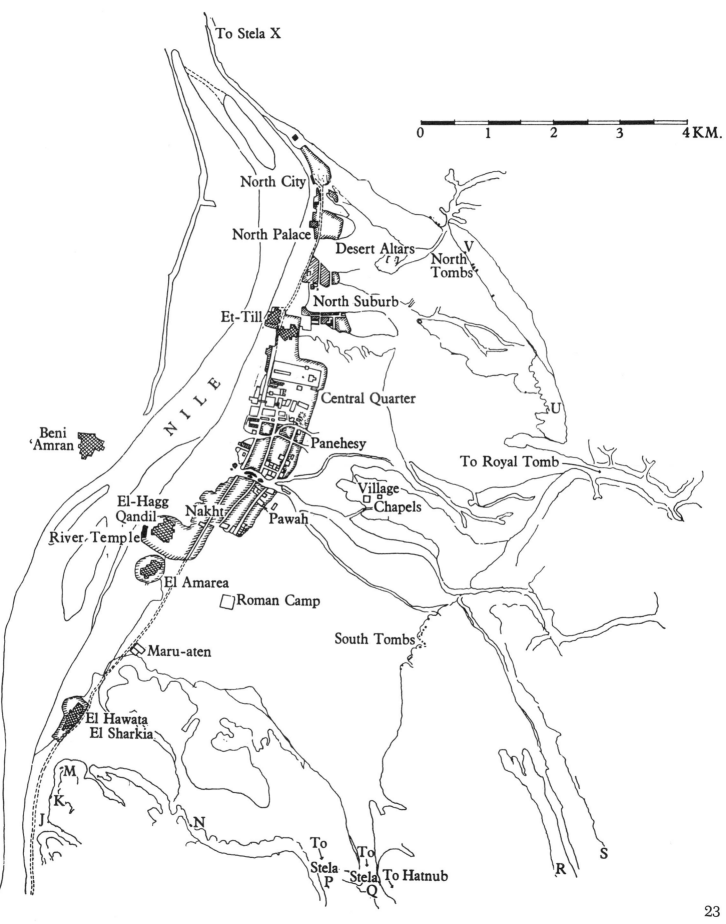

To Stela X

North City

North Palace

Desert Altars

North Suburb

V

North Tombs

Et-Till

N I L E

Central Quarter

U

Beni 'Amran

Panehesy

To Royal Tomb

Village Chapels

El-Hagg Qandil

Nakht

Pawah

River Temple

El Amarea

Roman Camp

South Tombs

Maru-aten

El Hawata El Sharkia

M

K

J

N

To Stela P

To Stela Q

To Hatnub

R

S

0   1   2   3   4 KM.

23

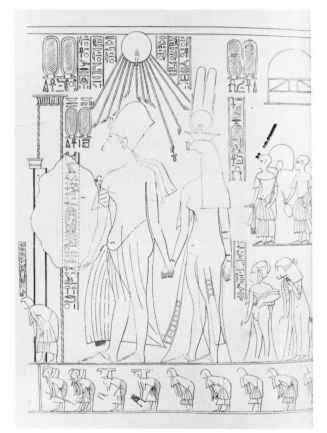

Fig. 8. Relief in the tomb of Huya at Tell el Amarna, showing Akhenaten leading his mother by the hand into her "sunshade" temple. She is followed in the upper register by her retinue and in the lower by her daughter Beketaten with her attendants. After a line drawing by Norman de Garis Davies (Davies 1905b, pl. IX). Reprinted with the permission of the Egypt Exploration Society.

("Incarnation [?] of the Aten")[28] and the Queen had augmented her name by the addition of the epithet Neferneferuaten ("Fair is the Goodness of the Aten"). These changes seem to have taken place at the time when the titles of the Aten were altered to indicate that the god had celebrated another jubilee.[29] A codicil on ten of the later Boundary Stelae is dated to Year 8 and informs us that Royalty paid another visit to the City in that year for the purpose of inspecting the boundaries on the southeastern frontier and repeating the dedication of the township to "the Father, the Living Aten, forever."

The next great event of the reign for which we have any evidence is dated to Year 12, but before this occurred the didactic name of the Aten was changed so as to remove any therio-anthropomorphic and pantheistic ideas that may have clung to it. The falcon symbol used to spell out "Re-Herakhty" was replaced by abstract signs to give an equivalent, "Re, Ruler of the Horizon," while a phrase in the second cartouche was altered to remove an ambiguity that could refer to Shu, the old god of the void. The name in its amended form now reads, "Re, the Living, Ruler of the Horizon in his Aspect of the Sunlight."[30] This change appears to have coincided with an alteration in its epithets suggesting that the Aten had celebrated a third jubilee.[31] These modifications are in the direction of a more abstract and exclusive view of the godhead and probably coincided with the substitution of phonetic spellings for words like "truth" and "mother," which had up to then been determined by hieroglyphs that could also suggest goddesses. The plural form of "god" was also avoided. The precise moment at which these developments took place is not known for certain, but thus far no one has found it necessary to question the view that they occurred in Year 9.[32] They show that Akhenaten's religious ideas were moving toward a more uncompromising monotheism and an intolerance of other gods than the Aten.

The last event of the reign for which we have any specific date is the great reception that was held in Year 12. Representations of this ceremony in two of the later tombs at Tell el Amarna show that Akhenaten and Nefertiti were carried in gold-covered state palanquins, more appropriate for this time-honored occasion than the great chariots of state, from the Palace to a gilded baldachin which had been set up in the City. There, with their six children in attendance, they received delegates from "Syria and Kush (the North and the South), the East and the West, and from the Islands in the Mediterranean, all lands being united so that they might receive the King's blessing."[33]

The representatives of the different nations are shown being ushered into the royal presence and proffering characteristic gifts. Such scenes with similar texts are not uncommon in the Theban tombs earlier in the Dynasty; and I have sought to show that they record an event which took place on the occasion of a king's accession or of his jubilee, when the great and small nations of the Near East paid homage to a new king or a rejuvenated old monarch.[34] The Amarna scenes, according to this view, commemorate Akhenaten's accession to sole rule.

It was probably in this same Year 12 that the Dowager Queen Tiye paid a visit to Amarna (Fig. 8), where Akhenaten had built her a "sunshade" temple (No. 13) for the daily rejuvenation of her powers. She may in fact have taken up long-term residence at Tell el Amarna, since references to her house have survived, and also to the house of her daughter, Beketaten, who accompanied her. Tiye's Chief Steward Huya was granted a tomb which was among the last to be cut in the northern cliffs. The King evidently planned that his mother should be buried in his own tomb in the Royal Wadi, for there fragments of a sarcophagus have come to light inscribed with her name as well as with his own and that of his father.[35] He also had made for her a large funerary shrine of gold-covered wood, in the reliefs of which he figures prominently, making offerings to the Aten with her in attendance. This equipment was supplied despite the fact that Amenhotep III must already have provided all of Tiye's burial furniture and installed some of it, at least, in his own tomb at Thebes. From this it would appear that Akhenaten's ideas were hardening against burial according to any vestiges of the old Osirian rites which were anathema to his reformed doctrine.

In the next few years he had several opportunities to exercise his principles in making burial arrangements for members of his immediate family. The first to die was his second daughter, Maketaten, who was buried in a suite of chambers leading from the main corridor of the Royal Tomb, which were decorated with unusual reliefs showing the royal family mourning over the bier of the dead princess. The presence of a nursemaid holding a baby and accompanied by a fanbearer outside the death chamber in these scenes has encouraged the belief that Maketaten died in childbirth, and if this is true, the event can hardly have happened before Year 14 at the earliest. Soon after this, Nefertiti herself disappears from history, and while her retiral has been attributed to a fall from the King's favor, it is much more likely to have been the result of her death.[36] The archaeologists who examined the Royal Tomb in 1931 found evidence that led them to believe that she had once been buried there.

The removal of the Chief Queen from the scene left a notable vacuum in the cult of the Aten. She had officiated as a sort of high priestess, a virtual equal of the King. He now tried to replace her by their eldest daughter, Merytaten, who took over some of her mother's monuments, such as her "sunshade." She is mentioned in the diplomatic correspondence of the day as an all-important person in the royal entourage.

A little later Smenkhkare, a younger brother of Akhenaten, reached manhood and, since the latter had no sons, was appointed co-regent and married to the royal heiress, Merytaten. He also took the epithet Neferneferuaten, which had formerly belonged to Nefertiti. This may indicate that Smenkhkare was expected to fill the role in the cult of the Aten that had formerly been taken by the Chief Queen. Only a few monuments have been recovered from Amarna showing both kings functioning together in the worship of the Aten accompanied by Merytaten or another of the princesses.[37] It is probable, however, that Smenkhkare spent much of his time at Memphis, which had always remained a great center and where there were important royal residences.

When Merytaten was married to Smenkhkare, Akhenaten is thought to have taken his next surviving daughter, Ankhesenpaaten, to be his consort, but the events of the last years of his reign are too crowded and confused for us to know the sequence in which the marriages occurred. It is at least clear from his skeletal remains that Smenkhkare died at about the age of nineteen, and thus, if he came to the throne at manhood, could not have enjoyed more than three years of rule.[38] An inscription mentioning that his mortuary temple was at Thebes and in the estate of Amun is, in fact, dated to his third regnal year, and this is taken to mean that he had reverted to the worship of the god of Thebes. Some authorities take the view that he would hardly have done so while Akhenaten was still on the throne, and that his return to orthodoxy indicates that he outlived the senior King.[39] If he did, it could only have been by a few months, since the following boy-king Tutankhaten, later named Tutankhamen, who married Smenkhkare's widow, had the names and symbol of the Aten inscribed upon his lion throne and royal scepters. The worship of the Aten would hardly have been revived, particularly by a child of nine, if Smenkhkare's return to the orthodox religion of Amun had been complete and functioning for some time. It would appear that Merytaten died before her husband, Smenkhkare, who then married the next heiress, her sister Ankhesenpaaten.[40] She cannot have been his wife for long, probably no more than a few months; on his death she married his younger brother Prince Tutankhaten, a boy half her age, and by this act of union brought him the throne of Egypt.

It is, however, possible that Smenkhkare died shortly before Akhenaten and that it was the senior partner who buried his co-regent in equipment that had originally belonged to Merytaten but had not been used for her burial.[41] It was brought out of storage and refurbished and adapted for her husband, perhaps in conformity with Akhenaten's views on purging funerary furniture of all Osiride elements. If Smenkhkare had reverted to the worship of Amun in his brief reign and had prepared funerary furniture for himself that was strictly in traditional style, as it appears to have been, judging from the articles that were usurped from it by Tutankhamen, it is difficult to see anyone other than Akhenaten burying him in equipment on which the prayers and symbols of the Aten religion figured so prominently.

Be that as it may, both kings died within a short time of each other or perhaps at the same time: we are unlikely ever to know.

In the last years of their father's reign, Merytaten and Ankhesenpaaten bore daughters who were called after their mothers, with the added epithet *tasherit* ("junior"),[42] and since it is clear that the father in each case was a king, the presumption is that he was Akhenaten, the divine royal family not being restricted by the incest tabus that operated in the case of ordinary mortals. The fate of these children is unknown, but they appear to have lived for only a very brief span.

An important event in Akhenaten's reign that is difficult to place is his outburst of iconoclastic fury. Agents were dispatched throughout the land to break up the images of the gods, particularly those of the influential Amun of Thebes, and to excise their names from the monuments, great and small. Since this profanation is usually supposed to have taken place at about the time of the removal to Tell el Amarna, references to Amun and other gods later in the reign must indicate at least a partial relenting in the campaign of vilification. It is difficult, however, to reconcile this policy of compromise with the later change of name of the Aten in Year 9, which indicates a more abstract and rigid conception of divinity. It may be that the desecration was perpetrated at about the same time as when the words for "mother" and "truth" were cleansed of their old associations and the plural form of the word "god" was avoided. But it could also be that the destruction was the last event of the King's reign. A final decision will have to await further evidence.

Akhenaten's highest regnal date is Year 17, written on fragments of wine jars found at Tell el Amarna, and it seems clear that he did not survive the vintage of the following year. His fate is obscure, but apparently he was not buried in the Royal Tomb at Tell el Amarna which he had prepared for himself.

During his reign the balance of power in North Syria decisively shifted. The kingdom of the Mitanni, which had been the traditional ally of Egypt for the two previous reigns, challenged the Hittites in Anatolia, and the struggle between the two powers disturbed the allegiance of Egypt's northernmost vassals on the borders of these great nations. The preoccupation of Akhenaten with religious affairs gave him little opportunity for an armed parade through his dominions such as had been the practice of his warlike ancestors when trouble threatened and the morale of vassal states had to be improved. While there seems to have been no widespread collapse of Egyptian power in the East, there was a definite erosion of its influence, particularly among the northern vassals who were inevitably drawn into the expansionist plans of the resurgent Hittites.[43] One by one the vassal states transferred their allegiance to the rising star of the energetic young Hittite monarch Shuppiluliumash, and it became the policy of subsequent pharaohs to win back these renegades. As a result Egypt embarked upon long and exhausting wars with the Hittites during Dynasty XIX.

Akhenaten's domestic policies, far more than his neglect of foreign affairs, brought confusion and distress into the Egyptian state. His transfer to the Aten of all the treasure and revenues of the temples of the other gods upset the economic basis of Egyptian life and damaged the prosperity of the land. His successor, the boy Tutankhaten, had no option but to abandon Tell el Amarna and to return to the ways of the past that had long stood Egypt in good stead. He had to admit the errors of his predecessor's ways and change his name to Tutankhamen as a sign of his reversion to orthodoxy. Later generations execrated Akhenaten far more viciously than he had denied the past. They not only damaged his monuments but even excised his name from the records. In the reign of Ramesses II his neglected and desecrated monuments at Tell el Amarna were dismantled and the stone was used for the foundations of new and orthodox temples, mainly across the river at Hermopolis. Thereafter the desert sands drifted over the ill-fated site, preserving what poor remnant was left for the spade of the archaeologist in our own age.

THE MONUMENTS OF
AKHENATEN AND NEFERTITI

Fig. 9. Fragmentary sandstone statue of Amenhotep IV, found in the remains of a peristyle court east of the Great Temple of Amun at Karnak. Emplacements for twenty-eight square piers were revealed together with fragments of colossi which had evidently been part of them. These were figures of Amenhotep IV, represented as a living king, standing with feet together, holding scepters in his hands, and wearing various crowns and headdresses. The astonishing feature of this example is that the King is shown naked and without genitals, although the sculpture is apparently finished. The androgynous nature of his physique is here emphasized by the voluminous breasts and hips and plump thighs. At the same time, the neck is lean and long and the collarbones prominent. The face is elongated and gaunt, the eyes narrow and slanting. If the lower limbs had survived, they would no doubt have shown the same spindle shanks as appear in the early reliefs (Fig. 34). Excavated by the Egyptian Department of Antiquities in 1926–1932. Early Period. Height 400 cm. Egyptian Museum, Cairo JE 55938.

In the early years of his reign, probably within a few weeks of ascending the throne, Akhenaten opened a new sandstone quarry at Gebel el Silsila ninety miles south of Thebes for the purpose of building a great temple to his sun god. Officials who were dispatched on this work have left records of the event in rock stelae at Zarnikh opposite Esna and at Gebel el Silsila.[44] In the latter place the King, wearing the Crown of Upper Egypt, makes offerings to Amun-Re, the god par excellence of Upper Egypt. The quarry was evidently in an area where the strata of rock ran in such a way that blocks measuring about one cubit in length (about twenty inches) by half a cubit in height could be easily prised out of their beds. These proved very useful building units for a large, untrained labor force to handle, for the small blocks could be carried and comfortably moved into position by one man. So rapidly, in fact, could these stones be built into walls that units of the same dimensions were used later in the reign when limestone was substituted for sandstone in the construction at Tell el Amarna. The unskilled masons must have found little difference between these blocks and the mud-bricks they used for their own houses. Since these sandstone blocks are roughly three handspans long, they have been dubbed *talatat* (from the Arabic for "three") by the workmen concerned with handling them today. This word has been adopted by archaeologists, who have sometimes applied it to limestone blocks of similar dimensions from Tell el Amarna.[45]

It is probable that another factor weighed with Amenhotep IV's architects. Amenhotep III was still reigning on the elevation of his son as co-regent, and the old King's massive constructions at Luxor and Western Thebes may have been absorbing most of the experienced stonemasons at the quarries and on the various sites. In order to organize and train his own artisans, Amenhotep IV had to treat his own constructions as major public works and to press his chief ministers into the task of mustering and controlling conscripted laborers.

The text on the stelae at Gebel el Silsila states that the stone was destined for the "great *ben-ben* of Re-Herakhty, in his aspect of the light which is in the Sun Disk, at Karnak."[46] Besides this sanctuary, at least seven other buildings for the Aten have been identified at Thebes, but until their remains have been studied and published, it is idle to speculate upon their design and purpose and to decide whether or not they were independent structures. Buildings bearing similar names, however, were subsequently erected at Tell el Amarna,[47] and if we are to judge by the evidence that has come to light on the latter site, the Theban temples might have been built on the same plan, though not necessarily in the same topographical relationship. Thus the temple at Karnak called "Aten Is Found" may have been at Tell el Amarna part of "The House of the Aten," which was the main temple, a vast complex consisting of several sections with different names. Though this also appears to be the case at

Thebes, where in Theban Tomb no. 55 "Aten Is Found" is said to be in "The House of the Aten,"[48] the latter name more likely refers to the domains of the Aten at Karnak upon which the different shrines, kiosks, and temples were erected. At Tell el Amarna "The Mansion of the Aten" was a separate building adjacent to the King's House, and it is probable that at Karnak, too, it formed an independent unit founded earlier than the reign of Akhenaten and perhaps undergoing a change of name with the new King. There is also mention of a building named "Jubilation in the Seat of the Aten,"[49] which may have had a palace attached to it, later called "The Stronghold,"[50] similar to the royal palaces attached to the Ramesseum and the great temple of Medinet Habu in Ramesside times. It would appear that it was here that the first jubilee of the Aten may have been celebrated. At Tell el Amarna the name "House of Jubilation" (or "Rejoicing") was attached not only to a part of the Great Temple but also to a portion of the Great Palace (No. 11).

Of all the buildings at Karnak, only the ground plan of a vast temple to the Aten has been traced in part about a hundred yards east of the present gate of Nectanebo I in the eastern boundary wall of the Great Temple of Amun.[51] So far, a colonnaded court has been excavated with the remains of colossal statues of the King standing against pillars (Figs. 9–12). This site has been identified, perhaps improperly, as the "Aten Is Found" in which stood "The House of the *Ben-ben*." The *ben-ben* was the pyramid-shaped stone of the ancient sun cult at Heliopolis. At Tell el Amarna the *ben-ben* took the form of a stela, and that this may already have been the case at Karnak is indicated by the hieroglyphic determinative on the stela at Gebel el Silsila which has the appearance of a badly made sign for a stela.[52]

The temples of the Aten at Karnak were dismantled in after years and their parts used as foundations and fill for several later constructions, such as the Hypostyle Hall, the Second, Ninth, and Tenth Pylons of the Great Temple of Amun, and for buildings at Luxor and Medamud.[53] Explorations at these places have recovered many thousands of sandstone blocks and more await retrieval. Unfortunately the sporadic way in which some of these excavations have been conducted has led to the removal and storage of many of the reliefs in a haphazard and piecemeal fashion. The present clearing of the Ninth Pylon at Karnak (Figs. 13–15), however, has followed a more systematic method. As it is clear that the Aten temples were demolished course by course from the top downward and usually transferred to new positions in more or less the same order, it has been possible to reconstruct some of the original scenes in their entirety and not in a mere tantalizing jumble of parts.

The rapid method of quarrying the *talatat* left rather rough edges, and thus a generous application of gypsum plaster was necessary to fill in the blemishes and the cracks between the joints and courses. The complete scenes recovered from the fill of the Ninth Pylon show that plaster was also spread as a layer over the entire surface to give the sandstone the appearance of white limestone and that much detail was added in paint. It is probable that originally all *talatat* were coated with a plaster layer which has fallen away in the damp subsoil where most of them have been preserved as foundations for

Fig. 10. Fragmentary sandstone statue of Amenhotep IV,
found in the remains of a peristyle court east of the Great
Temple of Amun at Karnak.
Excavated by the Egyptian Department of Antiquities in
1926–1932. Early Period.
Height about 400 cm. Egyptian
Museum, Cairo JE 49529.

Fig. 11. Upper part of a sandstone statue of Amenhotep IV, found in the remains of a peristyle court east of the Great Temple of Amun at Karnak. Excavated by the Egyptian Department of Antiquities in 1926–1932. Early Period. Height about 180 cm. Egyptian Museum, Cairo JE 49528.

Fig. 12. Upper part of a sandstone statue of Amenhotep IV, found in the remains of a peristyle court east of the Great Temple of Amun at Karnak. Excavated by the Egyptian Department of Antiquities in 1926–1932. Early Period. Height 150 cm. Egyptian Museum, Cairo 29/5/49/1.

Fig. 14. *Talatat* from a temple to the Aten reused as fill within the Ninth Pylon of the Great Temple of Amun at Karnak.

Fig. 15. *Talatat* from a temple to the Aten reused as fill within the Ninth Pylon of the Great Temple of Amun at Karnak.

Fig. 13. Ninth Pylon of the Great Temple of Amun at Karnak.

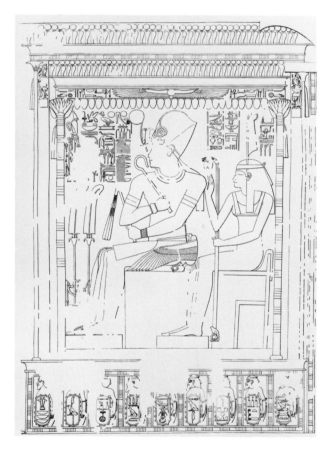

Fig. 16. Relief in the tomb of Ramose at Thebes, showing Amenhotep IV seated on a block throne under a baldachin with, beside him, the goddess Maat, who has the features of his mother, Queen Tiye. The King receives bouquets presented by the Vizier Ramose. After a line drawing by Norman de Garis Davies (Davies 1941, pl. XXIX). Reprinted with the permission of the Egypt Exploration Society.

other structures. The fact that fine detail was to be added to a coating of plaster may account, in part at least, for the rather summary treatment many of the blocks exhibit.

Over the years, a few blocks and fragments from Karnak, sawed into slabs for ease of transport, have found their way into the art market and have thence passed into museums and private collections (Nos. 25, 27, 36, 37, 40, and so forth). It appears that in the process a number of the blocks have been painted with modern pigment, in some cases perhaps enhancing traces of color that were already evident upon them.

Other monuments of the age of Akhenaten in the Theban area are now to be found only in the tombs of some of his officials. Of these, the most important are the reliefs in the tomb chapels of his Vizier Ramose (Figs. 16, 17; see p. 48) and of his Cupbearer and Master of Works Parennefer. Both of these chapels were evidently left unfinished on account of the early death of Ramose and of the transferal of Parennefer to Tell el Amarna.[54]

It is from this latter City of the Aten that most of the monuments of Akhenaten's reign have been recovered. The Boundary Stelae which were cut in the surrounding cliffs to demarcate the site still survive in a greatly mutilated state, and fourteen of them have been traced during the past century.[55] The best preserved of them (Stelae A, B, Q, S, and U) show in the upper part of each tablet confronted figures of Akhenaten followed by Nefertiti raising their hands in adoration below the sun disk, the Aten, which radiates upon them while two of their attendant daughters shake sistra (Nos. 8, 28; Fig. 18). At the foot of eleven of these stelae are mutilated groups of statuary, showing the King and Queen holding tablets in front of them (cf. No. 1) and smaller dyads of the senior princesses (No. 32). With the exception of three stelae of earlier pattern, all are dated to Year 6, when Akhenaten paid a state visit to the City in order to define its boundaries more precisely by erecting six additional stelae. During the length of time it took to carve these monuments, it was decided to increase their number by another five stelae, and the last of these were not ready before Year 8, when the King again visited the southeast boundary and repeated his oath to preserve the City within its boundaries and there to provide for his own burial and for those of his family and his court. Thus all eleven stelae, while dated to Year 6, have a codicil dated two years later reporting this event.

Three of the stelae (X, K, M), however, give the greatly damaged text of an earlier proclamation which recorded the founding of the City, and although their date has been lost, they have been dated to Year 4 by virtue of an internal reference to an event of that year in a context that makes it clear that Akhenaten is recounting all the evil things that have been said in the recent past, from the latest to the most remote.[56] But just as the stelae of Year 8 were all postdated in anticipation of a rededication at that future time, so it seems to me that the Year 4 in this earlier text could be equally anticipatory. Unfortunately the syntax of the inscription is of no assistance, for the active verbs can equally well be translated by the present as by the future tense.[57] It should be noted, however, that the only princess originally represented or mentioned is the eldest, Merytaten, and that

Fig. 17. Relief from the tomb of Ramose at Thebes, showing Amenhotep IV and Nefertiti at their Window of Appearances under the rayed sun disk of the Aten—the earliest manifestation of a new subject in the iconography of the reign. After a line drawing by Norman de Garis Davies (Davies 1941, pl. XXXIII). Reprinted with the permission of the Egypt Exploration Society.

Fig. 18. Boundary Stela S at Tell el Amarna. After a line drawing by Norman de Garis Davies (Davies 1908a, pl. XXVI). Reprinted with the permission of the Egypt Exploration Society.

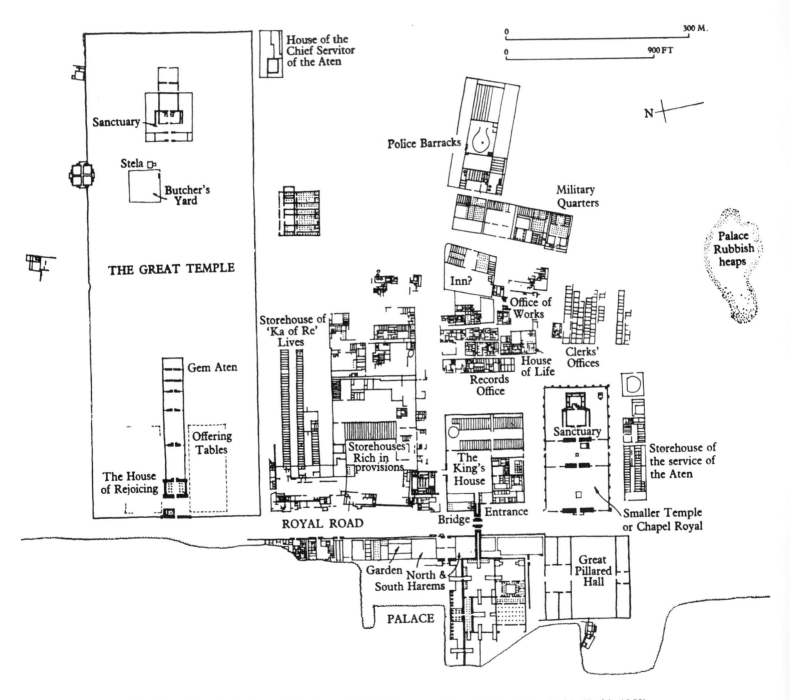

House of the
Chief Servitor
of the Aten

0   300 M.

0   900 FT

Sanctuary

Stela

Butcher's
Yard

N

THE GREAT TEMPLE

Police Barracks

Military
Quarters

Palace
Rubbish
heaps

Gem Aten

Inn?

Office of
Works

Storehouse of
'Ka of Re'
Lives

Clerks'
Offices

Offering
Tables

House
of Life

The House
of Rejoicing

Records
Office

Sanctuary

Storehouses
Rich in
provisions

The
King's
House

Storehouse of
the service of
the Aten

ROYAL ROAD

Bridge

Entrance

Smaller Temple
or Chapel Royal

Garden

North &
South Harems

Great
Pillared
Hall

PALACE

Fig. 19. Plan of the Central Quarter of Tell el Amarna, from W. Stevenson Smith (Smith 1958).
Reprinted with the permission of the Egypt Exploration Society.

even the figure of Makctaten has been inserted as a distinct after-thought. This suggests that, in whatever year the stelae were carved, a pattern was followed that had been fixed very early in the reign.

While the boundaries were being fixed, work began on the public and private buildings in the City (Fig. 19). Of the former, the most important were the temples, "The Mansion of the Aten" and the vast complex, "The House of the Aten," and the palace to which the name of "House of Rejoicing" appears to have been applied but which is referred to today as the "Great Palace."[58] All these structures were built or designed to be completed in stone, though mud-brick was also widely used. But in place of the standstone of Gebel el Silsila which had been used at Karnak, the limestone of Middle Egypt was employed at Tell el Amarna. The size of the Karnak *talatat* had proved so convenient for rapid building that the same dimensions were used for the roughly cut limestone blocks at Tell el Amarna. But while the main buildings could be run up rapidly, their decoration took much longer and was completed, if at all, only toward the end of the reign.

Some time after the death of Akhenaten, reliefs in these buildings were desecrated by hacking out the names and features of Akhenaten and Nefertiti and sometimes the Aten (Nos. 4, 116), though the figures of the princesses appear to have been generally spared. Later still, in the reign of Ramesses II, workmen were sent to the deserted site to demolish the stonework of the temples for use elsewhere. At the Great Temple ("The House of the Aten") excavation has failed to find more than one block *in situ* (No. 76). Similarly the statuary was deliberately smashed, presumably to retrieve any pedestals suitable for reuse in other monuments. The remaining fragments were buried in a dump on the southeast outskirts of the boundary wall of the Great Temple, where they were excavated by Flinders Petrie and Howard Carter in 1891–1892 (No. 4).[59] It is probable that it was in this same place that earlier visitors such as J. S. Perring picked up stray fragments on or near the surface (No. 2).

"The Mansion of the Aten," the smaller temple at Amarna, was subjected to the same violent destruction, and of its stonework scarcely anything has been recovered except small fragments of columns and statuary. Recovery of the ground plans and other data have revealed that the temples at Tell el Amarna seem to be adaptations of the primal sun temple of Heliopolis, the evidence for which is presumed to exist in the ruined Fifth Dynasty temple of Nyuserre at Abu Ghurab.[60] The essential feature of this temple is a colonnaded court with restricted entry which contained a cult image in the form of a *ben-ben* or pyramidal stone set upon a squat podium with an altar before it. In the Aten temples, which like other sun temples were orientated on an east-west axis, a much simpler ritual was appropriate for a god who did not exist in the form of a graven image; all that was required was the making of lavish offerings to the actual rays of the sun in an open sanctuary. Although the squat obelisk of the *ben-ben* was transformed into a stela at Tell el Amarna, the stela was not made the focal point of the open court; that distinction was conferred upon the altar set on a platform, to which a stairway with parapet ascended from the west.[61] Access to this altar was obscured

Fig. 20. Fragment of a painting showing the Princesses Neferneferuaten-tasherit and Neferneferure seated on cushions beside their mother's sandaled feet. Excavated by W. M. F. Petrie in 1891 in a room of the King's House at Tell el Amarna. Middle Period. Length 36 cm. Ashmolean Museum, Oxford 1893.1-41 (267).

Fig. 21. Reconstruction of a painting on a wall of the King's House at Tell el Amarna showing the royal family. Akhenaten sits on a cushioned stool within a kiosk. Opposite him, Nefertiti squats upon a cushion with one arm around her eldest daughters; the other may have supported the youngest child, Sotepenre, on her lap. The three eldest stand between their parents. Merytaten, in the middle, has one arm around the neck of Ankhesenpaaten on the right, who turns toward Sotepenre and allows the baby to grasp her finger. Maketaten, on the other side of Merytaten, clasps her sister's waist. The other two daughters play happily by their mother's feet. After a line drawing by Norman de Garis Davies (Davies 1921, pl. II). Reprinted with the permission of the Egypt Exploration Society.

by baffle walls, and subsidiary offering tables may have been placed in adjacent courts (No. 81).[62]

The Great Palace was partly explored in 1891 by Petrie, who conducted little more than a sondage in the area of this huge building, and some of the stonework which he recovered is in Cairo, Brooklyn, and Oxford (Nos. 18, 49). Later excavation by the Egypt Exploration Society has also succeeded in recovering fragments of the architectural stonework (Nos. 33, 48).

It will be convenient at this point to mention some fragments of wall painting in glue tempera recovered from palaces at Amarna, and a painted mud pavement found by Petrie in the *harim* quarter of the Great Palace which was spitefully destroyed in 1912.[63] The most important find, however, was the lower part of a mural painting in the "King's House" adjacent to the Small Temple. This remarkable picture when complete represented the King and Queen and their six daughters (Figs. 20, 21) and perhaps was a source of inspiration for the design of a number of the family stelae (Nos. 16, 56). With amazing skill, in view of his simple equipment, Petrie bewitched the largest fragment of this painting from the mud-brick wall and brought it to Oxford, where it forms one of the prized possessions of the Ashmolean Museum.

After a considerable number of stray Amarna blocks were found in earlier years, a welcome treasure of reliefs from public buildings at Tell el Amarna came to light in 1939. Toward the end of their tenth season at Hermopolis, a German expedition uncovered in the foundations of the west tower of a temple gateway erected by Ramesses II more than twelve hundred limestone blocks which had been brought across the river and used in much the same way as the sandstone *talatat* were reused in later constructions at Karnak. This large find could not be fully recorded by the Germans before they finished the season's work, and they had to be content with storing the blocks at the site. The war prevented the expedition from resuming the excavation, and since supervision was lax, illicit digging not only uncovered some of the hastily stored finds but also brought to light other reliefs in contiguous areas of the site. By the end of the war many of these blocks, now sawed into slabs and tricked out in modern pigments, were on the market, and some hundreds of them have found their way into private and public collections, mostly in the United States.[64]

Like some of their Karnak counterparts, these blocks were removed from their finding place in no orderly sequence, and until the whole site has been systematically excavated it would be premature to decide whether the Hermopolis finds can be put together to form larger scenes. So far only two blocks that are contiguous have come to light (No. 57). It would seem, in fact, that the transport across the river to Hermopolis, and perhaps to other sites, caused the various consignments of blocks to be jumbled and distributed to different reception points, in a manner unlike the more localized and more systematic transfer at Karnak.[65] It is also possible that, as in the Ninth Pylon at Karnak, the towers of the temple gate at Hermopolis were filled with these *talatat*, and that the denuding of the pylon also destroyed its contents.

Nevertheless, despite the random sampling of the Amarna temple reliefs now available, it is possible to reconstruct a good deal of their subject matter from parallel scenes in the private tombs. The private tombs, in fact, have been the prime source for our knowledge of Amarna history, art, and iconography since 1824 when Gardner Wilkinson copied scenes in the northern group. He was followed by other draftsmen, the last being Norman de Garis Davies, whose exemplary survey in six volumes was completed in 1908.[66] On the Boundary Stelae Akhenaten had promised his courtiers burial in the eastern hills at Tell el Amarna, and the tombs he bestowed upon them were evidently intended, like the tombs of Parennefer and Ramose at Thebes, to be splendidly decorated in painted relief. His ambitions, however, outran his resources. The tombs were hastily hewn in the foothills to the south and in the cliffs to the north of the Central Wadi. The rock in these regions is generally poor, and so the sunk relief is often little more than a core upon which the final surface was originally a coat of plaster that was manipulated while still soft with a modeling tool. This is a technique that had already been used in the Theban tomb of Parennefer, who was one of the King's chief craftsmen, besides acting as his cupbearer, and it is employed widely at Tell el Amarna, not only for relief but also for statues in the round; the famous bust of Nefertiti, for instance, is covered in places with a layer of plaster half an inch thick (Fig. 1).[67] The process has the advantage of speed in execution, precision in detail, and freedom in handling, and, as Davies pointed out, it makes possible that attention to facial expression that characterizes the scenes in these tombs.[68]

Despite these advantages, nearly all the tomb chapels are unfinished. Some were abandoned with partially hewn chambers and with walls left blank or decorated with mere preliminary sketches in line drawing. Clearly an attempt was made to supply a number of high officials with tombs at the same time, and as soon as one tomb was partially excavated the stonemasons were transferred to another, while the draftsmen moved in to decorate those walls that were ready and were followed in turn by sculptors and painters. So wealthy and influential an official as Ay, the Master of the Horse (Fig. 5), who began a tomb planned as the largest in the necropolis, managed to get no more than half his main hall excavated and only the entrance and part of one wall decorated. Of fourteen tombs whose owners can be identified, nine were started and left incomplete before regnal Year 9.

The Royal Tomb in the Central Wadi was also left unfinished. The main corridors and the burial chamber had been cut and two subsidiary suites prepared. The larger one was perhaps designed for the burial of Queen Tiye, the smaller evidently for the burial of the Princess Maketaten, to judge from reliefs on the walls showing the King and Queen mourning over her bier and other scenes of lamentation.[69] Here, too, the rock is of poor quality and much of the relief had to be supplemented with plaster which has now fallen away (No. 143).

It is from the Royal Tomb, however, that well over two hundred fragments of the King's *shawabti* figures in alabaster, granite, quartzite, limestone, sandstone, and faience have been recovered, mostly in the past century, and have passed into the art market (Nos. 161–175). Not a single example has been found intact, and the presumption is that the figures were deliberately destroyed in antiquity at the time when the sarcophagi and the King's canopic chest were broken up.[70] The latter object, from its unstained condition, shows that mummified viscera could never have been deposited in it, and it seems clear that the King was never buried there and that, despite their presence in the tomb, the *shawabti* figures did not accompany him to the grave.

The differing features of the *shawabti* heads have induced some scholars to question whether all the figurines represent Akhenaten, and attempts have been made to identify some of them as Smenkhkare. The problem is a somewhat difficult one, since it is clear that Smenkhkare resembled Akhenaten, who was his elder brother or half brother.[71] No evidence, however, has come to light that there was ever any intention of burying Smenkhkare in the Royal Tomb, which was reserved, according to the Boundary Stelae, for Akhenaten, Nefertiti, and their daughter. Moreover, on all the inscribed fragments no other name but that of Akhenaten appears. Since there is apparently some evidence that Nefertiti was buried in the Royal Tomb, it might be argued that some of the *shawabti* figures could represent her. Again, no fragment recorded from the tomb is inscribed with her name and titles or carries a queen's scepter or wears a queen's headdress. The presumption is that all her *shawabti* figures were removed when her burial was transferred elsewhere in the reign of Tutankhamen. It is true that the lower part of a *shawabti* of Nefertiti does exist in The Brooklyn Museum (33.51). That fragment was acquired in the Cairo market in 1933 together with three fragmentary *shawabtis* of Akhenaten and probably came from the Royal Tomb.[72] If that is the case it must have been broken at the time of transfer of Nefertiti's burial and left behind as useless. No other fragments that would fit it have so far come to light.

An examination of the four hundred or so *shawabti* figures from the tomb of Tutankhamen furnishes a useful comparison. Some of these are made in the same materials as the Akhenaten specimens, but they include in addition examples in wood, painted or gilded. They, too, vary in quality from the exquisite and fine to the crude and semifinished, while their portraiture ranges from the accurate to the perfunctory. It is clear that, like Akhenaten's examples, they are the work of craftsmen of different degrees of skill. There is no need, therefore, to question that the fragments from the Royal Tomb represent Akhenaten alone and that they were made by various hands at different times within his reign. They must be judged by the finest examples among them (No. 175) and not by the cruder specimens. No fragments of wooden *shawabtis*, either plain or gilded, were found among the debris of the Royal Tomb, but it is probable that such intrinsically valuable specimens would not be installed in the appropriate chamber until the day of the King's burial. They were either deposited with him elsewhere or were adapted for the use of his successor; perhaps some suffered one fate and the rest the other.

Undoubtedly the most spectacular source of art objects to have survived at Tell el Amarna is not in the wreckage of palaces and

Fig. 22. House of the "Favorite of the King, Chief of Craftsmen, the Sculptor Tuthmose," discovered by the Deutsche Orient-Gesellschaft in 1912 at Tell el Amarna. Photograph courtesy of the Centre of Documentation and Studies on Ancient Egypt, Cairo.

Fig. 23. Plaster mask of Akhenaten. Excavated by the Deutsche Orient-Gesellschaft in the studio of the Chief Sculptor Tuthmose at Tell el Amarna. Late Period. Height 30 cm. Ägyptisches Museum Berlin/DDR 21348.

temples but in the workshops of the sculptors. Several sculptors' studios were found by German and British archaeological expeditions near the wadi that separates the southern part of the Main City from the northern district.[73] Of these the most important was House P 47, 1–3 (Fig. 22), which, from a fragment of inscribed ivory found on its premises, has been identified as the workshop of the "Chief Craftsman, Sculptor, and Favorite of the King, Tuthmose."[74] The statuary recovered from the rooms of this house has given a new dimension to Amarna art, but perhaps provides an unbalanced view of the art of the period since no sculptors' studios from earlier or later periods have survived with their sketches, studies, and examples of work in progress as well as finished sculptures.

In the workshop of Tuthmose were found master portraits of royalty worked and finished by the hand of a chief sculptor, which, having been officially approved, served as models for lesser craftsmen who had the duty of producing portraits of royalty for one of the many enterprises under commission (No. 95). The painted bust of Nefertiti is a rare example of this kind of model sculpture (Fig. 1). It is cut off arbitrarily at the shoulders and thus could have served none of the ritual or official purposes of Egyptian statuary, but it has a resemblance in this respect to certain sculptor's models of royal busts, or, as some think, ex-votos, made for craftsmen engaged in the decoration of Ptolemaic and Roman temples.[75] Other models in the workshop were in the form of plaster casts from master portraits (Nos. 94, 111, 112; Figs. 23, 24). In addition there were heads in limestone, quartzite, and granite in various stages of production (Nos. 99, 103; Fig. 25), parts of composite statues (No. 88; Fig. 26), and a miscellaneous number of plaster masks of men and women (Nos. 108, 109; Fig. 27). The realism and uncharacteristic appearance of these masks have so confounded many critics and connoisseurs since their discovery that they have often been described as life masks or death masks, and attempts have been made to identify the sitters with historical characters (Nos. 95, 108).[76]

It should be emphasized that, while a single example of a death mask made in ancient Egypt has survived at Saqqara (Cairo 10/12/24/6),[77] objects such as this can have served no practical function. The funerary equipment of all who could afford such luxuries was made during their lifetimes, and coffin and mummy masks have the idealized features of the deceased as he hoped to appear in some eternal heyday.[78] Moreover, it is apparent that most of such equipment was supplied from stock and bore no resemblance whatever to the person it pretended to portray. If the features of the dead needed to be perpetuated, they were not immortalized in the manner of these so-called death masks with their hollow cheeks and wrinkled brows. The masks, moreover, have a muscular tension about the mouth and eyes that is in striking contrast with the collapsed orbits and relaxed muscles of the Saqqara death mask.

There is also no evidence that the masks were taken from life, those who support such views pointing indiscriminately to masks that show the sitter wearing a diadem and the parietal bulges of the Blue Crown (Nos. 94, 95), as though it were likely that the royal family would be content to have their faces smothered in a mess of crude

Fig. 24. Plaster mask of a king, probably Smenkhkare. Excavated by the Deutsche Orient-Gesellschaft in 1912 in the studio of the Chief Sculptor Tuthmose at Tell el Amarna. Late Period. Height 20 cm. Ägyptisches Museum, Berlin (West) 21354.

Fig. 26. Yellow-brown quartzite head of a princess, probably Merytaten. Excavated by the Deutsche Orient-Gesellschaft in 1912 in the studio of the Chief Sculptor Tuthmose at Tell el Amarna. Middle Period. Height 21 cm. Egyptian Museum, Cairo JE 44869.

Fig. 25. Granite head of Nefertiti. Excavated by the Deutsche Orient-Gesellschaft in 1912 in the studio of the Chief Sculptor Tuthmose at Tell el Amarna. Late Period. Height 25 cm. Ägyptisches Museum Berlin/DDR 21358.

Fig. 27. Plaster mask, perhaps a portrait-study of one of the foreign women in the King's *harim*. Excavated by the Deutsche Orient-Gesellschaft in 1912 in the studio of the Chief Sculptor Tuthmose at Tell el Amarna. Late Period. Height 27 cm. Ägyptisches Museum Berlin/DDR 21261.

gypsum plaster while they were still wearing the royal regalia. Moreover, most of the masks bear traces of a seam showing the join of the separate halves of the molds in which they were cast. This seam runs vertically down the center of the face, indicating an extraordinary and even perverse manner of making a mold of the human features whether from the living or the dead subject, and is contrary to the method used for the Saqqara mask. It is, however, the natural way of preparing a mold from an original made in an unyielding substance such as wood, stone, or clay. One, at least, of these masks, from the artificial nature of its fringe of hair, suggests that its archetype was a wooden statue (No. 112). None of the so-called life masks bears any traces to show that the subject was prepared for the molding process by having his eyes and the hair of his eyebrows protected and tubes inserted into his nostrils.

The late Günther Roeder, who had the unrivaled opportunity of examining these masks in detail, reached the conclusion that they are casts of originals modeled in clay,[79] and this writer is disposed to agree with this verdict. It must be accepted that at least as far as the royal family was concerned, the Egyptian sculptor was required to produce a fairly close portrait, idealized perhaps but recognizable, of his sitter. For this, training was necessary, and the ability of the sculptor to model rapidly a likeness of the new king or queen in some plastic substance, such as wax or clay, could have been acquired only by constant practice. We can see in the Amarna masks pupils' exercises in this exacting art. The most successful of them have been made more permanent by casting in plaster, another skill which every craftsman had to learn, for it was from casts of models made by the master sculptor that most of his carving was done. No sitter could pose long enough for his statue to be chipped in stone or chiseled in wood. It seems certain that most clients who were privileged to commission a statue from the royal workshops would have their portrait rapidly modeled in clay by the sculptor as an aid to his work in a more durable medium. Naturally, the finished statue cut in stone or wood with simple tools would not show the same free handling and plastic treatment as these masks exhibit. Some of the masks show a certain degree of realism and may therefore portray royal or private clients. Others may be mere fanciful creations, studies by the sculptor to perfect his training. Still others may be portraits of the artist's fellows, or his relations or acquaintances, made with no intention of ever carving a finished likeness.

It is at least highly probable that by the time the studio of Tuthmose was abandoned, the people whose portraits appear among the casts and sculptured heads found there were dead or disgraced if they had ever existed in the flesh. Otherwise the studies would have been removed, together with the sculptors' tools and equipment, for use at a new center of industry. We must not expect therefore to find among these abandoned works representations of the reigning king and queen and their advisers at the time of the removal. When the studio was abandoned, the artists left behind material that was out of date, and portraits of Amenhotep III and Akhenaten and of Nefertiti and Merytaten, besides those of other princesses as children, have been identified among the remains.[80] Since it can be presumed that the artists could not bring themselves to destroy the work of their hands, they abandoned them as they were, complete or unfinished or broken.

From other houses in the City have come statuettes of members of the royal family used like household gods in private shrines (Nos. 52, 96; Fig. 28). They too are representations of dead or disgraced royalty that were abandoned with other household possessions when the decision to leave the City was taken. Evidently family worship centered around a shrine in which a representation of the royal family was kept, sometimes behind wooden doors that could be opened to reveal the image.[81] Several of these icons in the form of reliefs have survived in part or in whole (Nos. 16, 56; Fig. 2). Some shrines were built inside the house,[82] but the more elaborate examples took the form of a chapel erected in the garden,[83] which resembled, on a miniature scale, a sanctuary of the Aten, with an altar placed before a stela showing the royal family at worship (No. 54).

Fig. 28. Painted wooden statuette of a king, who has been identified as Akhenaten, presumably from the slightly serpentine neck and the pronounced paunch. Provenance not known. Late Period. Height 25.3 cm. Ägyptisches Museum, Berlin (West) 21836.

THE DEVELOPMENT
OF
THE AMARNA STYLE—THE EARLY PERIOD

Although the objects in the present catalogue have been assigned to the Early, Middle, or Late Period of Amarna art, there are manifest difficulties in tracing the evolution of style during the age of Akhenaten. Not only have the monuments of the age survived in a greatly incomplete and damaged state, but their remains have also been so scattered as to make it hazardous to try to establish a proper sequence of artistic activity. In the past, scholars have been conditioned by the belief that Akhenaten ruled in Thebes, under the guidance of his mother, Queen Tiye, for the first four or five years of his reign before suddenly introducing a new creed and a revolutionary art and taking himself off to Amarna.[84] The art historians among them have therefore been tempted to date such traditional representations as the Louvre statue (Fig. 29) to the early years of his reign and to group the more unorthodox works into the period of the Aten heresy.

This view has been supported by the interpretation put upon the scenes in the Theban tomb of the Vizier Ramose, where on the west wall of the first hall there is an almost completed relief in the style of art prevalent during the reign of Amenhotep III. This is flanked by an unfinished companion scene showing all the mannerism of the revolutionary art and dominated by the emblem of the rayed disk of the Aten.[85] The incomplete state of this large tomb encouraged the inference that the revolutionary art had burst forth just at the moment of the move to Amarna, and that Ramose had time only to have a scene in the obligatory new style sketched on the wall of his tomb before work had to be suspended on his removal to the new capital. This view could still prevail, even after research had failed to find any trace of Ramose at Tell el Amarna.[86] The discovery of the Karnak *talatat*, however, has rather upset this view, for they testify that the revolutionary art was already well established at Karnak before the exodus of the King and his followers to the City of the Aten. It seems probable, in fact, that further research will push the appearance of this revolutionary style even earlier in Akhenaten's reign. To this writer it seems clear that to date the more traditional works of the period to a prerevolutionary phase is no longer tenable.

Another system used for dating the monuments of Akhenaten has been to take note of the number of princesses occurring on them. At Amarna the greatly damaged Boundary Stelae K, M, and X, dated to Year 4(?), appear to have only the eldest princess, Merytaten, represented, and certainly only she is mentioned in the text. Stela K shows also Maketaten, inserted as an afterthought. The later Stelae A and B, dated to Year 8, have a relief of Ankhesenpaaten added at the last moment.[87] A scene in the tomb of Meryre II at Tell el Amarna, dated to Year 12, shows all six surviving princesses.[88] From these data, a time scale has been devised, but even those who have used it have seen its shortcomings.[89]

The reconstruction of the wall painting found in a room in the

King's House and now in Oxford (Figs. 20, 21) shows Akhenaten and Nefertiti with all six daughters. The eldest three stand between their parents, the youngest, an infant, is held on her mother's lap, and the two others play together on a cushion by her footstool. Two fragments from the scene give the early name of the Aten and disclose, therefore, that all six daughters had been born before Year 9,[90] a fact that is not revealed by any other monument of the reign. Moreover, this dating system, which assumes that every incident in the life of the royal family was immediately reflected in iconography, ignores the way in which the ancient Egyptian craftsman worked, particularly during the Amarna Period. The artist was not concerned with recording the changing course of history but with eternal verities concerning kingship. The craftsmen employed on the many undertakings, both royal and private, had to work in haste, and it was natural that they should prefer subjects that had been in stock from earlier years of the reign and that they had perfected by constant copying. Moreover, the revision of the patterns or the introduction of new compositions would be the concern of the master craftsmen, who were too few and too busy with royal commissions to spend much time disseminating their new designs among the rank and file. The painting on the wall of a private room in the King's House must have been the work of a master craftsman and, as such, original and in advance of the fashion. The cartoon on which it was based might never have entered the repertoire of lesser artisans, although certain of the house stelae were perhaps modeled upon such pictures (Nos. 16, 56). It comes as no surprise, therefore, to find that in one of the two scenes dated to Year 12 six princesses are shown, and, in a different version of the same event, only three.[91] Moreover, representations that are dated to after Year 9 by the use of the later name of the Aten often show only one princess in the retinue.[92] It is unfortunately not possible, therefore, to date any Amarna scene according to the number of daughters accompanying Akhenaten and Nefertiti.

In these circumstances, the only reliable system to employ is to sort the monuments into some rough order by the form of the names of the King and Queen and the Aten. A letter dated to Year 5 still names the King as Amenhotep (IV), but on the Boundary Stelae of Year 6 he is called Akhenaten. At the same time Nefertiti seems to have added the epithet Neferneferuaten to her name. The name of the Aten was also changed at some time between Years 8 and 12, and most scholars agree that it must have been in Year 9.[93] This dating, however, must be used with caution, for the early names in texts were sometimes altered in antiquity to bring them up to date.[94]

Unfortunately, the three periods in the history of the reign do not coincide with stages in the development of the art, and different criteria, based upon stylistic analysis, will have to be employed if the course that art took during the life of Akhenaten is to be traced.

The monuments of his first years are extremely scanty and ruined. He is sometimes accredited with finishing the Third Pylon at Karnak, though Amenhotep III claimed it entirely as his own. Akhenaten appears greatly effaced on both the north and south walls of the porch, on the north wall smiting captives,[95] but it is most likely that he was merely associated with his father in the scenes on this pylon, in the

Fig. 29. Yellow steatite (?) statue of Akhenaten. The King is represented in the restrained style of the Late Period. Originally the Queen was beside him, on his right; her left arm is still around his waist. Acquired by Henry Salt, perhaps in the Memphis region, in 1826. Height 61 cm. Musée du Louvre, Paris, N. 831.

Fig. 30. Sandstone block carved with opposed figures of Re-Herakhty and Amenhotep IV. Early Period. Length 150 cm. Ägyptisches Museum Berlin/DDR 2072.

same way as he appears twice with him, but on a smaller scale, in the royal bark on the east face of the northern tower (Fig. 4).[96] The work is in the orthodox style of his father's reign and was doubtless executed by the designers and craftsmen of Amenhotep III.

There are also a small number of monuments in which Re-Herakhty appears as a falcon-headed man bearing the disk of the sun upon his head. The most accessible of these is the large sandstone block found in the Tenth Pylon, showing the King before Re-Herakhty, who bears the early didactic name of the Aten but not yet enclosed within cartouches (Fig. 30). It should be noted that this scene is cut in *low* relief in the style of Amenhotep III, and there is nothing, in fact, to show that it is not, like the Third Pylon, part of a monument belonging to that King. The block is of greater dimensions than the *talatat* and must come from a shrine decorated in the very first months of Akhenaten's association with his father. It has been claimed that the figure of the god and the names of the Aten replace earlier carvings, but this has been questioned.[97]

That the rayed disk of the Aten, and with it the revolutionary features of the new art, appeared very early in the reign is suggested by the equipoise of scenes in the tomb of Ramose, to which reference has already been made (see pp. 34, 48). On one side there is a relief of Akhenaten on a throne under a great baldachin receiving the gift of a bouquet of Re-Herakhty from Ramose (Fig. 16), an event which this writer has argued took place at the enthronement of the King as co-regent.[98] This scene had not been completed before the companion relief was drawn and partly cut in the new style and with the new

subject of Akhenaten and Nefertiti at their Window of Appearances (Fig. 17), albeit by the same craftsmen responsible for the traditional style of work.

The stela referring to the opening of the quarries at Gebel el Silsila has lost its date, if it ever had one, but in this writer's opinion it belongs to the very first months of the reign. Some time had to elapse while the actual structure of the Karnak temples was raised before their decoration could be started, perhaps a year or more. It was then that the epiphany of the new rayed sun disk coincided with its first jubilee and that there appeared a different style of art in which to express the new teaching. To this writer there seems a good case for considering that this revolutionary style existed in the imagination of Akhenaten from the very first and was imposed upon his chief designers at the beginning of his reign. A small interval would have to elapse between the conception and the execution, between the cartoon and the finished relief. The representations that exist before the appearance of the new art were probably commissioned by Amenhotep III, or at least done by artists belonging to his court.

The early style of the reign first appears on the Karnak *talatat*, and certain factors condition its character. In the first place, the King was in a hurry, as is seen in the way a labor force, probably including many army recruits, was conscripted to lever the sandstone building blocks out of their beds and to use them with the most superficial trimming. Gypsum plaster lavishly applied was used to fill holes, cracks, and deficiencies. In order to cover hastily built walls in the shortest possible time, the fine low relief, which had been an essential requirement for the decoration of temples built in soft stones earlier in the Dynasty, was replaced by sunk relief. This latter technique could cover large areas of wall space without the long and tedious process of sinking the background. But sunk relief, particularly if it required to be covered with a thin coat of plaster, had to be carved deeper than raised relief, and subtleties of modeling had to be sacrificed to more dramatic light and shade. Deep sunk relief can produce optical illusions when the drawing is not adjusted to compensate for this deficiency; limbs, for instance, can appear much more slender than they really are, and other distortions occur as a result of heavy shadows falling on modeled forms. It is thus partly an illusionary quality that gives the Karnak *talatat* their mannerist appearance.

The stone of some of these *talatat*, too, tends to be coarse. Fine work in it is hardly possible, and often all that the Karnak reliefs have bequeathed to us is little more than a summary core on which a plaster coating was meant to be modeled. The forms tend to be angular, emphatic, and rudimentary, but they make up in vigor and movement what is lacking in delicacy and fine draftsmanship.

Lack of subtlety, in fact, was due to a second factor, the shortage of experienced craftsmen at the King's command. It is virtually certain that at this early period in his reign the skilled masons of Egypt were largely employed on the gigantic work of Amenhotep III at Luxor, Western Thebes, and elsewhere, and these great enterprises must have absorbed the supply of stone quarried in large well-cut blocks. The workmen who could be spared for the undertakings of the co-regent were the sons of the older craftsmen, and not all were fully trained and experienced. It is probable that the traditional drawing of Egyptian reliefs, going back to archaic times, like hieroglyphic writing to which it was closely related, had to be learned as a mystery rather than an instinctive means of expression. It is indisputable that frequently in its history Egypt reverted to a sanctified style of the past, as though to keep its well of inspiration pure and undefiled.

The younger workmen, not fully steeped in the traditions of their craft, and with minds more sympathetic to experiment, could give full rein to certain tendencies that had already appeared in the popular, as distinct from the official, art of the time. In paintings in private tombs at Thebes this popular art makes its first appearance before Akhenaten in scenes of everyday life that left some personal memorial of the owner's activities on earth. The religious scenes—offerings at the tomb stela, entombment, and funerary rites—are usually traditional in their expression and correct and somewhat monotonous in their composition. We tend to pass them over in favor of the new themes of contemporary life, the military scenes, the raising and storing of crops and herds, the hunt from the chariot, the foreign gifts and their bearers, the display of the equipment prepared for the new pharaoh, and the ceremonies before the king seated upon his throne.[99] All these subjects gave the artists an opportunity for a freer and more original approach to novelties and acted as an encouragement to them to use the same fresh vision on some of the more traditional subjects, such as the scenes of banqueting, fishing and fowling, and the harvest.

It is in these representations that the Egyptian artist in the middle years of Dynasty XVIII betrays a short-lived delight in the world around him, and in the whimsical observation of human behavior within it—the quarreling gleaners pulling each other's hair, the girl plucking a thorn from her companion's foot, the field laborer playing his flute in the shade of a tree while another takes a pull from a waterskin slung under a bough. Occasionally this new freedom could lead to bold innovations, such as the representation of singers and dancers shown full face in a novel frontal view, or the twisting posture of the dance, or the woman turning to invite her fellow diner to taste the fruit she holds in her hand. These passages in the paintings in the tombs of Nakht, Menna, Djeserkaresonb, Sobekhotep, Nebamun, and others are the most precious among the legacies that ancient Egypt has bequeathed us, and they testify to a new force gathering beneath the fabric of Egyptian art that was shortly to erupt. When Akhenaten did away with the concrete representation of his god and replaced its image by the symbol of the rayed sun disk, he also banished most of the traditional iconography of temple reliefs. New subjects had to be invented, and for this the new vision of artists not fully trained in the Egyptian way of art had full scope to find appropriate expression. The result often has been described as "realistic" or "naturalistic" or "truthful." However, just as the reliefs in the Fifth Dynasty sun temples were concerned with the yearly cycle of life under the beneficent rule of the sun god, so the new subjects for representation, as we shall see, were concerned with life under the beneficent rule of the new sun god. For these scenes the same lively expression was instinctively chosen as had already appeared as modest asides in the Theban tomb paintings.

There was another important factor, and probably the most influential in determining the early style of the reign, and that was the intervention of Akhenaten himself. Bek, his chief sculptor at this period, insists that he was the apprentice whom the King himself taught, and the main impact of his teaching was probably on the choice of subject matter to be represented, and certainly on the way in which the royal family was to be depicted. With the arrival of the symbol of the sun disk, there also appears a grotesque manner of portraying the King and Queen which no artist in ancient Egypt would have dared to initiate, even if it had ever occurred to him to break with the idealistic tradition of representing the god-king as a perfect being. Just as effigies of the sun god were prohibited, so figures of the King as an ideal man were abandoned. The King was now represented with a receding forehead, a lined and haggard face, a long nose, thick lips, slanting eyes, a hanging overgrown jaw, and hollow cheeks (Nos. 3, 6, 15). His neck was shown as lean and arching, emerging from pronounced collarbones (Figs. 9, 31). His breasts were prominent, his paunch pendulous, his buttocks large, and his thighs inflated above spindle shanks. The extraordinary distortions in which Akhenaten chose to have himself represented have raised speculation in the minds of pathologists that if he bore any resemblance in life to his appearance on the monuments, he must have suffered from a malfunctioning of the pituitary gland.[100] The abnormal features of his anatomy are shown at their most distinctive on the colossi recovered from the ruins of a temple to the Aten at East Karnak (Figs.

Fig. 31. Fragment of an alabaster slab carved in sunk relief with a figure of Akhenaten offering a pot of unguent to the Aten. Excavated by W. M. F. Petrie in 1891 at Tell el Amarna. Early Period. Height about 50 cm. Egyptian Museum, Cairo 26/6/28/8.

9–12). In particular the statue showing him naked without any genitals (Fig. 9) has invited much comment, and various unconvincing attempts to explain the peculiarities away have been made by suggesting that it is unfinished, or awaits the fitting of clothing in another material, or is covered by a form-hugging gown, or is a deliberate attempt to create a hermaphrodite—the mother and father of mankind.[101] The epicene nature of Akhenaten's physique as represented by his artists has sometimes made it difficult to distinguish between fragmentary statues of himself and those of Nefertiti on anatomical grounds alone (Nos. 5, 20).

It is inexplicable that Akhenaten should have instructed his artists to portray him with such a pathological appearance, which belongs to neither normal men nor women, if he did not suffer from some disturbance of the endocrine system. His complaint, however, does not seem to have been severe enough to interfere seriously with his procreative powers. The skulls of his putative brothers, Smenkhkare and Tutankhamen, are long and broad,[102] a trait which they probably inherited from their ancestor Yuya.[103] The presumption is that Akhenaten and his daughters had similar heads which, perhaps in order to class him apart from mere mortals, he had depicted in an exaggerated manner. It is, however, clear that his followers immediately adopted the same fashion in which to have themselves represented. The Vizier Ramose, for instance, suddenly appears in his tomb with the elongated shaved skull, the lean face, hanging jaw, and long thin neck of the elect, in contrast to his orthodox appearance on the opposite side of the same wall.[104]

We cannot say whether Nefertiti's appearance underwent a comparable change, since no representation of her is known before the advent of the new style, but it seems likely. She was in any case portrayed with similar exaggerations, which are mitigated by the gown she wears and the natural feminine form of her anatomy. Both she and the princesses in their more mature representations are shown with slender waists and enormous buttocks and thighs, which we have suggested are an attempt, like the epithets that are applied to her, to create an erotic symbol in the cult of the Aten (Nos. 22, 31, 53). Her features take on something of the aspect of her husband's but are more angular in their details, whereas his are more rounded. Her nose is smaller, her chin more pointed, her lips more sharply chiseled, and there is often a pronounced bulge along the ridge of her cheekbone (Nos. 26, 91; Fig. 1). A curious fashion of the age is the adoption by the womenfolk of the short Nubian hair style, which has a military origin and recalls the masculine urchin or gamin cuts, the shingles and Eton crops of a more recent past.[105] The appearance of the Queen or a princess in this style of hair dressing has often resulted in their being confused with men (No. 48). In this charade Akhenaten by contrast can appear in a loose gown, like a woman's, unconfined by a sash, though this habit was also worn by Amenhotep III in his later years and was not uncommon in Ramesside times.[106] It may be that the representation merely gives an up-to-date picture of contemporary dress and has no transvestite significance. Nefertiti, however, does appear in a tall blue cap, which, although known as headgear worn by certain female sphinxes, seems specially chosen to match the Blue Crown that was the King's usual headwear.

The princesses are represented during this early phase with shaved heads showing extraordinarily elongated skulls perched upon long slender necks (Nos. 35, 130). The rest of their anatomy is an adolescent version of their mother's (Nos. 34, 90), although some of the statues, such as those at the Boundary Stelae, can show them with the inflated thighs and spindle shanks also to be observed in contemporary statuettes of girls found at Medinet Ghurab.[107] One of the innovations of the Amarna Period was the representation of children as persons in their own right and not as adults on a miniature scale. No better examples of this exist than the early painting of children from a wall in the King's House (Fig. 20), although the statuettes surmounting the gold and silver sticks of Tutankhamen show that the idea is still very much alive at the end of the reign.[108]

The greatly misshapen skulls in the representations of the royal princesses (Fig. 32) have encouraged the same urge to "explain" them as exists in the case of the epicene colossus of Akhenaten (Fig. 9). The excessive elongation has been attributed to intentional deformity by head binding, a practice for which there is no evidence in Egypt.[109] Another interpretation that has been offered is that it is a form of hairdressing.[110] There seems no doubt that it is purely a mannerism of the new art style, and while, for instance, Ankhesenpaaten under Akhenaten appears with the fashionably distorted cranium, under Tutankhamen her neck and head, even in a skullcap, are shown as normal.[111]

Apart from these distortions in the portrayal of members of the royal family, Akhenaten did not specify a single change in the traditions of Egyptian drawing. The human figure continued to be rendered in the same visual terms as had come down from the Archaic Period, when the forms of art were established at the conceptual stage of its evolution in the service of the divine kingship. Thereafter art observed the same sanctified conventions for as long as Egyptian kingship lasted. Akhenaten introduced changes in the choice of illustrative material, but the age-old artistic vision in which those subjects were rendered was retained. Only a willful distortion in the drawing of the human figure was new, and that distortion was limited to representations of the royal family and their retinue. Soldiers, servants, foreigners, and the commonfolk are shown without such marks of distinction. The canon of proportion was slightly adjusted internally to take account of a longer face and neck, but otherwise the artists felt it unnecessary to make any changes in the manner of representing the human form, though they could already draw the statue of a man, as distinct from the man himself, in a more naturalistic style of illusion.[112] In this context, therefore, it is wrong to speak of realism or naturalism in Amarna art: one kind of mannerism was replaced by another. When the sculptor Bek spoke of being the apprentice whom the King himself taught, all that this declaration means is that Akhenaten specified the way in which he and his immediate family were to be drawn, and what events were to be recorded on the monuments of his reign.

This new style erupts at Karnak with the first great work of the King's early years as co-regent, but it is seen to full effect in the

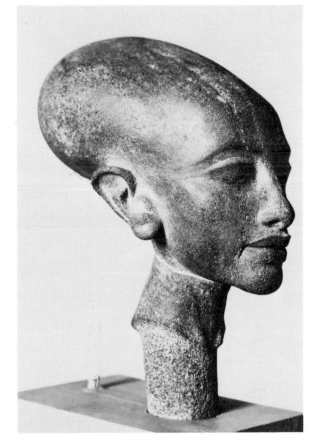

Fig. 32. Yellow-brown quartzite head of a princess. Excavated by the Deutsche Orient-Gesellschaft in 1912 in the studio of the Chief Sculptor Tuthmose at Tell el Amarna. Middle Period. Height 19 cm. Egyptian Museum, Cairo JE 44870.

Fig. 33. Fragment of an alabaster slab carved in relief with figures of Akhenaten and Nefertiti offering to the Aten while Merytaten shakes her sistrum. Excavated by W. M. F. Petrie in 1891 at Tell el Amarna. Early Period. Height 105 cm. Egyptian Museum, Cairo 30/10/26/12.

Boundary Stelae and the groups of sculpture that accompanied them.[113] These are mostly dated to Year 6, but some were being carved as late as Year 8, albeit in the same style and pattern as the earlier examples. It must be appreciated that, owing to the gigantic building operations of the King and to the shortage of skilled supervisors, cartoons and patterns produced early in the reign could still be copied much later. It seems to this writer that the extreme style of the Boundary Stelae may well have been fixed early in the reign before Year 4, which appears to be the date of inaugurating the earliest of them. It was then accepted as the standard design for all the stelae, even at a date when the style was undergoing some modification.

Several famous fragments of alabaster parapets, found by Petrie in the ruins of the Great Palace and now in the Cairo Museum (Figs. 31, 33), show the excesses of the new style at their most extravagant. This style has been a fertile source of inspiration to many modern forgers, who have failed to appreciate its subtleties but have produced from its exaggerations a whole series of travesties in relief and statuary. The fragment from a similar parapet in The Brooklyn Museum (No. 18) has the cartouche of Nefertiti in its early form, so dating it to before Year 6 and putting it among the earliest monuments raised at Tell el Amarna. The carved slab found by Barsanti in the Royal Tomb in 1891 (Fig. 34) and evidently squared up for copying, shows from the names of the Aten and the King that it must date to between Years 6 and 9, though it is rather less competently carved in the softer stone. Also belonging to this early phase is the family stela in West Berlin (No. 16). All these monuments exhibit the mannerist characteristics of an art style that had been developed before Year 4 and was still valid as late as Year 9.

The direction that this early style took, however, must have owed as much to the King's chief sculptor as to Akhenaten's intervention, and there the King was fortunate in having an artist of genius at his call. This man may perhaps be recognized as the Chief Craftsman and Sculptor of the King, Bek, the son of Men, who discharged similar functions for Amenhotep III.[114] He has left us a quartzite naos-stela showing his wife and himself in the fashionable distortion with the prominent breasts and paunch of his King (Fig. 6). He is almost certainly responsible for the design of the Karnak colossi, which are among the most impressive masterpieces of the age, with their suggestion of a brooding, fanatical power tensed beneath the calm coherence of their sculptural masses (Figs. 9–12). They still have the ability to disturb and move the onlooker by the interpenetration of their sophisticated meaning and their primitive force. It was the genius of Bek that took the pathological distortions prescribed by Akhenaten and integrated them into an artistic triumph, creating effigies of the King that reveal him as superhuman.

Another work that may be accredited to Bek or his school is the quartzite head of a princess found in the workshops of Tuthmose (No. 88) and probably a leftover model from the earlier years of the reign. This also is among the masterpieces of the period, taking the peculiarities specified for the representation of the princesses, with their long deformed skulls upon slender necks, merely as a point of departure, and infusing them with a transcendental quality that transforms them into impressive symbols with a life of their own. The creation of new symbols to replace the old was, in fact, one of the main concerns of the artist in this early phase. The innovations and discoveries of the new style could quickly become formulae, especially in the hands of the less inspired artists. Thus the portrait of the King soon lost its individual quality and took on the status of a symbol. This is seen in the reduction of the neck to an arched column with exaggerated tendons,[115] the rendering of the perforated lobe of the ear as a mere ring of flesh, and of the streamers on the crowns as floating decorative motifs. They have lost their primal significance and become the mannerism of a fashionable mode.

Bek was active at Tell el Amarna as well as at Karnak, for the joint stela he erected with his father at Aswan,[116] and dated to before Year 9, describes him as "Chief of Sculptors on the Mighty Monuments of the King in the House of the Aten at Akhetaten." We may therefore accredit to him the fragments of broken sculpture found there by Petrie and Carter in 1891 (Nos. 4, 5, 20). His influence would also persist in the work of the craftsmen whom he had trained and inspired for some time after his removal from the scene. This retirement came probably with his death, for which we have no particulars but which seems to have occurred about Year 8, when new influences began to make themselves felt.

Fig. 34. This limestone slab, found by the Egyptian Department of Antiquities in 1891 in a room of the Royal Tomb at Tell el Amarna, shows the royal family offering to the Aten. A grid of red lines has been ruled over the surface, suggesting that the relief was to serve as a model for craftsmen carving the walls of the burial chamber. The drawing, in the extreme mannerist style of the Early Period, may have been regarded as out-of-date when the time came to decorate the other chambers of the tomb, and it was apparently abandoned among debris. Height 51 cm. Egyptian Museum, Cairo 10/11/26/4.

OVERLEAF: Fig. 35. Reddish-brown quartzite slab carved in sunk relief with Akhenaten and a princess, probably Merytaten, offering to the Aten. Clothing, altars, and offerings have been cut out, evidently for the insertion of polychrome glass or faience inlays or inlays in other stones. Perhaps from Heliopolis. Late Period. Given by Mrs. Jones Wister to the Philadelphia Museum of Art in 1900 and transferred to the University Museum, Philadelphia, in 1931. University Museum, Philadelphia E 16230.

THE DEVELOPMENT
OF
THE AMARNA STYLE—THE LATER PHASES

The contribution of Bek and his colleagues to the development of Amarna art lay in giving artistic expression to the King's ideas, in formulating an iconography, and in marshaling and training the necessary craftsmen from what we have assumed was a relatively inexperienced labor force. The capacity for organizing his affairs on specialist lines, which had become almost an instinct with the ancient Egyptian, now induced him to meet the need for a great burst of artistic activity by the methods of mass production. It was not only the opulence of the Amarna age that encouraged architects to inlay their buildings with decorative motifs in multicolored glass and faience, in the manner of cloisonné jewelry, or to substitute stone, glass, and faience inlays for the details of figures and inscriptions in the stone and mud-brick buildings (Nos. 86, 158, 159; 91, 134). Such inlays could be cast in great numbers in clay molds, or carved by specialists in the quiet of their studios. All that the workman on the site was required to do was to cut out silhouettes in intaglio into which these brilliant and detailed prosthetics could be cemented (Fig. 35).

Similarly, the Amarna Period invented the composite statue, which allowed specialists to perfect their skill in carving one particular part only for final assembly, so that we find feet, hands, arms, and heads in quartzite, granite, and jasper for fixing to clothed bodies of white limestone (Nos. 104, 87, 21; Fig. 36). All these novelties were ingenious solutions to the problem of making sculpture of high quality in the shortest possible time, but they did not survive the reign of Akhenaten. The reversion to orthodoxy encouraged a return to the traditional methods of carving statuary.

We can see other evidence of this specialization in the carving of the Amarna limestone reliefs that have been recovered from Hermopolis. The scenes in which the King and Queen and their immediate retinue appear are evidently the work of master hands or experienced craftsmen (Nos. 92, 117, 122), but the quality deteriorates toward the edges of the pictures, where genre scenes, often set in landscape, fill gaps in the composition or assist in binding the various elements into a unity.[117] These genre scenes are often novel in their choice of subject matter and lively in conception, but their execution is usually perfunctory and sometimes even inept. They are the work, we may conclude, of the beginners and improvers or, at least, the nonspecialists, since their often unusual composition and execution have evidently not been standardized by frequent copying (Nos. 64, 71).

There is another factor that influences considerably the style of the Amarna reliefs. The temples and public buildings of Tell el Amarna and the tombs were made in limestone, not the sandstone used at Karnak. More detailed work could be done in the finer, harder, and more compact white limestone of Tell el Amarna which did not need to be covered with a skin of plaster, except in some areas of bad

PRECEDING PAGE: Fig. 36. Unfinished brown quartzite head of a queen, probably Nefertiti. Excavated by the Egypt Exploration Society in 1932 in a sculptor's studio at Tell el Amarna. Late Period. Height 33 cm. Egyptian Museum, Cairo JE 59286.

Fig. 37. Yellow quartzite head of Nefertiti. Excavated at Memphis in 1915 by the Eckley B. Coxe, Jr., Expedition of the University of Pennsylvania. Late Period. Height 18 cm. Egyptian Museum, Cairo JE 45547.

rock where the tombs were cut. Blemishes might be filled with gypsum (Nos. 11, 73), but the ability of the sculptor to carve this stone in a suaver and more precise manner softened the asperities and starkness of the Karnak style. The impact which material had upon style can be seen in the limestone relief of the jubilee scene in Cambridge and the sandstone version in Boston (Nos. 11, 7). The deeper and more summary cutting of the sandstone slab gives a harsher, more vigorous, and more extreme aspect to drawing which is essentially similar in both reliefs, even though one came from Karnak and the other probably from Memphis.

When the sculptors turned to limestone, therefore, they were less tempted to depart far from the conventions of traditional carving in this medium. Nevertheless, what they had learned at Karnak was not forgotten. The Boundary Stelae, the alabaster parapets, and the carved slab from the Royal Tomb (Figs. 18, 31, 34) show that, if need be, they could transfer the deep-cut relief and the exaggerated style developed in dealing with coarse sandstone to work executed in the finer limestone.

The character of the Early Period of Amarna art suffers a change in about Year 8, which we ascribe to the disappearance of Bek from the scene. Much of the tradition that he created continued by its own momentum, but side by side with it can be traced new tendencies which ultimately are to become the style prevalent at Thebes and Memphis during the last reigns of Dynasty XVIII. This more conventional phase may, in fact, show the impact of the Memphite style, always influential from earliest days and no less a potent factor in Dynasty XVIII, when Ptah, the god of Memphis, could be hailed as "The Creator who has made things with his two hands as satisfaction for his mind."[118] Not that the High Priest of Ptah, the Greatest of Craftsmen, whose office had been held by Akhenaten's elder brother early in the reign of his father, would have had any religious influence on the sun cult of Akhenaten. Nevertheless, in the Amarna Period Memphis was still an important capital with its great palace complex in the foundations of which a statue head of Nefertiti has come to light (Fig. 37),[119] and where monuments of Smenkhkare have been found.[120] It was at Memphis that the great tradition of carving in limestone had developed from earliest days. The distinctly Memphite character of the tomb reliefs of Apuia, excavated at Saqqara and probably made in the co-regency of Amenhotep III and Akhenaten,[121] already have many of the traits of later Amarna art.

We may postulate that this later style, which is easier to isolate in the last years of Akhenaten's reign, owed its character to the appointment of a successor to Bek, who, if he did not come from Memphis, was conversant with its artistic traditions. Between the earlier phase and this later phase, there is a transitional period which overlaps them and bridges the gulf between, for instance, the work of Bek and that of Tuthmose, between the Karnak colossi and the portrait studies from House P 47, 1–3 at Tell el Amarna.

The transition is already seen toward the end of the Early Period in the reliefs in the tomb of Ay at Tell el Amarna.[122] These cannot have been started much before Year 6, when the new series of Boundary Stelae were being carved; yet work on them ceased before Year 9,

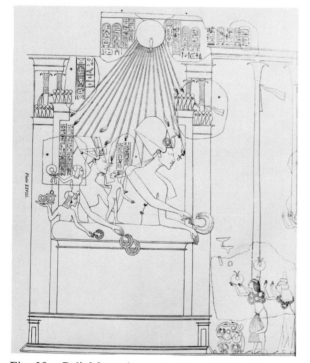

Fig. 38. Relief from the tomb of Ay at Tell el Amarna, showing the royal family at the Window of Appearances. Akhenaten and Nefertiti lean over a cushioned parapet to throw down gold collars and other gifts to an honored courtier, Ay, and his wife, Tiy. Nefertiti fondles the head of Ankhesenpaaten, who strokes her mother's chin. The other daughters hold trays piled with gifts. After a line drawing by Norman de Garis Davies (Davies 1908b, pl. XXIX). Reprinted with the permission of the Egypt Exploration Society.

since the name of the Aten in the tomb is given only in its early form. Ay, as the King's putative father-in-law, was granted a tomb that was designed to be the most magnificent in the necropolis, but work on it did not proceed very far and was halted when only the entrance corridor and one wall had been partly decorated in relief. Yet the figures of the royal family (Fig. 38) are shown with none of that haggard and aged appearance of the earlier style (No. 27). Akhenaten's features are bland, and some restraint has been exercised in representing his anatomy without a prominent paunch or a slender arched neck. Nefertiti's appearance is gracious and natural, while the figures of her three eldest daughters have little of the extravagance of earlier representations. The portraits of Ay and his wife, Tiy, are individual and lack the obvious Amarna mannerisms (Fig. 5); it seems probable that they were able to call upon the services of an important sculptor in the royal workshops for the carving of these reliefs. The same restrained hand is evident in the reliefs in the tomb of Tutu, whereas Parennefer has employed a sculptor well versed in the conventions of the early style. These three tombs were started and partially decorated at about the same time.

The gilded wooden shrine, made by Akhenaten for his mother, Queen Tiye, and found in the tomb of Smenkhkare in the Valley of the Kings at Thebes, is dated by the name of the Aten to after Year 9.[123] It was probably made after Year 12, and the relief of the Queen Mother still surviving at the time of its discovery showed none of the mannerism of the early style. Nefertiti's figure is often elongated, as are those of women in crowd scenes in Amarna tombs and on the Karnak *talatat*,[124] and her head can sometimes be small in relation to her body (Fig. 34). On this shrine, however, the proportions of Tiye's figure are normal, but she already has that somewhat overlarge head that characterizes the post-Amarna paintings in the tombs of Tutankhamen and of Huy, his Viceroy of Kush.[125] Only in her long nose and hanging jaw are the early Amarna traits present.

A similar design, perhaps from the same master cartoon, was used for reliefs of Tiye in the tomb of her Steward Huya at Tell el Amarna, where the proportions of the ladies in waiting should be compared with their counterparts on the Karnak *talatat* to appreciate the change in style.[126] Since the tomb of Huya dates to after Year 9 and the reliefs in question probably to after Year 12, it would not be too rash to date to this latter year the change in style from the Early Period to the Late Period.

Between the two periods falls the transitional stage of the Middle Period to which we have already referred and which may be identified in the reliefs in the tomb of Ay at Tell el Amarna. In this intermediate style the characteristics and momentum of the Early Period still prevail but are losing their power and are in process of being transformed. What brought this change about is problematical, but probably an influx of skilled workmen, experienced in the orthodox art of Amenhotep III, coincided with the suspension or completion of work on the old co-regent's monuments and may have altered the composition of the labor force. There may also have been a shifting of interest on the part of Akhenaten, and a less direct concern with the manner of his artists, provided that subject matter was not changed. We tend to think of the pharaoh as ubiquitous and all-knowing, but many innovations may have been introduced by zealots more royalist than their King, and never seen or approved by him. As the reign wore on, the first fine careless rapture of his courtiers was doubtless fading. Changes were abroad and are discernible in the Amarna tombs. Whereas, for instance, in the earlier chapels the owner tends to have at least one relief of the royal family offering to the Aten in the thickness of the doorway, in the later examples there is a reversion to the figures of the owner alone worshiping the rising and the setting Aten.[127]

The latest phase of Amarna art, which we have attempted to isolate as coinciding with the appointment of a new master craftsman whom we may perhaps identify for ease of reference as the Chief Sculptor Tuthmose, saw a more purposeful direction given to these less revolutionary tendencies. The achievement of this phase was to tame the exuberance and bravura of the work of Bek into a more elegant and sophisticated style. Most of the sculptures from the workshop of Tuthmose show the latest manifestations of this phase (Nos. 88, 75, 99, 103, 109). So also do many of the reliefs from Hermopolis that belong to the later years of the reign, as is shown by inscriptions recovered with them referring to events and personalities active in Akhenaten's last years.[128] The figures of the senior princesses, who filled important roles at the court of their father in the later part of his reign, also appear not infrequently in these reliefs (Nos. 116, 122, 124). They are characterized by a more refined taste and by more careful drawing than are evident in the earlier examples, but they lack something of their movement and vitality.

Probably the qualities of the late style are best appreciated from the sculptors' model reliefs that have survived. It is, for instance, instructive to compare an example showing a portrait of the King in the late style with one in the early manner (Nos. 121, 15; 115, 12). The profile has become less angular and the forms softer and rounder. The hollow cheek and raised cheekbone have disappeared; so has the sharp line of the jaw running up to the ear. The neck has lost its lean, muscular appearance, while the creases in it are more pronounced. The perforation of the ear is no longer circular but has become an oval slit, and the lobe has lost the aspect of an independent boss. At the same time the mode of representing the eye has been changed: it is less elongated, less slanting, and takes an isolated position within the face, following to some extent the same design as is used in sculpture in the round. The lines running from the corners of nose and mouth are still delineated, but more sensitively. On the whole, the features are less gaunt and more plump. This could be accredited to a change in the physique of the King as he got older, and certainly the body of the Louvre statue suggests no little adiposity, though in those same places that had already been singled out for emphasis in the early reliefs (Figs. 29, 34). This softening of style, however, seems merely to be the substitution of an earlier exaggerated mannerism by a more restrained naturalistic interpretation of that mannerism.

The same tendencies are at work in the statuary of the last years. The Curtis group in the Louvre (Figs. 39, 40) is dated by the form

Figs. 39–40. Painted limestone pair statuette of Akhenaten and Nefertiti. Perhaps originally from Tell el Amarna. Late Period. Height 23 cm. Musée du Louvre, Paris E. 15593.

Fig. 41. Limestone statuette of the royal family. Excavated by W. M. F. Petrie in 1891 at Tell el Amarna. Early to Middle Period. Height 13.5 cm. University College London 004.

of the names of the Aten written on the back slab to after Year 9; it shows a similar departure from the extravagance of the earlier statue of Nefertiti (No. 22). The headless, unfinished group in University College London (Fig. 41), which is about the same date or a little earlier, shows a similar basic treatment of form. The adiposity of the two adult figures, however, has been slightly exaggerated, since it has yet to be mitigated by the carving of pleated clothing or by its application in modeled gesso. Also in the same genre are the statuettes of Akhenaten recovered from house ruins at Tell el Amarna (Nos. 52, 96). It might be argued that these small-scale works, designed for the house shrines, would not in any case show the virtuosity of the great statues made for the temples of the Aten. A statuette, however, from Tell el Amarna and probably from a domestic shrine, shows on a miniature scale all the early stylistic features of the damaged statues of the Great Temple and the Boundary Stelae (No. 1). It should be compared with an example of the later statuary found in a sculptor's studio and now in the Cairo Museum (Fig. 42). This shows Akhenaten holding a table of offerings and displays the same restrained realism as is evident in the more famous seated statue and the limestone bust, both in the Louvre (Figs. 29, 43). Whatever developments were taking place in the spheres of religion and politics during the last years of Akhenaten's reign, it is clear that the convulsive spasms of the Amarna revolution in art were over.

The Karnak colossi representing Akhenaten introduced at a blow a number of novelties that entered into the conventions of Egyptian sculpture and remained there for a century or so. Certain features derived from the previous reign, such as the double curve on the medial line of the lips and the main S-shaped coil of the uraeus on the brow, remained unaltered, but practically all else was changed by more plastic treatment of forms. The eyes ceased to be mere decorative ovals; they were deeply modeled, with the upper lids carved to catch the light, and the thick cosmetic lines extending from the outer corners were abandoned in favor of a more natural fold of the upper lids over the lower. The eyebrow, too, instead of being an elegantly arched appliqué, followed a more naturalistic course. The ears became more fleshy, with the upper and lower tips curving from the side of the head (Nos. 99, 102) and the perforations of the lobes boldly indicated as a round hole or crater. Lips were rounder and thicker and sometimes shaped like a Cupid's bow (Nos. 3, 97). The tendons of the neck, the sternal notch, and the collarbones were boldly modeled (No. 4), and usually a double fold on the throat was indicated by incised lines.

An invention of the Bek school was the carving of statues in such a way as to reveal the forms of the body beneath a heavily pleated gown. This is especially evident in sculptures of women (Nos. 22, 106), but statues of the King were similarly treated.[129] The convention persisted into later reigns and was particularly popular in Ramesside times.

In the later periods of Amarna art all these stylistic innovations develop on more conservative lines. The collarbones do not project so harshly and are often hidden beneath a deep collar which becomes fashionable (No. 106). The perforation of the earlobe tends to change

Fig. 42. Yellow limestone statue of Akhenaten holding an offering table. Excavated by the Deutsche Orient-Gesellschaft in 1911 in a house at Tell el Amarna. Late Period. Height 40 cm. Egyptian Museum, Cairo JE 43580.

Fig. 43. Limestone bust of Akhenaten. Probably originally from Tell el Amarna. Late Period. Height 58 cm. Musée du Louvre, Paris E. 11076.

into a slit. The lines running from the corners of the mouth and nose are less pronounced when not suppressed. Occasionally they are developed into more expressive folds, giving an air of tired disillusion to the features (Figs. 29, 44),[130] distinct, however, from the haggard appearance of the King and Queen in some of the early reliefs (Nos. 16, 25). The exaggerations in the proportion of the figure give way to a more traditional canon, as is particularly evident in the statuary recovered from the workshop of Tuthmose and the now headless statues of the King and Queen in Silsila sandstone from a garden shrine at Tell el Amarna, and now in Oxford.[131] All date to the later years of the reign.

Fig. 44. Limestone statuette of Nefertiti. Excavated by the Deutsche Orient-Gesellschaft in 1912 in the studio of the Chief Sculptor Tuthmose at Tell el Amarna. Late Period. Height 40 cm. Ägyptisches Museum Berlin/DDR 21263.

ICONOGRAPHY

When Akhenaten early in his reign abolished the graven image of his sun god Re-Herakhty as a falcon-headed man and substituted for it an elaboration of the hieroglyph for "sunlight," with many rays in place of the symbolic three, he thereby banished many of the subjects for representation on temple walls. During Dynasty XVIII the large temples that had been built at Thebes, Memphis, and elsewhere had developed a decoration that followed a prescribed pattern. The theme was the exaltation of the pharaoh as the son of the deity living within the shrine, and as the intermediary between gods and men. The pylon and the outer walls were covered with reliefs showing the king as a mighty warrior smiting the northern and southern foes of Egypt, as on the Seventh and Eighth Pylons at Karnak, and thereby driving by magic all manifestations of evil away from the holy precincts.

Occasionally the hostile forces might take the form of the animals of the wild to be hunted by the pharaoh in his chariot. From the reign of Amenhotep III we have scarabs issued to commemorate the King's cattle and lion hunts, and the later Pharaoh Ramesses III is represented hunting on the rear of the southern tower of the First Pylon of his mortuary temple.[132] The motif of the hunting pharaoh occurs on the painted box of Tutankhamen, the lid and sides of which are covered with pictures of the King as the champion of Egypt, repelling its enemies,[133] and Tutankhamen must also have been represented hunting on the walls of Karnak, to judge from the decoration of blocks still lying near the Ninth Pylon.

Insufficient evidence has survived from the reliefs at Karnak and at Tell el Amarna to inform us whether this warlike theme was considered proper for the decoration of the girdle walls of the Aten temples, but it seems likely. Akhenaten as co-regent had been portrayed in relief on the Third Pylon at Karnak in the attitude of smiting the northern foes, and the same design has survived on a sandstone *talatat*[134] and in the decoration of royal kiosks on the state barges (Nos. 55, 57). Some *talatat* from Karnak showing Akhenaten, Nefertiti, and Merytaten on a very large scale[135] probably came from a pylon and suggest that under Akhenaten the decoration of the towers would have shown him smiting the appropriate foe under the rays of the Aten, accompanied by his wife and daughter, precisely as he appears on the cabin of the royal barge. This design still persists during the reign of Tutankhamen.[136]

Akhenaten retained another protective device for the temple threshold in the form of the sphinx, perhaps because it was a manifestation of Re-Herakhty or, in his case, an image of the King as an incarnation of Re-Herakhty. Sphinxes have been found at Tell el Amarna,[137] and blocks carved with recumbent sphinxes in relief from a "sunshade" kiosk and other temples have also been unearthed (No. 13). The sphinxes doubtless flanked the entrance to the precincts and protected them from unauthorized intruders.

Whether battle scenes appropriate to the temenos walls were carved on them is doubtful, the virtual absence of such warlike themes perhaps being due to chance (cf. No. 148). It seems to this writer that the subject of the hunt of the creatures of the wild is more likely. Fragments of scenes in which animals, such as hyenas,[138] antelopes, and cattle, appear, some evidently in motion (No. 149), probably belong to a scene of the chase analogous to that on the painted lid of the box of Tutankhamen,[139] but another interpretation in respect to the cattle may be more plausible.

Connected with such scenes of the hunt are reliefs showing the royal family engaged in fishing and fowling in the marshes, a subject that survived as a decoration for temple walls until Ptolemaic and Roman times, as at Esna.[140] The Amarna version included at least a trio of the royal family if we can judge from mere fragments (Nos. 126, 150). The subject, however, remained in the repertoire during the reign of Tutankhamen, and it is not, in fact, possible to interpret one Hermopolis relief showing the spearing of fish and fowl (No. 150) without reference to the complete version that exists carved as an ivory appliqué upon a box of Akhenaten's successor, Tutankhamen.[141]

This scene suggests that one of the main contributions which Akhenaten made to new designs for his temple walls was the association of his wife and daughter with himself in all his representations. Instead of the king smiting foes before the god, he slaughters them in the presence of his queen and daughter under the Aten disk. In place of the lonely pharaoh dealing with the affairs of state before the god of the temple, every act is performed by Akhenaten in company with his consort and his eldest daughter or daughters. This emphasis upon a divine family officiating in the holy precincts is to our mind a conscious or subconscious effort to appeal to that concept of family so dear to the Egyptian psyche. A feature of the earlier dynasty had been the association of gods into trinities, and this tendency progressed steadily throughout the history of Egypt.

An idea of what some of the vanished reliefs of the temples of Tell el Amarna comprised can be obtained from another parallel from the tomb of Tutankhamen. This is a small gold-covered shrine which has reliefs on its sides, back, and doors concerned with the King, not in the presence of the gods but with his wife, who is probably identified with the goddess "The Great Enchantress." The royal couple are engaged in affairs of their daily life, such as fowling, shooting with the bow, pouring perfume into the Queen's cupped hand, anointing, tying on collars, and so forth.[142] Only one relief, the presentation of the symbols of myriad years of jubilee, has any analogy with traditional designs;[143] the rest are novel and presumably derived from similar scenes of the preceding reign. Such scenes are suggested by fragments of relief from Hermopolis which reveal that the complete subject was the royal family engaged at some purely domestic function within a kiosk (No. 142).[144] Such conversation pieces can be reconstructed on the basis of corresponding scenes in tombs and on house stelae (Nos. 16, 56) at Tell el Amarna.[145] It is clear that an important element in the new iconography was the domestic life of the royal family, but that this was displayed on the outer walls of temples is doubtful. It is more likely that it formed the subject for the decoration of interior walls.

Sometimes, however, such scenes of purely domestic import have a deeper significance. Temple reliefs, showing the god in the shrine being adorned, particularly by having a collar put around its neck, had appeared earlier in the Dynasty,[146] but whereas then it was the king who clothed the god, now it is the Queen who adorns Akhenaten (Fig. 45), just as it is Ankhesenamen who ties the collar on Tutankhamen.[147] Much of the traditional subject matter, in fact, was retained in the Amarna religion; it was the form it took that was new. Thus the former scenes in which a pharaoh makes offerings to the gods, is received by the gods of the temple, embraced by them, and given the breath of life, were proscribed, once the concept was introduced that divinity could not be represented in the form of an image. Nevertheless, the same ideas were expressed in the scenes of offering made by the royal pair to the Aten, whose rays embrace them and bring the breath of life to their nostrils. What is a sequence of acts in the old style becomes a simultaneous event in the new.

Other themes in which the gods participated are generally ignored. The scenes of the divine birth of the king resulting from the union of the sun god with the chief queen, an incident which involved a traditional pantheon of gods, is not illustrated in the Amarna Period, although Amenhotep III had used it as the decoration of a chamber in his temple at Luxor.[148] Yet one wonders whether the significance of the "sunshade" temples in the case of the queens and senior princesses was not the daily union of the royal women with the god by means of the sunbeams. Other traditional scenes that apparently disappear from view are the lustration (ceremonial purification) of the pharaoh by gods of the four quarters, the coronation of the king by the god, and the inscribing of his name on the sacred *ished* tree by Atum, Thoth, or Seshat. Only a fragmentary lustration scene, unfortunately too incomplete to give much information, does exist in the case of the royal princesses.[149] Perhaps, therefore, one should be prepared to encounter a similar scene in which the king is "baptized." The coronation of the king in the conventional style, with the god adjusting the crown, is also unknown. Yet the symbol of the rayed disk, busy with its many hands, that Akhenaten had created, was able to carry out such functions daily as it received offerings or caressed the limbs of the royal pair. In one instance, at least, it holds out protection and sovereignty to the uraeus on the King's brow,[150] and in some representations the hands of the Aten adjust the crowns of both Akhenaten and Nefertiti.[151]

Another scene common in temple reliefs is the image of the god carried in its sacred bark mounted on a litter supported on the shoulders of priests.[152] Such a representation was, of course, entirely inappropriate to so intangible a god as the Aten. But a fragment from Hermopolis has survived which suggests that the King or the royal pair was towed in a bark upon a canal in a rite analogous to the river festivals of some of the old gods (No. 138). From all the Amarna versions of the traditional temple reliefs, the images of the gods have been banished, but there is more than a suspicion that the new image of the sun god is his "beautiful child," the King, who replaces the old personifications of divinity.

The position of the god in the earlier temple scenes of the Dynasty is thus taken by the King and his family. He is the manifestation of

Fig. 45. Fragment of a painted limestone house stela from Tell el Amarna. The entire scene would have shown Akhenaten seated on a throne, one elbow resting on the cushioned backrest, while Nefertiti, standing before him, leaned forward to tie a collar or pectoral around his neck. Late Period. Height 12 cm. Ägyptisches Museum Berlin/DDR 14511.

the Aten, and it is the cycle of his daily life with his family that becomes the theme for the decoration of the palace as well as of the temple. The most important of the King's functions was the daily worship in the temple, when lavish offerings to the Aten were made by the royal family, acting on behalf of all the people over whom the sun disk ruled. Since the god did not exist in iconic form, none of the usual daily ceremonies concerned with the wakening, purifying, adorning, lustrating, fumigating, anointing, and feeding the god was called for, and only offerings, fresh or burnt, upon an altar in an open court were appropriate. At this function Nefertiti officiated on equal terms with her husband, while the children assisted by rattling their sistra (Nos. 17, 49).

This theme became the main decoration of the inner temple reliefs, ensuring by magic means that even in absence the royal family would continue the daily worship. The scene is preserved completely in the Amarna tombs,[153] where we can see that the main incidents are the emergence of the royal family from their palace (No. 63), the drive to the temple with their retinue, some of whom run on foot (Nos. 51, 73, 140), the reception by the jubilant temple staff (Nos. 36, 37, 66), the procession to the temple gates, and the making of offerings in the altar court (Nos. 17, 49, 116). Whether or not this theme was a reinterpretation of earlier temple scenes is unknown, since similar decoration has not survived, but it is significant that the temples of Ptolemaic and Roman times, which have best preserved such scenes, perpetuate the motif of the pharaoh leaving his palace to enter the temple and make offerings to the gods.[154] The temples of the Aten were shown in some detail, though probably not with reliable accuracy (Nos. 81, 82), and on the verges of the main composition there is abundant detail to fit the main scene into an appropriate setting of landscape and onlookers (Nos. 63, 66, 131). The resulting genre scenes are novel and, though often more vigorous than accomplished, add many lively touches to the compositions. At the same time they are usually incised rather than fully carved in relief, and their linear quality gives them an evanescence, so that they do not impinge upon the main feature of the composition.

It is with the aid of the scenes in the Amarna tombs that we can reconstruct into some coherence the tantalizing glimpses that we receive from the Karnak and Hermopolis fragments. There is one subject, however, which, though essential in the tomb, was inappropriate in the temple, and that was the scene of the rewarding of the tomb owner by the royal family at their Window of Appearances.[155] In compensation, there are scenes, especially from the Karnak temples, which found no echo in the tomb reliefs, such as the incomplete and enigmatic rites of the jubilee, which must have been reinterpreted to make them apply to the Aten (Nos. 7, 11). We can also identify the theme of the founding of the temple, known earlier from reliefs at Amada, for instance,[156] and much later in the Ptolemaic temples.[157] Of such a scene all that has survived to hint at its existence are three or four reliefs showing men engaged in construction work carrying the stones of which the temples at Karnak and Amarna were built (No. 68). At least one such fragment has survived from Karnak to suggest that the subject belongs to the first years of the reign.[158]

There are, however, a number of fragments that have no parallel in earlier or later scenes, and of these not the least ambiguous are the reliefs in which cattle are seen browsing in the open (Nos. 80, 145). It is uncertain whether these belong to a great hunting scene in which the animals of the wild are rounded up by the pharaoh in his chariot, or whether they are parts of a pastoral scene, which showed goats as well as cattle in the domains of the Aten (No. 72), all contented in their rushy meadows under the beneficent rays of the Disk. A scene in the Royal Tomb showed the sun rising upon the temple and ostriches and gazelles rousing themselves from their sleep.[159] This theme was surely not unique, but was probably inspired by an archetype occurring in the decoration of temple walls. It is possible that it was a sculptural representation of the sentiments expressed in the Hymn to the Aten, showing the entire cycle of the day under the rule of the sun god. At his rising, "all cattle are at peace in their pastures; the trees and herbage grow green. The birds fly from their nests with wings [raised] in praise of your spirit. All animals gambol. . . . When you set in the western horizon, the earth is in darkness . . . men pass the night indoors with head covered. . . ."

This last phrase may explain reliefs in Brooklyn and Boston (Nos. 70, 65) in which men are seen sleeping beside fires, perhaps in the open, but possibly in a chamber. For further information and a definite opinion we shall have to await the discovery of more reliefs from Hermopolis or Karnak, and their full publication.

THE CHARACTER OF AMARNA ART

The extent and nature of the revolution in Egyptian art that occurred in the early years of Akhenaten's reign can be readily discerned by comparing a relief such as the Berlin house stela (No. 16), made between Years 6 and 9, with any relief from the Theban tombs of Khaemhet, Amenemhet called Surer, or Kheruef carved in the last years of Amenhotep III.[160] The first gives a visual rendering in sunk relief of an abnormal aspect of the human form, by bold rather than careful drawing. The others are traditional in presenting the human form as an intellectually perceived ideal, and in expressing that perfection by meticulous drawing and exquisite carving in low relief. It is the inevitability of the existence of Khaemhet, Amenemhet called Surer, and Kheruef in some world beyond human care that moves us to admire and pay homage. By contrast, the family of Akhenaten on the Berlin stela is very much alive in a transient world of human emotion and suffering. The time represented is not eternity but a brief moment in the lives of five beings as they are caught in an act of mutual affection under the daytime disk of the Aten, with the north wind fluttering the streamers on their dress. The space in which they exist is the circumscribed world of a garden pavilion built of slender reeds and rushes, having no symbolic meaning in this context. Our main reaction is not of wonder or awe but of sympathy with the King and Queen in the human predicament in which they are represented.

These are the obvious distinctions between the reliefs of Akhenaten and those of Amenhotep III (Fig. 46) made only a few years earlier or perhaps even contemporaneously. There are, however, other differences so fundamental that these reliefs might be the work of separate cultures rather than of different artists. The tomb carvings show man as a symbol, with both feet seen in their interior aspect and each pair of hands appearing as two identical versions of the same hand. They are, in fact, *symbols* of feet and hands, and as such had existed since Egyptian drawing had crystallized into an accepted canon in archaic times. In the Berlin stela, however, the left and right feet are carefully differentiated, and the hands of the children also appear to be distinguished, though the scale of the latter is too small for certainty. What is clear, however, is that while the sidelock of Merytaten is shown in detail worn on her right side, those of the other children are obscured, since they are facing left. In other words, the artist conceived of his figures as existing within the reality of space and not within the two-dimensional confines of the picture. This is an entirely new vision on the part of the sculptor, which is rare in the ancient world, though there is a hint of it in a painting in London (British Museum 37984) and a somewhat ambiguous representation earlier in Crete.[161] Its arrival can almost be pinpointed. The distinction between left and right feet is not made in the nearly contemporary tomb at Thebes, nor in those of Ramose and Parennefer dating to the first years of Akhenaten's reign.[162] It is not used on the early parapets at Tell el Amarna, though it puts in a sporadic appearance on the Boundary Stelae[163] and is fully established on the stela from the Royal Tomb (Fig. 34) and on the Berlin house stela (No. 16), both dating to between Years 6 and 9. It appears to be an innovation of the King's sculptors, because it is confined to figures of the royal family (No. 58); for the rest, the old conventions prevailed, as is evident in the reliefs on the walls of the private tombs at Tell el Amarna. The same distinction is made in the Memphite tomb of Haremheb,[164] and in the paintings in the tomb of Tutankhamen it is confined to the feet of the living. That it was considered alien is seen in the reversion to the traditional assemblage of parts in the reliefs of Ramesside times, such as the detailed low reliefs of Sety I in his temple at Abydos, where both feet are carved with two inner profiles.

This might be accredited to a resumption of the old conventions with an antiquarian return to the orthodox art of the past, but that it was really a reversion to ancient Egyptian instincts is seen in the change of design in the sarcophagi of the immediate post-Amarna kings. Tutankhamen has a sarcophagus with one of the goddesses of the four quarters standing at each exterior corner in such a position that half her body falls vertically on the long side, and the other half on the short end.[165] This is a continuation of a design which was new for sarcophagi and apparently an innovation of the Amarna Period, to judge from a fragment in which Nefertiti plays the part of a goddess.[166] It reveals that space was conceived as a totality and not as the contiguity of adjacent planes.

That this new concept was outside the natural experience of the Egyptian artist is suggested by the sarcophagus of Haremheb which, although only a few years later in date, shows that the position of the goddesses has been shifted slightly so that two are fully revealed on each long side, only one of their winged arms being visible at the head and foot ends.[167]

The same management of space, but comprehended from within rather than from without, is seen in the reliefs carved on the walls of the tomb chambers at Tell el Amarna, which, as we have pointed out earlier, almost certainly copy designs used in the decoration of the temples. In place of the former extracts from the pattern books assembled according to the taste of the patron in a medley of subjects, each wall is considered as an entity and covered with one complete scene. In a chamber in the Royal Tomb one scene is spread over two adjacent walls, and a room in the Northern Palace at Tell el Amarna was apparently decorated with bird life in a continuous marshscape spread over all walls.[168]

Moreover, the composition on each wall is put into an appropriate spatial setting that may be either landscape or architecture. The action portrayed is not conceived as existing in some absolute dimension, but within a prescribed limit of time and place. Thus two compositions of the royal family at meat in the tomb of Huya show on the one wall the eating of food in the palace by day, and on the other the drinking of wine there by night.[169] The reliefs of men asleep are also new in this sun-drenched world of the Aten and can only have been devised to signify time (Nos. 65, 70). Every scene has its appropriate architectural or landscape setting. It is true that larger-scale single-subject compositions do appear on the walls of tombs in the last years of Amenhotep III and that some of them are

Fig. 46. Relief in the tomb of Khaemhet at Thebes, showing officials receiving jewels at an investiture before Amenhotep III on the occasion of his first jubilee. Reprinted with the permission of The Metropolitan Museum of Art. Photography by Egyptian Expedition.

placed in their proper context, whether before the baldachin of the King or in the sporting world of the marsh goddess,[170] but at Tell el Amarna no picture can easily be divorced from its setting, whether it is the palace, the Window of Appearances, the temple, the chariot roadway, or the police barracks.[171] One is aware that the action is taking place in a specific part of the City of the Aten and not in some indeterminate other world.

This attempt to give verisimilitude to activity centered in the world of the living may be a reflection of that more concrete conception of existence that the sun cult of the Aten promoted. The eternal life for which the courtiers prayed was not in the shadowy Osirian netherworld, for Osiris had been banished from the burial, but at sunlit Tell el Amarna near their King, "as the patron of the dead, in whose control all privileges and means of happiness for both worlds lay."[172] It would appear that the Great Temple of the Aten, with its forest of offering tables, functioned for the souls of the dead as well as for the living, for many of the burial petitions pray that the deceased may receive libations and offerings in the Temple of the Aten.[173]

The worship of the royal family as the intermediary between the god and mankind was often conducted in the house shrine at Tell el Amarna, with the stela as the focal point of the cult (Nos. 16, 56). It is a feature of the new concept of a divine family that each member of it should be distinctive. Akhenaten and Nefertiti on these stelae are not shown in exactly the same pose, and the figures of the daughters are carefully differentiated except when they participate as sistrum players at the worship of the Aten. This emphasis upon individuality, particularly in children, is a new feature of Egyptian art and is perhaps an expression of that delight in personal achievement that is characteristic of the age. The infant is no longer represented as a symbol like a hieroglyph, a naked child with a sidelock and a finger in its mouth, or as an adult on a miniature scale. He becomes a person in his own right with the disproportionately large head of the child (Nos. 35, 130), a feature which is retained during the early reign of Tutankhamen in the figures of the King that surmount his gold and silver staves.[174] The child's index finger is taken out of its mouth and used to caress a companion (Fig. 20; No. 130), or to indulge in the typically childish gesture of pointing (No. 16).

The visual representation of man as an individual is seen to advantage in the management of crowd scenes at Tell el Amarna. The best reliefs and paintings at all periods of ancient Egypt furnish examples of the felicitous representations of assemblies of people in a variety of poses. The Amarna artists, however, excelled in the portrayal of groups, delighting in the different rhythms and patterns that were created by placing heads and bodies in individual postures (Nos. 74, 139; cf. No. 93). The old device of the overlapping contours, which, for instance, so disturbs our appreciation of the crowd of mourners in the tomb of Ramose,[175] is used only on the verges of compositions where onlookers are represented acting as units, cohorts of troops, squads of scribes, embassies of foreigners, or bevies of ladies in waiting (No. 139). In the scene of mourning in the Royal Tomb,[176] all the weepers are carefully distinguished by posture, a remarkable achievement in a composition which invariably called for groups of professional mourners. In the case of the main actors and even of the minor actors in the scenes represented at Tell el Amarna, there is a conscious attempt to show them as individuals with their distinctive physiques (Nos. 72, 75). They may reveal the signs of age or corpulence, in such frankness probably following the example of their King, who did not scruple to have the peculiarities of his curious anatomy blatantly paraded.

When these individuals are banded together in groups, they are seldom enclosed in the separate "frames" of traditional Egyptian composition, in which a square or rectangle can be drawn around the various parts to resolve them into the units from which they were constructed. Instead, the various groups, isolated at their different activities, are connected by linkages to form a completely co-ordinated scene. Frankfort, in an acute study,[177] has drawn attention to this feature, which can be seen even in the traditional processions of tribute bearers, in which figures kneel or prostrate themselves with outflung arms, or captors haul their charges forward, to break up the conventional pose and placing of a row of foreigners.[178] But it can be seen particularly vividly in the reliefs and paintings in which Akhenaten and Nefertiti dandle their children (Nos. 16, 92). The unity of the family is emphasized by a completely integrated composition, in one case by the daring device of placing Nefertiti in her husband's lap with the children disposed between them (No. 56). We have only to compare the Theban tomb paintings of tutors with several of their royal charges seated stiffly in echelon on their knees[179] to see what the new vision has done to such a theme. In the process the royal family has gained humanity at the expense of regal dignity, and it is perhaps significant that when Ankhesenpaaten reaches up to play with the ornament on her mother's crown in the Berlin stela (No. 16), we should be reminded of a vignette in the Theban tomb of Menna, where the baby of a nameless peasant woman seated under a tree lifts her hand in the same way to touch her mother's earring.[180]

Thus each part of the grand composition is integrated in the same way as the whole. The result is a dramatic performance represented within space as upon a stage with the City of the Aten as its setting. The scenes on tomb and temple walls show the passing pageant as full of the tension of a moment of time—the excited and jubilant arrival at the temple, the pride and joy of the presentation of awards at the Window of Appearances, and the vibrant fervor of the actual worship (Fig. 47).[181] All the actors in the play are individuals, even the children. Nowhere else in Egyptian art do we get so vivid an impression of the excitement of a bold experiment in living and worship. The significance of this drama is conveyed by another innovation—the visual expression of emotion. Egyptian art had always been concerned with transmitting ideas and information by means of symbols. In the Amarna Period symbols were not discarded, but transmuted. Joy was expressed by something more than the raising of both hands on high; each arm is held at a different angle and the fingers are recurved in an expectant tension.[182] At the same time the face is directed upward in a kind of ecstatic vision. The King and Queen raise their eyes to the Aten (Nos. 14, 31); their courtiers raise their eyes to them (Nos.

Fig. 47. Relief in the tomb of Ipy at Tell el Amarna, showing the royal family offering to the Aten. After a line drawing by Norman de Garis Davies (Davies 1906). Reprinted with the permission of the Egypt Exploration Society.

138, 139). The technique of modeling the relief in plaster has often assisted the sculptor in achieving an individual cast to features and distinct facial expression.[183] An emotion such as joy or tension (No. 118) is shown not only by the principals; the onlookers too may burst into wild capering in their excitement.[184] One of the discoveries of Amarna artists was the importance of the hand in conveying a mood as well as an action (Nos. 18, 35, 118, 130). The fingers of Amarna hands are made long and are recurved in an elegant sensitivity. The gestures of these hands assist in the dramatic presentation of a scene, just as they do in paintings of seventeenth-century Europe, which were greatly influenced by the stage with its expressive posing of the hands in mime. At Tell el Amarna the gestures of the hands also assist in the dramatic presentation of a scene, and the artists had something more to do than to practice the carving of a few stereotyped actions of the hand (Nos. 146, 147). For one thing, the left and right hands of the royal family and their retainers are usually differentiated, like their feet, particularly in the reliefs of the later reign (Nos. 74, 118, 137, 139).[185]

During the reign of Akhenaten the old subjects for illustration were proscribed. They might be modified, but the need for new interpretation was in itself a revolutionary idea that demanded revolutionary treatment. The attempt of the artists to show the scenes of contemporary life as though set upon a stage at Karnak or at Tell el Amarna is hardly unconscious. The main actors, the King and Queen and their retinue, hold the center of the stage, and the subsidiary players are grouped in the wings. There is none of the untidiness of real life in these compositions. The scenes are organized so as to present an event dramatically, with all extraneous detail carefully excluded. But this presentation is made in visual terms, the actors are put in their proper places and their natural setting, and their relationship to one another by gesture or other linkages is expressed by purely artistic means. If the artist's equipment was too limited for him to attain the complete illusion for which he was striving—and this could only have been achieved by the use of perspective—he made some shift with a kind of "cavalier perspective," as Frankfort has demonstrated.[186] As such it was a notable achievement in the art of the ancient world. It vanished under the forces of reaction, together with the vision that had given it birth, though echoes of it persisted in battle scenes on Ramesside temple walls.

Amarna art in the integration of its compositions betrays the same mental processes that in the sphere of religious thought brought about a simpler eschatology, a more joyous acceptance of the natural world, and a more rational belief in a universal sole god.

1. Breasted 1948, pp. 356, 392.
2. Aldred 1971, pp. 4–5.
3. Aldred 1971, pp. 37–39.
4. Aldred 1971, pp. 29–30.
5. Piankoff 1964, p. 218.
6. Anthes 1952; Westendorf 1966.
7. Hayes 1962, pp. 3–5.
8. Gardiner 1947, p. 190*.
9. Aldred 1971, p. 32.
10. Hayes 1962, p. 4.
11. Cf. Davies 1943, p. 81 (18).
12. Gauthier 1912, pp. 335–336 C III, B.
13. Aldred 1970, p. 111.
14. Aldred 1968, pp. 88–89.
15. Aldred 1971, pp. 32–33.
16. Aldred 1971, p. 41.
17. Gardiner 1961, p. 217.
18. May was its steward; see Davies 1908a, pl. IV.
19. Cf. Bennett 1965, pp. 207 ff.
20. See Aldred 1971, p. 6 for references to these examples of antiquarian interest during the reign of Amenhotep III.
21. Gardiner 1961, p. 228.
22. Sa'ad 1970, p. 192.
23. Aldred 1968, Chap. VII.
24. Aldred 1968, pp. 88–89.
25. Gunn 1923, pp. 170–72.
26. Davies 1908a, pl. XXIX, column X.
27. Davies 1908a, pp. 19–33.
28. Aldred 1968, p. 185.
29. Aldred 1959a, p. 30.
30. Cf. Bennett 1965, p. 209.
31. Aldred 1959a, p. 30.
32. Fairman 1951, p. 153.
33. Davies 1905a, pls. 37–40; 1905b, pls. 13–15.
34. Aldred 1970, pp. 105 ff.
35. Engelbach 1931, p. 102, n. 2.
36. Aldred 1968, pp. 242–43.
37. Roeder 1969, pl. 16, 406 VII A, p. 274 G.1.
38. Harrison 1966, pp. 111–12.
39. Cf. Fairman 1972, p. 17.
40. Roeder 1969, 826/VIII A, p. 169, 5 d.
41. Aldred 1961c, pp. 48–49.
42. Roeder 1969, 54, N1 H (i); 58, N4 (d) and (i).
43. Aldred 1971, pp. 37–38.
44. Porter and Moss 1937, pp. 171, 220.
45. Nims 1968, p. 544.
46. Legrain 1902, pp. 262–63.
47. Fairman 1951, pp. 191–97; Doresse 1955.
48. Davies 1941, pl. 33.
49. Fairman 1951, pp. 195–97.
50. Hayes 1951, p. 180.
51. Porter and Moss 1972, p. 253.
52. Legrain 1902, p. 264.
53. Porter and Moss 1972, p. 586, V "talatat".
54. Davies 1923a, pp. 136–45; Aldred 1959c, pp. 116–20.
55. Davies 1908a, p. 19.
56. Helck 1958, p. 300, n. 7.
57. Fairman 1951, p. 190, n. 1.
58. Cf. Fairman 1951, p. 197.
59. Petrie 1894, pp. 1, 18.
60. Bissing 1905–1928.
61. Badawy 1968, pp. 200–201.
62. Pendlebury 1951, pls. 4, 6A, 6B.
63. Petrie 1894, pp. 12–13; Bissing and Reach 1906.
64. Cooney 1965, pp. 1–3.
65. Sauneron and Sa'ad 1969.
66. Davies 1903–1908.
67. Anthes 1954, pp. 6–8.
68. Davies 1903, p. 18.
69. Bouriant 1903, pl. 6.
70. Hamza 1941.
71. Aldred 1968, p. 97; Fairman 1972, p. 18.
72. Aldred 1968, p. 243.
73. Porter and Moss 1934, pp. 202–204, 206.
74. Found in House R47.2 (Berlin Museum no. 21.193). Borchardt 1923, p. 31, n. 1.
75. Young 1964.
76. de Wit 1950, pls. 4–5, 54–55.
77. Quibell 1909, pl. 55.
78. Quibell 1908, pls. 4–5, 10, 12.
79. Roeder 1941.
80. Schäfer 1931, pls. 8, 13–14, 20–21, 32, 34–36.
81. Borchardt 1923, pp. 20–24.
82. Frankfort 1927, p. 213.
83. Lloyd 1933, pp. 1–2.
84. Breasted 1948, Chap. 18.
85. Davies 1941, pls. 29, 33.
86. Davies 1941, p. 4.
87. Davies 1908a, p. 24.
88. Davies 1905a, pl. 38.
89. Davies 1903, p. 42.
90. Davies 1921, p. 5.
91. Davies 1905a, pl. 38; 1905b, p. 10, pl. 13.
92. Frankfort 1927, pls. 45, 47.
93. Fairman 1951, p. 153.
94. Weigall 1922, pp. 199–200.
95. Sa'ad 1970, p. 189.
96. Sa'ad 1970, p. 192.
97. Smith 1958, p. 276, notes 17, 18.
98. Aldred 1970, pp. 112–13.
99. Porter and Moss 1960, Appendix A, pp. 463 ff.
100. Aldred 1962, pp. 293 ff.
101. Samson 1972, p. 23; Vandier 1958, p. 337, n. 2; Smith 1958, p. 180; Westendorf 1963, pp. 269 ff.
102. Harrison 1966, pp. 114–15.
103. Quibell 1908, p. 70.
104. Davies 1941, pls. 30–31, 34, 36.
105. Aldred 1957b.
106. Davies 1941, pl. 33; Hayes 1959, fig. 142; Scamuzzi 1963, pls. 57–59.
107. Chassinat 1901, pp. 226–27.
108. British Museum 1972, no. 22; Aldred 1956, pl. II, 5.
109. Aldred 1953, pp. 194–95.
110. Murray 1934, pp. 65–66.
111. British Museum 1972, no. 25.
112. Davies 1943, pls. 36, 37.
113. Davies 1908a, p. 23.
114. Habachi 1965, pp. 85 ff.
115. Cooney 1965, p. 22.
116. Habachi 1965, fig. 11.
117. Cooney 1965, nos. 56–57.
118. Davies 1936, pl. 70.
119. Aldred 1968, pl. 8.
120. Newberry 1928, p. 8.
121. Quibell and Hayter 1927, pp. 10–11, pls. 8–13.
122. Davies 1908b, pls. 29, 38, 39, 42.
123. Davis 1910, pls. 29, 32, 33.
124. Smith 1958, pl. 124 (b).
125. Davies 1926, pls. 27, 28.
126. Davies 1905b, pl. 9, and Cat. nos. 150, 172.
127. Davies 1905a, pp. 6, 30–31; 1905b, pp. 2–3; 1908b, pp. 3, 15–16, 26.
128. Roeder 1941, pp. 379–81; Kap. VII E.6–11.
129. Griffith 1931, pl. 23.
130. E.g. Berlin no. 21.63 (Pl. no. VI); Louvre no. 891 (Pl. no. XXIX).
131. See note 129 above.
132. Nelson 1932, pls. 116–17, 130; Groenewegen-Frankfort 1951, pl. XLVIII.
133. Davies 1962, pls. I–V.
134. Sa'ad 1970, p. 190.
135. Smith 1958, pl. 181; Smith 1967, p. 26.
136. Davies 1912, p. 128, fig. 4.
137. Pendlebury 1951, pls. XLI, 2, 3; LVIII, 3; LXVIII, 3–6.
138. Smith 1967, p. 30 (described as a jackal).
139. Davies 1962, pl. III.
140. Lepsius 1848–1859, Part 4, pls. 88–89.
141. British Museum 1972, no. 21.
142. British Museum 1972, no. 25.
143. Cf. Hayes 1959, p. 243, fig. 147.
144. Cooney 1965, nos. 62–63.
145. Davies 1905a, pl. 32.
146. Lepsius 1848–1859, Part 3, pls. 35c, 52.
147. British Museum 1972, no. 25.
148. Porter and Moss 1972, pp. 326 ff. (Room XIII).
149. Cooney 1965, no. 17.
150. Davies 1908b, pl. 4.
151. Davies 1905b, pl. 32A; 1906, pl. 22; 1908a, pl. 26; 1908b, pls. 4, 29.
152. For a pre-Amarna version see the bark shrine of Hatshepsut (Porter and Moss 1972, p. 66, V. 44).
153. Davies 1903, pls. 10, 10A; 1905a, pl. 13.
154. Porter and Moss 1939, p. 46 (17)–(19); p. 47 (21)–(27); p. 132 (85)–(91).
155. E.g. Davies 1908b, pls. 4, 19, 29.
156. Porter and Moss 1951, p. 72 (69)–(70).
157. Porter and Moss 1939, p. 50 (43)–(51); p. 131 (77)–(81); p. 132 (83)–(84).
158. Leclant 1955, pl. 21, fig. 8.
159. Bouriant 1903, pl. 1.
160. Porter and Moss 1960, no. 48, pp. 87 ff; no. 57, pp. 113 ff.; no. 192, pp. 298 ff.
161. Davies 1936, pl. 70; Evans 1928, figs. 454, 483.
162. Davies 1941, passim; Davies 1923a, pp. 22–26.
163. Davies 1908a, pls. 26, 33.
164. Boeser 1911, pls. 23, 24.
165. Carter 1927, pls. 64, 65.
166. Schäfer 1931, pl. 56.
167. Hornung 1971, pls. 62, 65.
168. Frankfort 1929, pp. 58 ff.
169. Davies 1905b, pls. 4, 6.
170. Wreszinski 1923, 88 b (1), 206: I, 2a, 423.
171. Davies 1905b, pls. 33, 34; 1908b, pl. 29; 1903, pl. 25; 1905a, pl. 13; 1906, pl. 26.
172. Davies 1903, p. 46.
173. Davies 1908b, p. 35; 1905b, pp. 17–18.
174. See note 108 above.
175. Davies 1941, pl. 25.
176. Bouriant 1903, pl. VI.
177. Frankfort 1929, pp. 9–10.
178. Davies 1905a, pl. 38.
179. Davies 1923b, p. 42, fig. 3.
180. Mekhitarian 1954, pl. on p. 79.
181. Davies 1905a, pl. 13; 1903, pl. 8; 1905a, pl. 12.
182. Davies 1908b, pl. 4.
183. Davies 1905a, p. 18.
184. Davies 1908b, pl. 29; 1905a, pl. 38 (lowermost register).
185. Cooney 1965, no. 20.
186. Frankfort 1929, p. 14.

No. 19
Head of Queen Tiye

No. 22 Torso of a queen

No. 25
Nefertiti presenting
an offering (detail)

No. 72
Herdsman
with goat (detail)

No. 88   A princess

No. 146
An olive branch for the Aten (detail)

No. 175
Head and shoulder of a *shawabti*

No. 99
A youthful queen

THE CATALOGUE
NOS. 1–175

Bibliographical entries marked with an asterisk (*) are selective. The publications chosen are primarily those that are most easily accessible to the greatest number of readers and/or that contain useful illustrations. Each entry not accompanied by an asterisk is either complete or contains, it is hoped, references to all works in which the piece in question is illustrated.

No. 1
STATUETTE OF AKHENATEN
Early Period

Collection: Ägyptisches Museum, Berlin (West) 21835

The King is dressed in a short pleated sash and wears the Blue Crown. He holds a stela upright before him, and his figure is supported by a back pillar.

Material: Fine hard white calcite ("alabaster").

Color: Minute trace of blue pigment on crown.

Measurements: Height 12 cm. Width of King 3 cm. Height of head with crown 2.6 cm. Height of face 1.1 cm. Height of base 0.8 cm. Width of base 2.6 cm. Depth of base 5.8 cm. Height of stela 6.7 cm. Width of stela 2.5 cm.

Condition: Fragment from right-hand side of stela missing.

Provenance: Tell el Amarna. Excavated by the Deutsche Orient-Gesellschaft in 1912, in House N 48, 15, in town north of Main Wadi.

COMMENTARY: This statuette, probably contained in a small shrine, was evidently part of the furnishings of a private chapel in the house where it was found. Such features as eyes, ears, and uraeus appear not to have been fully carved, but details of these were perhaps once supplied in color. To judge from the particle of bright blue pigment on the crown, the statuette may once have been fully painted, but the pigment has not survived on the hard, polished surface of the stone. Inscriptions on the stela and back pillar (perhaps including the names of the Aten) were probably once written in ink, but all traces of these have also been removed by time. The overall style of the piece and the frankly feminine features of the King's physique suggest the early years of Akhenaten's reign. The statuette appears to be a replica on a miniature scale of one of the statues of near life size in the Great Temple of the Aten (No. 20).

Bibliography: Porter and Moss 1934, p. 205. Add: Fechheimer 1922a, pl. 85; Murray 1930, pl. XXXIII; Hermann and Schwan 1940, p. 83, illus.; Murray 1949, p. 157, pl. LXI; Berlin West 1967, p. 67, no. 744, illus.

No. 2
FRAGMENT OF A ROYAL HEAD
Early Period

Collection: British Museum, London 13366

The head is preserved only from below the eyes to the base of the neck, and what remains has been battered, but characteristic features point to its identification as an early portrayal of Akhenaten.

Material: Indurated limestone, much fissured.

Color: Grayish; no added color.

Measurements: Height (above modern base) 15.8 cm. Width 11 cm. Depth 13.8 cm. Height of preserved part of face 9.7 cm.

Condition: Upper part of head, ears, and back of skull, together with most of nose and chin, now missing; remains of deep vertical drill hole at rear of head.

Provenance: Tell el Amarna ("Alabastron"); presumably from the southeast area of the Great Temple. Presented to the British Museum in 1853 by J. S. Perring.

COMMENTARY: It was not unknown for parts of statues to be broken off during the making (cf. No. 52), and this head was apparently parted from its body in antiquity and rejoined to it by a dowel of wood or metal (cf. No. 22). The fissured stone of which it was made seems to have been particularly brittle and subject to fracture. The sensuous mouth with its fleshy lips resembles that of Akhenaten. Although the cheeks are rounded and youthful, there is a slight indication of a line running from nostril to chin on the right-hand side. There is no indication of an Adam's apple, and the neck shows no wrinkles, although a tendon may be traced on the left. The chin, largely reconstructed, is deep in profile, however, and a line along the edge of the right cheek probably indicates the *afnet* headdress, and thus confirms the identification of the head as that of the King rather than the Queen. The piece was said to have been found in the ruins of a temple at "Alabastron," the name given to Tell el Amarna by early travelers on account of the nearby alabaster quarries at Hatnub. The exact findspot is said to have been "El Tell," which suggests that it was picked up near the surface of the mounds covering the Great Temple, probably at or near the dump where Petrie and Carter later unearthed the Amherst fragments (see No. 4).

Bibliography: Porter and Moss 1934, p. 197. Add: Petrie 1894, p. 18; Budge 1923, pl. VIII facing p. 80; Vandier 1958, p. 336.

No. 3
FRAGMENT OF THE KING'S
FACE

Early Period
Collection: The Metropolitan Museum of Art, New York 26.7.1395 (Carnarvon Collection, 1926; Gift of Edward S. Harkness, 1926)
A fragment from a statue that was about two-thirds life size shows the exaggerations characteristic of the early years of Akhenaten's reign.
Material: Indurated limestone.
Color: No trace.
Measurements: Height 8.1 cm. Width 5.1 cm. Depth ca. 4.5 cm.
Condition: Fragmentary but without flaws.
Provenance: Tell el Amarna. Excavated by Carter and Petrie in 1891–1892 on the southeast side of the Great Temple. Formerly in the Amherst and Carnarvon collections.
COMMENTARY: Though in the Early Period there is often little to distinguish portraits of Akhenaten from those of Nefertiti, this piece, attributed by Petrie to Nefertiti (Petrie 1894, pl. I, 15), certainly portrays the King. It is superbly modeled by a master's hand, and the marblelike stone lends perfection to the small fragment.

* *Bibliography:* Porter and Moss 1934, p. 234. Add: Amherst 1921, p. 75, no. 842, and pl. XIII; Burlington 1922, p. 81, no. 40a, and pl. VI; New York 1937, no. 17, illus.; New York 1945, 17th pl.; Hayes 1959, p. 286, fig. 174; New York 1962, p. 28, fig. 35; Posener, Sauneron and Yoyotte 1962, p. 270, illus.; Fischer 1965, p. 175, fig. 10.

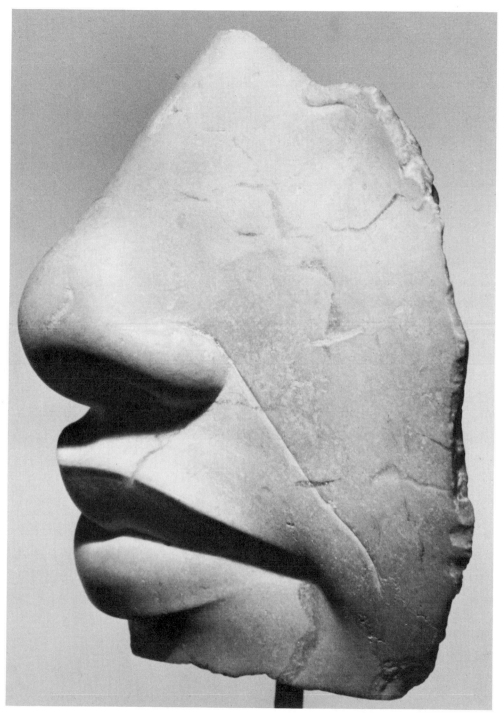

No. 4
TORSO OF AKHENATEN
Early Period

Collection: The Brooklyn Museum 58.2

The bare, armless torso of the King is preserved from the base of the neck nearly to the waistline; at the back is a portion of a pleated sash with an inscribed band giving the early name of the Aten. The front of the torso shows the beginning of the sinewy neck, the pronounced collarbones, and the effeminate breasts characteristic of the King; a short, shallow channel, the median line, leads down to the navel. On the chest are three almost obliterated pairs of cartouches with the names of the Aten. At the rear of the torso is a back pillar with its surface hacked away below the fanlike end of a pigtail that once belonged to an *afnet* headdress.

Material: White indurated limestone.

Color: No trace.

Measurements: Height 55.1 cm. Width 44.3 cm. Depth 41 cm. Width of back pillar, top 2.9 cm. Width of break at neck 16.5 cm. Depth of break at neck 23.9 cm. Width of break at waist 32.9 cm.

Condition: Fragmentary; deliberate damage to cartouches of the Aten.

Provenance: Tell el Amarna. Excavated by H. Carter and W. M. F. Petrie in 1891–1892.

COMMENTARY: The Brooklyn torso was found with other fragments dumped in a heap on the southeast side of the Great Temple at Tell el Amarna. These fragments all passed into the possession of Lord Amherst, who had contributed to the cost of the excavation, and when his collection was dispersed in 1921 they were sold at auction in thirteen lots. Most of the fragments were eventually acquired by The Metropolitan Museum of Art (Nos. 5, 20). The great torso, however, passed through several collections in Paris before it came to The Brooklyn Museum. It is probable that all the statues represented by these fragments received two consecutive mutilations before they were buried, the first being the elimination of the more prominent cartouches of the Aten and the desecration of the features of the King, and the second being the overthrow of the sculptures for the sake of the stone of their pedestals. This final destruction may have been effected in Ramesside times, when the Great Temple appears to have been demolished to provide fill for a new construction at Hermopolis on the opposite side of the Nile. Traces at the sides of the torso show that the arms did not hang free and indicate that they may have been bent at the elbows to present a stela or an offering table (Pendlebury 1951, pl. LXIV, 4–6, and No. 1).

Bibliography: Petrie 1894, mentioned vaguely on p. 18; Amherst 1921, p. 75, no. 838; Sambon 1931, pl. III; Cooney 1965, pp. 102–106, illus.; Scott and Scott 1968, p. 84, illus.; James 1973, no. 307.

No. 5
FRAGMENTARY SCULPTURE OF AKHENATEN

Early Period

Collection: The Metropolitan Museum of Art, New York 21.9.3 (Gift of Edward S. Harkness, 1921)

The King is represented with characteristic prominent neck tendons and collarbones and heavy, effeminate breasts. The body above the waist is naked, but traces of a pleated sash, bearing the names of the Aten, run diagonally across the right hip. At the rear is part of a back pillar giving a second cartouche of the Aten and the epithet "Given life forever and ever." Three pairs of cartouches containing the early names of the Aten are incised on the chest and diaphragm, and part of still another cartouche is preserved on the remains of the King's upper right arm.

Material: White indurated limestone.

Color: No trace.

Measurements: Height 33.3 cm. Width 26.9 cm. Depth at waist (slant) ca. 27 cm. Intracolumnar width 7 cm. Height of cartouche on back pillar 12.2 cm. Width of break at neck ca. 10.6 cm. Depth of break at neck with back pillar ca. 17 cm. Width of break at back pillar, upper and lower 11.3 cm.

Condition: Diagonal break upward from waist; head, legs, and arms missing.

Provenance: Tell el Amarna. Excavated in 1891–1892 by H. Carter and W. M. F. Petrie on southeast side of the Great Temple. Formerly in the Amherst Collection.

COMMENTARY: This piece was found in the same context as No. 4 and is of similar design to that fragment, although on a smaller scale. It is evident that the arms of the King were held at his sides and not bent at the elbows to hold an offering table. Traces on the back indicate that he wore the *afnet* headdress.

* *Bibliography:* Porter and Moss 1934, p. 197. Add: Amherst 1921, p. 75, no. 839; Vandier 1958, pp. 336, 340; Hayes 1959, p. 285, fig. 173, right; Aldred 1968, p. 184, pl. 88, right.

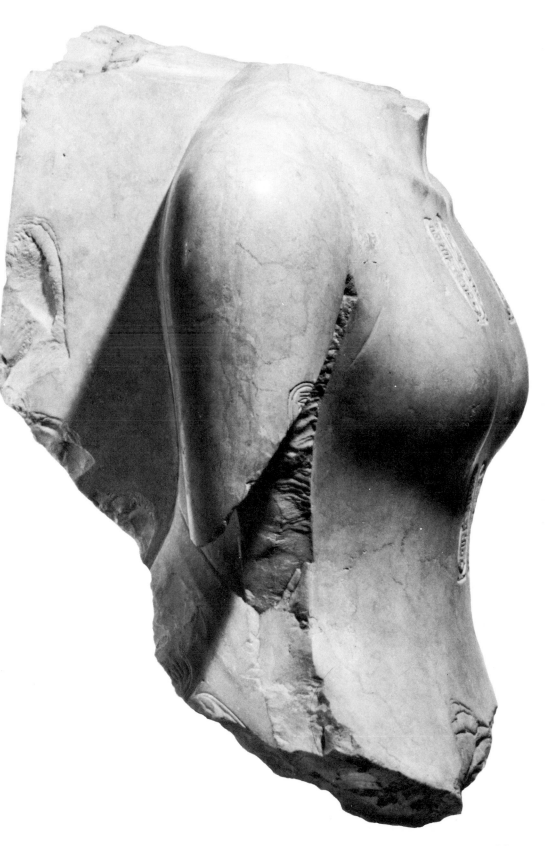

No. 6
FACE OF AKHENATEN
Early Period
Collection: Ägyptisches Museum, Berlin (West) 14512
Fragment of sunk relief, with head of the crowned Akhenaten facing right.
Material: Limestone.
Color: No trace.
Measurements: Height 15.4 cm. Width 11.1 cm. Thickness ca. 3.2 cm. Height of face to edge of crown 8.3 cm.
Condition: Sawed from larger block; upper part broken away.
Provenance: Not known. Acquired in 1900.
COMMENTARY: The fragment evidently once formed part of a large relief in which the King was shown in side view raising both hands in adoration, a pose known from the Boundary Stelae (No. 8). The headdress worn here, however, seems most likely to have been the White Crown, which was probably elongated to balance the exaggerated proportions of the lower part of the King's face. All the distortions of the early style of Akhenaten's reign are here shown in a manner that verges on caricature: The narrow slanting eye, with the upper edge of the lid contoured, the long nose with slightly bulbous tip, the thick everted lips, the folds of flesh running from the nostrils toward the corners of the mouth, the elongated hanging jaw, and the serpentine neck—these are all conventions characterizing portraits of the King in the Early Amarna Period. Even the hole in the royal ear has been exaggerated to such an extent that the lobe has become a mere ring of flesh.

* *Bibliography:* Porter and Moss 1934, p. 233. Add: Fechheimer 1922b, pl. 155; Schäfer 1928, p. 57, fig. 68; Hamann 1944, p. 241, fig. 258; Ghalioungui 1947, p. 37, fig. 9; Lange 1951, p. 136, and pl. 12; Wolf 1957, p. 518, and p. 514, fig. 491; Berlin East 1961, pl. 37; Berlin West 1967, p. 66, no. 742, illus.

No. 7
A ROYAL JUBILEE
Early Period
Collection: Museum of Fine Arts, Boston 67.922.

The fragment of sunk relief shows the head of Akhenaten, with the Red Crown, under the rays of the Aten. Traces remain to show that the King was followed by Nefertiti and a bowing retinue.

Material: Sandstone.

Color: Traces of red pigment on faces.

Measurements: Height 20.6 cm. Width 53.1 cm. Thickness ca. 3.9 cm. Height of head to top of crown 11 cm. Height of face 5 cm. Intracolumnar width, left 4.3 cm., right 4 cm.

Condition: Edges abraded; lower portion missing.

Provenance: Karnak.

COMMENTARY: The King is not named on this fragment, but since his features are unmistakable and the Queen who so closely follows him is designated as Nefertiti, there can be no doubt that he is Akhenaten. He is shown in the earliest years of his reign celebrating a jubilee, almost certainly that of the Aten (cf. No. 11). Similar fragments, probably from an early Aten temple at Karnak, which are now in Paris (Louvre E. 26103 and E. 26104: Vandier 1969, p. 45, figs. 6, 7; also Clère 1968, pp. 51–54), enable us partially to reconstruct the scene. When complete, it would have shown Akhenaten, wearing the short jubilee cloak and carrying crook and flail, beneath the abundant rays of the Aten. Here, only the tips of the plumes on Nefertiti's crown are visible, but they indicate that she was represented on a much smaller scale than the King. The inscription over her head describes her as "Chief Wife of the King, Mistress of the Two Lands"; her name appears in its earlier form. The bowing dignitaries who accompany the King and Queen follow in such close proximity to the royal pair as to make it unlikely that any of the princesses participated in the scene, which was doubtless complementary to another representation showing Akhenaten in the White Crown of Upper Egypt.

Bibliography: Boston 1967b, p. 63, illus.

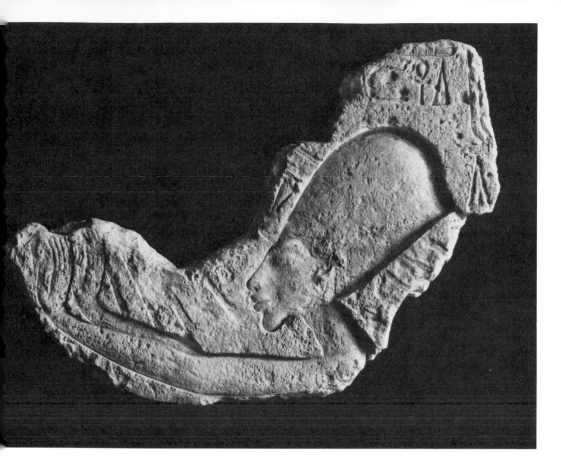

FRAGMENT OF A BOUNDARY
STELA

Early Period, Year 6
Collection: Albright–Knox Art Gallery, Buffalo 37:6
The head and shoulders of Akhenaten raising his hands in praise of the Aten, which sends the blessing of its rays, are here preserved in a fragment of one of the Boundary Stelae erected by the King to define the limits of the god's City.
Material: Nummulitic limestone.
Color: No trace.
Measurements: Height 55 cm. Width 74.5 cm. Height of head to top of crown 30 cm.
Condition: Fragmentary; nose, lips, and chin restored.
Provenance: Tell el Amarna; from Boundary Stela N on the cliffs halfway along the southern border of the City.
COMMENTARY: This fragment is a small part of the stela which was hewn in the living rock at the southern boundary of Akhet Aten, the "Horizon of Aten," as the ancient City was named. This, with some fourteen other Boundary Stelae, was carved in Year 6 of Akhenaten's reign, when the occupation of the new City began. In 1843–1845 the Prussian Expedition headed by Richard Lepsius visited the Amarna region twice and made copies and a squeeze of Stela N as it then existed (Fig. 48), and sixty years later it was again copied in a line drawing by Norman de Garis Davies, so there is no doubt of the origin of the present fragment. The complete relief, like those on the other Boundary Stelae, pictured the royal family with all the extreme mannerisms of the early style—wasp waists, enormous buttocks and thighs, emaciated features. In this fragment such distortions are still to be sensed in the exaggerated length of the Blue Crown and the thick lips, pendulous chin, skinny, sinuous neck, and almost clawlike hands of the King. It is such idiosyncrasies that have been copied, or rather parodied, by the many modern forgers of Amarna art. On Stela N, as on the other Boundary Stelae, the King and Queen, accompanied by one or two princesses, were depicted before an offering table, under the rays of the Aten to whom they raised their hands in adoration. The Buffalo fragment shows at the top, below the first cartouche of the Aten, part of an inscription, "Given life forever [and ever]," and, at the extreme right, the edge of the King's cartouche and the words "Given life."

Fig. 48. Squeeze of Boundary Stela N made in 1843–1845 by the Prussian Expedition headed by Richard Lepsius.

* *Bibliography:* Porter and Moss 1934, p. 231. Add: Lepsius 1848–1859a, pl. 295, fig. 45; Lepsius 1904, p. 129; Schäfer 1928, p. 55, fig. 65; Schäfer 1931, pl. 12; Schäfer 1936, pl. 26; Buffalo 1938, p. 90, illus.; Cooney 1939; Roeder 1961, pl. 2.

No. 9
TRIAL PIECE

Early Period

Collection: Musées Royaux d'Art et d'Histoire, Brussels E. 3051

Even if other evidence were lacking, the irregular shape of this random flake of stone would make it clear that the relief of a king's head carved upon it was the work of an apprentice.

Material: Limestone.

Color: No trace.

Measurements: Height 13.9 cm. Width 9.7 cm. Thickness 2.6 cm. Height of face 4.6 cm.

Condition: Apparently complete; sporadic dendritic markings.

Provenance: Said to be Tell el Amarna.

COMMENTARY: The head carved on this block shows most of the mannerisms of the Early Period of Amarna art, and the person represented is evidently Akhenaten. Although the King wears a short Nubian wig of military cut with only some rudimentary scratches indicating a uraeus, the features are the familiar narrow slanting eye, long nose, hollow cheeks, thick lips, and hanging chin. The edge of the jaw is indicated, as are the folds of the neck, but the S-shaped contour of the back of the neck is not pronounced. The carving of the wig is unfinished.

* *Bibliography*: Capart 1908, p. 84, fig. 10; Capart 1909, pl. 71; Capart 1911, pp. 31–34, and fig. 10; Maspero 1912, p. 184, fig. 337; Capart 1927, pp. 36–37, and pl. 50; Brussels 1934a, pl. 47; Weynants-Ronday 1940, p. 63, fig. 5; Pijoán 1945, p. 300, fig. 399; de Wit 1946, fig. 100 opposite p. 169; Brussels 1963a, pl. XII; Brussels 1963b, pl. XI; Gilbert 1966, pp. 70–71, no. 41, illus.; Brussels 1969, p. 9, illus.

No. 10
STUDY FOR A ROYAL HEAD

Early Period

Collection: Musées Royaux d'Art et d'Histoire, Brussels E. 3052

This trial piece was carved on the back of an earlier study on a larger scale, of which only the tips of nose, lips, and chin remain. While the representations on both sides of the fragment have the features of Akhenaten, there is no trace of a uraeus on the more fully preserved side of the fragment.

Material: Limestone.

Color: Red guideline visible in places.

Measurements: Height 15.2 cm. Width 13.1 cm. Thickness 1.7 cm. Height of face 6.6 cm.

Condition: About half of original block missing; remainder broken into three pieces and rejoined; top and right-hand edges worked.

Provenance: Said to be Tell el Amarna.

COMMENTARY: While the pupil who made this practice piece has caught most of the characteristics of the early Amarna style, he has been none too happy in his placement of the eye and has failed to note its downward slant. He has, however, meticulously rendered the curls of the short wig worn by the King.

* *Bibliography*: Capart 1908 pp. 85–86, figs. 11–12; Capart 1911, pp. 31–34, and figs. 11–12; Capart 1927, pp. 36–37, and pl. 50; Brussels 1934a, p. 17, fig. 31; Coremans 1936, p. 51, fig. 3; Bille-de Mot 1937, p. 82, fig. 6; Pijoán 1945, p. 300, fig. 398; Brussels 1963b, pl. X.

No. 11
JUBILEE SCENE
Early Period
Collection: Fitzwilliam Museum, Cambridge 2300.1943
A sunk relief shows Akhenaten in jubilee attire. At the left, he offers a jar of ointment to the Aten before an altar piled with food; at the right, beyond an open door, he walks in procession with scepters in his hands, attended by bowing attendants and blessed by the rays of the Aten.
Material: Limestone.
Color: Traces of red pigment.
Measurements: Height 23 cm. Width 53 cm. Thickness 6.5 cm.
Condition: Right-hand corner missing; damage to edges; blemishes on surface, some filled in modern times with plaster, of which traces remain.
Provenance: Not known; perhaps Memphis. Formerly in the Gayer-Anderson Collection.
COMMENTARY: Akhenaten, wearing a short cloak and the White Crown with a band and streamers, is probably celebrating a jubilee of the Aten rather than his own (see No. 7). In the scene at the left, which takes place within a court or roofless shrine with open door, the King offers unguent before an altar loaded with wine, bread, geese, grapes, cucumbers, and bouquets. A statuette of the King in a pose of offering is part of the altar's furnishings. An inscription in minute ill-formed hieroglyphs gives part of the titulary of the Aten and the place name "Jubilation in the Horizon [or Seat] of the Aten." In the right-hand scene the Pharaoh, holding a flail and a long-handled version of the *heka* scepter, walks in a procession under the rays of the Aten, whose hands hold alternate *ankh* and *was* signs. He is immediately preceded by a

bowing lector priest, garbed in a kilt and short wig and holding a writing palette or a papyrus roll, and by another figure almost completely destroyed. The latter can, however, be identified, on the basis of both parallel representations on similar *talatat* and the remains of an inscription, as "The Chief Seer of Re-Herakhty [etc.] in the House of the Aten in Karnak." Following the King is an *imy khent* (probably Tutu) with a kilt and shaved head, who carries a box or footstool and a staff from which sandals hang by their thongs. Both attendants wear bands with floating streamers around their heads. The rearmost is said to be, in addition to an *imy khent,* the "Chief Prophet" of the King, and this suggests that Akhenaten was at this time already considered to be a god with a cult of his own. The text stating that the Aten is within "Jubilation in his Seat or Horizon" must be a reference to a part of the temple complex of the Aten at Karnak where the jubilee ceremonies of the god were conducted. "The House of Jubilation" was the name given to the palace in which the Pharaoh celebrated his jubilee, and at Tell el Amarna it was used to designate both the official portion of the Great Palace and part of the Great Temple (Fairman in Pendlebury 1951, p. 197; Hayes 1951, pp. 177–181). By analogy it may be presumed that "Jubilation in the Seat of the Aten" was the name given to the equivalent portion of that Aten temple at Karnak, where according to all the evidence the first jubilee of the Aten was observed. Confirmation of this is provided by the fact that the King's name in the Cambridge relief has been changed from its Amenhotep form. This indicates that both the relief and the place named thereon date from early in

the reign, and that the Aten's first jubilee, unlike his later ones, which were presumably celebrated at Tell el Amarna, was celebrated at Karnak because the new capital had not yet been built. It is not yet possible to determine the provenance of the Cambridge relief with absolute certainty. Several sandstone *talatat* with scenes of the first jubilee have survived at Karnak (No. 7). The Cambridge relief and two others formerly in the Musée Guimet (Louvre A.F.6757–58) (Doresse 1955, pp. 121–122) are the only examples known in limestone. We therefore must presume that they are either the sole survivors of an otherwise unknown limestone structure at Karnak, or that they did not, despite the fact that two of them were originally purchased at Luxor, come from Karnak. The latter theory is by far the more attractive of the two, since similar limestone blocks of the Amarna Period have been discovered at Memphis (Engelbach 1915, pl. LIV) and since Gayer-Anderson acquired most of his collection in Cairo, a city close to Memphis. The Cambridge relief is carved in the somewhat bleak style current during the early part of Akhenaten's reign, but the more tractable limestone has encouraged the sculptor to execute his figures in a less angular and exaggerated manner than those carved by his contemporaries at Karnak. The quality of the carving is poor, as can be seen, now that the plaster "correction" has fallen out of the original incisions, in the changes made in the shape of the White Crown on the left.

* *Bibliography:* Griffith 1918; Schäfer 1919; Sethe 1921, pp. 123–124; Weigall 1922, p. 195; Griffith in Weigall 1922, pp. 199–200; Doresse 1955, p. 122; Aldred 1959b; Aldred 1968, p. 128, pl. 49.

No. 12
MODEL HEAD OF AKHENATEN
Early Period

Collection: Royal Scottish Museum, Edinburgh 1969.377

Akhenaten is pictured in sunk relief wearing the Blue Crown which is decorated with roundels and has ribbed streamers floating from the rear. Near the left edge of the slab is a neatly drilled round hole, doubtless made to suspend the model for future reference.

Material: Soft white limestone.

Color: No trace.

Measurements: Height 26.3 cm. Width 21.3 cm. Thickness 4.3 cm. Height of face 8.8 cm.

Condition: All edges worked and back roughly adzed in antiquity; slab broken in half across the line of the eye and rejoined; pink ferrous patination except in areas where efflorescence of salts affected original surface.

Provenance: Tell el Amarna; said to have been found in vicinity of Stela X.

COMMENTARY: That the relief is a model made by a master sculptor for the use of lesser craftsmen seems evident from its rectangular shape and worked edges, which differentiate it from the odd fragments of limestone employed by pupils for practice, generally known as trial pieces (Nos. 9, 10, 119). The present relief should be compared with a similar master relief in The Brooklyn Museum (No. 121), which also has a hole for suspension, one head carved to end just below the clavicles, and a similar rough tooling on the reverse. Here the resemblance ends. The Edinburgh specimen emphasizes the neck muscles, the collarbones, the edge of the jaw, and the vertical furrow on the cheek— all features that were suppressed in later models (No. 115). Earlier reliefs also show a prolongation of the edge of the upper eyelid, whereas later examples treat eye and lid as an independent ovoid, and, as here, examples from the beginning of the reign treat the earlobe as a circular boss with a hole rather than a slit in the center. All these details suggest that the model under discussion may belong to the Early Period and may have been used by one of the sculptors who worked on the Boundary Stelae. This is the only such relief known to this writer in which the Blue Crown has been finished in detail, with its roundels and the ribbing of its streamers carefully indicated. Near the lower right-hand corner of the slab are two circular cuts, evidently to show how the roundels should be made. This crown, unlike the *afnet* headdress specified in other models (Fig. 49), reveals the double curve of the back of the King's neck, a peculiarity of Akhenaten's anatomy as rendered by his artists (No. 117).

Bibliography: Spink 1964, no. 6, illus.

No. 13
AKHENATEN AS SPHINX
Early Period

Collection: N. Koutoulakis, Geneva
A sphinx with the features of Akhenaten is carved in sunk relief on this nearly complete slab. Its forelegs are in the shape of arms holding between their long-fingered hands a libation vessel which asperges a floral offering at the left. From the upper left-hand corner, the disk of the Aten sends its rays to accept the offering and bring life to the donor. Across the upper part of the panel, beneath a *pet* sign denoting "heaven," runs an inscription giving the names and titularies of Aten, Akhenaten, and Nefertiti.

Material: Limestone.

Color: Traces of red in the rays of the Aten and blue on body of sphinx.

Measurements: Height 58.5 cm. Width 92.5 cm. Thickness ca. 7 cm. Length of sphinx 63.2 cm. Height of head 13.8 cm. Height of face 7.8 cm.

Condition: Broken into three pieces and rejoined; damage at left-hand edge; blemish on cheek of sphinx partly restored. Top and right side cut in modern times.

Provenance: Not known.

COMMENTARY: As a manifestation of the sun on the horizon, Re-Herakhty, the sphinx was not anathema to Akhenaten, and he was not infrequently pictured in the guise of this strange animal with lion's body and human head. Other relief representations of him in this form are to be found, for example, in Cairo (JE 65926: Leibovitch 1943, p. 258, fig. 16; Hassan 1953, pp. 179–180, with fig. 117), Boston (64.1944: Boston 1964b, p. 48. illus.), Hanover (Kestner Museum 1964.3: Woldering 1964, p. 53, fig. 25), and Brooklyn (36.881: Pendlebury 1951, pl. LXVIII, 3), and fragments of several of his sphinxes sculptured in the round have been found at Tell el Amarna (Pendlebury 1951, p. 17, and pl. LVIII, 3). On the present relief, the name of the Aten appears in its earliest form, although the names of the royal pair occur in a later version that places the relief somewhere between Year 6 and Year 9 of the King's reign. In the inscription the Aten is said to be "within the Sunshade in [the temple called] Fashioner of the Horizon of the Aten in Akhetaten" (i.e. Tell el Amarna). This temple has thus far not been identified, but the "sunshades" were apparently kiosk-like structures in which members of the royal family may have received a periodic recharge of their divine power (Pendlebury 1951, pp. 203–204). Although the only "sunshades" so far known are those of royal women, the one named on this slab may have belonged to the King, who is referred to as the "fashioner [or builder] of the Horizon [or Seat] of the Aten." Sphinxes, as protectors of thresholds, were probably located so as to flank the entrances to "sunshades." The companion pieces in Boston and Hanover are undoubtedly from the same building as the one for which the present block was carved.

Bibliography: None.

Fig. 49. Sculptor's model relief carved with portrait heads of Akhenaten (left) and Smenkhkare. Excavated by the Egypt Exploration Society in 1932 on the site of the Great Temple at Tell el Amarna. Egyptian Museum, Cairo JE 59294.

No. 14
AKHENATEN WEARING THE
ATEF CROWN

Early Period
Collection: The Metropolitan Museum of Art, New York 66.99.41 (Fletcher Fund, 1966 and The Guide Foundation, Inc., Gift, 1966) In this fragment, perhaps from a stela, a more than usually attenuated figure of the King is shown making an offering to the Aten, whose name appears in three pairs of cartouches inscribed on the royal chest and diaphragm.
Material: Quartzite.
Color: Natural dark reddish brown of stone.
Measurements: Height 24.5 cm. Width 16 cm., in front 14 cm. Thickness ca. 7.6 cm. Height from chin to sun disk 8 cm.
Condition: Eye, mouth, and nose deliberately damaged; cartouches untouched.
Provenance: Said to be Tell el Amarna, Great Temple of the Aten; acquired in Cairo, 1939. Formerly in the Gallatin Collection.
COMMENTARY: This is the only representation known to the writer in which Akhenaten appears wearing the single *atef* crown—a signal refutation of the idea that this headdress is peculiar to Osiris, a god whom the King pointedly ignored. It is likely that the relief showed Akhenaten in a ceremony connected with a jubilee of the Aten, perhaps the first such celebration, to judge from the style of the King's figure and the early form of the Aten's names inscribed on his body. What remains of Akhenaten's hand indicates that he may be pouring burning incense on offerings to the god. Ancient damage to the surface of the fragment gives the illusion that the lower part of the King's body is in raised relief, but the entire carving is actually in sunk relief.

Bibliography: Gallatin 1950, pl. IV, opposite p. 38; Cooney 1953, p. 11, no. 47, and pl. XXXIV; New York 1961, p. 17, no. 78, and pl. 22; Fischer 1967, p. 255, fig. 2; Young 1967, pp. 277 and 278, fig. 7.

No. 15
UNFINISHED PORTRAIT OF THE KING

Early Period
Collection: The Metropolitan Museum of Art, New York 66.99.40 (Fletcher Fund, 1966 and The Guide Foundation, Inc., Gift, 1966) The relief shows Akhenaten in profile, looking to the right and wearing the *afnet* headcloth. It appears to be the exercise of a student-sculptor, who has tapered off the lower edge of neck and headdress and left uncut the uraeus on the brow.
Material: Limestone.
Color: No trace.
Measurements: Height 34.8 cm. Width 23.4 cm. Thickness ca. 4 cm. Height of head 18 cm. Height of face 11.7 cm.
Condition: Surface lightly pitted; back of slab sawed off in modern times.
Provenance: Tell el Amarna. Excavated in 1891–1892 by W. M. F. Petrie, probably in sculptor's workshop north of the Great Palace. Formerly in the Amherst and Gallatin collections.
COMMENTARY: The drawing is in the exaggerated style of the Early Period with the elongated, slanting eye, the thick lips, and the hollow cheeks especially emphasized, and the earlobe rendered virtually as a perforated boss. Although this study is evidently the work of a skilled and experienced pupil, such details as the furrows on neck and face have been omitted.

* *Bibliography:* Amherst 1921, p. 76, no. 847, and pl. XIV; Steindorff and Hoyningen-Huene 1945, p. 114, illus.; Cooney 1953, pp. 10–11, no. 46, and pl. XXXI; Harvard 1954, p. 18, no. 9, and pl. IV; Aldred 1961b, p. 81, and pl. 132; Arab Information Center 1967, illus. on cover; Fischer 1967, illus. on cover.

No. 16
THE ROYAL FAMILY
Early Period, about Year 8
Collection: Ägyptisches Museum, Berlin (West) 14145

A rectangular stela carved in sunk relief shows Akhenaten, Nefertiti, and three of their infant daughters within a light kiosk under the rayed disk of the Aten. The royal pair sit facing each other upon cushioned stools, their sandaled feet resting upon hassocks. The King wears a short kilt with sash and the Blue Crown circled by uraei and with ribbed streamers at the back. He holds the Princess Merytaten, naked except for an ear ornament, as if to kiss her. She strokes his chin with one hand and points with the other to the group opposite. The Queen, wearing a long robe with ribbed sash and her characteristic tall crown with ribbed streamers and a circlet ornamented with uraei, holds the second daughter, Maketaten, seated on her lap, while the third child, Ankhesenpaaten, climbs on her arm and toys with one of the uraei pendant from her mother's crown. Both princesses are naked, but Maketaten wears an earplug and her hair is gathered into a sidelock that falls over her right ear. Behind the King is a garniture of four pairs of wine jars linked by flower garlands. Inscriptions at the top of the stela give the early names and titles of the Aten as well as those of the royal pair. Three other inscriptions identify the daughters and name Nefertiti as their mother.

Material: Limestone.

Color: No trace.

Measurements: Height 32.5 cm. Width 38.7 cm. Thickness 3.8 cm. Height of King's face 3 cm. Height of Queen's face 2.6 cm. Width of long column of text 1.5 cm.

Condition: Broken across middle and rejoined; lower legs and feet of Ankhesenpaaten and top left-hand corner of slab missing. Back and edges mostly covered with a discolored ancient plaster which probably once held the stela in position within a niche.

Provenance: Probably Tell el Amarna; acquired in Cairo in 1898.

COMMENTARY: This stela is one of the small number of icons surviving from shrines erected in private houses at Tell el Amarna (see also Figs. 2, 3, 39, 40). These shrines were probably made of mud-brick, with the painted face of the stela protected by wooden doors. By the time of the New Kingdom, worship of a trinity of deities forming a family group had become popular, appealing as it did to the strong love of family characteristic of the Egyptians. When the old gods were abandoned under Akhenaten, the royal family replaced the earlier

kinship groups as a focus of worship, and private shrines in houses at Tell el Amarna bear witness to the cult. The present example is the most celebrated of its kind, and surely no more appealing domestic conversation piece has survived from antiquity. The relief is cut in the bizarre style of the Early Period. The serpentine necks and drawn features of the King and Queen and the elongated skulls of the princesses are characteristic of that time. Care has been taken, however, to indicate correctly the left and right feet and to show the sidelock on the right side of the head. The usual equipoise of Egyptian composition has been maintained by the opposition of the figures of King and Queen and by the rays of the Aten descending from the central focus of the sun disk, but within this traditional composition there is a *contrapposto* of different elements, especially evident in the pose of the two elder daughters, who, while turning their backs to each other, are linked by the childish gesture of

the pointing forefinger, thus creating a psychological unity to reinforce the artistic cohesion of the design. An unusual feature of this stela are the two *ankh* signs held to the nostrils of the royal pair by the rays of the Aten. It is also to be noted that Nefertiti sits alone on her own stool decorated with the symbols of the United Two Lands. Is this to emphasize that she is equal to her husband in power and right to rule?

* *Bibliography:* Porter and Moss 1934, p. 232. Add: Spiegelberg 1903, p. 67, fig. 62; Sandman 1938, p. 156, no. CLXV; Ghalioungui 1947, p. 36, fig. 8; Groenewegen–Frankfort 1951, p. 105, and pl. XXXIXB; Lange 1951, p. 136, and pls. 14, 15; Basel 1953, p. 44, no. 95, and fig. 16; Anthes 1954, p. 22, illus.; Aldred 1961b, p. 76, and pl. 116; Berlin West 1967, p. 68, no. 749, illus.; Aldred 1968, pl. 54; Lange and Hirmer 1968, p. 459, and pl. 184; Wenig 1969, p. 50, and pl. 57; Müller 1970a, p. xxxvii, and pl. 124.

No. 17
ROYAL WORSHIPERS
Early Period
Collection: Museum of Fine Arts, Boston 67.637
A fragment of a column, carved in sunk relief, shows Akhenaten, Nefertiti, and Merytaten adoring the Aten, whose rays bring life.
Material: Limestone.
Color: Traces of red and blue pigment.
Measurements: Height 22.4 cm. Width (diameter) 52.5 cm. Circumference 59.5 cm. Thickness 6.1 cm. Height of head of Nefertiti 6.1 cm. Height of face of Nefertiti 3.8 cm. Height of head of Merytaten 4.5 cm. Intracolumnar width ca. 3.4–3.5 cm.
Condition: A curved slab, evidently used for cladding a rounded core of a different material (No. 26); all edges original; broken and repaired; damage to upper edge and lower right-hand corner.
Provenance: Tell el Amarna; found at Hermopolis.
COMMENTARY: The complete scene, carried on adjacent slabs, would have shown a balanced composition in which Akhenaten and Nefertiti make offerings of formal bouquets on an altar under the rays of the Aten, while their eldest daughter Merytaten assists by rattling her sistrum. This slab gives a right-hand portion of the scene. On it, Akhenaten, probably clad in the typical royal kilt, is wearing a short curled wig (of the Nubian type?) with floating ribbons at the back; Nefertiti wears her accustomed tall cap and pleated robe and shawl. She is titled "Mistress of the Two Lands," and her name appears in its early form. Rays of the Aten enfold her upper body, support her elbow, and bring life to her nostrils. Behind her, at the left end of the slab, Merytaten, with the typical sidelock pendant from her elongated skull, is twice pictured, back to back, her figures separated by a vertical line. Other curved slabs probably showed the altar and repeated and completed the figures of the officiants (cf. No. 34).

Bibliography: Boston 1967b, p. 62, illus.; Terrace 1968, p. 54, fig. 10; Roeder 1969, p. 386, no. 245/VII, and pl. 3; Boston 1972, p. 17, no. 6, illus.

No. 18
FRAGMENT OF A PARAPET
Early Period

Collection: The Brooklyn Museum 41.82

The parapet, carved on both sides in sunk relief, shows parts of the figures of Akhenaten and Nefertiti making offerings to the Aten, whose rayed hands bring life to their nostrils. Above, a hieroglyphic inscription in several columns gives parts of the names and titularies of the royal pair. The upper edge of the parapet is carved as a capping with smooth double-cambered surface.

Material: White indurated limestone.

Color: No trace.

Measurements: Height 41.8 cm. Width 44.6 cm. Thickness, top 12.1 cm., bottom 13.9 cm. Height of head of Queen 5.3 cm. Height of face of Queen 3.8 cm. on both sides. Height of Maat (without crown) 5.9 cm.

Condition: Greatly damaged, but no deliberate mutilation to names and figures of King and Queen is apparent. Some natural fissures and other blemishes in the stone were doubtless originally filled with plaster.

Provenance: Tell el Amarna. Excavated by W. M. F. Petrie in 1891–1892 in the ruins of the Broad Hall of the Great Palace.

COMMENTARY: The parapet and its history have been described at length by Cooney and Simpson (see bibliography), who offer a tentative reconstruction of the scene pictured on its two faces. On both sides of the fragment that remains, a large, deep-cut figure of the King is followed by a smaller representation of the Queen. Of the King's figures little is left, while those of the Queen are fairly well preserved down to the waist. On what may arbitrarily be called the obverse of the parapet nothing of the King's figure remains except part of one upraised upper arm, his neck, chin, and lower lip, part of his chest, and the ribbed streamers hanging from the back of his crown. His arm and chest are ornamented with cartouches bearing the early name of the Aten. So is the body of the Queen, who follows him bearing aloft a pair of cartouches mounted on a *heb* sign, which are also inscribed with the names of the Aten. The Queen wears the short Nubian wig with double uraei on the forehead and streamers floating from the back and is evidently clad in her accustomed floating robe and shawl. On the reverse of the parapet she adds a broad collar to her costume, as well as a pectoral with the Aten's cartouches, and offers a little figure of herself (as the goddess Maat?), which bears the cartouches in a *heb* sign flanked by *ankh, djed,* and *was* signs. These objects recall the double

perfume container found in the tomb of Tutankhamen (Cairo T. 223: Desroches–Noblecourt 1963, pl. XIII), and are probably to be identified as similar holders for scented oils (cf. Davies 1906, pl. XXXI). It is to be presumed that Akhenaten made such an offering on the lost part of the parapet. His figure on the reverse of the piece is slightly more complete than that on what we have called the obverse, for it shows part of his features and a portion of the Blue Crown, but it gives no hint of the offering he presented to the god, nor do the fragmentary inscriptions at the tops of the two sides provide a clue. The inscriptions on both sides of the parapet are similar, giving with some variations names, titles, and epithets of Akhenaten and Nefertiti. On the reverse are the remains of the prenomen of the King and the titles "Son of Re, living in Rightness, Lord of Crowns, Akhenaten, whose lifetime is long; [and] the

Hereditary Princess, Great of Favor, Lady of Love, Mistress of Upper and Lower Egypt, the [Chief] Wife of the King, [His Beloved] Nefertiti," but on the obverse she is called "Mistress of All Lands, Pure of Hands." The early form of the Queen's name suggests that this parapet was among the first monuments erected at Tell el Amarna. It may even have been part of that altar at which Akhenaten made his·vows when, as the Boundary Stelae tell us, he founded the City as the seat of the Aten.

A small wedge-shaped fragment of this parapet has been kindly lent to The Brooklyn Museum by The Metropolitan Museum of Art and bears the number L49.13a-b.

Bibliography: Porter and Moss 1934, p. 195. Add: Petrie 1894, pp. 8, 11, 19, and pl. XII; Hearst 1939, p. 8, no. 28, and pl. 3; Comstock 1941, pp. 29–30, illus.; Cooney and Simpson 1951, pp. 1–12, illus. (incl. cover); James 1973, no. 306.

its close resemblance to a schist sculpture of that Queen found by Petrie on Sinai and now in the Cairo Museum (JE 38257: Aldred 1961b, pp. 66–67, and pls. 83–84). Both have the same shape of face, arched eyebrows, and pouting expression, and evidently both belong to the last years of Amenhotep III, when portraits of the Queen departed from the style prevalent in the earlier years of the reign. A similar wooden head is shown in process of being carved by a craftsman in the studio of the Queen's chief sculptor Yuti, which is represented in a relief in the tomb of her steward Huya at Tell el Amarna (Davies 1905b, pl. XVIII). Since the Dowager Queen Tiye lived on into the reign of her son Akhenaten, it is possible that the head was carved during his reign, although it lacks the mannerism of the style of his early years. As the head is finished along the line of a missing necklet or collar, it was evidently intended for insertion into a separately made body, perhaps of a different material. Apparently at some time in its life it has undergone modifications. Beneath the present wig apparently lies an electrum *afnet* headdress, which has been exposed on the brow, at the nape of the neck, and in a gash near the crown of the head. The pigtail of this underlying headdress has been broken off and is missing. It is probable that a second earring is still hidden under the wig at the right ear. It would appear that the original head was provided with only one uraeus, the hole for which at the center of the brow has been filled in. Later, when the composition wig was added, two uraei were substituted. At the same time, the wooden spike at the crown of the head was also added, probably to carry a circlet of uraei surmounted by horns and plumes. Of the small blue glass ring beads that originally ornamented the wig, only a patch remains. Why all these alterations were made can only be a subject of speculation, but it seems that there are several instances of alterations to the coiffures of royal women at this period (No. 124).

* *Bibliography:* Porter and Moss 1934, p. 113. Add: Fechheimer 1922b, pl. 90; Erman 1936, pl. 26; Hamann 1944, p. 237, and 238, fig. 253; Lange 1951, p. 135, and pl. 5; Basel 1953, p. 46, no. 103, and fig. 12; Anthes 1954, p. 14, illus.; Wolf 1957, pp. 441–442, and p. 440, figs. 398–399; Smith 1958, p. 155, and pl. 117; Vandier 1958, pp. 322, 330, and pl. CVII, 5, 7; Aldred 1961b, p. 67, and pl. 86; Berlin West 1967, p. 61, no. 676, illus.; Aldred 1968, p. 69; Lange and Hirmer 1968, pp. 444–445, and pl. 157; Yoyotte 1968, p. 98, and p. 97, illus.; Wenig 1969, p. 50, and pl. 59; Müller 1970a, p. xxxvi, and pl. 117.

No. 19
HEAD OF QUEEN TIYE
*Late Reign of Amenhotep III–
Akhenaten*
Collection: Ägyptisches Museum, Berlin (West) 21834
The royal lady wears a short curled wig with a spike at the vertex. A diadem with indications of two uraei at the brow crosses the forehead. The eyes are inlaid and the eyebrows hollowed to take a paste filling. A single earring is exposed at the left side.

Material: Head boxwood; eyes black and white glass set in ebony rims; eyebrows with traces of black paste filling; diadem gesso with remains of leaf gold overlay; wig probably cloth covered with a compound of mud, resin, and wax, originally impressed with a reticulation of blue glass beads; earring gold and lapis lazuli.
Color: The boxwood is now of a red-brown tone. This may be due to the patina of age rather than to deliberate staining, although the convention of representing women's skin as light in color was frequently ignored in the Amarna age.
Measurements: Height 9.5 cm. Width 7.9 cm. Depth 8.1 cm. Height of face 4.3–4.7 cm. Width of break at neck 3.0 cm. Depth of break at neck 2.9 cm.
Condition: Gashes over right eyebrow; front of diadem and two uraei missing; wig broken to expose the left earring and also at a spot near the vertex to reveal electrum (?) underneath.
Provenance: Said to be from the ruins of a palace at Medinet Ghurab.
COMMENTARY: This head is usually identified as a portrait of Queen Tiye, chiefly on account of

No. 20
TORSO OF QUEEN NEFERTITI
Early Period
Collection: The Metropolitan Museum of Art, New York 21.9.4 (Gift of Edward S. Harkness, 1921) The much mutilated fragment is part of a statue that undoubtedly once formed a counterpoise to a sculpture of Akhenaten. It shows the Queen in a diaphanous pleated robe that is passed over her left shoulder and knotted under her right breast, leaving that breast and shoulder bare. Although her collarbones and neck tendons are less pronounced than her husband's, we hardly need her name inscribed on the side of the back pillar of this fragment to tell us that the person represented is Nefertiti. The inscription adds, "May she live forever and ever."
Material: White indurated limestone.

Color: No trace.
Measurements: Height 28.3 cm. Width across arms 30.3 cm. Depth from breast to back pillar 20.2 cm. Intracolumnar width 6.8 cm. Depth of bottom break ca. 19.5 cm. Width of bottom break of back pillar ca. 11.1 cm. Width of break at neck ca. 10.1 cm. Depth of break at neck 13.5 cm.
Condition: Fragment, from neck to below the waist; lower arms missing; damage to both breasts.
Provenance: Tell el Amarna; see No. 4, Commentary.
COMMENTARY: Five pairs of car-

touches bearing the early name of the Aten are incised on the Queen's chest, diaphragm, and upper arms, and the surface of the inscribed back pillar bears parts of similar cartouches. The breaks on the fragment indicate that it may once have been part of a dyad representing the royal pair.

* *Bibliography:* Porter and Moss 1934, p. 197. Add: Amherst 1921, p. 75, no. 839; Vandier 1958, pp. 336, 340; Hayes 1959, p. 285, fig. 173, left; Aldred 1968, p. 184, pl. 88, left.

No. 21
FRAGMENTARY FACE IN YELLOW JASPER

Early Period

Collection: The Metropolitan Museum of Art, New York 26.7.1396 (Carnarvon Collection, 1926; Gift of Edward S. Harkness, 1926)

The face is undoubtedly from a composite statue which must have been one of the most spectacular achievements of antiquity.

Material: Jasper.

Color: Yellow, highly polished.

Measurements: Height 12.6 cm. Width 12.7 cm. Depth 11.5 cm.

Height from chin to upper lip ca. 5.2 cm.

Condition: Fragment: only mouth and chin and part of neck preserved; upper lip chipped.

Provenance: Probably Tell el Amarna. Formerly in the Carnarvon Collection.

COMMENTARY: This face certainly belongs to the Amarna Period. The folds of flesh in the neck could indicate a date late in the reign of Amenhotep III, but more probably the statue was one of a series made by Akhenaten for his mother, Queen Tiye (cf. No. 101). The full underlip characteristic of that Queen and the small, round, slightly double chin exclude Nefertiti as the original of this portrait. The high polish, which gives the illusion that the lips are of a different color from that of cheeks and neck, is not the least remarkable feature of this sculptural tour de force.

* *Bibliography:* Burlington 1922, p. 80, no. 40, and pl. VI; New York 1937, fig. 16; New York 1945, 16th pl.; Hayes 1959, pp. 259–260 with fig. 156; Aldred 1961, p. 68 and pl. 90; New York 1962, p. 28, fig. 34; Bille-de Mot 1966, pl. XIII; New York 1970, p. 91, no. 25, illus., and p. 27, illus.

No. 22
TORSO OF A QUEEN
Early Period
Collection: Musée du Louvre, Paris
E.25409
The fragmentary sculpture of a
woman with back pillar, her left
leg striding forward, is clothed in
a clinging pleated robe which
passes over the left shoulder and
is knotted under the right breast,
leaving the right shoulder bare.
While the sculpture is not inscribed, it doubtless represents
Nefertiti, and there is evidence that
it once formed part of a group.
Material: Dark red quartzite.
Color: No added color.
Measurements: Height 29.4 cm.
Width 13 cm. Depth 12.6 cm.
Width of back pillar, upper 4.8
cm., lower 5.1 cm. Width of break
at neck 3.5 cm. Depth of break at
neck with back pillar 9.8 cm.
Condition: Head, right arm, left
hand, legs below knees, and top of
back pillar missing. Two drill holes
in right shoulder, one containing
the stump of a metal dowel.
Provenance: Not known.
COMMENTARY: The sharp carving
of the clavicles and the manner in
which the neck is joined to the
torso show that this sculpture belongs to the Early Period. At that
time it could only represent Nefertiti, for it is clothed, while the
princesses, still children, would
have been shown in the nude and
wearing a sidelock, of which no
trace exists. The stump of the
right arm indicates that it was
stretched out to encircle the waist
or shoulders of another figure,
which was probably carved as a
separate entity on a contiguous
block of stone. The relaxed, precisely indicated folds of the gown
on the right-hand side of the sculpture suggest that the two statues
could not have been attached at
the shoulder (cf. No. 106) but that
they were carved independently,
with perhaps only half the arm of
the Queen appearing as part of the
figure she embraced (cf. No. 90).
The luxuriant curves of the Queen's
body, with its slender waist and
ample thighs, and enormous buttocks emphasize her significance
as an erotic symbol. The carving
of female figures in such a manner
as to reveal a naturalistic form beneath the clothing was an innovation of the Amarna sculptors, who
reached a high degree of accom-
plishment to be reflected in statuary of Dynasty XXI, Dynasty XXV,
and the early Ptolemaic Period.

* *Bibliography:* Vandier 1958, pp.
340, 351–352; Desroches-Noblecourt 1961, no. 54, illus.; Harris
1966, p. 38, and pl. 29; Paris 1967,
p. 22, no. 108, with illus. on p. 32;
Vandier 1967, p. 307, fig. 8; Yoyotte 1968, pp. 102–103, illus.;
Wenig 1969, p. 50, and pl. 65.

No. 23
KING OR QUEEN?

Early Period

Collection: The Cleveland Museum of Art 59.188

The royal personage here depicted under the rays of the Aten is wearing a short Nubian wig with floating ribbons at the back.

Material: Sandstone.

Color: Traces of red on face and neck.

Measurements: Height 26.7 cm. Width 28 cm. Thickness 6.4–7.7 cm. Height of face 14.6 cm.

Condition: Broken into three pieces and rejoined.

Provenance: Karnak.

COMMENTARY: The head on this relief is carved in the sharp angular style developed at Karnak during the first years of Akhenaten's reign in the decoration of temples built for the Aten. The rather coarse granular stone employed demanded deep cutting and bold treatment, with the elimination of finicky detail. Although the masons, like their King, were in a hurry, they rose to the occasion and, as this head bears witness, produced impressive works. The question of whether it represents the Queen or the King has arisen. In this writer's opinion, the person pictured is Nefertiti, wearing the short Nubian wig she so often affected (Nos. 18, 48). The sharp chin is a little unusual in this early phase, but it is evidently a summary version of the King's pendulous jaw (Nos. 25, 27), and the narrow, sloping eye and the lines running down from the nostril and the corner of the mouth are characteristic. That there is no vestige of a double curve at the back of the neck is also in favor of seeing the subject as Nefertiti. A ray of the Aten passes behind her head to caress her shoulder. This is a feature not unusual in the Early Period, particularly when the Queen stands at the Window of Appearances, as she does, for instance, in the tomb of Ramose at Thebes (Fig. 17), where she is also pictured in the Nubian wig.

Bibliography: Cleveland 1966, p. 4, illus.; Cooney 1968, pp. 3, 7–8, 17, and illus. on cover; Porter and Moss 1972, p. 40.

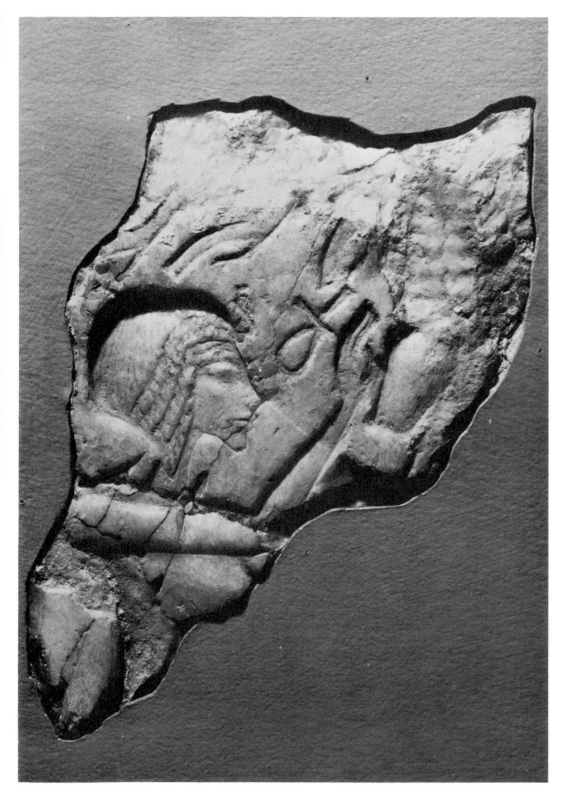

No. 24
THE QUEEN OFFERING A LIBATION

Early Period

Collection: Museum of Fine Arts, Boston 37.3

Nefertiti, pictured in sunk relief with a libation jar in one hand and with her other hand raised in adoration, pays homage to the Aten.

Material: Alabaster.

Color: No trace.

Measurements: Height 18.7 cm. Width 15.2 cm. Height of head 4.5 cm. Height of face 3.1 cm.

Condition: Very fragmentary; surface fissured in places.

Provenance: Tell el Amarna. Excavated in 1935 by the Egypt Exploration Society in the Broad Hall of the Great Palace. Excavation no. 35/280.

COMMENTARY: That the royal person represented is Nefertiti, wearing the short Nubian wig with streamers at the back and two solar uraei on the brow (cf. No. 18), is clear from the ribbed streamers pictured in the top right-hand corner of the fragment, which hang from the crown of a taller figure preceding her, who must have been Akhenaten. The Queen, doubtless repeating the King's gesture, raises a libation jar, and a ray of the Aten holds an *ankh* to her nostrils.

Bibliography: Dunham 1937, p. 13, illus.; Pendlebury 1951, p. 68; Dunham 1958, p. 74, fig. 49; Smith 1960, p. 118, and p. 119, fig. 77; Boston 1964a, pp. 192–193, illus.; Boston 1967a, no. 27, illus.

No. 25
NEFERTITI PRESENTING AN
OFFERING

Early Period

Collection: Christos G. Bastis, on
loan to The Brooklyn Museum
L69.38.1

The Queen is shown in sunk relief
in profile at right and facing right,
with hands upraised to present an
offering. She wears a long curled
wig with lappets, which is bound
by a fillet with a uraeus at the
forehead. A large earplug ornaments her visible ear, and traces
of cartouches of the Aten on her
upper and lower arms probably
represent the decorative bezels of
bracelets. A ray of the Aten ends
in a hand that holds an *ankh* to
the Queen's nostril. An incomplete
panel of inscription back of the
Queen refers to her daughter
Merytaten, who was doubtless once
represented as standing behind
her mother.

Material: Sandstone.

Color: Traces of red on the Queen's
flesh and of blue on her wig.

Measurements: Visible height 20.9
cm. Visible width 42.3 cm. Thickness ca. 3.8 cm. Height of face 8.3
cm. Intracolumnar width 9.4 cm.

Condition: Upper and lower edges
damaged; about a fifth of the block
sawed off at the right. Back cut in
modern times.

Provenance: Karnak.

COMMENTARY: This relief appears
to be the major part of a *talatat*,
or one of the blocks from one of
the temples to the Aten built at
Karnak during the early years of
Akhenaten's reign. Here, as so
often, the emaciated features of
the Queen, her hollow cheeks, slit
eyes, lined jaw, and hanging chin,
duplicate the characteristics of her
husband's face. Such likenesses
often result in a confusion of
identity, but in general a sharp
chin distinguishes the early portraits of Nefertiti (No. 23), and
her jaw, as here, is less deep than
that of her husband. A similar
piece with the Queen's head, undoubtedly from the same monument, is in the Cleveland Museum
of Art (59.186: Cooney 1968, p. 7,
fig. 6).

Bibliography: Fazzini 1972, p. 48,
fig. 16.

No. 26

THE ROYAL COUPLE WITH
OFFERINGS

Early Period

Collection: The Brooklyn Museum
71.89

A curved slab shows, at the left,
Nefertiti in her tall cap and filmy
gown offering a bouquet of lotus
to the Aten. She follows an incomplete figure of the King, pictured on a larger scale, who wears
the Blue Crown, of which only the
back edge and floating ribbons are
visible. An inscription at the top
gives parts of the names and titularies of Akhenaten and the Aten.

Material: Limestone.

Color: Traces of blue on inscriptions, flowers, and crowns; red on
bodies and on arms of Aten.

Measurements: Height 23.5 cm.
Width, following circumference
38.1 cm, straight 37.7 cm. Thickness 1.2–4.1 cm. Height of Queen's
head with crown 9.5 cm. Height
of Queen's face 4.3 cm.

Condition: Lower left-hand corner
broken off and replaced; other
edges chipped and some damage to
surface. Back cut in modern times.

Provenance: Tell el Amarna; found
at Hermopolis.

COMMENTARY: Excavators for the
Egypt Exploration Society, who
uncovered the Weben Aten of the
Great Palace, remarked that the
columns had been only roughly
finished and accordingly were designed to be overlaid with curved
stone slabs of finer quality. The
present slab, convex on its carved
surface, is obviously an example
of such a revetment for a column
(see also No. 17). Although part
of the epithets that usually accompany the names of the Aten
and Akhenaten is visible at the
upper margin, the cartouches of
the royal pair are missing. Nevertheless the queen must be Nefertiti, for the representation shows
all the characteristics of her portrayals during the Early Period—
long, thin neck with prominent
tendons, well-defined jaw, lined
face, circular perforation in earlobe, and especially the long, nervous fingers of the hands.

Bibliography: None.

No. 27
BREAD FOR THE ATEN
Early Period

Collection: Dr. Rëuben Hecht, Haifa

A royal personage in short Nubian wig with uraeus on the brow and floating ribbons at the back offers a tray with bread to the Aten, whose rays accept the gift and bless the giver. Cartouches of the Aten are incised like bracelets on the arms of the suppliant.

Material: Sandstone.

Color: No traces; grayish stone.

Measurements: Height 24.1 cm. Width 45 cm. Depth 6 cm. Height of face 9.7 cm.

Condition: Broken across and rejoined; lower right-hand and upper left-hand corner missing; some damage to face.

Provenance: Karnak.

COMMENTARY: The differences between the features of Akhenaten and Nefertiti as rendered by artists of the Early Period have been discussed in Nos. 23 and 25. While the royal pair often are represented as on this slab in the same Nubian wig and with similarly exaggerated features, there are usually subtle differences between the faces of the King and Queen. Akhenaten's face is longer, his chin larger, his lips more everted and their profile less sharp; his neck, with prominent muscles, is sinuous and shows a pronounced double curve at the rear. Such characteristics enable us to identify the person pictured on this relief as the King himself. That the offering he brings is a tray with bread is evident from other representations of the period (Davies 1906, pl. XXIII).

Bibliography: Kibbutz Hazorea 1969, p. 10, no. 76.

No. 28
FRAGMENT FROM A
BOUNDARY STELA

Early Period, Year 6

Collection: William Rockhill Nelson Gallery of Art, Atkins Museum of Fine Arts, Kansas City, Missouri 44–65

A fragment of Boundary Stela N, contiguous to that shown in No. 8, represents Nefertiti wearing a pleated robe and her tall cap surmounted by a disk and double plumes. She raises her hands in adoration of the Aten, one of whose rays touches a feather of her crown and another holds an *ankh* to her nostrils. Cartouches of the Aten adorn the bracelets on the Queen's arm. Behind her is the diminutive figure of a princess in a long gown, who carries a sistrum in her right hand.

Material: Nummulitic limestone.
Color: No trace.
Measurements: Height (visible) 48.6 cm. Width (visible) 65.1 cm. Depth (visible) 3.5 cm. Height of Queen's head 19.4 cm. Height of Queen's face 9.5 cm.
Condition: Fragmentary; some restoration to face and neck of Queen; rectangular block with head of princess missing.
Provenance: Tell el Amarna; from Boundary Stela N on the cliffs halfway along the southern border of the City.

COMMENTARY: On the original rock-cut stela, Nefertiti stood behind and slightly below her husband, with her fingertips almost touching the streamer of his crown. Behind her stood her two eldest daughters, Merytaten on groundline and Maketaten, apparently as an afterthought, in the space above her sister. The figure of the latter is preserved at the extreme right of this stela, but a stone slab used to patch a flaw in the rock has fallen away, taking her likeness with it. The head of Nefertiti earned an early fame, for it was published by Richard Lepsius in his *Denkmaeler* (Lepsius 1848–1859a, pl. 295, fig. 48; Lepsius 1904, p. 129) as a typical portrait of the Queen.

Bibliography: Porter and Moss 1934, p. 231. Add: Cooney 1939, illus.; Kansas City 1959, p. 20, illus.

No. 29
QUEEN CROWNED WITH DISK
AND PLUMES

Early Period

Collection: University College London 038

Nefertiti is pictured in this fragment wearing a long lappet wig and a modius with large uraeus, which is surmounted by a disk set in horns and long plumes. While the Queen's head is in profile, her crown is shown in front view. A sleeve on her right arm remains to show that she was clothed.

Material: Discolored indurated limestone.

Color: No trace.

Measurements: Height 12.5 cm. Width 4.2 cm. Thickness 3.1 cm. Height of worked surface 10.9 cm. Height of head from base of neck 3.2 cm.

Condition: Chips on surface; fissures filled with dirt giving false impression of black lines.

Provenance: Tell el Amarna. Excavated in 1891–1892 by Howard Carter and W. M. F. Petrie, probably in the area of the Great Palace.

COMMENTARY: This fragment may have been found among the broken remains of the parapets discovered by Petrie in the Broad Hall of the Great Palace (No. 18). The style points to the early years of Akhenaten's reign, when representations of the Queen (who must be Nefertiti) reflected the features of her husband. Such details as the large circular perforation of the earlobe, the furrow running from the nostril, and the impressionistic uncut eye are all characteristic of the early phase of Amarna art.

Bibliography: Pendlebury 1951, p. 224, and pl. CV, 10; Samson 1972, pp. 41–42 with pl. 18.

No. 30
QUEEN WITH SCEPTER

Early Period

Collection: Staatliche Sammlung Ägyptischer Kunst, Munich ÄS 4231

Only the upper part of the figure of a queen is preserved on this slab. She wears a wig with long lappets and a double uraeus on the brow. Her head is surmounted by a much eroded crown that is apparently encircled by a frieze of uraei, and probably bore ram's horns, sun disk, and feathers. She carries over her left shoulder a scepter of the "fly-whisk" type. Rays of the Aten descend from the right of the slab, and at the left edge are traces of the queen's retinue.

Material: Sandstone.

Color: Traces of red on body of attendant.

Measurements: Height 18.7 cm. Width 27.2 cm. Thickness 4.4 cm. Height of queen's head 5.5 cm. Height of queen's face 3.6 cm.

Condition: Fragmentary and with surface eroded in places, especially around crown.

Provenance: Karnak.

COMMENTARY: The queen represented in this early relief from a temple at Karnak is clearly not Nefertiti, and the features, especially the distinctive lips and short chin, point irresistibly to Queen Tiye. The symbols held in the hands of the Aten suggest that the fragment comes from one of the early jubilee scenes (Nos. 7, 11), in which, as this relief shows, the Queen Mother evidently played a part. She is apparently accompanied by attendants, but whom did she follow? It could hardly have been Nefertiti, and presumably it was a king. But which king?

Bibliography: Müller 1963, pp. 217–218, illus.; Barta 1966, pp. 1–2, with fig. 1; Munich 1966, no. 52, ÄS 4231, illus.; Aldred 1968, p. 128, pl. 48; Munich 1970, no. 52, ÄS 4231, and pl. 31; Munich 1972, p. 65, and pl. 35; Porter and Moss 1972, p. 190.

No. 31
NEFERTITI IN CEREMONIAL ATTIRE

Early Period, about Year 8
Collection: Ashmolean Museum, Oxford 1893.1–41(71).
The curved surface of the slab indicates that it formed part of a column drum. The Queen is depicted in her usual diaphanous gown, but her tall cap with its fluttering streamer is topped by horns, disk, and two long plumes. She lifts a formal bouquet toward the Aten, one of whose rays touches the uraeus on the front of her cap. Behind her follows one of her daughters, of whom only the head and a hand holding a sistrum are preserved.
Material: Hard white limestone.
Color: Traces of red; traces of blue in the inscriptions.
Measurements: Height 36.2 cm. Width (straight) 30 cm. Depth 12.8 cm.
Condition: Fragmentary, but with no sign of deliberate mutilation.
Provenance: Tell el Amarna. Excavated by W. M. F. Petrie in 1891–1892, perhaps in the area of the Great Palace. Formerly in the Kennard Collection.
COMMENTARY: Columns of text in front and behind the Queen, naming her as "Mistress of the Two Lands," make her identification certain. The daughter following her must be Merytaten, as indeed the remaining signs of an inscription over her head seem to indicate. The later form of the Queen's name must mean that the relief is to be dated after Year 5 (see page 24), but the features of the Queen are carved in the exaggerated style of the early reign. The addition of the horns and tall plumes of the King's *ibes* crown (Gardiner 1953, p. 27, note 5) to the Queen's tall cap is unusual, but it is also found on the heads that form the finials of the rudders of her state barge (No. 55). A unique representation of Akhenaten in an almost identical crown appears on a fragment of a limestone parapet found by Petrie in the Great Palace and now in Cairo (JE 13415). This and the Ashmolean fragment provide the only known examples of a nontraditional crown worn by both King and Queen. The implication seems to be that the two are to be considered equal, even if they are often depicted on differing scales (see No. 16). The salient feature of this relief is, however, its apparent eroticism. The exaggeration of the breast, buttocks, and pubic mound must have been a deliberate emphasis on the part of the artist and his patron.

Bibliography: None.

No. 32
HEAD FROM A BOUNDARY STELA

Early Period, about Year 6
Collection: H. E. Smeets, Weert, Holland
A princess wearing a heavy sidelock and large ear studs is represented in this fragment from a Boundary Stela. The sculpture from which it comes must originally have been of life size.
Material: Nummulitic limestone.
Color: No trace.
Measurements: Height 20.3 cm. Width 16 cm. Depth 20.3 cm. Height of face to eyebrows 8 cm.
Condition: Nose and large portions of cheeks restored.
Provenance: Tell el Amarna; from an unidentified Boundary Stela. Formerly in the collection of J. Eisenberg.

COMMENTARY: It is difficult to determine from which of the numerous Boundary Stelae erected by Akhenaten the present head was taken. It seems that most of the heads of the sculptured groups flanking the stelae were knocked off in antiquity and left lying where they fell; some have been picked up in modern times, but most have been lost. The best preserved of the groups today is that of Stela A, which marks the northern boundary on the bank of the Nile opposite the City of Akhenaten, but the present head could as well have come from one of the

now greatly dilapidated statues of Stelae B, N, P, Q, R, S, or U. The stelae themselves, as well as the sculptured figures, have suffered damage. At the turn of the century Stela P was blown up by peasants who thought that it marked the entrance to a cave containing untold treasure, and Stela N has lost parts of sculptures in modern times (Nos. 8, 28). The groups of statuary on either side of the bases of the stelae usually show Akhenaten and Nefertiti standing and holding before them tablets inscribed with the names of the Aten (Nos. 1, 4, 20). The King and Queen are flanked by a pair of statues of their two eldest daughters, holding hands or with their arms around each other's waist (cf. No. 89). These groups are carved into the solid rock and attached to it by a spine of stone. The present head of a princess is from one such group, in which the royal daughters were shown nude and wearing the sidelock on their elongated skulls. The limestone into which they were carved was full of fossil shells and thus demanded a bold, sometimes summary treatment. After the statues had been hewn, however, they were probably covered with a skin of plaster and painted. No traces of this finish now remain; in fact, the surface of the stone has been polished by long exposure to wind-driven sand. In their original state the eyes of this fragment were probably modeled in plaster on what is now little more than a slightly convex orb. A similar technique is found on statues of the owners of rock tombs at Tell el Amarna, which were rough-carved from the coarse rock of the region and carefully worked in the plaster overlay (Davies 1906, p. 21). While the Smeets head should represent either Merytaten or Maketaten it is impossible, in spite of a certain individuality of profile, to say which of the two it portrays. For a general discussion of the Boundary Stelae at Tell el Amarna see page 34.

Bibliography: Royal-Athena 1964, pp. 26–27, no. 126, illus.

No. 34
THE PRINCESS ROYAL
Early Period
Collection: The Brooklyn Museum 35.2000

The convex surface of this block indicates that it is a fragment from a column, and the figures carved upon it, back to back, apparently represent one and the same princess. Both figures are shown wearing the youthful sidelock and a long pleated robe knotted under the breast, and their features are almost identical. A deep vertical line divides the two representations.

Material: Limestone.

Color: Traces of red paint on flesh parts, of yellow on garments, of blue on dividing line.

Measurements: Height 17 cm. Width 25.1 cm. Thickness 5.4 cm. Height of left princess's head 2.8 cm. Height of left princess's face 2.2 cm. Intracolumnar width for left princess 8.2 cm., for right princess 9.5 cm.

Condition: Damage to upper middle section, including parts of backs of heads.

Provenance: Tell el Amarna. Excavated in 1934 by the Egypt Exploration Society in the Weben Aten (or chapel) of the Great Palace. Excavation no. 34/126.

COMMENTARY: Since remains of a pleated robe at the right-hand edge of this fragment indicate that the princess is following a much taller woman than herself, it must be assumed that the woman can only be Nefertiti and that it is her eldest daughter Merytaten who attends her. This assumption is supported by the inscribed column section in Boston (No. 17), where Merytaten is pictured in identical fashion, in the train of her royal father and mother. The coiffure of the figure on the left of the Brooklyn fragment indicates that the princess is wearing a curled wig with the addition of a sidelock, a feature also found on the sculptured head of a princess in Paris (Fig. 50).

Bibliography: Pendlebury 1935b, p. 134, and pl. VIII, 5; Pendlebury 1951, p. 62, and pl. LXV, 10.

No. 33
PRINCESS WITH SIDELOCK
Early Period
Collection: Museum of Fine Arts, Boston 37.1

A carving in the typical Amarna style shows only the head of an unidentified princess in sunk relief.

Material: Limestone.

Color: Traces of red and blue pigment.

Measurements: Height ca. 19 cm. Width ca. 14.8 cm. Height of head 6.2 cm. Height of face ca. 5 cm. Intracolumnar width 6.4 cm.

Condition: Surface flaws.

Provenance: Tell el Amarna. Excavated in 1935 by the Egypt Exploration Society in the Broad Hall of the Great Palace. Excavation no. 35/264.

COMMENTARY: The remains of the two columns of hieroglyphs give in both cases the ends of inscriptions referring to Nefertiti, to whose name is often appended the benediction "May she live forever and ever." The larger size of the *heh* sign in the first column suggests that this referred to Nefertiti herself as Queen, whereas in the second column she is referred to as the mother of the daughter who is shown below. In the complete relief, therefore, Nefertiti was immediately followed by her eldest daughter, doubtless holding a sistrum. This fragment, therefore, must represent the features of Merytaten in the mannerism of the early style.

* *Bibliography:* Dunham 1937, p. 13, illus.; Smith 1942, p. 120, and p. 119, fig. 78; Pendlebury 1951, p. 68, and pl. LXXIII, 1; Boston 1956, p. 21, illus.; Smith 1960, p. 134, and p. 133, fig. 85.

Fig. 50. Painted limestone head of a girl, possibly Ankhesenpaaten. Perhaps originally from Tell el Amarna. Late Period. Height 15.3 cm. Musée du Louvre, Paris E. 14715.

No. 35
NURSING CHILD

Early Period

Collection: The Brooklyn Museum 37.405

A fragment of sunk relief bears part of the figure of a woman who offers her breast to an infant princess, whose head and hand only are preserved.

Material: Limestone.

Color: Traces of red pigment on flesh, especially hands, and of blue inscription.

Measurements: Height 11.4 cm. Width 28.2 cm. Thickness 6.2 cm. Intracolumnar width, left 4.1 cm., right 4.7 cm.

Condition: Generally good but with surface blemishes.

Provenance: Tell el Amarna. Excavated in 1936–1937 by the Egypt Exploration Society in the Great Palace, South Section, Central Halls west of axis. Excavation no. 36/20.

COMMENTARY: Despite the precedent set at Deir el Bahri by representations of Hathor suckling Hatshepsut, there is, to this author's knowledge, no scene in which a queen is shown nursing her infant. At Tell el Amarna the princesses are invariably suckled by wet nurses (Bouriant 1903, pls. VII, IX). This scene, therefore, probably represents a nurse who is feeding one of the infant daughters of Nefertiti. Since the inscription seems to indicate that at least one other princess was shown pre-

ceding the nurse with the baby, it is likely that the present fragment is part of a processional scene in which the senior princesses were followed by an attendant with the latest daughter.

Bibliography: Cooney 1938, p. 93, and p. 95, illus.; Pendlebury 1951, p. 72, no. 36/20; Brooklyn 1952, no. 41, illus.; James 1973, no. 299.

No. 36
ACCLAIMING THE KING

Early Period

Collection: The Brooklyn Museum 64.199.1

A woman carved in sunk relief raises her hands in the gesture of greeting and jubilation. She wears a pleated gown and a long wig. On her head is an ointment cone embellished with a lotus flower and bud.

Material: Brown sandstone, probably originally covered with a lime wash and painted.

Color: Red coloring on arms, face, and cone.

Measurements: Height 21.1 cm. Width 28.7 cm. Thickness 3.6 cm. Height of head without cone 6.6 cm. Height of face 4.5 cm. Height of cone 4.2 cm.

Condition: Sawed from a block, about half of which is missing; upper and lower edges trimmed.

Provenance: Karnak.

COMMENTARY: This fragment from one of the early Aten temples at Karnak shows a summary, angular carving of the granular stone, which is one of the several characteristic styles of that site. That the figure is one of a group is clearly indicated by the fact that one of her raised arms overlaps the arm of another woman who was doubtless pictured beside her. Parallels for groups composed of temple women are found in Amarna tomb reliefs that show the royal party acclaimed at the entrance to the Great Temple (Davies 1903, pl. XIII). The present slab, however, bears a design that seems to be peculiar to Karnak.

Bibliography: Brooklyn 1966a, pp. 16–17, illus.; Hofstra 1971, no. 15, illus.

No. 37
A ROYAL RECEPTION

Early Period

Collection: The Brooklyn Museum
67.175.1

A fragment of a slab deeply carved in sunk relief bears the upper part of the reception accorded to the royal family arriving on a state visit. At the right is seen the rear contour of the head of a fanbearer, followed by a fan set in the characteristic papyrus umbel at the top of a staff. Behind is the fully preserved head of another fanbearer who kneels and raises a hand in adoration, and at the extreme left is a military standard in the form of a boat, the cabin of which is surmounted by a fan.

Material: Sandstone.

Color: Traces of red pigment on face and hand.

Measurements: Height 16.7 cm. Width 26.4 cm. Thickness 4.5 cm. Height of head 5.9 cm. Height of face 3.9 cm. Height of band at top 1.1–1.2 cm.

Condition: About half the slab missing; all four corners broken and lacking. Back cut in modern times.

Provenance: Karnak.

COMMENTARY: We have here part of a scene in which fan- and standard-bearers greet the arrival of the royal family at the entrance to a temple. They kneel and raise one hand in adoration, while grasping in the other hand the staffs of their fans or standards. There were at least two fanbearers

represented here, although the head of only one is fully visible. That he was, like most such men, a Nubian is evident from his deeply lined face and Negroid features and the typically Nubian style of his wig. The boat standard was a common emblem for marine detachments throughout Dynasty XVIII.

Bibliography: Brooklyn 1969a, p. 130.

No. 38
STUDENT'S EXERCISE

Early Period

Collection: Musées Royaux d'Art et d'Histoire, Brussels E. 7232

A pair of confronted heads represent a queen and a king. The former, at the left of the slab, is probably Nefertiti; the latter, facing her from the right, seems to be Akhenaten. Over and between the two profiles the student-sculptor has carved an outstretched hand.

Material: Limestone.

Color: No trace.

Measurements: Height 15.3 cm. Width 18 cm. Thickness 3.7 cm. Height of left face 4.6 cm. Height of right face 5.8 cm.

Condition: Surface near top edge damaged; ancient breaks at sides.

Provenance: Tell el Amarna. Excavated in 1891–1892 by H. Carter and W. M. F. Petrie; said to have been found in a house. Formerly in the Amherst Collection.

COMMENTARY: Like Nos. 9, 10, 59, and 119, this piece appears to have been made by a pupil who, although not a beginner, lacked the skill imparted by experience. The Queen wears the short Nubian wig, and the King the *afnet* headdress, but in both cases the uraeus is lacking. The features of Nefertiti are less exaggerated than those of her husband, her eye better placed and less slanting, her mouth smaller and her jaw shorter. Her shoulder is shown in perspective— a convention that appears at Tell el Amarna only on the Boundary Stelae, where the royal pair raise empty hands in adoration of the Aten (Nos. 8, 28). Certain peculiarities, such as the defined angle of the King's jaw and the mechanical drill hole in his earlobe, suggest that the pupil was here copying work of an earlier period. The hand is a rather pedestrian rendering of the typical Amarna hand with its long, elegant fingers and thumb (cf. No. 147).

Bibliography: 1935a, p. 564, fig. 2; Pendlebury 1935b, p. 134, and pl. VIII, 4; Pendlebury Bille-de Mot 1937, p. 83, fig. 7; Pendlebury 1951, p. 61, and pl. LXV, 8.

No. 39
TWO SOLDIERS

Early Period

Collection: Fitzwilliam Museum, Cambridge 4514.1943

The soldiers, of whom only the upper parts of the figures are preserved, run toward the right. The foremost has a thick shock of hair; he apparently carries his shield under his arm and holds in his hand a looped rope. The second soldier, his shield slung over his shoulder, carries a spear in the right hand and a battle-axe in the left. His head is shaved in front to the crown of his head and falls in a thick mass behind. The hand of a third man appears at the left edge.

Material: Limestone.

Color: No trace.

Measurements: Height 17.5 cm. Width 25 cm. Thickness ca. 6 cm.

Condition: Stone stained a light umber, perhaps through long contact with mud; surface much worn and pitted; sawed and split from a larger block.

Provenance: Not known; probably region of Memphis. Formerly in the Gayer-Anderson Collection.

COMMENTARY: The quality of the limestone and the condition in which it has survived suggest a site near Memphis rather than Hermopolis as a findspot for this block. Subject matter and treatment recall scenes in tombs at Tell el Amarna, where the King's bodyguard runs beside the royal chariot (Davies 1903, pl. XV; Davies 1905a, pl. XVII; Davies 1905b, pl. XXXI), but this design differs in detail: the looped rope is perhaps a sling, and the battle-axe is carried blade forward.

Bibliography: None.

No. 40
OBSEQUIOUS ATTENDANT

Early Period

Collection: Fitzwilliam Museum, Cambridge 4529.1943

A man with shaved head who carries a staff over his shoulder is one of a procession of bowing figures in attendance upon the King.

Material: Sandstone.

Color: Body of man painted red; kilt and background white.

Measurements: Height 22.3 cm. Width 43.5 cm. Thickness 4.6 cm.

Condition: Broken vertically and rejoined; eye of man repainted; damage at edges and piece missing from center above man's back. Back cut in modern times.

Provenance: Not known, but probably Karnak; formerly in the Gayer-Anderson Collection.

COMMENTARY: Traces of another figure in front of this bowing man indicate that he is part of a procession of officials welcoming the royal family as they enter a temple. The staff he carries is probably the stock of a fan; that it is not a spear is shown by his unmilitary shaved head. The sunk relief is deeply carved in the rather coarse stone, and the features of the man are boldly modeled.

Bibliography: None.

No. 41
WORKERS

Early Period

Collection: The Cleveland Museum of Art 59.187

A slab carved in low relief pictures portions of six men engaged in some unknown task of field or river.

Material: Sandstone.

Color: Red paint on the bodies and traces of black on the wigs.

Measurements: Height 26.7 cm. Width 58.5 cm. Thickness 6.4–7.7 cm.

Condition: Upper and lower edges broken very roughly; some surface blemishes.

Provenance: Karnak.

COMMENTARY: That this slab is in raised relief indicates that it may have formed the interior portion of a larger composition; the part preserved, however, presents a rhythmic pattern of bodies bent in toil, and it is to be noted that the treatment of the figures of the workmen is much more conventional than that of the royal family and their entourage during this Early Period. In the absence of any comparable composition, the meaning of this scene must remain an enigma. Possibly we have here a fishing scene with men on a boat or on the bank of the river hauling up fish traps; the man with outstretched arms may be holding the rope of a dragnet. In this case the legs in the upper left-hand corner could belong to a man on the riverbank who is concerned with some background activity, as, for instance, the gardener and the shipwright in the boat scene in No. 71.

Bibliography: Cooney 1968, pp. 9–10, with fig. 7; Porter and Moss 1972, p. 40.

No. 42
LADEN SERVANT

Early Period

Collection: Royal Scottish Museum, Edinburgh 1963.240

An attendant bowing under the weight of a large vessel is shown in sunk relief on a fragment with fine rhythmic line.

Material: Sandstone.

Color: Flesh tones red; traces of black on hair; garment and background white, and traces of white on vessel.

Measurements: Height 23 cm. Width 28.2 cm. Thickness 4 cm.

Condition: Sawed from a block; fragment broken in half vertically and rejoined.

Provenance: Karnak.

COMMENTARY: As is usual in representations of humble folk, this servant is shown in a more naturalistic fashion than is the case with members of the royal family and their entourage. The traces of white on the bowl may indicate that it was made of silver, and the position of the bearer's hand suggests that the contents of the vessel were heaped above the rim. Rather exceptionally, the servant wears a short-sleeved garment; men engaged in menial tasks usually are clothed only in kilt or loincloth that leaves the upper body bare.

Bibliography: None.

No. 43
LADIES OF THE COURT
Early Period
Collection: Royal Scottish Museum, Edinburgh 1960.906
The relief shows the upper bodies of two ladies in waiting, facing right. They wear wigs with sidelocks and carry their fans of office over their right shoulders.
Material: Sandstone.
Color: Traces of red pigment.
Measurements: Height 15.3 cm. Width 13.4 cm. Height of near woman's head 5.8 cm. Height of far woman's head 4.2 cm.
Condition: Some surface damage at rear of heads, near breast, before arms.
Provenance: Probably Karnak.
COMMENTARY: The ladies, pictured in echelon with overlapping profiles, are shown by the position of their forearms to be passengers in a chariot who grasp the front rail of the vehicle for support. They are probably driven by a groom. This motif, well known at Amarna, was thus already fixed at Karnak. The relief doubtless comes from a scene in which the royal family, with their retinue, ride in chariots from the palace to the temple. As befits such an occasion, the ladies in waiting wear wigs with elaborate sidelocks (cf. Nos. 44, 106) and carry their fans of office.

Bibliography: None.

No. 44
LADIES IN WAITING
Early Period

Collection: Staatliche Sammlung Ägyptischer Kunst, Munich ÄS 4863

Three ladies carrying fans follow a figure at the right which is now missing; only part of the large sunshade he carries is visible at the upper right-hand corner of the slab. The ladies in waiting wear short wigs; the first and the last of the group have massive sidelocks falling over their right shoulders.

Material: Sandstone.

Color: Traces of red body color and yellow on clothing.

Measurements: Height 22.7 cm. Width 43.1 cm. Thickness 4.8 cm. Height of heads 7.2 cm. Height of faces 4.3 cm.

Condition: Incomplete block with right-hand portion missing.

Provenance: Karnak.

COMMENTARY: In its original state, as shown in an old photograph, the relief included two sunshade bearers with shaved heads preceding the ladies (cf. No. 137). This is the Karnak prototype of a subject that occurs frequently at Tell el Amarna, and it should be noted that at neither place are these minor actors in the royal pageant depicted with the distortions characteristic of the royal family.

Bibliography: Barta 1966, pp. 2–3, with figs. 2–3; Munich 1966, no. 52, ÄS 4863, illus.; Munich 1970, no. 52, ÄS 4863, and pl. 32; Munich 1972, p. 66; Porter and Moss 1972, p. 190.

No. 45
HOMAGE TO THE KING
Early Period

Collection: Milton Lowenthal, New York

A fragment from a *talatat* shows a man with arms raised in a gesture of acclaim. His thick mop of hair with a feather stuck into it proclaim him a Nubian, and traces of other figures behind him and in a second register over his head indicate that he formed part of a group.

Material: Sandstone.

Color: Traces of black on feather and of red in flesh areas, probably modern.

Measurements: Height 23.3 cm. Width 18.2 cm. Thickness 6.2 cm.

Condition: Modern oblique cut at right-hand edge; all other edges damaged.

Provenance: Probably Karnak.

COMMENTARY: This fragment comes from a scene in which onlookers render obeisance to the royal family. Not only his feathered coiffure but also his features and his lined face declare the man pictured to be a black from Kush, and indications of a sleeve on his outstretched arm suggest that he may have been a person of rank, perhaps belonging to the corps of foreign delegates attached to the court of Akhenaten (cf. Davies 1905a, pl. X).

Bibliography: None.

124

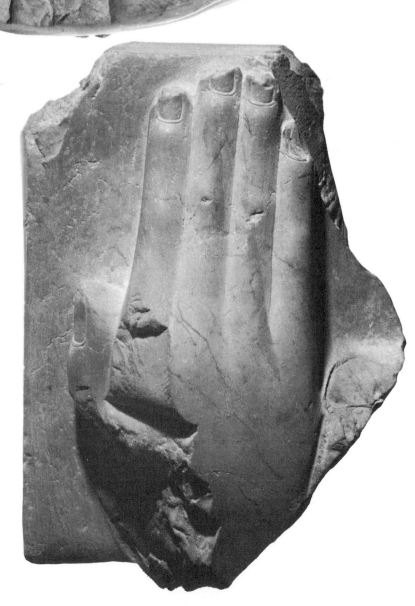

No. 46
RIGHT HAND FROM A LIFE-SIZE
STATUE

Early to Middle Period
Collection: The Metropolitan Museum of Art, New York 68.134 (Gift of Joseph V. Noble, 1968)
The hand, with fingers extended, supports a rectangular offering tray, which was held in front of the completed figure.
Material: Indurated limestone.
Color: No trace.
Measurements: Height 9.8 cm. Width 13.8 cm. Depth 19.7 cm. Thickness of slab 4.4–5.5 cm. Height of break with hand 9.4 cm.
Condition: Two fragments broken from wrist and replaced; damage to back of hand and to fingertips; right-hand corner of tray missing and upper edge damaged; remaining edges smoothly finished.
Provenance: Probably Tell el Amarna.
COMMENTARY: This fragment is evidently from a statue of the King or Queen presenting an offering (cf. No. 4). Similar fragments were found by the Egypt Exploration Society in the dump outside the southeast boundary wall of the Great Temple, two of them also of life size (Pendlebury 1951, pl. LXI, 3), and it is very probable that the present fragment comes from the same place. The upper surface of the offering tray bears no trace of the offerings usually carved in low relief (see Fig. 42: Cairo JE 43580). The hand has been carved with a considerable understanding of anatomical structure, but although the nails and the quick have been shown with great fidelity, the wrinkles across the joints have not been indicated.

Bibliography: Parke-Bernet 1968, p. 12, no. 85.

No. 47
AKHENATEN AND THE ATEN
Early to Middle Period
Collection: Ägyptisches Museum, Berlin (West) 2045
Rectangular tablet with rounded upper corners incised on one face with two cartouches containing the early name of the Aten upheld by a squatting figure of Akhenaten in the pose of the god Heh. The King wears an *afnet* headdress and is flanked by his name and titles and those of Nefertiti.
Material: Fine white alabaster.
Color: Traces of black pigment filling part of the inscriptions.
Measurements: Height 8.8 cm. Width 4.2 cm. Thickness 1.3 cm. Height of King 2.7 cm.
Condition: Lower left corner chipped and discolored.
Provenance: Not known. Formerly

in the collection of C. R. Lepsius.
COMMENTARY: The design of this piece is known from a fragmentary scarab in University College London, which gives the King's name in its Amenhotep form, thus dating it to before Year 6 (Petrie 1917, pl. XXXVI, 1; Samson 1972, pp. 98–99). This Berlin plaque, giving the names of the King and Queen in their later forms, must date to a time between Years 6 and 9, with a bias toward the earlier date. The tablet may have been an ex voto or part of a foundation deposit for a building dedicated to the Aten, perhaps at Tell el Amarna.

Bibliography: Porter and Moss 1934, p. 232. Add: Berlin 1899, p. 129; Berlin 1924, p. 253; Sandman 1938, p. 157, no. clxix (called clix); Berlin West 1967, p. 67, no. 745, illus.

No. 48
RELIEF FROM THE GREAT PALACE
Early to Middle Period, about Year 8
Collection: The Brooklyn Museum 35.1999
A fragment of a column drum is carved in sunk relief with the head of a queen who wears the short Nubian wig with a uraeus at her forehead and a streamer at the nape of her neck. A ray of the Aten brings life for her to breathe. Over her head are the remains of an inscription.
Material: Sandstone.
Color: Extensive remains of blue pigment on wig; traces of red on face.
Measurements: Height 29.2 cm. Width 29.5 cm. Thickness 6.8 cm. Height of head 11.1 cm. Height of face 7.7 cm.
Condition: Patches of lime wash that formed a ground for painting remain on wig and background. Back and right side cut in modern times.

Provenance: Tell el Amarna. Excavated by the Egypt Exploration Society in 1934 in the Broad Hall of the Great Palace. Excavation no. 34/167.
COMMENTARY: The convex surface of this fragment suggests that it formed part of the drum of a column. Since it was found in the Broad Hall of the Great Palace, which was built before Year 9, the person represented is not likely to have been Smenkhkare or indeed any other king. The portrait is clearly of Nefertiti (cf. No. 121), although her features have been somewhat sharply defined by the deep cutting in the granular stone. Remains of inscription refer to epithets of the Aten and Akhenaten.

Bibliography: Pendlebury 1935a, p. 565, fig. 8; Pendlebury 1935b, p. 133, and pl. XII, 1; Pendlebury 1951, p. 65, no. 167, and pl. LXVII, 1; Aldred 1957a, p. 37, note 5; Silverberg 1964, 14th pl. following p. 80; Bille-de Mot 1966, pl. XV; James 1973, no. 295.

No. 49
ROYAL FAMILY AT WORSHIP
Early to Middle Period

Collection: Ashmolean Museum, Oxford 1893.1–41 (75)

A slab from a column with the greater part of standing figures of the King and Queen followed by a princess of whom only the head and outstretched arm with sistrum remain. Incomplete inscriptions give the names and epithets of Akhenaten and Merytaten.

Material: Hard white limestone.

Color: No trace.

Measurements: Height 24 cm. Width, straight 28 cm., following curvature 29 cm. Thickness 9.7 cm.

Condition: Extensive surface damage; face of Queen undamaged, but hand of Aten holding *ankh* to her nostrils destroyed, probably with intention.

Provenance: Tell el Amarna. Excavated in 1891–1892 by W. M. F. Petrie in well of garden of the Harim of the Great Palace. Formerly in the Martyn Kennard Collection.

COMMENTARY: The Queen, wearing her tall cap with streamers and her usual robe floating open at the front, follows the King, who is clothed in a tight kilt bound with a sash tied well below the abdomen; the pair are attended by Merytaten. Nefertiti, holding a *kherep* baton in her raised right hand, repeats the gesture of her husband, who probably stretched a similar baton over an altar piled with offerings to the Aten. The same design appears on a relief in the tomb of Panehsy at Tell el Amarna (Davies 1905a, pl. VII). Stylistic features to be noted here are the folds of flesh on the necks of all three figures, the treatment of the Queen's perforated earlobe as though it were a separate boss (cf. No. 31), and the bull's tail hanging from the back of the King's belt.

Bibliography: Petrie 1894, p. 10, and pl. X.

No. 50
NEFERTITI WITH FLOWERS
Early to Middle Period
Collection: Ashmolean Museum,
Oxford 1893.1–41 (171)
A fragment of a column portrays
the Queen in tall crown and
pleated gown holding aloft in both
hands the stems of bunches of
flowers.
Material: Yellow sandstone.
Color: Traces as follows: crown
blue; streamers red upon white;
upper part of collar white.
Measurements: Height 18.5 cm.
Width 30.5 cm. Thickness 9.7 cm.
Condition: Surface intact, but en-
crusted with salt efflorescence.
Provenance: Tell el Amarna. Excavated in 1891–1892 by W. M. F.
Petrie, probably in the Great Palace.
COMMENTARY: To judge from her
tall cap, the Queen is doubtless
Nefertiti. The style of this fragment is similar to that of No. 48,
and both pieces probably come
from the same area. The Queen
was presumably preceded by her
husband, who stood before an altar
of the Aten. The same design is on
a carved slab from the Royal Tomb
which is now in Cairo (Fig. 34:
Cairo 10/11/26/4: Aldred 1968,
p. 72, fig. 5).

Bibliography: None.

No. 51
A STATE CHARIOT
Early to Middle Period
Collection: The Brooklyn Museum
60.28. (Gift of the New Hermes
Foundation)
Pictured in sunk relief on this slab
is a chariot drawn by two gallop-
ing stallions driven by a groom.
The head of the nearer horse is
shown in frontal pose.
Material: Limestone.

Color: Traces of red base line; the
carved portions all painted red,
probably in recent times.

Measurements: Height 23.3 cm.
Width 53.5 cm. Thickness 3.2 cm.
Height of horse's head 5.9 cm.

Condition: Slab evidently complete, but only part of chariot
shown. Some damage to face of
driver; worn channel in front of
him. Back cut in modern times.

Provenance: Tell el Amarna; found
at Hermopolis.

COMMENTARY: Recently recovered
scenes from a temple of the Aten
at Karnak indicate that the decoration of its outer walls included a
visit to the temple by the royal
pair and their court mounted in
state chariots and attended by
their retinues. Such scenes evidently also embellished the walls
of the Great Temple at Tell el
Amarna, and scenes pictured in
the chapels of the tombs of Meryre
and Panehsy near the City provide
a useful control for the iconography. The relief shown here pictures a groom driving a presumably empty chariot in the train of
the Queen and King. He crouches
with whip and reins in one hand
and the slack of the reins in the
other. He wears a kilt and a wig
with pointed lappets. Although his
face has been damaged, his aquiline features are clear and seem
to indicate that he, like so many
professional charioteers of Egypt,
may have been an Asiatic. That
the pole of the chariot is capped
by a sun disk makes it evident that
the vehicle belonged to an important personage, though hardly to a
member of the royal family, whose
horses are usually crowned with
plumes. A clue to the owner of the
equipage may be found in the
sandals slung by their thongs over
the charioteer's arm. Since similar
grooms are pictured both wearing
sandals and carrying them (Davies
1903, pl. XXIV), the man represented here may be both sandal
bearer and charioteer to a high
functionary, almost certainly the
Vizier or the Mayor of the city
Akhetaten, who on state occasions
were obliged to run beside the
royal chariot and often discarded
their hampering sandals (Davies
1903, pl. X a; Davies 1906, pls.
XX–XXI). The frontal view of the
horse's head is one of those frequent breaks with tradition in
which Amarna art delights.

Bibliography: Aldred 1961b, pp.
69–70, and pl. 95; Brooklyn 1962,
p. 69, and p. 32, illus.; Schulman
1964, p. 53, note 17; Cooney 1965,
pp. 52–54, no. 30, illus.; Roeder
1969, p. 405, no. P.C. 30, and
pl. 175.

No. 52
STATUETTE FOR A SHRINE
Middle Period (?)
Collection: Musées Royaux d'Art et d'Histoire, Brussels E. 6730
The figure, with narrow back pillar, shows the King in broad collar and pleated kilt girded by a sash with ribbed ends hanging down in front.
Material: Fine white limestone.
Color: Red on flesh areas; very faint traces of painted collar preserved.
Measurements: Height (above modern base) 10.7 cm. Width 5.4 cm. Depth 3.6 cm. Width of break at neck 1.4 cm. Depth of break at neck 2.6 cm. Width of break at back pillar 1.1 cm.
Condition: Fragment preserved from base of neck to knees; right wrist and hand missing.
Provenance: Tell el Amarna. Excavated in 1931 by the Egypt Exploration Society in the southwest corner outside the boundary wall of the Small Temple. Excavation no. 31/435.
COMMENTARY: Here we have another example of a figure of the King such as was worshiped in household shrines in observance of the cult of the royal family, for when complete this small figure must have resembled No. 96. The fall of the kilt at the back, however, indicates that the present figure was shown with one leg

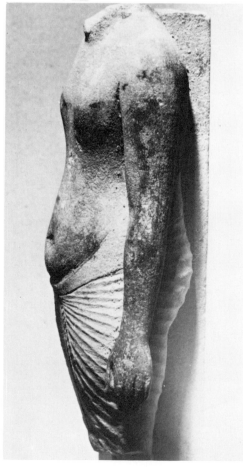

advanced, a more usual convention that is also to be seen on a statuette of Akhenaten in the Ashmolean Museum (1924.162: Porter and Moss 1934, p. 206, "House L. 50. 12"). In this Brussels piece the belly is more protuberant than in No. 96, and the arms, held farther away from the body, lend the figure a more relaxed air in spite of its striding pose. These two small sculptures are of about the same size and both were apparently "decapitated." The Brussels example shows an ancient dowel hole in the neck which indicates that it had been broken in antiquity and carefully repaired.

Bibliography: Brussels 1934a, pl. 11; Brussels 1934b, p. 23, fig. 1; Bille-de Mot 1937, p. 84, fig. 8; Pendlebury 1951, p. 100, and pl. LXXV, 6; Vandier 1958, pp. 336, 348; Bille-de Mot 1966, pl. XIX.

No. 53
PRINCESS WITH FRUIT
                    Middle Period (?)
Collection: William Rockhill Nelson Gallery of Art, Atkins Museum of Fine Arts, Kansas City, Mo. 47–13

A nude, childish figure, identified as a princess by her sidelock, stands on a rectangular base with left leg advanced. Her left arm hangs relaxed at her side; her right arm is bent to hold a piece of fruit, perhaps a pomegranate, beneath her breasts. Neither the base nor the narrow back pillar is inscribed.

Material: Soft white limestone.

Color: Black guidelines on back pillar, top of base, and around neck.

Measurements: Height 39.6 cm. Width at elbows 10.2 cm. Depth at base 18.8 cm. Height of head 8.7 cm. Height of face 5.8 cm. Height of base 3.4 cm. Width of base 8 cm.

Condition: Repairs to neck, knees, and above ankles; nose damaged.

Provenance: Not known; probably Tell el Amarna.

COMMENTARY: This is one of few reasonably complete sculptures of princesses that have survived (cf. Fig. 51). For the rest, we have to be content with torsos or heads or the greatly damaged groups that remain *in situ* at some of the Boundary Stelae, notably Stela A (Porter and Moss 1934, p. 230). The child represented here has the characteristic elongated skull of the royal daughters, with a huge sidelock at the right. Her features are childlike, her body plump. Although the sculpture is almost complete, the presence of a few guidelines indicates that some finishing touches remained to be added. Perhaps the eyes were to be more carefully cut, and certainly the whole surface was to be painted and the child was to be identified by inscriptions on base or back pillar or both. It would today be rash to try to guess her name. One can only hazard that she may be one of the younger princesses and that this portrait was carved rather late in Akhenaten's reign. One of the achievements of Amarna artists was the representation of children as children and not, as had been customary in Egypt, as adults on a miniature scale (cf. No. 110). This statuette, with the disproportionately large head of infancy, the legs firmly braced back, and the chubby body, gives an impression of immature charm and innocence, which does not require conventional symbols, such as sidelock or finger in the mouth, to lend conviction. It is in the Amarna age that figures of maidens holding fruit or birds or small animals make their appearance. When the royal family assembled to receive the tribute of the nations in Year 12, the younger daughters carried baby gazelles in their arms, and at the same ceremony Ankhesenpaaten was shown holding pomegranates, one of which she offered to Maketaten (Davies 1905a, p. 39, pl. XXXVIII; Lepsius 1848–1859a, pl. 99b). The pomegranate, introduced into Egypt from Asia during the earlier New Kingdom, may have had some deeper signifiance, suggesting the protection of a goddess of love and fertility. At Tell el Amarna, of course, no such goddesses were recognized, although the age spoke much of love, but perhaps it was the women of the royal family who were regarded as natural substitutes for such deities.

Bibliography: Kansas City 1949, p. 16, illus.; Kansas City 1959, p. 20, illus.; Hall 1968, p. 17, fig. 20.

Fig. 51. Red-brown quartzite statuette of a princess. Excavated by the Deutsche Orient-Gesellschaft in 1912 in the studio of the Chief Sculptor Tuthmose at Tell el Amarna. Middle to Late Period. Height 22 cm. Egyptian Museum, Cairo JE 44873.

No. 54
AKHENATEN WITH FORMAL BOUQUET

Middle Period

Collection: Ägyptisches Museum Berlin/DDR 22265

The head and parts of the arms of the King are here pictured in sunk relief. He holds between his raised hands a bouquet of lotus flanked by leaves of lettuce (?), which the rays of the Aten reach down to receive; two of these rays bring life to the King and to the uraeus of the Blue Crown he wears. At the right is part of an inscription giving the early name and an epithet of the Aten.

Material: Limestone.

Color: Red on face and arms; blue on crown and inscription.

Measurements: Height 14 cm. Width 15.7 cm. Thickness 4 cm. Height of King's face 2.6 cm. Width of cartouche ca. 2 cm.

Condition: Back of slab and right-hand edge worked; other edges fractured.

Provenance: Tell el Amarna. Excavated in 1911–1912 by the Deutsche Orient-Gesellschaft in House P 49,1, in town north of Main Wadi.

COMMENTARY: This slab probably formed part of an architectural element in a private chapel similar to that in the house of Panehsy at Tell el Amarna (Fig. 52). The early cartouche of the Aten shows that the scene was carved before Year 9, but the excesses of the early style are already on the wane. The elegance of the King's recurved fingers and the elongated thumbs should be noted. Here, as so often, the rays of the Aten and the hands in which they terminate seem to have been carved by a less experienced artist than the one employed on the main figure.

Bibliography: None.

Fig. 52. Left-hand side of the façade of a shrine (partly restored) showing Akhenaten, Nefertiti, and Merytaten making offerings to the Aten. Excavated by the Egypt Exploration Society in 1926–1927 in the house of Panehsy at Tell el Amarna. Late Period. Height 110 cm. Egyptian Museum, Cairo JE 65041.

No. 55
A VESSEL OF THE ROYAL
FLEET

Middle Period (?)
Collection: Mr. and Mrs. Norbert
Schimmel, New York
This slab, showing a vessel moored
on the bank of the river or a canal,
is apparently related to two reliefs
in Boston (No. 57), although it
does not adjoin them. Like them,
it depicts a royal vessel; nearby,
on the bank, is a man with a
bundle of oars and, at upper right,
is a garden.

Material: Limestone.

Color: Modern red-brown painting
on sunk areas.

Measurements: Height 24 cm.
Width 54.2 cm. Thickness 3.5 cm.

Condition: Top edge damaged;
other minor flaws.

Provenance: Tell el Amarna; found
at Hermopolis.

COMMENTARY: That the ship pictured here may be a warship seems
evident from the shields of its
marines seen resting on its gun-
wales. The boat is secured to the
bank by lines attached to two
mooring posts, and a man carrying
a bag has just ascended a gang-
plank and stepped on deck. From
the prow a streamer flutters in the
wind. The forecastle, with its
frieze of cobras, has a side panel
showing the King, accompanied by
his wife and daughter and under
the protection of the Aten, in the
act of smiting a foe. The forecastle takes the form of a kiosk,
which opens toward the stern, and
the artisan, ignoring perspective,
has spread out the opening for
the viewer to see that it has a
cushioned parapet and a fringed
awning and is flanked by pillars
supporting the roof. An interesting
feature of this relief is the *sheduf*

resting on two forked poles which
is shown in the garden at the
upper right. The *sheduf* is an age-
old irrigation device still used in
Egypt but rarely pictured in antiquity. Here, hastily sketched, it
lacks its long sweep with attached
jars to lift water from canal or
river. It has apparently been dismantled, and what seem to be
sweep and jars lie beside it. The
garden, fenced by a lattice on its
landward side, contains a different
plant in each of its plots. Near it,
a large bird, probably a crane, flies
over the water.

Bibliography: Hoffmann 1964a,
no. 119, illus.; Cooney 1965, pp.
80–81, no. 50, illus.; Hamburg
1965, p. 26, no. 42, and fig. 31;
Bille-de Mot 1966, fig. 32; Jerusalem 1967, no. 21, illus.; Roeder
1969, p. 405, no. P.C. 55, and pl.
182.

Fig. 53. Suggested restoration of the design of No. 56. After a line drawing by Norman de Garis Davies (Davies 1923b). Reprinted with the permission of The Metropolitan Museum of Art.

No. 56
INTIMATE FAMILY SCENE
Middle Period

Collection: Musée du Louvre, Paris E. 11624

A fragment of a stela preserves the lower part of a domestic scene in which Nefertiti is pictured with two of her children, all seated on the lap of her enthroned spouse. She wears a long pleated robe with fringed hem, and the King is clothed in a pleated kilt; his feet rest upon a hassock. The scene takes place within an arbor or a kiosk supported by posts made of bundled reeds, and before the royal family is a stand on which rests a bowl heaped with fruit and flowers.

Material: Limestone.

Color: Remains of red on flesh, especially of King, and of white on garments.

Measurements: Height 24.7 cm. Width 34 cm. Thickness 4.9 cm.

Condition: Fragmentary, but with lower edge and remaining parts of sides worked; back adzed to rough finish; gashes on legs of King.

Provenance: Tell el Amarna. Excavated in 1891–1892 by H. Carter and W. M. F. Petrie; said to have been found in a house. Formerly in the Amherst Collection.

COMMENTARY: The stela of which this fragment is a part was doubtless installed in a chapel devoted to the cult of the royal family in a private house (cf. No. 16; Figs. 2, 3). The subject of the scene, which has been plausibly reconstructed (Fig. 53: Davies 1923b, p. 42, fig. 4), is unprecedented. Even at Deir el Bahri, where Queen Ahmose is shown in dalliance with her divine spouse, Amun, the proprieties are observed (Porter and Moss 1929, p. 118). The subject is again found at Luxor, where Queen Mutemwiya is represented on the lap of her consort, Amun (Porter and Moss 1929, pp. 106–107). The Paris stela not only is expressive of that love of family which is one of the abiding features of Egyptian character but it provides evidence of the extent to which worship of the royal and divine family had replaced the long-established cults of trinities composed of god, goddess, and their offspring, which had grown in popularity during the earlier New Kingdom. When complete, the stela would perhaps have shown the cornice of the kiosk broken by the rayed symbol of the Aten. Despite its small size, what remains of the stela gives evidence of great confidence and precision in the carving, such details as the distinction between right and left foot being carefully observed, even in the minute extremities of the children.

* *Bibliography:* Porter and Moss 1934, p. 207. Add: Capart 1942, pl. 543; Koefoed-Petersen 1943, pl. 15b; Paris 1948, p. 64, and pl. XIV, upper; Spiegel 1950, pl. 2; Paris 1961, p. 68, and pl. XIV, upper; Drioton and du Bourguet 1965, p. 286, fig. 62; Bille-de Mot 1966, fig. 46.

Fig. 53.

No. 57
RIVER SCENE WITH ROYAL
BARGES
                    Middle Period (?)
Collection: Museum of Fine Arts,
Boston 64.521 and 63.260
Two adjacent slabs show a scene
of royal barges rowed by oarsmen
along the river or a canal.
Material: Limestone.
Color: Blue and pinkish-red pigment apparently applied in modern times.
Measurements: 64.521: Height
23.9 cm. Width 54 cm. Height of
faces on the oars 2.1 cm. Height
of faces of attendants 1.1–1.3 cm.
63.260: Height 23.4 cm. Width
53.1 cm. Thickness 3.3–3.6 cm.
Height of faces of oarsmen ca.
1.2 cm. Width of water channel at
breaks, left 3.7 cm., right 3.8 cm.,
bottom 9.9 cm.
Condition: Virtually intact.
Provenance: Tell el Amarna; found
at Hermopolis.
COMMENTARY: By a happy acci-
dent two adjacent blocks have survived to provide continuation of
a single scene. Representations of
state barges are not unknown at
Tell el Amarna; a scene of such
vessels sketched in the tomb of
May (Davies 1908a, pl. V) shows
them at anchor beside the quay of
the Great Palace. They are recognizable by the hulls and also by

the finials of their great steering
oars, which are carved in the likeness of King or Queen. In this
representation appears the stern
of Nefertiti's barge, with its stern
castle in the form of a kiosk on
the wall of which Nefertiti is depicted under the protective rays
of the Aten as smiting a foe. That
the foe is a Syrian *woman* is evident from her sidelock and cape-
like garment. As Nims has pointed
out (Nims 1968, p. 546), there is
a parallel to this scene on the
throne of Queen Tiye in the tomb
of Kheruef (Fakhry 1943, pl.
XXXIX). The steering oars terminate in the head of Nefertiti,
who wears the tall cap surmounted
by a disk and plumes. Her crew is
busy rowing, and the steersmen
stand at tillers under the protection of the royal panther skin (No.
126). The deferential attitude of
the guards standing on the cabin
roof suggests that the royal party
is aboard, probably in the forecastle. In the lower slab the prow
of a second barge is shown to the
left with the leadsman at his
sounding pole. The scene on this
cabin apparently depicts Akhenaten smiting a foe (Cooney 1965,
p. 84), and thus the barge is indicated as the King's. In the lower
left-hand corner of this second
barge are the tops of two plumes

that must belong to the steering
oars of a third barge. This is
unlikely to be Akhenaten's vessel
as Miss Chapman's reconstruction
(in Cooney 1965, p. 82) would
suggest, for according to the scene
in the tomb of May, the King's
steering oars were surmounted by
his sculptured head wearing the
atef (see also the model barge
from the tomb of Tutankhamen:
Carter 1933, pl. LXIII, A). Another
contemporary relief in the Cairo
Museum (JE 91723: Keimer 1947,
pp. 117–125, pls. I–II) has the
finial of the steering oar in the
form of the King's head wearing a
short wig, with a circlet carrying
the uraeus, surmounted by the
Double Crown. There is no certainty, however, that the state
barge in the representation belonged to Akhenaten in preference
to Amenhotep III or Smenkhkare.
We must presume, therefore,
either that the tops of the plumes
in the lower left-hand corner of
the Boston relief belong to another
queen (probably Tiye) or that
Nefertiti's barge was shown both
at rest and in motion.

Bibliography: Terrace 1964, p. 53,
fig. 6; Cooney 1965, pp. 82–85,
nos. 51 and 51a, illus.; Smith
1965, figs. 194–195; Roeder 1969,
p. 406, no. P.C. 67, and pl. 191.

No. 58
BEAUTIFUL ARE THY FEET IN
SANDALS
Probably Middle Period
Collection: The Brooklyn Museum
60.197.7
The feet and ankles of a royal
lady and the edge of her long
pleated robe are all that remain
on this beautifully carved slab
which must have formed part of
a large-scale figure.

Material: Limestone.

Color: Areas of pinkish red not
ancient.

Measurements: Height 23.4 cm.
Width 55.6 cm. Thickness 3.3 cm.
Length of foot 26 cm.

Condition: Broken down the middle and reassembled; lower right-
hand corner with part of foot
deeply chipped; minor chips at all
edges. Back cut in modern times.
Provenance: Tell el Amarna;
found at Hermopolis.

COMMENTARY: The arguments for
attributing this fragment to a representation of Queen Nefertiti
have been well adduced by Cooney,
although the same reasoning might
be employed in identifying the person pictured as Queen Merytaten
(No. 120). Whoever was portrayed, the slab is a small masterpiece. It might be noted that the
artist has carefully distinguished
the left foot from the right. Such
differentiation, lacking in earlier
Egyptian art, is characteristic of
the Amarna Period and its after-
math.

Bibliography: Cooney 1965, pp.
23–24, no. 13, illus.; Roeder 1969,
p. 404, no. P.C. 29, and pl. 173.

No. 59
SCULPTOR'S TRIAL PIECE
Middle Period
Collection: University College London 011
On a stone slab the profile of a
queen has been drawn in ink; lips
and chin have been partially
carved.
Material: Grayish-white limestone.
Color: Outlines in black ink.
Measurements: Height 8.7 cm.
Width 7.5 cm. Thickness 1.6 cm.
Condition: Upper and right-hand
edges worked; left-hand portion
and probably part of lower edge
missing.
Provenance: Tell el Amarna. Excavated in 1891–1892 by H. Carter
and W. M. F. Petrie; no precise location given.

COMMENTARY: The person represented is probably Queen Nefertiti,
wearing her tall cap with uraeus.
The cutting has begun with philtrum, lips, and chin; the nostril
and the muscle at the corner of
the mouth have been defined. A
start has been made on the earlobe, at which point the relief has
been cut to its full depth. The
diadem, including the semicircular
notch in front of the ear, has been
provisionally cut. Ink lines define
the contour of the jaw and the
folds of the neck.

Bibliography: Mentioned vaguely
in Petrie 1894, p. 30, no. 72; Burlington 1922, p. 64, no. 2; Pendlebury 1951, pp. 225–226, and pl.
CV, 3; Samson 1972, pp. 42–43,
with pl. 19.

No. 60
A PRINCESS PRAYING
Middle Period
Collection: Museum of Fine Arts, Boston 36.96
The head and shoulders of a young woman remaining on this fragment identify her as a princess. She wears the sidelock, large ear stud, and pleated dress characteristic of the daughters of Akhenaten and raises her hands in the familiar gesture of adoration.
Material: Granite.
Color: The natural color of the stone, black speckled with pink.
Measurements: Height 10.5 cm. Width 13.8 cm. Height of head 2 cm. Height of face 1.5 cm. Height of broad band 0.9 cm.
Condition: Surface unblemished.
Provenance: Tell el Amarna. Excavated by the Egypt Exploration Society in 1934 in the North Harim of the Great Palace. Excavation no. 34/69.

COMMENTARY: Although the excavators described this fragment as part of a stela, it is difficult to determine the type of monument from which it came. The inscription above the head of the princess, which includes the name of Akhenaten, must have extended for some distance to her left and thus, since the top of her head is in close proximity to the border of the inscription, would allow no space for taller representations of her parents, who might be expected to precede her. Accordingly it may be assumed that this monument is concerned only with the princess, and such an assumption seems to be confirmed by the pose of the figure with both hands raised in adoration. When the royal daughters are shown with their parents, they are usually represented holding a sistrum. Of the two-column inscription in front of the princess, only a mention of the Queen is preserved. It is possible, therefore, that the figure represents Merytaten and that the fragment may very well come from her "sunshade," which was a division of the Great Palace, as an inscription on a statue base in London (British Museum 1000: British Museum 1939, pp. 27–28, pl. XXIV; Pendlebury 1951, pp. 193 c, 201 f) informs us. The princess also had another "sunshade" in the Maru Temple in the southern part of the City, which had earlier belonged to Queen Nefertiti (cf. No. 13).

Bibliography: Dunham 1936, p. 24, illus.; Pendlebury 1951, p. 45, and pl. LXIII, 4.

No. 61
CLEARING THE WAY FOR ROYALTY
Middle Period
Collection: Elie Borowski, Basel
A slab with parts of two registers depicts, above, portions of bowing men who rest the ends of their staves on the ground, and, below, the plumed heads of two spans of horses held by grooms.
Material: Limestone.
Color: Blue on horses' plumes, black on wig of groom, pale red on horses, men, and staves; all probably modern.
Measurements: Height 22.7 cm. Width 53 cm. Height of groom's head ca. 6 cm.
Condition: Damage to left-hand side and upper corners and edge of block.
Provenance: Tell el Amarna; found at Hermopolis. Formerly in the collection of Mr. and Mrs. Leon Pomerance.

COMMENTARY: While this slab bears part of a scene of royal progress such as is common enough at Tell el Amarna, the whifflers pictured in the upper register lend an added detail. They bow low and touch the ground with the ends of their long staves to salute the passing of the King and his retinue. The plumes on the head of the first span of horses indicate that the chariot they draw is a royal one. The grooms try to quiet the restive steeds by stroking their noses.

Bibliography: Cooney 1965, pp. 58–59, no. 35.

No. 62
ADORATION OF THE KING
Middle Period (?)
Collection: Museum of Fine Arts, Boston 62.1168
The worshiper, kneeling on his left knee, raises his hands toward a cartouche inscribed with the prenomen of Akhenaten.
Material: Limestone.
Color: No trace.
Measurements: Height 26.3 cm. Width 24.6 cm. Thickness 3.2 cm. Height of head 5 cm. Height of face 3.7 cm.
Condition: Surface flaws; all sides except bottom cut in modern times.
Provenance: Probably Tell el Amarna.
COMMENTARY: The man pictured, who is described as the Overseer of Works, User-Seth, is "praising the living Aten." His hair reaches to his shoulders, and he wears a tunic with a flounced apron—a common Amarna fashion. The first column of the inscription reads, "The Lord of the Two Lands, Neferkheprure-waenre, given life." The fragment probably comes from the lintel of a house, for similar architectural elements often show the owner kneeling to praise the name of the King, Queen, and the Aten (see Berlin East 21597: Schäfer 1931, pl. 55). No house at Tell el Amarna, however, has yet been identified as belonging to this Overseer of Works.

Bibliography: Boston 1962, pp. 44–45, illus.; Terrace 1964, p. 52, fig. 5.

No. 63
THE WINDOW OF APPEARANCES
Middle Period (?)

Collection: Museum of Fine Arts, Boston 63.427

This window, or balcony, wherefrom time to time the King showed himself to the multitude, dominates a scene in a palace courtyard, in which servants are at work and doorkeepers stand guard.

Material: Limestone.

Color: Details in red and blue indicate modern repainting.

Measurements: Height 23.8 cm. Width 52.9 cm. Thickness 3.3 cm.

Condition: Some abrasions and blemishes; lower right-hand corner missing.

Provenance: Tell el Amarna; found at Hermopolis.

COMMENTARY: The Window of Appearances is shown in every private tomb at Tell el Amarna, with the royal family leaning over its cushioned sill to throw down gifts to their favorites. Several locations for this window have been proposed, including one on the bridge that linked the Great Palace with the King's Estate. This, however, seems unlikely, and not in conformance with the representations on reliefs. If the analogies provided by the palaces at the Ramesseum and at Medinet Habu are reliable guides, the Window of Appearances must have looked onto a colonnaded court, which at Tell el Amarna was probably the Broad Hall of the Great Palace. The present relief shows part of a court, entered by a gateway at the right and containing a kiosk with a frieze of solar cobras (see No. 155), a light canopy that af-forded protection from the sun. Entrance to the kiosk was through the two doors pictured at its right and left, which doubtless gave access to a ramp (not shown) which led to the balcony with its cushioned parapet and shutters that could be closed when the window was not in use. At the left a servant with a broom pauses in his task of sweeping the courtyard to chat with a companion; another, to the right, brings a jar full of water with which to lay the dust. Above him an overseer with a stick advances from a corner where the guards have stacked their axes, shields, and spears.

Bibliography: Terrace 1964, p. 54, fig. 7; Cooney 1965, pp. 77–78, no. 48, illus.; Smith 1965, fig. 204; Roeder 1969, p. 407, no. P.C. 127, and pl. 191.

No. 64
HOUSES ON A CANAL
Middle Period (?)
Collection: Museum of Fine Arts, Boston 63.962
While the shorthand of this representation is somewhat difficult to decipher, a little study reveals that it depicts modest dwellings, very like those in Egyptian villages of today.
Material: Limestone.
Color: Traces of blue, red-brown, and pinkish-red paint, all probably modern.
Measurements: Height 23.4 cm. Width 52.8 cm. Width of red band near the body of water 1.4–1.5 cm. Thickness ca. 4 cm.
Condition: Top edge damaged at middle; all edges slightly chipped.
Provenance: Tell el Amarna; found at Hermopolis.
COMMENTARY: At left, three women, raising their arms aloft, dance on tiptoe before a group of houses pictured on a much smaller scale as bordering the river or a canal. These houses have been identified as part of the service quarters of the Great Palace, but their position and details are hard to reconcile with excavated remains and with representations of such quarters in certain tombs at Tell el Amarna. The position of the houses in relation to the water pictured at the top of the relief does not conform to the situation of the Palace on the bank of the Nile. Cooney argues persuasively that the water is more likely to be a canal than the river, but his conclusion makes the identification of the two separate houses as part of the Palace complex even more difficult to understand. It seems to this writer that this slab is simply a scene of village life. Probably the state barges are sailing along the waterway and some of the inhabitants of the hamlet have turned out to greet the passage of the flotilla, as they would do in Egypt today, while others continue at their daily tasks. In the main room of the first house, a man tends a brazier; in an adjacent larder are pictured wine jars and rushwork stands bearing pottery beer bottles and bread and vegetables. A flight of stairs leads from a courtyard to the roof, where there is a curious barred object, plausibly identified by Cooney as a pigeon trap. The second house includes a bedroom with mattress and coverlet and headrest on the bed and a pair of sandals hanging on the wall. In an adjacent room, shown below, a woman is grinding grain in a mortar. This house too has its well-filled larder, and also a third room, where a woman is bent over some unknown task. The remains of actual houses similar to those pictured on this slab have been excavated at Tell el Amarna by both British and German expeditions, and related small houses in the ruins of a workmen's village at Deir el Medineh have been particularly well examined by the French (for references, see Badawy 1968, pp. 110 ff.)

Bibliography: Cooney 1965, pp. 74–75, no. 47, illus.; Terrace 1968, p. 52, fig. 5; Roeder 1969, p. 407, no. P.C. 116, and pl. 189.

No. 65
ASLEEP BY THE CAMPFIRE
Middle Period
Collection: Museum of Fine Arts, Boston 67.921

This fragment of sunk relief pictures a recumbent man sleeping under a coverlet. Below, left, are the knees of a second man, and traces of campfires are visible.

Material: Limestone.

Color: Traces of red paint on man's face.

Measurements: Height 22.6 cm. Width 37.2 cm. Thickness 4.8 cm. Height of head 5.1 cm. Height of face 3.9 cm.

Condition: Edges broken; about a quarter of slab missing at left.

Provenance: Tell el Amarna; found at Hermopolis.

COMMENTARY: This scene is related to or may be a continuation of No. 70. The sleeper lies with knees raised; his head is supported by a block headrest; he lies on one arm with the other arm flung across his body. His heavy mop of hair and his thick lips suggest that he may be a Nubian soldier and that this, too, is a scene of camp life. The tuyeres for blowing up a fire are seen at the left, and below are the flames of another fire.

Bibliography: Boston 1967b, p. 62.

No. 66

AWAITING THE ROYAL RET-
INUE

Middle Period (?)
Collection: Museum of Fine Arts,
Boston 1971.295
Fanbearers and grooms are pic-
tured in a temple courtyard, wait-
ing beside a chariot for the royal
retinue to emerge from worship.
Material: Limestone.
Color: Traces of red pigment.
Measurements: Height 23.8 cm.
Width 53.6 cm. Thickness 6 cm.
Width of baseline 0.7 cm.
Condition: Damage to lower right-
hand corner and middle of upper
edge.
Provenance: Tell el Amarna; found
at Hermopolis.
COMMENTARY: Similar scenes are
not uncommon in tomb reliefs at
Tell el Amarna. Here Nubian fanbearers stand at ease, while a
driver restrains the restive' stallions of a chariot to the right. The
absence of plumes on the horses'
heads suggests that the equipage
may belong not to a member of
the royal family but to someone
in the King's retinue. In the background (the incomplete upper
register) is evidently an entrance
to the temple with its double doors
folded open against the gate towers. An unusual feature of this
relief is the offering table with
incense burners to the right and
a small kiosk to the left, which
stand in what must be the dromos
of the temple. Are we to assume
that these were erected outside the
sacred precincts for the offerings
of the common people who had no
right of entry to the inner courts?
Bibliography: None.

No. 67
FEEDING A CALF
Probably Middle Period

Collection: The Brooklyn Museum 60.197.4

On this slab of sunk relief a herds-man wearing a short Nubian wig is forcibly feeding a stalled calf by thrusting a pellet of food down its throat; beyond are three other tethered calves waiting to be fed, their halters held in the man's left hand. To the left are the hind-quarters of a much larger animal.

Material: Limestone.

Color: Scattered traces of original red-brown paint on the cattle and of black on the herdsman's hair, but extensively repainted.

Measurements: Height 23.6 cm. Width 54 cm. Thickness 3.4 cm. Height of herdsman's head 5.3 cm. Height of herdsman's face 3.9 cm.

Condition: Lower corners chipped. Back cut in modern times.

Provenance: Tell el Amarna; found at Hermopolis.

COMMENTARY: The fragment comes from a scene in which the slaughterhouse adjacent to the Great Temple is represented. The cattle being fattened for sacrifice are tethered to a common tether-ing block. This representation is unusual in distinguishing calves from the full-grown oxen generally depicted in feeding scenes (Davies 1903, pl. XXIX). A veterinarian, however, has suggested that the man represented here may be re-moving the cud from the calf's mouth.

Bibliography: Cooney 1965, p. 62, no. 38, illus.; Roeder 1969, p. 405, no. P.C. 33, and pl. 175.

No. 68
BUILDING THE GREAT TEMPLE
Middle Period (?)

Collection: The Brooklyn Museum 61.195.1

The upper part of a laborer carry-ing a block of stone and, above him, the legs of two other work-men are all that remain of a swarming crew engaged in erect-ing the walls of the Great Temple of the Aten.

Material: Limestone.

Color: Traces of original red paint on bodies of workmen and of yel-low on the stone walls.

Measurements: Height 22 cm. Width 27.4 cm. Thickness 3.6 cm. Height of workman's head 4 cm. Height of workman's face 3 cm.

Condition: Left end of block broken away and missing; upper register greatly eroded. Back cut in modern times.

Provenance: Tell el Amarna; found at Hermopolis.

COMMENTARY: The scene in sunk relief of which this fragment in raised relief probably once formed the inner part may have repre-sented the construction of a por-tion of the temple complex, and Dr. Nims's suggestion that the ob-ject carried by the workman in the lower register is one of the stone blocks used in that edifice is al-most certainly correct (Nims 1968, p. 546). This laborer, with his heavy shock of hair and thick lips, may have been a Nubian or a Negro soldier who formed part of a contingent engaged in con-struction, and the legs shown in the upper register of the block may be those of men belonging to the same task force. Another block found at Hermopolis (Roeder 1969, pl. 58, 203–VII) pictures a procession of three workmen car-rying similar blocks up an incline. A similar scene at Karnak may also be compared (Leclant 1955, pl. XXI, 8).

Bibliography: Brooklyn 1963, p. 109; Cooney 1965, pp. 90–91, no. 54, illus.; Roeder 1969, p. 405, no. P.C. 58, and pl. 176.

143

No. 69

THE PALACE KITCHENS
Probably Middle Period
Collection: The Brooklyn Museum
62.149

A spirited scene in sunk relief gives a glimpse of the busy kitchen quarters of the Great Palace of Akhenaten.

Material: Limestone.

Color: The pinkish-red enhancement of figures and details is modern.

Measurements: Height 22 cm. Width 54.3 cm. Thickness 3.7 cm. Width of bottom band 1.1 cm.

Condition: Chipped and abraded at edges. Back cut in modern times.

Provenance: Tell el Amarna; found at Hermopolis.

COMMENTARY: This scene is part of a detailed, though probably inaccurate, representation of the Great Palace. At the left are two vaulted bakehouses, probably constructed of mud-brick. In the outermost of these, a man puts circular loaves upon an oven; behind him, on a rushwork stand, are five freshly baked loaves. A breadboard, a mixing bowl, and a water pot are on the floor, and a stick for poking the fire seems to lean against the wall. In the innermost bakehouse the baker pokes the fire with one hand while shielding his face from the flame with the other. The loaves he has baked are conical, and he is surrounded by molds for shaping them and by bowls and water jars. The incomplete register above the bakehouses shows what are evidently the lower parts of two brewhouses, separated from the bakeries by a passageway with doors. The bellows here used for stimulating the flame is worthy of note (cf. No. 70). Other rooms of the kitchen quarters are shown to the right. Through one of them two men carry a large wine jar, slung in a net from a pole. These rooms open on a courtyard through a portal with open doors, outside of which is a small cupboard containing five pairs of sandals evidently belonging to the kitchen staff. In the courtyard is a small plot of three flower beds, and a man with a short-handled broom eternally sweeps the path to the door.

Bibliography: Brooklyn 1964, p. 115; Cooney 1965, pp. 73–74, no. 46, illus.; Duke 1965, no. 11; Roeder 1969, p. 406, no. P.C. 84, and pl. 184.

No. 70
SLEEPING MEN

Middle Period
Collection: The Brooklyn Museum
64.148.3
The two reclining male figures
here shown in sunk relief one
above the other were actually re-
posing side by side. Between them,
at one end of a rectangular object,
is a fire; at the right is a vertical
channel.
Material: Limestone.
Color: Ground stained yellow-
brown; traces of paint on the
men's faces, the rectangular object, and the vertical channel.
Measurements: Height 23.3 cm.
Width 36.6 cm. Thickness 5.8
cm. Height of top man's head 4.7
cm. Height of top man's face
3.2 cm.
Condition: Right third of slab
missing; flaws on edge of lower
pallet and on vertical channel.
Back, left side, and bottom cut in
modern times.
Provenance: Probably the region
of Tell el Amarna.

COMMENTARY: Although no information about its exact provenance is obtainable, the height and
material of the slab suggest the
Amarna region, and the unusual
character of the subject as well as
its treatment is wholly in the spirit
of the genre scenes produced at
that place. The lower man reclines
on a pallet, his knees drawn up
and his neck supported by a headrest of block form. Although his
eye appears to be open, it was presumably the intention of the artist
to show him sleeping. Beside him
reposes a second man stretched
full length, his head supported by
his hands; he, too, appears to be
asleep. Both figures are framed
within enclosures representing bed-
covers, which take different shapes
in conformity with the different
postures of the men. The block
between the men is a hearth of
bricks or stones from which the
flames emerge. Two long objects,
probably a form of bellows or
tuyere, are represented as leading
into the fire. A brazier with two

similar tubelike implements is to
be seen in the tomb of Mahu,
Chief of Police at Amarna (Davies
1906, pl. XXVI). The purpose of
the vertical channel on the right
of the slab is difficult to determine;
it may simply be part of the enclosure in which the scene is set.
The sleepers recall a passage in
the Great Hymn to the Aten which
refers to the setting of the sun in
the western horizon, when "men
spend the night indoors with the
head covered, the eye not seeing
its fellow." The scene, however,
probably represents part of an encampment. Anticipating the lively
details of Ramesside camp scenes,
it may portray the eternal vigi-
lance of the police force that
guarded the city Akhetaten. If it
were indeed part of a military
scene, its warlike theme would be
a distinct departure from the
usual subjects of Amarna iconography (see also No. 65).

Bibliography: Brooklyn 1966a, p.
63.

No. 71
RIVERSIDE SCENE
            Middle Period (?)
Collection: The Brooklyn Museum
65.16
The bow and forecastle of a boat
moored beside a clump of reeds
appear in the lower register of this
slab, which also depicts a gardener
and a shipwright at their occupations on the riverbank.
Material: Limestone.
Color: Traces of red, probably not
ancient.
Measurements: Height 23.8 cm.
Width 38.5 cm. Thickness 4.3
cm. Height of man's head 1.5 cm.
Inside dimension of squares 2.7
cm.
Condition: Piece broken away
diagonally and missing from left
of slab; top surface chipped and
blemishes at lower right-hand
corner. Back cut in modern times.
Provenance: Tell el Amarna; found
at Hermopolis.
COMMENTARY: A genre scene in
the lively and impressionistic, if

somewhat careless, style characteristic of such representations.
That the complete scene probably
pictured the river near the Great
Palace, with state barges and other
shipping moored to poles along its
bank, is suggested by a similar
scene sketched in the tomb of May
at Tell el Amarna (Davies 1908a,
pl. V). In the present relief a gardener, naked except for a loincloth
and with two replenished water
pots suspended from a yoke across
his shoulders, mounts the bank toward a number of square garden
plots pictured on its crest. In the
upper part of the relief is an
enclosure where a shipwright
crouched on a three-legged stool
shapes a spar with an adze upon
a chopping block. Beside him are
a bowl and a water jar on a stand.
Outside the enclosure lie three
finished spars.

Bibliography: Bröoklyn 1966a, p.
63; Roeder 1969, p. 409, no. P.C.
277, and pl. 209; Hofstra 1971,
no. 16, illus.

No. 72
HERDSMAN WITH GOAT

Middle Period (?)

Collection: Anonymous Loan to The Brooklyn Museum L71.8.1

A goat nibbling at a tuft of herbage is followed by a herdsman who carries a staff in his right hand and a jar slung at the end of a stick over his left shoulder; in the background are two trees. A raised tongue along the right edge indicates that the slab was once fitted into the inside corner of a structure.

Material: Limestone; discolored.

Color: No trace.

Measurements: Height 22.4 cm. Width 45.1 cm. Thickness without raised tongue 6.1 cm. Depth of raised tongue 2.1–2.2 cm. Height of herdsman's head 5 cm. Height of herdsman's face 3.7 cm.

Condition: Upper edge chipped and flaws in upper part of background; face of goatherd damaged; about one-fifth of slab missing from left. Back and right side cut in modern times.

Provenance: Said to be from south Tell el Amarna.

COMMENTARY: This genre scene is carved with greater boldness and competence than is usually found in subsidiary representations. The figure of the goat with wrinkled muzzle tearing at the herbage is particularly striking. The goatherd with unkempt hair, drawn features, and protruding belly with prominent navel is the Amarna version of a traditional figure. Similar herdsmen from the desert tribes bordering the Nile Valley are pictured in Egyptian art at least as early as Dynasty XII. A parallel to the present representation is to be found on the dado of the main scene on the west wall of the tomb chapel of Huya at Tell el Amarna (Davies 1905b, pl. VII), and also on a block from Hermopolis where goats are shown browsing in a pastoral setting (Roeder 1969, pl. 99, 439–VII).

Bibliography: Brooklyn 1971, p. 19.

No. 73
COURT LADIES IN CHARIOTS
Middle Period (?)
Collection: Mr. and Mrs. Norbert Schimmel, New York
Two ladies in waiting stand upright in chariots drawn by rearing steeds. They hold their fans of office in one hand and clutch the chariot rail with the other for support.
Material: Limestone.
Color: Red in all sunk areas, probably modern.
Measurements: Height 24 cm. Width 55.3 cm. Thickness 3.8 cm. Height of faces, top 2 cm., bottom 1.5 cm.
Condition: Upper part of head of horse at left, faces of women and of right-hand groom restored in plaster.
Provenance: Tell el Amarna; found at Hermopolis.

COMMENTARY: Ladies in waiting riding in chariots in the train of the royal family are frequently pictured in tombs at Tell el Amarna. They are usually shown, as here, bolt upright, with a groom crouched before them holding the reins. On one occasion the drivers seem to huddle in light cabins, perhaps of rushwork, in order to avoid contact with their jolted, swaying passengers (Davies 1903, pl. XIX).

Bibliography: Hoffmann 1964a, no. 120, illus.; Cooney 1965, pp. 56–57, no. 33, illus.; Hamburg 1965, p. 26, no. 43, and fig. 34; Bille-de Mot 1966, fig. 28; Jerusalem 1967, no. 13, illus.; America–Israel Cultural Foundation 1968, pp. 121–122, no. 420, illus.; Roeder 1969, p. 404, no. P.C. 18, and pl. 172; Müller 1970a, p. xxxviii, no. 128, and pl. 129.

No. 74
GIRL MUSICIANS
Middle Period (?)
Collection: Mr. and Mrs. Norbert Schimmel, New York
Here we have, in raised relief, a slab from the central portion of a large scene in sunk relief, which probably pictured the royal family entertained while at meat by young women.
Material: Limestone.
Color: All worked areas painted red in modern times; a few traces of ancient pigment.
Measurements: Height 22.6 cm. Width 53.1 cm. Thickness 3.2 cm.
Condition: Slight diagonal crack toward left end and some wearing at edges; otherwise virtually intact.
Provenance: Tell el Amarna; found at Hermopolis.
COMMENTARY: The five musicians are equipped with a harp, lutes, flute, and lyre. The lutes are played with plectrums attached to the instruments by strings, and one of the women has apparently ceased her strumming, perhaps in order to sing. The musicians were not nude, as they now appear to be. They wore diaphanous garments which were undoubtedly once indicated by painting. As Cooney has pointed out, the character of this orchestra shows that it comes from a scene in the Great Palace rather than in a temple. Parallels exist in tombs at Tell el Amarna (Davies 1905b, pls. V, VII, XXXIII), and we are probably to visualize this troupe as facing a kiosk in which the royal family dines. The disposition of the figures in this composition, the varied rhythm of the intervals between them, the arabesque of the differently posed hands and strings, all reveal the supremacy of Amarna artists in handling groups (see also No. 139).

Bibliography: Hoffmann 1964a, no. 116, illus.; Cooney 1965, pp. 66–67, no. 42, illus.; Hamburg 1965, p. 25, no. 39, and fig. 40; Bille-de Mot 1966, fig. 74; Jerusalem 1967, no. 17, illus.; America–Israel Cultural Foundation 1968, pp. 130–131, no. 450, illus.; Michalowski 1968, p. 397, fig. 446; Roeder 1969, p. 404, no. P.C. 10, and pl. 171.

No. 75
AGED COURTIERS
Middle Period (?)
Collection: Mr. and Mrs. Norbert Schimmel, New York

A procession in which three older courtiers take part is here pictured as approaching the King. Each old man carries a curious notched stick with lines radiating from its top.

Material: Limestone.

Color: Modern red paint on figures.

Measurements: Height 23.8 cm. Width 54.3 cm. Thickness 3.7 cm. Height of head of middle courtier 6.6 cm. Height of faces ca. 5.4 cm.

Condition: Virtually intact.

Provenance: Tell el Amarna; found at Hermopolis.

COMMENTARY: The bowing courtiers appear to be proceeding along a way flanked by wickerwork stands holding bowls and amphorae that contain food and drink; vestiges of these are preserved in the upper register (cf. Davies 1905b, pl. IX). The remark-able features of this scene are the individuality of the faces of the men, unmistakably furrowed by age, and the curious notched sticks they carry in their hands. The men wear the usual Amarna dress of tunic and kilt with full front panel. The more fully preserved figure wears a wig with long lappets. That the first man, whose torso only remains, is also elderly is suggested by the folds depicted around his middle. The face of the figure bringing up the rear, with half-open lips, is that of an eager old man; the central figure, somewhat less individualized, has the sunken cheeks and drooping mouth of the aged. The notched sticks with pronged tips that these men carry remain an enigma. They have been variously interpreted as flaming torches and goads, and have been likened to papyrus stalks and canes. Cooney has drawn attention to other reliefs from Hermopolis in which bowing and erect courtiers appear to be giving similar notched sticks to the King. It was a custom, not infrequently illustrated in tombs of Dynasty XVIII, for court dignitaries to present bundles of papyrus stalks or other bouquets to a king on festal occasions, especially on his birthday, and it may be this customary offering that is pictured here, although the lack of detail (which may have been added in paint) makes it impossible to determine what plants were considered appropriate for such an occasion at Tell el Amarna. The bouquets offered to Amenhotep IV at his advent have the traditional form and are described as of Re-Herakhty, Mut, and Khonsu (Davies 1941, pls. XXX–XXXI). Perhaps a special type of bouquet was considered appropriate in the City of the Aten.

Bibliography: Hoffmann 1964a, no. 113, illus.; Cooney 1965, pp. 92–93, no. 55, illus.; Hamburg 1965, p. 24, no. 36, and fig. 47; Jerusalem 1967, no. 23, illus.; Woldering 1967, p. 230, no. 66, illus.; Roeder 1969, p. 404, no. P.C. 14, and pl. 171.

No. 76
THE ROYAL CORTEGE
                    Middle Period (?)
Collection: The Metropolitan Museum of Art, New York 27.6.1 (Gift of Egypt Exploration Society through the generosity of Mrs. Fahnestock Campbell, 1927)
In this familiar scene of waiting chariots, only one entire vehicle, with its attendant groom and spirited span, and the rear of a second are preserved.
Material: Limestone.
Color: Traces of red on horses and on faces and bodies of attendants.
Measurements: Height 23.5 cm. Width 54 cm. Thickness 4.2 cm.
Condition: Slab complete, but broken and mended; some chips at edges.
Provenance: Tell el Amarna. Excavated in 1927 by the Egypt Exploration Society in the Sanctuary of the Great Temple.
COMMENTARY: This is one of the very few complete slabs that survived the efforts of the Ramesside quarriers to remove the masonry of Tell el Amarna and reuse it elsewhere, especially at Hermopolis. In addition to the chariots, a second register at the bottom of the slab shows the upper parts of figures participating in temple ceremonies; these include singers, and a lute and a flute player.

* *Bibliography:* Porter and Moss 1934, p. 195. Add: Steindorff and Hoyningen-Huene 1945, p. 116, illus.; Winlock 1947, p. 156, and pl. 26; Phillips 1948, fig. 41; Pendlebury 1951, p. 12, no. 26/79, and pl. LX, 2; Hayes 1959, p. 287, fig. 175; Yadin 1963, p. 213, illus.

No. 77
BULL CALF WITH ATTENDANT
Middle Period (?)
Collection: Leon Pomerance, New York

A bull calf is led by a halter held in the hand of an attendant. Although this slab is complete, it presents only the head and part of the body of the animal and the kilt and lower arm of its keeper.
Material: Limestone.
Color: Modern pinkish-red color on worked surfaces.
Measurements: Height 22.6 cm. Width 52.1 cm. Thickness 3.6 cm.
Condition: Minor blemishes; otherwise perfect. Back cut in modern times.
Provenance: Tell el Amarna; found at Hermopolis.

COMMENTARY: This carefully worked slab apparently formed part of a scene in which attendants bring forth fat sacrificial cattle to greet the royal party on its arrival at the temple (Davies 1903, pl. XIV). The modeling of the animal is in the fine classical tradition of early Dynasty XVIII, and indeed, as Cooney has pointed out, there is nothing of the Amarna style in this relief save the voluminous kilt of the attendant (cf. No. 137).

Bibliography: Cooney 1965, pp. 58–59, no. 36, illus.; Brooklyn 1966c, pp. 62–63, no. 69, illus.; Roeder 1969, p. 405, no. P.C. 32, and pl. 175; Finch 1971, p. 38, illus.

No. 78
WAITING CHARIOT
Middle Period (?)
Collection: Mr. and Mrs. Norbert Schimmel, New York
Scenes of chariots waiting for the royal family or high officials at the gate of temple or palace are frequent at Tell el Amarna. On this slab only the front of the chariot is pictured, but the horses are shown with exceptional skill.
Material: Limestone.
Color: Horses light yellow; modern overpaint removed.
Measurements: Height 23.2 cm. Width 52.5 cm. Thickness 3.5 cm.
Condition: Broken in two places and rejoined; lower right-hand and upper left-hand corners damaged.
Provenance: Tell el Amarna; found at Hermopolis.
COMMENTARY: The action of the near horse, shown as biting his itching foreleg, adds a special touch to this spirited relief. The pose is known from a sketch on a limestone flake, probably of later date, in The Metropolitan Museum of Art (23.3.33: Hayes 1959, p. 393, fig. 248). The harness, with breastband, girth, saddle, and headstall, is clearly shown, and part of the reins remain. The pole with its stay, however, has been omitted, and the lid of the bow case strapped to the chariot covers part of the tails of the horses. The absence of a disk on the saddle and of plumes on the horses' heads indicates that the chariot belonged to a lesser official in attendance upon the royal party.

Bibliography: Hoffmann 1964a, no. 122, illus.; Hoffmann 1964b, p. 276, fig. 3; Cooney 1965, p. 49, no. 27, illus.; Hamburg 1965, p. 27, no. 45, and fig. 33; Mitten 1965, p. 30, fig. 2; Bille-de Mot 1966, fig. 33; Jerusalem 1967, no. 18, illus.; Littauer 1968, pl. V, a; Roeder 1969, p. 404, no. P.C. 7, and pl. 171; Müller 1970a, p. XXXVIII, and pl. 129.

No. 79
DETAILS FROM A CAVALCADE
Middle Period (?)
Collection: Mr. and Mrs. Norbert Schimmel, New York
Two heads of spirited horses to the left and part of a face to the right remain from a procession of chariots, probably two abreast, on the royal road at Tell el Amarna.
Material: Limestone.
Color: Traces of red on horses and on face of man.
Measurements: Height 22.3 cm. Width 26.5 cm. Thickness 3.7 cm. Height of head 6.1 cm.
Condition: Half of slab missing at the right.
Provenance: Tell el Amarna; found at Hermopolis.
COMMENTARY: The heads of the horses have hogged manes and their nostrils are split to compensate (as the Egyptians thought) for the restricted breathing imposed by the nosebands of ancient harnesses, which pressed on the animals' nostrils (Littauer 1969, p. 293). The headstalls are shown in some detail, revealing the cheekpiece and the bit in the mouth. The face of the man at the right is probably that of an official who is in a chariot driven alongside but in advance of that drawn by the horses here pictured. Under the man's chin are what appear to be two tassels, perhaps floating from the headgear of a groom, now missing, who crouched before him.

Bibliography: Cooney 1965, pp. 50–51, no. 28, illus.; Littauer 1969, p. xli, b; Roeder 1969, p. 404, no. P.C. 16, and pl. 176.

No. 80
HEAD OF A BULL
Middle Period
Collection: Galerie Maspero, Paris
A slab in sunk relief shows only the head of the animal, tongue protruding and ear laid down on cheek.
Material: Limestone.
Color: Entire surface covered by possibly modern red-brown wash.
Measurements: Height 21.2 cm. Width 36.1 cm. Thickness 4.5 cm.
Condition: Fragmentary; damage in region of horn. Back cut in modern times.
Provenance: Said to be Tell el Amarna.
COMMENTARY: At first glance it might appear that this fragment formed part of a scene showing animals being forcibly fed in the stockyard of a temple (cf. No. 67), but further examination makes it doubtful that such was the case, and the absence of a halter indicates that the bull was not being led in procession or otherwise held in restraint. This suggests that the animal was in the wild and that we may have here a part of a scene similar to the wild cattle hunt of Ramesses III pictured in his mortuary temple at Medinet Habu (Nelson 1932, pl. 117). Although the stalk of a plant before the muzzle of the bull and the ear folded forward make it also possible that on the present piece the animal is browsing peacefully in a pasture, it is nevertheless probable that the fragment belongs to a great hunting scene, of which other portions exist (Nos. 144, 149). Such a scene could well include some animals browsing in the thickets before the hunt had caught up with them (see also No. 145).

Bibliography: None.

No. 81
THE SANCTUARY OF THE GREAT TEMPLE

Middle Period (?)

Collection: Museum of Fine Arts, Boston 63.961

The Holy of Holies is pictured in sunk relief, its altars heaped with offerings for the Aten.

Material: Limestone.

Color: Numerous traces of red paint.

Measurements: Height 22.7 cm. Width 26.9 cm. Thickness 3.2 cm.

Condition: Half of slab missing from the left; chipped at edges and considerably damaged at right-hand corners.

Provenance: Tell el Amarna; found at Hermopolis.

COMMENTARY: The scene here represented is doubtless, as Cooney has demonstrated, the Sanctuary of the Great Temple. The main altar, heaped with offerings of meat, bread, and wine and garnished with bouquets, is flanked by statues of the King with offering trays; below it (or perhaps surrounding it) are smaller altars and incense burners. Doorways on the left lead to chapels that are also furnished with altars and incense stands. On the right are the remains of a columned portico, one of two flanking the entrance into the Sanctuary through baffle walls. The excavations of the Egypt Exploration Society at the Great Temple furnished evidence of shrines on three sides of the court, but Amarna artists were interested in giving an aspective impression rather than an accurate architectural rendering. It might be noted that the statues of the King flanking the main altar are not shown in other reliefs that depict the Sanctuary of the Great Temple. For the reconstruction of the Great Temple see Pendlebury 1951, pp. 9 ff., and pl. VIII.

Bibliography: Smith 1964, p. 144, illus.; Cooney 1965, pp. 100–101, no. 61, illus.; Smith 1965, fig. 207; Roeder 1969, p. 408, no. P.C. 260, and pl. 207.

No. 82
A TEMPLE COURTYARD
Probably Middle Period
Collection: The Brooklyn Museum
61.195.3
A sunk relief gives an idea of a court in the Great Temple of the Aten at Tell el Amarna. It shows a triple colonnade with offering tables flanking a sanctuary with doors.
Material: Limestone.
Color: Original colors lacking; traces of modern red pigment.
Measurements: Height 24.5 cm. Width 54.1 cm. Thickness 4.4 cm. Height of colonnade 6.5 cm.
Condition: Damage at middle of upper edge and at both lower corners. Back cut in modern times.
Provenance: Tell el Amarna; found at Hermopolis.
COMMENTARY: This representation, one of a series depicting the Great Temple of the Aten, doubtless formed part of a scene in which the royal family arrived in chariots for a state visit to the chief center of sun worship at Akhetaten. As Cooney has pointed out, such schematic renderings as this cannot be reconciled with the plan of the Great Temple recovered by excavation; while we can thus find no close parallel to the courtyard here depicted, the scene suggests a colonnade sheltering altars heaped with flowers and food offerings and flanked by incense burners. This colonnade seems to lead to a pillared chapel or sanctuary with open door, which was also furnished with altars and incense burners.

Bibliography: Cooney 1965, pp. 99–100, no. 60, illus.; Hawkes 1965, p. 80, illus.; Roeder 1969, p. 408, no. P.C. 253, and pl. 206.

No. 83
VINE WITH GRAPES
Middle Period (?)
Collection: Mr. and Mrs. Norbert Schimmel, New York
A fragment showing a vine bearing leaves and fruit probably once formed part of a scene representing an arbor that sheltered one or more members of the royal family.
Material: Limestone.
Color: Post bluish; grapes black; vine trunk and branches and parts of leaves reddish brown; traces of yellow on leaves.
Measurements: Height 23.1 cm. Width 42.3 cm. Thickness 4.4 cm.
Condition: Some chips at edges.
Provenance: Tell el Amarna; found at Hermopolis.
COMMENTARY: The fragment evidently comes from a representation of an arbor similar to that pictured on an ivory plaque in the Louvre (E.14373: Desroches-Noblecourt 1968, pp. 82–88, pl. XIV). At the left the trunk of the vine climbs up a post of the arbor; the branches are less deeply carved, and the veined leaves are still more faintly etched, some of them so delicately as to seem to recede into the background. The grape clusters, in contrast, are so boldly and deeply carved as to give weight and substance to the ripened fruit. The sculptor has shown here not only his preoccupation with texture but also his skill in indicating depth by establishing spatial relationships between the several parts of the growing vine.

Bibliography: Hoffmann 1964a, no. 127, illus.; Cooney 1965, p. 98, no. 59, illus.; Hamburg 1965, p. 28, no. 50, and fig. 52; Bille-de Mot 1966, fig. 42; Jerusalem 1967, no. 22, illus.; Roeder 1969, p. 404, no. P.C. 5, and pl. 170.

No. 84
INLAY IN POLYCHROME FAIENCE
Middle Period (?)

Collection: British Museum, London 58480

A lotus flower, consisting of a mosaic of glazed faience elements, once formed part of the wall decoration of a house at Tell el Amarna.

Material: Glazed faience.

Color: Sepals of calyx green; petals light and dark blue on white; petaloids red.

Measurements: Width at top 8.5 cm. Width of break 2 cm. Thickness 1 cm.

Condition: Two of the larger petals and three petaloids missing; base of calyx broken off and lacking.

Provenance: Tell el Amarna. Excavated in 1926 by the Egypt Exploration Society in House U. 37. 22 in the North Suburb. Excavation no. 26/386.

COMMENTARY: The lotus flower was built up of elements with colored glazes applied to a grayish faience body. It was found in a small house, but may possibly have been carried there anciently from a more pretentious dwelling in which elaborate faience borders might be expected to have occurred.

Bibliography: Frankfort and Pendlebury 1933, p. 21, and pl. XXX, 3.

No. 85
POLYCHROME FAIENCE TILE WITH GRASSES
Middle Period (?)

Collection: British Museum, London 59290

A clump of grass or reeds is pictured on a tile, probably originally of semicircular shape.

Material: Glazed faience.

Color: Leaves pale green outlined in brown on cream-colored ground.

Measurements: Height 11 cm. Width 12.8 cm. Thickness 1 cm.

Condition: Fragmentary; made up of four connecting pieces.

Provenance: Tell el Amarna. Excavated in 1929 by the Egypt Exploration Society in Houses U. 36. 20 and U. 36. 37 of the North Suburb. Excavation nos. 29/10 and 29/11.

COMMENTARY: The suburb in which these fragments were found presented a mixture of slum dwellings and small houses, together with a sprinkling of somewhat more pretentious abodes. Houses U. 36. 20 and U. 36. 37, in which parts of this fragment were found, were among the poorest. The excavators have speculated that the many faience fragments scattered among the humble dwellings were perhaps pieces of broken ornaments gleaned from the scrap heaps of rich houses.

Bibliography: Frankfort and Pendlebury 1933, pp. 17–18, and pl. XXX, 1.

No. 86
CATTLE AMONG RUSHES
Middle Period
Collection: Musée du Louvre, Paris
E. 17357
A fragment of a polychrome faience tile pictures a spotted bull calf gamboling amid flowering rushes. At the left are the hindquarters of another bovine.
Material: Glazed faience.

Color: Ground white; leaves of plant green outlined in black; flower tufts red and brown; calf white with black spots; larger animal outlined in brown.

Measurements: Height 10.8 cm. Width 11.4 cm.
Condition: Fragmentary; surface undamaged.
Provenance: Probably Tell el Amarna. Formerly in the Alphonse Kann Collection.
COMMENTARY: The theme of a bull calf frolicking in a swampy pasture was already a decorative element in the Malqata Palace of Amenhotep III in Western Thebes (Smith 1958, pl. 122, B), and it may have been inspired by that King's famous hunt of wild cattle in his second regnal year. The subject was a popular one at Tell el

Amarna, where it was used as a motif not only in painted pavements but also in tile decoration. In 1926 the Egypt Exploration Society found a tile very similar to the present specimen in the official residence of the Chief Servitor of the Aten, Panehsy (Frankfort 1927, pl. LI, 2; Pendlebury 1951, pl. LXII, 3; now in the Cairo Museum).

Bibliography: Vandier 1950, p. 25, fig. 1; Desroches-Noblecourt 1963, p. 165, fig. 97; Paris 1967, p. 23, no. 107, with illus. on p. 34; Vandier 1967, p. 308, fig. 11.

No. 87
CLASPED HANDS
Middle to Late Period
Collection: Ägyptisches Museum Berlin/DDR 20494
A right hand clasped by a left hand evidently comes from a group statue made in a royal workshop.
Material: Fine-grained quartzite.
Color: Natural light brown of stone.
Measurements: Length of right hand 9.2 cm. Length of left hand 8.4 cm. Width of right hand (at root of thumb) 3.4 cm. Width of left hand (at root of thumb) 3.6 cm. Width across both breaks 7.8 cm. Thickness 3.2 cm.
Condition: Unblemished; clean breaks at wrists.
Provenance: Tell el Amarna. Excavated in 1911–1912 by the Deutsche Orient-Gesellschaft in House no. P 49,6 in town north of Main Wadi.

COMMENTARY: This charming pair of hands, broken from a group sculpture representing at least two persons, is carved entirely in the round. The nails are indicated by D-shaped depressions, probably for inlaying with colored stone or glass (cf. No. 104). The underpart of the left hand is carved to show the division of the fingers but is otherwise summarily finished. That the fragment represents the hands of two figures seems clear, for the thumb of the left hand is more slender than that of the right and apparently belonged to a younger person or to a woman (cf. No. 110, although there the grasp is somewhat different and the back of one hand is lost in the mass of the stone). In royal pair statues of this period, it is usually the hand of the Queen which grasps the passive hand of the King (Fig. 41), or the hand of an elder princess which holds the hand of a younger sister. It is impossible to tell from what sort of group these hands come. If they are from a composite statue, one must visualize a very complicated substitute of two arms or forearms (cf. Berlin 20495: Schäfer 1931, pl. 48) joined at an acute angle at the hands. One can only admire the *maîtrise* of the sculptor who fashioned them.

Bibliography: Borchardt 1912, p. 32, and p. 34, fig. 25; Ross 1931, pl. 179, c; Lange 1951, p. 143, and pl. 64; Vandier 1958, p. 350; Berlin East 1961, pl. 38; Yoyotte 1968, p. 104, illus.

No. 88
A PRINCESS
Middle to Late Period

Collection: Ägyptisches Museum Berlin/DDR 21223

One of the best known of Amarna sculptures, this head of a princess shows the traits characteristic of the royal children. That it comes from a composite statue is clear from the remains of a tenon at the base of the neck. Eyebrows and eyes have been hollowed to receive inlays, probably of colored glass, and the usual cosmetic lines have been prolonged almost to the ears. The earlobe turns slightly outward and is pierced by an oval hole; the philtrum is indicated and the medial line of the lips shows a double curve; a line under the chin indicates a fold. The outward curve of the right ear should be especially noted, for it is a characteristic feature of Amarna art which persisted into the reign of Tutankhamen (Cairo CG 42091, 42097: Legrain 1906, pls. LVIII, LXII).

Material: Brown quartzite, with high polish.

Color: Traces of red on lips.

Measurements: Height 21.4 cm. Width 13.3 cm. Depth 17.5 cm. Height of face to top of eyebrows 10 cm.

Condition: Most of tenon broken away and missing; damage to tip of nose and to left ear and adjacent parietal area.

Provenance: Tell el Amarna. Excavated in 1912–1913 by the Deutsche Orient-Gesellschaft in House P 47,1 or 2 in town north of Main Wadi.

COMMENTARY: This sculpture clearly depicts the curiously elongated skull common to the princesses, with its bulges in the parietal areas, its slight division between the muscles under the occiput, and its indication of the vertebra at the base of the neck. Many attempts have been made to explain these overlong and overlarge skulls, but it seems to this writer that they are simply renderings of family peculiarities that existed but were greatly exaggerated by artists as a mark of the elect. The identity of the original of the sculpture is hard to establish, although the determined chin suggests Merytaten. Whoever she may have been, the head must be placed among the masterpieces of the Amarna Period, impressive alike for the consummate handling of the gem-hard intractable stone and for the impression it gives of an aloof and unselfconscious juvenile charm.

Bibliography: Porter and Moss 1934, p. 203. Add: Fechheimer 1922a, pls. 82–83; Whittemore 1925, p. 61, illus.; Otto 1939, pl. 97, 2; Schäfer and Andrae 1942, pl. 349; Hamann 1944, p. 242, fig. 259; de Wit 1950, pp. 46–47, no. 46–47, illus.; Lange 1951, p. 138, and pl. 27; Wolf 1957, p. 457, fig. 427; Vandier 1958, pp. 334, 343–344, and pl. cxii, 7; Firchow 1959, pl. 14; Aldred 1961b, p. 75, and pl. 113; Berlin East 1961, p. 63; Bille-de Mot 1966, fig. 68; Gerhardt 1967, illus.; Aldred 1968, p. 183, pl. 85; Michalowski 1968, p. 399, fig. 457; Wenig 1969, p. 51, and pl. 70; Giles 1970, pl. XI, upper left; Müller 1970a, p. xxxviii, and pls. 126–127.

No. 89
THE PRINCESS MAKETATEN
Middle to Late Period
Collection: The Brooklyn Museum
16.46
Of this delicately modeled sculpture of an adolescent girl only the torso remains. The figure, probably from a group, was evidently shown standing with feet together, left arm with clenched hand crossing below the breasts and right arm held downward and outward to touch another figure, now missing, on the right. At the rear, a back pillar with a columnar line on its left-hand side gives the name and titles of Maketaten.
Material: Quartzite.
Color: Stone originally pale brown.
Measurements: Height 30.2 cm. Width at shoulders 15.2 cm. Width of break at neck 4.1 cm. Depth of break at neck (slant) 8.6 cm. Width of bottom break, front (slant) 11.5 cm. Depth of bottom break, center 8.5 cm. Intracolumnar width 7.7 cm.
Condition: Head, legs, and parts of arms missing; minor chips and scratches; the stone discolored by an application of oil in 1933.
Provenance: Tell el Amarna (?); acquired by Charles Edwin Wilbour at Akhmim on January 8, 1890.
COMMENTARY: The statue of the princess shows her in the plumpness of early adolescence. The left hand clenched on the right breast was probably perforated to hold a flower or a sistrum. The back pillar, when complete, gave in its one preserved column the full titles, name, and affiliation of Maketaten, the second daughter of Nefertiti. It is not possible to say how many figures composed the group, but traces suggest that at least one other person was carved from the block, and it may be presumed that the eldest princess, Merytaten, stood next to her sister.

Bibliography: Revillout 1907, pp. 110–111; Taggart 1931, pp. 104–109, with illus. on p. 105; Capart 1936a, p. 12, and pl. IV, 3; Capart 1936b, p. 544 and following pl.; Capart 1949, fig. 34; de Wit 1950, p. 48, no. 51, and fig. on p. 49; Vandier 1958, pp. 343, 353, and pl. CXII, 4; Brooklyn 1967, pp. 68–69, illus.; Brooklyn 1970, pp. 50–51, illus.; James 1973, no. 290.

No. 90
TORSO OF A GIRL
Middle to Late Period
Collection: University College London 002

This fragment preserves a sculpture of a princess from the base of the neck to above the knees. The left-hand edge is worked to a flat finish as if to adjoin a block on which other figures were carved.

Material: Pale reddish-brown fine-grained quartzite.

Color: No added color.

Measurements: Height 16 cm. Width 7.8 cm. Depth 12.2 cm. Height of torso 14.7 cm. Width of break at neck ca. 4 cm. Width of bottom break (back of legs) 6 cm.

Condition: Head and lower part of legs, both arms, left shoulder, and back of block missing.

Provenance: Tell el Amarna. Excavated by W. M. F. Petrie in 1891–1892, but not precisely located.

COMMENTARY: The remains of the right arm show that it was bent at the elbow and turned to touch a person represented on a contiguous block. The left arm, to judge from surviving traces of the filling, was placed downward and outward to grasp the hand of a smaller figure standing well to the rear or more probably carved on the adjacent face of the same block. In other words, the monument from which this figure comes was composed of two or more blocks assembled in such a way as to resemble a cubical or rectangular monolith. On the outer face of each block was carved one or more figures, in such high relief as to be virtually freestanding, each holding the other by the hand. In support of this view it may be mentioned that the rear of the figure under discussion shows no trace of a back pillar but only a thick mass of stone, terminating in a fracture. Thus, this monument may have resembled the monolithic groups of Tuthmosis III and deities in London (British Museum 12: Hornemann 1969, pls. 1486–1487), and at Karnak (Barguet 1962, pl. XL a). It is difficult to decide whether or not one of the thighs of the present fragment is in advance of the other, but it would appear that the left foot may have been slightly forward. The "bridge" on the left-hand side of the figure is worked to a fine finish. The evidence is therefore that the fragment came from a monument that probably showed the King and Queen flanked at left and right by two or more of their daughters, just as they are sculptured on Boundary Stelae A and N (Davies 1908a, pls. XLI, XLIII; XXXIII, XL), but instead of being strung out in line, the figures formed two or three or even four sides of a monument composed of two or more blocks of stone. The torso is that of an adolescent female with undeveloped breasts and heavy buttocks, a slit along the belly defining the navel, and a roll of flesh accenting the pubic mound (see Nos. 31, 89). An argument has recently been advanced (Samson 1972, pp. 24–28) that this torso is from a statue of Nefertiti, largely because a similar fragment in the Ashmolean Museum (1893.1.41 [260]: Samson 1972, p. 27, pl. 9) is inscribed on its back pillar with part of the name of that Queen. The position of the name, however, shows that it refers to the affiliation of a princess who, as was usual, was named and then described as "born of Nefertiti." The fact remains that no representation of Nefertiti has come to light in which she is shown completely naked.

*Bibliography: Burlington 1922, p. 81, no. 43, and pl. IX; Fechheimer 1922b, pl. 94; Schäfer 1931, pl. 23; Schäfer 1936, pl. 32; Schäfer and Andrae 1942, pl. XV; Pendlebury 1951, pp. 226–227, and pl. CVI, 1; Capart 1957, p. 214, fig. 61; Wolf 1957, p. 459, fig. 430; Vandier 1958, pp. 343, 353, and pl. CXI, 5; Westendorf 1963, p. 277, fig. 8; Wenig 1969, p. 50, and pl. 66; Samson 1972, pp. 24–28 with pls. 8a–8b.

No. 91
INLAY FACE OF A KING OR QUEEN

Middle to Late Period

Collection: The Brooklyn Museum 33.685

Modeled in low relief, this face, shown in profile looking to the right, was made to be inset into a contrasting material. The eye and eyebrow have been hollowed out to receive inlays.

Material: Fine-grained red quartzite.

Color: Lips painted red.

Measurements: Height 12.1 cm. Width 11.8 cm. Thickness 4.3 cm.

Condition: Neck broken off and missing; nose abraded.

Provenance: Tell el Amarna. Excavated by the Egypt Exploration Society in 1932 in the Per Hai of the Great Temple. Excavation no. 32/61.

COMMENTARY: A decorative feature of buildings at Tell el Amarna was the lavish use of inlays of colored stones, glass, and faience, often in brilliant contrast, as on the capitals of palm columns (Petrie 1894, pl. VI). Human figures were frequently partly or entirely represented in a mosaic of variously colored elements. This head, found in a trench adjacent to a wall of the Great Temple, probably fell out of its setting when the wall was demolished in Ramesside times for the sake of its stone. It was designed to be set into a background of white limestone, and would have been completed perhaps by a Blue Crown in faience and certainly by inlays of glass in eyes and eyebrows. The subtle rendering of the facial muscles, the exquisite modeling of lips and ear belong to the later phase of Amarna art. The face has variously been identified as that of Akhenaten and of Smenkhkare, but the diadem could have belonged to a queen as well as to a king, and this writer has little doubt that the gentle thrust of the chin, the tight, pursed lips with their sharp profile, and the ridge of buccal muscle running from ear to nose all belong to representations of Nefertiti.

Bibliography: Pendlebury 1933a, p. 633, fig. 11; Pendlebury 1933b, p. 116, and pl. XVI, 1; Pendlebury 1951, pl. LVII, 4; Brooklyn 1952, no. 36, illus.; Pritchard 1954, p. 140, and p, 296, fig. 403; Roeder 1958, p. 54, item e; Peterson 1964, p. 25, note 70; Bille-de Mot 1966, fig. 64.

Detail

No. 93
GRAIN FOR THE HARVEST
                    Middle to Late Period
Collection: Mr. and Mrs. Norbert
Schimmel, New York
The field of grain pictured here in
raised relief may once have
formed part of a large harvest
scene.
Material: Limestone.
Color: Traces of blue and black in
sunk areas.
Measurements: Height 23.6 cm.
Width 52.9 cm. Thickness 4.6 cm.
Condition: Upper corners damaged; minor flaws, especially at
edges.
Provenance: Tell el Amarna; found
at Hermopolis.
COMMENTARY: The mastery of the
Amarna artists in presenting a
traditional subject is strikingly evident in this relief that pictures a
stand of wheat or barley. In place
of the conventional zone of ripened
grain with ears in a uniform hori-
zontal band, such as was represented in reliefs of the Old Kingdom and recurred with little varia-
tion in harvest scenes of Dynasty
XVIII, we have here an informal
arrangement of bearded ears moving in the breeze. The heights of
stalks and lengths of ears are
varied to form a subtle pattern,
set off against the hatchings
formed by the beards of the grain.
The rhythm is interrupted by a
few swordlike leaves, growing
from the stalks or perhaps belonging to tares mixed in with the
wheat. Growing grain is not infrequently represented at Tell el
Amarna. In the tomb of Huya
(Davies 1905b, pl. V) gleaners are
represented as standing in the
midst of it, but here it may have
some connection with the ritual
gathering of a sheaf, such as is
shown in a Brooklyn relief (No.
125).

Bibliography: Hoffmann 1964a,
no. 128, illus.; Hoffmann 1964b, p.
273, fig. 4; Cooney 1965, p. 96,
no. 57, illus.; Hamburg 1965, p. 28,
no. 51, and fig. 51; Mitten 1965,
p. 30, fig. 1; Bille-de Mot 1966,
fig. 43; Jerusalem 1967, no. 24,
illus.; Woldering 1967, p. 226, no.
54, illus.

No. 92
A MOTHER'S KISS
                    Middle to Late Period
Collection: The Brooklyn Museum
60.197.8
Only head and shoulders of the
fond pair are preserved in this
panel of sunk relief. The Queen
wears a short curled wig with
streamers floating from the back
and encircled by a diadem carrying a uraeus; a large earplug ornaments her ear. The child wears a
similar oversize earplug, and a
long plaited sidelock hangs over
its ear. A long ray coming from
the right upper corner ends in a
hand holding an *ankh* to the
Queen's nostrils. Under this are
the remains of three columns of
inscription.
Material: Limestone.
Color: Traces of red on flesh and
of blue on coiffures and inscription.
Measurements: Height 23.2 cm.
Width 45.2 cm. Thickness 3.4 cm.
Height of Queen's head 15 cm.
Height of Queen's face 10 cm.
Height of daughter's head 6.2 cm.
Intracolumnar width, left to right
4.4 cm., 4.4 cm., 4.7 cm.
Condition: Broken across middle
and rejoined; about one-fifth of
slab missing at right; face of
Queen and much of inscription
deliberately hacked out. Back cut
in modern times.
Provenance: Tell el Amarna; found
at Hermopolis.
COMMENTARY: This relief gives
one of the few representations of
kissing that are known in ancient
Egyptian art (cf. Fig. 54; and see
No. 123). Since the damaged inscription evidently bore the names
of her three eldest daughters, the
Queen represented here must be
Nefertiti, and the daughter she
kisses may be the eldest, Merytaten, whose name is preserved in
the first column of inscription, just
beyond the end of her lock of hair.
The remaining two princesses may
have been seated on the Queen's
lap (see Nos. 16 and 56). Other
interpretations are, however, possible, and the suggestion that the
princess portrayed here is the
fourth daughter, Neferneferuaten-
tasherit, is attractive to the author of this catalogue. If this were
the case, her elder sisters would
be grouped behind her.

Bibliography: Cooney 1965, pp.
20–22, no. 12, illus.; Hawkes 1965,
p. 87, illus.; Roeder 1969, p. 404,
no. P.C. 28, and pl. 172; James
1973, no. 309.

Fig. 54. Unfinished limestone statue of Akhenaten kissing one of
his daughters, probably Merytaten. Excavated by the Deutsche
Orient-Gesellschaft in 1912 in a sculptor's studio at Tell el Amarna.
Late Period. Height 42 cm. Egyptian Museum, Cairo JE 44866.

No. 94
LIFE-SIZE HEAD OF AKHEN-ATEN

Late Period

Collection: Ägyptisches Museum, Berlin (West) 21340

The plaster head, fully modeled and intact, extends from the level of the collarbones to the diadem. The backs of the ears are still embedded in the pour, and eyebrows and eyes are hollowed for inlaying.

Material: Gray-white plaster.

Color: No trace.

Measurements: Height 20 cm. Width 14.7 cm. Depth 13.2 cm. Height of face 12 cm.

Condition: Damage to right eyebrow; other blemishes received in casting.

Provenance: Tell el Amarna. Excavated by the Deutsche Orient-Gesellschaft in 1912, in House P 47,2, Room 19, in town north of Main Wadi.

COMMENTARY: The head has been cast from the rear into an open mold, and the excess of plaster at the back has been roughly tooled. The diadem is carefully delineated by a seam along the upper edge and around the semicircular bulges over the ears, which mark the springing of the Blue Crown. That the person represented is Akhenaten is indicated by the long triangular face, with its prominent chin and drooping mouth. The modeling, however, is in the restrained style of the King's later years, and that the cast has doubtless been made from a somewhat idealized original is revealed by the presence of the diadem and the Blue Crown and the absence of pronounced tendons, double folds of flesh, and Adam's apple from the neck.

Bibliography: Roeder 1941, p. 149, fig. 6, and passim; Berlin West 1967, pp. 71–72, no. 770, illus.

No. 95
HEAD OF A KING

Late Period

Collection: Ägyptisches Museum, Berlin (West) 21351

Life-size head, modeled to include the neck from the level of the collarbones to the diadem that follows the hairline. Remains over the ears indicate that the King was wearing the Blue Crown. The ears are fully modeled, but the holes for the earrings in the lobes appear only as faint depressions. Down the back of the neck is a raised wedge representing the streamers hanging from the rear of the diadem.

Material: Gray-white plaster.

Color: Eyebrows and outlines of eyes black; folds of skin along upper eyelids, at inner canthi of eyes, and from wings of nose to lips indicated by black lines; traces of black lines around nostrils, contours of lips, and lower edge of diadem.

Measurements: Height 26 cm. Width 16.3 cm. Depth 19.5 cm. Height of head 18.2 cm. Height of face 15 cm.

Condition: Flakes broken from above right brow and from lower neck between clavicles.

Provenance: Tell el Amarna. Excavated by the Deutsche Orient-Gesellschaft in 1912 in House P 47,2, Room 19, in town north of Main Wadi.

COMMENTARY: This sculpture was cast in a two-piece mold, the join of which can be detected in a slight ridge running down the center of the diadem, forehead, nose, philtrum, lips, chin, and neck. This feature, as well as the remains of roundels on the left parietal bulge of the Blue Crown, suggests that the object was cast from a finished sculpture, either one that had been accepted as a master portrait or one that was considered by the artist to be particularly successful. The fully modeled, sensitive lips, the hanging chin, hollow cheeks, and lined face indicate that the sitter must have been Akhenaten, portrayed in the restrained style of the last years of his reign.

Bibliography: Porter and Moss 1934, p. 203. Add: Fechheimer 1922b, pl. 84; Roeder 1941, p. 151 and passim; Lange 1951, pp. 137–138, and pl. 23; Anthes 1954, p. 15, illus.; Vandier 1958, p. 335; Hamburg 1965, pp. 18–19, no. 15, and figs. 3–4; Berlin West 1967, pp. 66–67, no. 743, illus.; Aldred 1968, pl. 1; Lange and Hirmer 1968, p. 460, and pl. 187.

No. 96
STATUETTE OF A KING
Late Period
Collection: The Brooklyn Museum
29.34
The king stands against an uninscribed back pillar, feet together, arms against his sides. He wears the Blue Crown with diadem and uraeus, a broad collar, kilt, apron, and sandals.
Material: Limestone.
Color: Crown blue with gilded diadem and uraeus; traces of red on streamers; red flesh tones; eyes white with black pupils; collar gilt, blue, white, blue; belt and apron gilded.
Measurements: Present height 21.9 cm. Width 4.8 cm. Depth 4.4 cm. Height of head 5.3 cm. Height of face 2.4 cm.
Condition: Head broken from body at neck and replaced; feet and base restored from the ankles downward; colors rubbed.
Provenance: Tell el Amarna. Excavated by the Egypt Exploration Society in November 1923, in House Q. 44. 1, Room 8, in town north of Main Wadi.
COMMENTARY: In the absence of any inscription this king has to be identified largely by the portraiture. Owing to its boyish appearance, it has been tentatively ascribed to Tutankhamen. It seems to this writer, however, that the prominent jaw, long nose, and pronounced paunch belong rather to Akhenaten, whose features have been somewhat softened to conform to the style of the Late Period. It is possible that the small sculpture was enshrined in the house in which it was found and discarded by the owner upon the death of Akhenaten and the abandonment of the City.

Bibliography: Porter and Moss 1934, p. 201, "House Q. 44. 4." Add: Whittemore 1925, pp. 59–65, illus.; Brooklyn 1952, no. 34, illus.; Vandier 1958, pp. 336–338, 348–349, and pl. CX, 4; Aldred 1961b, p. 82, and pl. 137; Peterson 1964, p. 19.

No. 98
FRAGMENT OF A FINE
SCULPTURE
Late Period or Reign of Tutankhamen
Collection: Anonymous Loan to The Brooklyn Museum L67.26.1
Only the lower half of a face, together with parts of the neck and ears, remains from what was once a masterpiece of royal sculpture.
Material: Fine white limestone, now discolored.
Color: Traces of red on lips and of black in corners of eyes.
Measurements: Height 4.9 cm. Width 5.1 cm. Depth 6.2 cm. Width of break at neck 2.9 cm. Depth of break at neck ca. 3 cm.
Condition: Mouth and chin intact; pitting on left cheek.
Provenance: Not known; indirectly acquired from the European art market.
COMMENTARY: The fragmentary nature of this head, from which so many stylistic criteria are missing, makes exact identification difficult.
That it portrays a member of the Amarna royal house nevertheless seems clear. Evidence of a diadem indicates that the person represented was most likely wearing the Blue Crown supported by a back pillar. The distinctive, heavily modeled mouth, with its Cupid's-bow form, resembles that of a well-known head (Fig. 55: Berlin East 20496). The eye, comparatively small and almond shaped, suggests the style of the reign of Tutankhamen (Cairo CG 42091: Legrain 1906, pls. LVII–LVIII), and the lower part of the face resembles that of a head in New York (The Metropolitan Museum of Art 50.6: Simpson 1955, pp. 112–114, illus.), which is usually accredited to the same King. This writer is inclined to identify this fragment as from a sculpture representing Smenkhkare or his younger brother Tutankhamen, with a bias in the latter's favor.

Bibliography: Brooklyn 1969a, p. 54, illus.

No. 97
FRAGMENT OF A HEAD
Late Period (?)

Collection: The Metropolitan Museum of Art, New York 66.99.34 (Fletcher Fund, 1966 and The Guide Foundation, Inc., Gift, 1966) Of this fragment, from which so many features are missing, little can be said except that it is certainly in the Amarna style and that the fine hard stone employed and the skillful carving indicate that it portrayed a member of the royal family.

Material: Fine-grained quartzite.

Color: Lips painted red; remainder of fragment in natural purplish brown of stone.

Measurements: Height 5.8 cm. Width 11.2 cm. Depth 10 cm.

Condition: Abrasion to upper lip and to remains of nose.

Provenance: Not known. Formerly in the Gallatin Collection.

COMMENTARY: The loose, fleshy lips and the remains of lightly traced furrows depending from the nostrils are in favor of an ascription to Akhenaten, although the possibility that the piece might come from a statue of Merytaten should not be excluded.

Bibliography: Cooney 1953, p. 12, no. 55, and pl. XXXV B; Harvard 1954, p. 18, no. 10.

Fig. 55. Limestone bust of a king, probably Smenkhkare. Excavated by the Deutsche Orient-Gesellschaft in 1912 in a sculptor's studio at Tell el Amarna. Late Period. Height 20 cm. Ägyptisches Museum Berlin/DDR 20496.

No. 99
A YOUTHFUL QUEEN

Late Period

Collection: Ägyptisches Museum Berlin/DDR 21220

That this head portrays a queen seems evident from the diadem across the brow. The tenon arising from the top indicates that the crown she wore was made of a contrasting material, and that the body was also fashioned from a different stone is clear from part of another tenon remaining at the base of the neck. The ears are unusually projecting; the eyes are large and the lips full; a shallow philtrum marks the short upper lip, and the full lips are divided by a triple curve. Two folds in the neck are indicated by a light scoring and black paint, and there is a faint depression at the base of the neck. The head is slightly elongated and gives the impression of being thrust forward.

Material: Yellowish-brown quartzite.

Color: Outlines of diadem, eyebrows and eyes, nostrils, folds of ears and perforations in earlobes all indicated in black paint; lips painted red.

Measurements: Height (above modern base) 22.4 cm. Width 15 cm. Depth 14.6 cm. Height of face 12.5 cm. Width of tenon 6.2 cm. Depth of tenon 5.3 cm.

Condition: Front of upper edge of top tenon broken away and restored.

Provenance: Tell el Amarna. Excavated in 1912–1913 by the Deutsche Orient-Gesellschaft in House P 47,2 in town north of Main Wadi.

COMMENTARY: Although the head was almost completed, a few details remained to be finished, and in the opinion of this writer the black lines on the sculpture represent guides to alterations that were needed before the piece was ready for the final polish. In its unfinished state the head has a juvenile appearance that has led some scholars to identify it as representing Merytaten, but the height and mass of the tenon at the top show that the crown designed for the sculpture must have been the tall cap of Nefertiti—a headdress never worn by any of her daughters—and the elongated neck contributes to the impression that we have here a portrait of the Queen. Even in its unfinished state, the head is one of the masterpieces of the Amarna Period, giving promise of a work of great subtlety.

Bibliography: Porter and Moss 1934, p. 203. Add: Borchardt 1917, p. 13; Fechheimer 1922b, pls. 88–89; Ranke 1936, fig. 126; Schäfer 1936, pl. 30; Schäfer and Andrae 1942, pl. 351; de Wit 1950, pp. 40–41, no. 36, illus.; Lange 1951, p. 137, and pls. 18, 20; Wolf 1957, p. 456, and p. 455, fig. 423; Vandier 1958, pp. 334, 340, 342, 351; Aldred 1961b, p. 78, and pl. 121; Berlin East 1961, p. 64, pl. 36; Bille-de Mot 1966, fig. 50; Yoyotte 1968, p. 114, illus.; Wenig 1969, p. 50, and pl. 60.

172

No. 100
UNFINISHED HEAD OF NEFERTITI

Late Period

Collection: Ägyptisches Museum Berlin/DDR 21352

The head, preserved from the top edge of the diadem to the base of the neck, was made to be fitted with a crown and inserted into a body of a different substance.

Material: Hard white limestone.

Color: Black lines and marks to scrve as indications for alterations.

Measurements: Height 29.8 cm. Width 18 cm. Depth 20.8 cm. Height of face 18.5 cm.

Condition: Damage to chin, left ear, and tenon at top of head.

Provenance: Tell el Amarna. Excavated in 1912–1913 by the Deutsche Orient-Gesellschaft in House P 47,1-3 in town north of Main Wadi.

COMMENTARY: That this head was in process of being carved is evident from the guideline that extends through the philtrum and down the center of the lower lip. The parts to be given special attention at the next cutting have been indicated by black brush marks. They include a ridge running from nose to ear on the left side, marks on the right cheekbone, depressions on each side of the nose near the inner corners of the eyes, the corners of the mouth, and the ends of the jaws. The lower edge of the diadem has not yet been fully cut, and the ears are still summarily sketched; the tendons of the neck have been defined by two diverging channels running from below the throat to the corners of the jaw. The sculptor has apparently copied the painted master portrait of Nefertiti (Fig. 1), but has made the mouth of the Queen appreciably larger—a fault that might have been corrected by further cutting. The head is in too rudimentary a state to decide whether it is the product of an apprentice working under the supervision of a master sculptor who would supply the finishing touches, or the incompleted work of an experienced craftsman.

Bibliography: Porter and Moss 1934, p. 203, lines 6–7 (museum no. not given and ref. to Kees to be deleted). Add: Borchardt 1923, pp. 34–35 with fig. 31; de Wit 1950, pp. 40–41, illus.; Bille-de Mot 1966, fig. 66.

No. 101
HEAD OF A QUEEN
Late Period (?)
Collection: The Metropolitan Museum of Art, New York 11.150.26 (Rogers Fund, 1911)

The statue from which this head comes was evidently made up of different materials. There is a rebate along the hairline for the reception of a wig or headdress of contrasting stone, and the eyes and eyebrows are hollowed for inlays, which were probably of naturalistic colors.

Material: Reddish-brown quartzite.
Color: No trace.
Measurements: Height 13.8 cm. Width 11.6 cm. Depth 12.1 cm. Height of face 11 cm. Width of break at neck 6.7 cm.
Condition: Broken off at neck; damage to ears and nose; abrasions above left eyebrow.
Provenance: Said to be Tell el Amarna; acquired in Cairo.

COMMENTARY: This head was formerly identified as representing Akhenaten or Smenkhkare. It surely portrays a woman, however, and it bears so close a resemblance to the head of Queen Tiye found by Petrie at the temple of Serabit el Khadim on Sinai (Cairo JE 38257: Aldred 1961b, pp. 66–67, and pls. 83–84) that it may confidently be ascribed to that Queen. This portrait has the same arched eyebrows, the identical lines running from the nostrils, the pouting lips, and the firm, slightly double chin that are characteristic of Queen Tiye. Especially the chin is quite different from Akhenaten's overlong lower jaw. The head was probably covered by a long, curled wig, perhaps made of blue faience, which fell behind the ears and over the shoulders as in the Sinai example. The neck may have ended in a tenon for fitting it into a body of contrasting stone. If the provenance is correctly given as Tell el Amarna, this sculpture would appear to belong to Tiye's later years, when she visited that City and indeed may have had a residence there. In the tomb of Huya she is shown on a visit to the sunshade temple built for her by Akhenaten. In the colonnades and sanctuary of that temple are represented statues of her with her royal husband (Davies 1905b, pl. X), and it is from one of these sculptures that this head may have come.

* *Bibliography:* Porter and Moss 1934, p. 234. Add: New York 1912, p. 14, "Floor 1, Wing E"; Bull 1926, p. 173, fig. 5; New York 1945, 18th pl.; de Wit 1950, pp. 30–31, no. 20, illus.; Roeder 1958, p. 60, no. D V 7, and pl. IV, b following p. 46; Vandier 1958, pp. 336, 338; Hayes 1959, p. 288, fig. 176; New York 1962, p. 29, fig. 37; Aldred 1968, p. 82, pl. 21; New York 1970, p. 91, no. 26, illus.

No. 102
HEAD OF A PRINCESS
Late Period

Collection: Ägyptisches Museum Berlin / DDR 14113

A head of a young woman, presumably one of the royal daughters, is broken from a statue. The broad, elongated skull rises rapidly from a receding forehead; the mouth, with a slight double curve on the medial line, droops at the corners; the heavy-lidded eyes are small and almond shaped; the earlobes have oval slits; the neck recedes into the clavicles, and thus the face seems to thrust forward.

Material: Limestone.

Color: Traces of red on flesh and of brighter red on lips; eyes with black pupils on white.

Measurements: Height 13.5 cm. Width 9 cm. Depth 10.8 cm. Height of face to top of eyebrows 6 cm. Width of back pillar 2.2 cm. Width of break at neck 5.7 cm. Depth of break at neck 4.8 cm.

Condition: Point of chin and middle of lower lip restored in plaster; rims of both ears broken; damage above right ear.

Provenance: Not known but probably Tell el Amarna; acquired in Cairo in 1898.

COMMENTARY: Although the back pillar supporting the head is uninscribed, the soft, unlined features of this head indicate that it represents one of the senior princesses, perhaps Ankhesenpaaten. The treatment of the eyes (cf. No. 98) and earlobes belongs to the later phases of the Amarna style, as does the somewhat idealized form of the skull (cf. No. 88). The drooping mouth and the heavy-lidded eyes, which lend a melancholy air to the head, recall the work of the sculptor who carved the statue of Nefertiti (Fig. 44: Berlin East 21263).

* Bibliography: Porter and Moss 1934, p. 234. Add: Borchardt 1911, p. 13, fig. 11; Fechheimer 1922b, pl. 91; Ranke 1936, pl. 137; Lange 1951, pl. 51; Wolf 1957, p. 457, fig. 429; Vandier 1958, pp. 343–344; Schäfer 1963, pl. 49; Bille-de Mot 1966, fig. 69; Lange and Hirmer 1968, p. 460, and pl. 189.

No. 103
A DAUGHTER OF AKHENATEN
Late Period
Collection: Ägyptisches Museum, Berlin (West) 21245
The stone head presented here probably comes from a composite statue. It is made with a rabbet at the upper edge to receive a wig of a different material, which would have covered the ears and the back of the neck, and there was presumably a tenon at the base of the neck for insertion into a body that was perhaps fashioned from a contrasting stone.
Material: Brown quartzite.
Color: Lips painted red; eyebrows, eyes, nostrils, and juncture of lips outlined in black.
Measurements: Height 11.2 cm. Width 7.2 cm. Depth 8.4 cm. Height of face 7.8 cm. Width of break at neck 4.4 cm. Depth of break at neck (slant) 5.7 cm.
Condition: Face well smoothed; lower part of neck broken away and missing.
Provenance: Tell el Amarna. Excavated by the Deutsche Orient-Gesellschaft in 1912–1913 in House P 47,2 in town north of Main Wadi.
COMMENTARY: The rather coarse granular stone in which this head was carved did not encourage a highly detailed finish, and the consequent rather summary treatment lends a dreamy quality to the features, with their heavy, relaxed lips and "Amarna eyes." The impressionistic effect, however, is fortuitous. Although a polish was given to the face, it seems probable that the black outlining of eyes, nostrils, and lips was an indication to the stonecutter to sharpen up those features with final touches. The head seems to have been discarded, however, before it could be finished, perhaps because the breaking away of the neck had rendered it useless. The sculpture seems clearly to represent one of the elder princesses, probably Merytaten, to judge from the pronounced chin, and it may even have been made during the early months of her reign as Queen of Smenkhkare.

* *Bibliography:* Porter and Moss 1934, p. 203. Add: Fechheimer 1922a, pl. 76; Hamann 1944, p. 243, fig. 261; Lange 1951, p. 138, and pl. 26; Basel 1953, p. 46, no. 104, and fig. 13; Vandier 1958, pp. 340, 342, 351; Berlin West 1967, pp. 68–69, no. 751, illus.

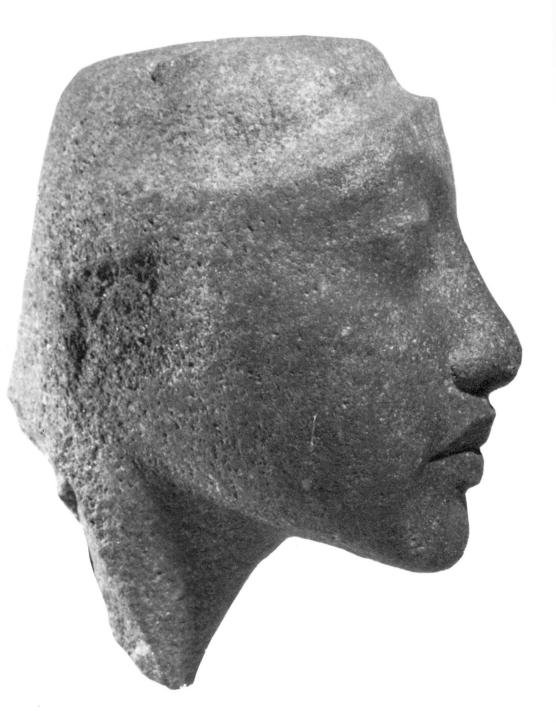

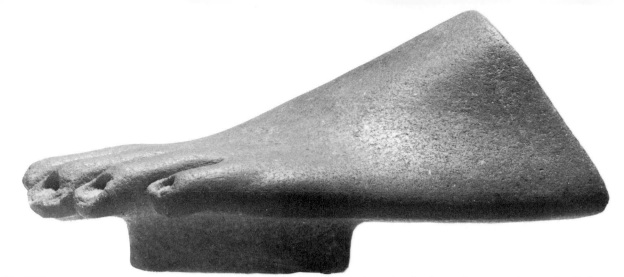

No. 104
FOOT FROM A COMPOSITE STATUE

Late Period

Collection: Dr. K. J. Stern, London This piece shows the forepart of a woman's left foot anterior to the ankle joint. The toenails are cut in intaglio to receive inlays, and a rectangular tenon on the sole indicates that the sculpture was set into a base.

Material: Yellowish-brown quartzite.

Color: Traces of gold on instep.

Measurements: Height 8.2 cm., of foot only 6.7 cm., of tenon 1.5 cm. Width 8 cm. Depth 17.5 cm. Height of cut (slant) 6.9 cm. Width of bottom at cut 6.5 cm.

Condition: Tip of big toe broken away at distal joint; nail bed of second toe chipped at tip; tips of other three toes damaged.

Provenance: Probably Tell el Amarna; said to be from Hagg Qandil. Formerly in the Collection of Gisela Müller–Reinhardt.

COMMENTARY: Feet from composite statues are rare, and the present one is a nearly complete example. It has been cut back from the base at an angle of about 45 degrees so that it could peep out from the hem of a trailing gown, which was probably carved in white limestone in imitation of the ubiquitous long white linen robes of the period. The areas of the toenails have been hollowed to receive inlays, probably of red stone or faience. In the cleft between the first and second toes is a drilled hole into which a sandal strap was probably fitted, and indeed at the posterior end of the foot a band of lighter shade about a half-centimeter wide can be traced from the dorsum down both sides to the sole. Specks of gold still adhering to the surface in this area are all that remain of what was probably a gilded sandal strap, perhaps once partly covered by the overhanging limestone dress. The foot is most skillfully carved, with careful indication of the folds in the skin, and Dr. Stern has no doubt that its anatomical features are those of a woman. The design of composite statues was such as to permit a specialist to concentrate on each separate part and thus to ensure the perfection of the whole.

Bibliography: Essen 1961, p. 103, no. 98, illus.

No. 105
HEAD FROM A STATUETTE

Late Period

Collection: The Metropolitan Museum of Art, New York 31.114.1 (Gift of Mrs. John Hubbard and Egypt Exploration Society, 1931) The young woman portrayed wears a short Nubian wig. Remains of the back pillar once behind the figure are uninscribed, and thus the woman's identity remains uncertain.

Material: Limestone.

Color: Flesh painted red; wig and eyes black.

Measurements: Height 3.5 cm. Width 3.1 cm. Depth 3.3 cm. Height of face 2.1 cm. Width of back pillar 0.6 cm. Width of break at neck 1.4 cm. Depth of break at neck 2 cm.

Condition: Paint rubbed; slight damage to tip of nose and chin.

Provenance: Tell el Amarna. Excavated in 1930 by the Egypt Exploration Society in House T. 68 of the North Suburb. Excavation no. 30/300.

COMMENTARY: From the moment of its discovery there has been a dispute about whether this head represents a man or a woman. This has been partly due to the red flesh tint, but it can be shown that at Amarna red was not always confined to portrayals of men, and to this writer the soft features, untouched by age, appear to be decidedly feminine. The style of wig, though again not exclusively a woman's fashion, was one particularly affected by the daughters of Akhenaten (cf. No. 124). The profile seemed to the excavator to resemble that of Ankhesenpaaten as represented on the back panel of a throne of Tutankhamen (Cairo T. 1: Aldred 1968, pl. 10), and certainly the head bears a family likeness to Akhenaten's daughters. The complete statuette may have formed part of a group of members of the royal family kept as a cult image in the house where it was found.

* *Bibliography:* Porter and Moss 1934, p. 200. Add: Aldred 1957b, p. 141, illus.; Vandier 1958, p. 518, note 5; Hayes 1959, p. 289, fig. 177.

No. 106
PRINCESS IN GALA DRESS
Late Period

Collection: University Museum of the University of Pennsylvania, Philadelphia E 14349

A statue of a princess, lacking head and feet, shows her standing with left leg advanced, right arm hanging at her side, and left arm bent upward and outward to touch a neighboring figure, now missing. The princess wears a clinging pleated robe and a broad collar, and the remainder of a sculptured lock of hair falls over her right shoulder.

Material: Limestone.

Color: Traces of black on hair, of red on right arm.

Measurements: Height 31.1 cm. Width 12.4 cm. Depth 10.4 cm. Width of back slab, top 8 cm., bottom 5.7 cm. Width of break at neck 2.7 cm. Depth of break at neck (slant) 4.5 cm., at feet 8.1 cm.

Condition: Head, feet, and parts of right hand and forearm missing; lower right-hand corner of back pillar broken off and replaced.

Provenance: Not known; probably Tell el Amarna. Formerly in the Fouquet Collection.

COMMENTARY: The sculptor has shown great skill in revealing the forms of the body underlying the filmy garment; even the clavicles beneath the collar are evident, as well as the navel, the pubic mound, and the rounded knees. The soft stone of which the statue was made lent freedom to the carving, and fill-ins between the upper and lower left arm and behind the left hand were retained to provide adequate support. While the figure, though clothed, bears some resemblance to the nude princess in Kansas City (No. 53), especially in the firm bracing of the legs, it shows a more traditional approach. The remainder of the sidelock seems to indicate that it was a style worn by somewhat older women, and thus the head of the statue may have resembled that of a girl in Paris (Fig. 50: Louvre E. 14715). It may have represented one of the senior princesses during the later years of Akhenaten's reign or even one of the royal relatives, such as Mutnodjem, the sister of Nefertiti. Of the alternatives, the first seems more likely. The statue was evidently, like No. 90, once accompanied by another figure on an adjacent block. The rough adzing of its left-hand edge, apparently ancient, provided a surface to hold a plaster joining between two pieces. The fact that the left edge of the back pillar is out of plumb conforms to ancient Egyptian practice, since the contiguous block would have been trimmed to compensate for the slope. The fact that this statue was made as a

separate part, probably of a dyad, has enabled the sculptor unrestricted access to the left-hand side, which has been carved and finished with great care. The loss of the left hand, however, makes it difficult to determine the pose of the completed figure. The young girl represented may have raised her hand in praise or have held a sistrum of metal or wood. If this was the case, it is doubtful that the adjacent figure was that of another princess, and it seems much more likely that it was of the King, who perhaps held before him an offering table or some such ritual object. An unfinished quartzite statuette of a princess in private possession shows the same kind of treatment of the upraised arm (Hamburg 1965, p. 20, no. 21).

Bibliography: Chassinat 1922, p. 20; Fouquet 1922b, p. 3, no. 11, and pl. II; Ranke 1950, pp. 67–68, with fig. 42; Vandier 1958, pp. 343–344, 352–353, and pl. CXII, 6; Philadelphia 1960, 11th p., illus.

No. 107
HEAD OF A MAN
Late Period
Collection: Ägyptisches Museum Berlin / DDR 21228
A cast, poured from the back into an open mold, shows the face of a man from base of neck to hairline. His brows are drawn into a slight frown; he has prominent cheekbones and hollow cheeks. The muscular nexus around the lips is emphasized, as is the ball of the chin, and the joining of the lips forms a straight line. The ears are correctly placed, and the lobes are apparently not perforated.
Material: Coarse gray-white plaster.
Color: No trace.
Measurements: Height 23.8 cm. Width 18 cm. Depth 15.4 cm. Height of face 19 cm.
Condition: Left side of nose and point of chin chipped; suggestion of an ancient repair on left cheek.
Provenance: Tell el Amarna. Excavated in 1912–1913 by the Deutsche Orient-Gesellschaft in House P 47,2 in town north of Main Wadi.
COMMENTARY: The cast is evidently a more complete version of the mask described in No. 109, but while it represents the same man, it was probably made in a different mold.

* Bibliography: Porter and Moss 1934, p. 203. Add: Hall 1927, p. 471, fig. 8; Roeder 1941, p. 148 and passim, with figs. 13–14 on p. 161; de Wit 1950, pp. 50–51, no. 56, illus.; Berlin East 1954, pl. 12; Capart 1957, p. 217, fig. 64; Wolf 1957, p. 461, fig. 434; Aldred 1961a, pp. 253–254, and fig. 45; Bille-de Mot 1966, fig. 70.

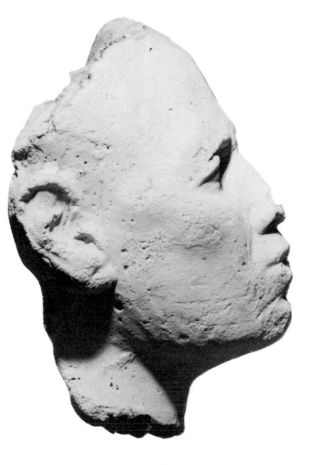

No. 108
PORTRAIT MASK OF A MAN
Late Period
Collection: Ägyptisches Museum, Berlin (West) 21350
This life-size cast shows a man's face modeled in depth from hairline to junction of neck and torso, but excluding the ears. The eyebrows are slightly in relief, and five furrows are indicated in the forehead. The folds of the upper eyelids are marked by six parallel lines.
Material: Brown-white plaster.
Color: Traces of black on brows; areas on upper lip and left eye marked in red.
Measurements: Height 27.5 cm. Width 13.7 cm. Depth 14.3 cm. Height of face 19.4 cm.
Condition: Discolored; minor chips.
Provenance: Tell el Amarna. Excavated by the Deutsche Orient-Gesellschaft in 1912–1913 in House P 47,2 in town north of Main Wadi.
COMMENTARY: This distinctive face, with its strong jawline, rather prominent cheekbones, and muscular neck, has been identified as representing Ay. While in profile it does to some extent resemble Ay as pictured in a relief from his tomb (Fig. 5), it is not possible to be categorical or to go further than to say that the mask must portray an important member of King Akhenaten's entourage. The cast was made in a two-piece mold the join of which can be traced down the center of the lips, although care was taken to eliminate it elsewhere. Such a careful plaster study seems to mark a stage in the preparation of an approved portrait, in which a likeness has been caught and is being carefully worked over, using such devices as the rather mechanical indications of furrows on the brow and wrinkles on the eyelids. The eyes have been rather summarily hollowed, presumably to contain inlays, but a correction for the left eye and an adjustment of the upper lip, both indicated in red paint, show the care that was taken with this plaster model.

* Bibliography: Porter and Moss 1934, p. 203. Add: Fechheimer 1922b, pl. 93; Otto 1939, pl. 97, 4; Roeder 1941, p. 151 and passim, with figs. 23–24 on p. 167; Schäfer and Andrae 1942, pl. 353; Hamann 1944, p. 239, fig. 255; Lange 1951, p. 138, and pls. 28–29; Wolf 1957, p. 461, fig. 432; Smith 1958, p. 206, and pls. 134–135; Vandier 1958, p. 335; Aldred 1961b, p. 78, and pl. 123; Berlin West 1967, p. 72, no. 772, illus.; Lange and Hirmer 1968, pp. 460–461, and pl. 190.

No. 109
MASK OF A MAN
Late Period
Collection: Ägyptisches Museum, Berlin (West) 21356
The mask shows a man with rather prominent cheekbones, hollow cheeks, and sunken eyes. The right eyebrow is ridged, and the inner eyepits are so deeply modeled that both eyes seem to turn inward.
Material: Gray-white plaster.
Color: No trace.
Measurements: Height 17.8 cm. Width 13.8 cm. Depth 12.9 cm.
Condition: Slight damage to tip of nose.
Provenance: Tell el Amarna. Excavated in 1912–1913 by the Deutsche Orient-Gesellschaft in House P 47,2, Room 19, in town north of Main Wadi.
COMMENTARY: The mask was cast in a one-piece mold in two stages, poured from the back. It appears to have been made in the same mold as No. 107, which was found at the same site and obviously represents the same man. These castings have been taken to be death masks, and Borchardt identified the man portrayed as Amenhotep III. This, however, seems unlikely, since the evidence afforded by the mummy of that King and by certain reliefs and statues of his later years indicates that he was grossly obese at the time of his death. The hollow cheeks of this mask are not those of a corpulent man, and there is, moreover, a certain muscular tension about the mouth that does not suggest the complete relaxation of death. An ancient Egyptian death mask surviving in a mold found by Quibell near the pyramid of King Tety of Dynasty VI (Cairo 10/12/24/6: Quibell 1909, pp. 112–113, and pl. LV) shows collapsed features, closed eyelids, and a remoteness far removed from the brooding introspection of these two masks which must have been made from an original modeled after life in clay or wax and then cast in plaster to serve as study pieces.

* *Bibliography:* Porter and Moss 1934, p. 203. Add: Roeder 1941, p. 151 and passim, with fig. 20 on p. 165; Lange 1951, p. 139, and pls. 34–35; Vandier 1958, pp. 320, 335, and pl. CV, 2; Hamburg 1965, p. 19, no. 16, and fig. 11; Berlin West 1967, pp. 69–70, no. 763, illus.; Aldred 1968, pl. 86; Lange and Hirmer 1968, p. 461, and pl. 191.

No. 110
FAMILY GROUP

Late Period

Collection: The Metropolitan Museum of Art, New York 11.150.21 (Rogers Fund, 1911)

A father (center), shown hand in hand with his son, casts a protecting arm around the neck of a naked child, who is probably his grandson.

Material: Limestone.

Color: Red on exposed flesh; black on hair.

Measurements: Height 17 cm. Width 12.5 cm. Height of dressed man 15.2 cm., his head 2.6 cm., his face 1.8 cm. Height of man with shaved pate 15 cm., his head 2.7 cm., his face ca. 2 cm. Height of boy 10.9 cm., his head 2.1 cm.

Condition: Damage to left side and legs of boy.

Provenance: Said to be Gebelein; acquired in Cairo.

COMMENTARY: The later years of Dynasty XVIII saw one of those periodic revivals of interest in the past that occur in the art of ancient Egypt throughout its long history. A statuette in The Brooklyn Museum (No. 96), found in a house at Tell el Amarna, has more than an echo of the Old Kingdom in its rigid stance, and this triad from Gebelein (?) similarly owes much of its pose and grouping to Old Kingdom sources. The feeling, however, is entirely that of the Amarna Period, which makes itself evident in the rather morose expressions of the faces and the elongated forms of the clasped hands. The fashions of dress and coiffures also bespeak Amarna. The son's costume, from his curled wig to his tunic with pleated sleeves and his kilt with flounced front panel, can be dated fairly closely to the Amarna Period (cf. Nos. 62, 137). The kilt of the father, although more restrained, as befits an older man, can also be duplicated in sculptures from Tell el Amarna. The rectangular slab against which these figures stand is uninscribed; so it is impossible to determine the names of the persons represented. This piece, however, is important as an outstanding example of a family group in a period in which private sculpture is otherwise almost nonexistent. It may well have been carved at Tell el Amarna and carried off to Gebelein when the populace of the former city was dispersed on its abandonment.

* *Bibliography:* Porter and Moss 1937, p. 164. Add: New York 1937, no. 15, illus.; New York 1946, no. 27, illus.; Scott 1948, p. 97, illus.; de Wit 1950, pp. 36–37, no. 32, illus.; Wolf 1957, p. 466, fig. 441; Vandier 1958, pp. 445, 481–482, 493, 497–498, 519, and pl. cxlvi, 5; Hayes 1959, p. 312, fig. 194; Aldred 1961b, p. 83, and pl. 141; Hornemann 1966, pl. 1403.

No. 111
MASK OF A WOMAN
Late Period

Collection: Ägyptisches Museum Berlin / DDR 21341

The cast shows a woman's head from the hairline to the base of the neck, including the left ear with a stud in the lobe. The eyebrows appear as ridges; the eyes are almond-shaped, with the upper lids indicated by faint incised lines; the medial line of the full lips shows the double curve, and the chin has a pronounced bulge.

Material: Coarse grayish-white plaster.

Color: No trace.

Measurements: Height 21 cm.

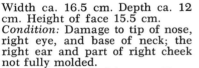

Width ca. 16.5 cm. Depth ca. 12 cm. Height of face 15.5 cm.

Condition: Damage to tip of nose, right eye, and base of neck; the right ear and part of right cheek not fully molded.

Provenance: Tell el Amarna. Excavated in 1912–1913 by the Deutsche Orient-Gesellschaft in House P 47,1–3 in town north of Main Wadi.

COMMENTARY: The woman portrayed here is apparently the same as the one of No. 112 (see Commentary under that number).

* *Bibliography:* Hall 1927, p. 470, fig. 3; Roeder 1941, p. 150; de Wit 1950, pp. 54–55, no. 63, illus.

No. 112
A WOMAN OF TELL EL AMARNA
Late Period

Collection: Ägyptisches Museum, Berlin (West) 21239

What appears as little more than a mask shows a woman's head from a fringe of stylized curls around the brow to the base of the neck. A boss at each ear seems to indicate a plug or earring.

Material: Gray-white plaster.

Color: No trace.

Measurements: Height 22.8 cm. Width 17.4 cm. Depth 14.6 cm. Height of face 13.8 cm.

Condition: Slight damage at right side of chin; neck broken through.

Provenance: Tell el Amarna. Excavated by the Deutsche Orient-Gesellschaft in 1912–1913, in House P 47,2, in town north of Main Wadi.

COMMENTARY: This head, virtually a mask, was poured into a one-piece mold from the back and tooled while the plaster was still wet. The details of each eye are shallowly incised on the protuberance of the underlying eyeball, a line defining the edge of the upper lid. Such treatment is too stylized to be anything other than the conventionalization of an established art form; it resembles the carving of the eyes of some of the statues of Tutankhamen (Cairo CG 42091: Legrain 1906, pl. LVIII). The mouth is modeled with a distinct double curve on the medial line of the lips. The neck, receding to the rear, makes the face appear to be thrust forward—a pose made familiar by the painted bust of Nefertiti (Fig. 1). The person represented in the present mask is again portrayed in another plaster cast which was found at the same site and is now in East Berlin (No. 111). The earplugs seem to indicate that both casts represent a woman and were made from a master copy, probably a wooden statue showing the owner in a stylized wig of the short Nubian type (No. 133). The sitter was probably one of the women of the royal house in the last years of Akhenaten's reign.

* *Bibliography:* Porter and Moss 1934, p. 203. Add: Fechheimer 1922b, pl. 92; Roeder 1941, p. 150 and passim, with fig. 7 on p. 149; de Wit 1950, p. 54, no. 62, and p. 55, illus.; Lange 1951, p. 139, and pl. 32; Vandier 1958, p. 335; Hamburg 1965, p. 19, no. 17, and figs. 8–9; Berlin West 1967, p. 70, no. 764, illus.

No. 113
SWIMMING GIRL
Middle Period (?)
Collection: University College London 006
This torso is evidently part of an object in which the girl in swimming pose originally held a tray or box between her outstretched hands; a hole between her shoulders was made to receive a separately made head and neck, perhaps of a different material. Objects of similar type have long been called "ointment spoons," "cosmetic spoons," or "toilet spoons," but their use remains uncertain, although the fine materials of which they were nearly always made and the care that was taken in their fashioning show that they were of some importance to the Egyptians who took them to their graves (Wallert 1967, pp. 50–53).
Material: Alabaster.
Color: No trace.
Measurements: Height 8.5 cm. Width 3.1 cm. Depth 2.6 cm. Diameter of hole 0.9 cm.
Condition: Head, arms from shoulders, and legs from knees missing.
Provenance: Tell el Amarna. Excavated in 1891–1892 by H. Carter and W. M. F. Petrie; precise findspot not given.
COMMENTARY: This fragment comes from a type of object which the luxurious taste of the age encouraged craftsmen to produce. The nubile girl it represents probably held before her an animal, a bird, a fish, or an aquatic plant, which was fashioned to serve as a container or scoop. A more complete fragment of about the same period in The Metropolitan Museum of Art (26.2.47: Hayes 1959, p. 268, fig. 162) shows the coiffure of the separately made head inlaid with black slate. While other similar examples exist, relatively few of them can be given an exact provenance and consequently an exact date. The present specimen, however, can be safely assigned to the Amarna Period, and indeed reflects the "Amarna Style" in the sensitive carving of the rounded forms of the youthful body. An interesting observation of the sculptor are the two dimples on the back above the gluteus muscles.

Bibliography: Pendlebury 1951, p. 227, and pl. CVI, 2, 6; Wallert 1967, p. 121, no. L65 UC 900; Samson 1972, pp. 30–31, with pls. 12a–12b.

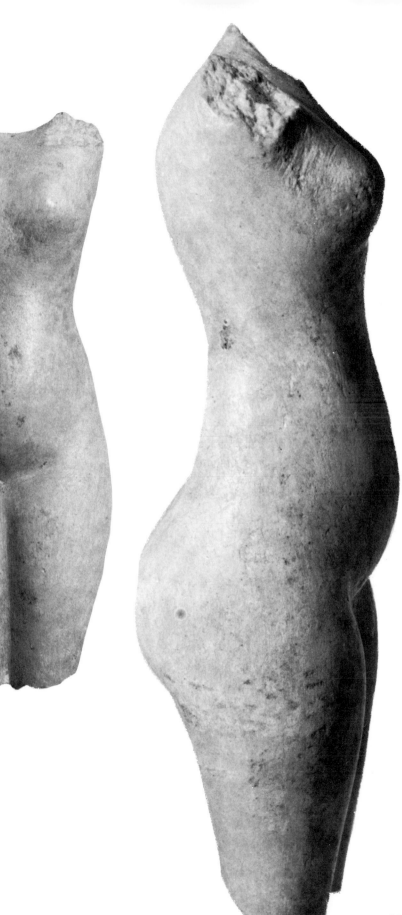

No. 114

TWO KINGS ENTHRONED

Late Period, Year 15 or later
Collection: Ägyptisches Museum
Berlin / DDR 17813

A stela in sunk relief depicts two kings seated side by side on cushioned thrones, their sandaled feet resting on hassocks. Before them is a table piled with typical offerings and a stand with wine jars. The king to the left wears a plain kilt and the Blue Crown with uraeus and ribbed streamers; his left arm embraces his companion; his right arm hangs straight at his side. The king at the right wears the Double Crown, also with uraeus and ribbed streamers. He turns his head toward his companion and caresses his chin with his right hand. Above the pair, the disk of the Aten sends down its life-giving rays.

Material: Limestone.

Color: No trace.

Measurements: Height 21.7 cm. Width 16.5 cm. Thickness 4 cm.

Condition: Faces of both kings mutilated; large chip broken from upper edge and restored in plaster.

Provenance: Not known; acquired in Egypt.

COMMENTARY: An incised inscription along the base of this stela indicates that it was "drilled by Pasi, captain of the state barge [?] Khaemmaat," and suggests that the piece was complete when dedicated, and that then the seven cartouches at the top were inscribed in ink to provide the names of the pictured rulers. The two cartouches at the left must have identified the king in the Blue Crown; the pair in the middle doubtless named the Aten; the three at the right probably gave the names of the king in the Double Crown and of his royal spouse. It is deplorable that these inscriptions have disappeared, for if preserved they would doubtless have told much concerning the final years of the rule of Akhenaten. As it is, the only inference possible seems to be that the stela represents a pair of co-regents seated side by side, the one on the left being Smenkhkare, and the other, Akhenaten, distinguishable by his characteristic profile. The intimacy suggested by the latter's caressing gesture led Newberry (Newberry 1928, p. 7) to postulate a homoerotic relationship between the rulers; but his suggestion has been rejected by scholars who have found such an idea upsetting and have proposed instead that the caress implies merely family approval or dynastic recognition. Whatever its implications, it seems incontrovertible that the scene provides strong evidence for a co-regency between Akhenaten and a junior partner, for both are shown in the guise of living pharaohs with distinctive crowns. It is worthy of note that the sculptor has attempted to differentiate the phys-

ical characteristics of the two rulers; while there is a family resemblance between them, Akhenaten has a thicker waist and a more pronounced paunch. For a sculptor's model showing the heads of these two kings, see Fig. 49.

* *Bibliography:* Porter and Moss 1934, p. 232. Add: Sandman 1938, p. 168, no. CXCV; Lange 1951, p. 140, and pl. 42; Roeder 1958, pp. 46, and 48, no. C III 4; Bille-de Mot 1966, fig. 81; Aldred 1968, p. 182, pl. 81; Giles 1970, pl. VIII, lower left.

No. 115
SCULPTOR'S MODEL
Late Period
Collection: Ägyptisches Museum Berlin / DDR 21683
A king wearing the *afnet* head-dress with uraeus is shown looking to the left. His lips seem to be slightly parted. Two lines cross the neck under the chin, and his earlobe is pierced with a large oval hole.
Material: Limestone.
Color: No trace.
Measurements: Height 21.4 cm. Width 21 cm. Thickness 4.1 cm.
Condition: Head of uraeus unfinished; slight damage to corner of mouth and rim of ear.
Provenance: Tell el Amarna. Excavated by the Deutsche Orient-Gesellschaft in 1914 in House O 47,15, in town north of Main Wadi.
COMMENTARY: This seems to be a model for an official portrait of the King made for the use of craftsmen engaged on royal commissions. The style is in the more restrained manner of the later years of the reign (cf. No. 121; also Cairo JE 59294: Cairo 1949, fig. 103), and that the King represented is Akhenaten seems clear from the shape of the chin and lips. It is to be noted that the upper rim of the eye is not prolonged, the contour of the jaw is not marked, and the vertical furrow in the cheek and the line from nostril to corner of the mouth are absent; there is also no indication of tendons in the neck. All these omissions point to a late date, which is further suggested by the deep oval hole in the earlobe.

* Bibliography: Porter and Moss 1934, p. 202. Add: Fechheimer 1922b, pl. 152; Lange 1951, p. 136, and pl. 13; Bille-de Mot 1966, fig. 80.

No. 116
A BOUQUET FOR THE ATEN
Late Period, Years 13–15
Collection: The Brooklyn Museum 60.197.6
Little more than a torso of the King and a vague outline of his lower face is preserved in this sunk relief picturing Akhenaten with raised arms offering a formal bouquet to the Aten, whose rays bring life to the royal donor and bless the gift laid upon an altar which was doubtless represented on an adjacent block. The King wears a crown, now missing, with a wide streamer hanging at the back. Behind him is a princess who holds a sistrum in her hand; only her head with its elaborately plaited sidelock and part of her hand with the sistrum are preserved. Above her is a large rectangular area where her name and titles have been deliberately erased. Vertical elements at each end of the block probably indicate that the offering took place within a chapel enclosed by doors.
Material: Limestone.
Color: Prevalent light red color is modern; traces of an original red pigment on King's chin and forehead and in cut edges along his arms and perhaps also the black of the wig may be ancient.
Measurements: Height 23.1 cm. Width 53.2 cm. Thickness 3.9 cm. Height of daughter's head 6.7 cm. Height of daughter's face ca. 5.5 cm.
Condition: Upper edge chipped at corners and in middle; deliberate damage to face of King, to cartouches on his body, and to inscription above princess. Back cut in modern times.
Provenance: Tell el Amarna; found at Hermopolis.
COMMENTARY: The King on this relief is undoubtedly Akhenaten, recognizable by his prominent jaw. A curved line descending from his lumbar region indicates that he was clad in a kilt, probably once painted white. His headdress was apparently the Blue Crown. The cartouches of the Aten outlined on his arms and body were probably inscribed in ink and were excised in ancient times. To judge from her stubborn little chin, the daughter officiating with the King was probably Merytaten, and the relief may have been made at a time when she was playing a prominent part in Amarna politics, after her mother's disappearance but before her own marriage to Smenkhkare. For the completion of this scene, see No. 122.

Bibliography: Cooney 1965, pp. 9–11, no. 4, illus.; Roeder 1969, p. 404, no. P.C. 24, and pl. 173; James 1973, no. 308.

No. 117
KING AKHENATEN

Late Period

Collection: Mr. and Mrs. Norbert Schimmel, New York

While only part of the head and shoulders of this royal personage has been preserved, enough of his distinctive features remains to identify him almost certainly as Akhenaten.

Material: Limestone.

Color: Pale red on flesh and streamers from crown; blue on lower part of crown.

Measurements: Height 21.9 cm. Width 35.3 cm. Thickness 2.9 cm.

Condition: About one-third of slab missing from left; large break at lower edge.

Provenance: Tell el Amarna; found at Hermopolis.

COMMENTARY: This slab has been inexplicably cut down in recent times. When it was first discovered by the Germans in their excavations at Hermopolis in 1938, the right arm of the King, extended to show the palm, was still preserved. This gesture, one of invocation or greeting, is frequent in the art of Amarna. The King, probably wearing the Blue Crown with fluttering ribbons at the back, has the sensuous lips, the prominent chin thrust forward, the thin neck, and the conspicuous collarbones characteristic of Akhenaten. The rather soft outlines and oval perforation in the earlobe (cf. No. 121) belong to the later phase of his reign.

Bibliography: Roeder 1938, p. 262, fig. 3; Roeder 1940, p. 62, and pl. 7, c; Hoffmann 1964a, no. 106, illus.; Cooney 1965, pp. 14–15, no. 7, illus.; Hamburg 1965, pp. 22–23, no. 29, and fig. 22; Bille-de Mot 1966, fig. 38; Jerusalem 1967, no. 6, illus.; America-Israel Cultural Foundation 1968, pp. 77–78, no. 286, illus.; Roeder 1969, p. 383, no. 255/VI, and pl. 5.

No. 118
A DUCK FOR SACRIFICE
Late Period

Collection: Mr. and Mrs. Norbert Schimmel, New York

The King, wearing the *afnet* head-dress, grasps a pintail duck by neck and pinions and offers it to the Aten. In the lower right-hand corner are the leg and part of the body of a second bird.

Material: Limestone.

Color: Blue on crown; red in other sunk areas.

Measurements: Height 25.1 cm. Width 54.7 cm. Thickness 3.7 cm. Height of face 14 cm. Height of cartouches 1.9–2.2 cm.

Condition: King's eye and upper face pitted; ear and left wrist damaged; upper right corner broken off and reattached.

Provenance: Tell el Amarna; found at Hermopolis.

COMMENTARY: This scene is interpreted by Cooney as one-half of an equipoise, in which the Queen, represented on a smaller scale, faced her husband and imitated his action in sacrificing a duck on the altar of the Aten. He regards the leg and body of the bird in the lower right-hand corner as belonging to a live duck held in the Queen's hand. Such equipoise of a king and queen in offering scenes is, however, unknown in the iconography of Amarna, and it seems to this writer that the Queen was behind her husband and that the fragmentary bird at the lower right is a duck already sacrificed and laid on the offering table. In any case, the position of the duck's leg and body does not suggest a composition in which the Queen

repeats the action of the King. The carving of the King's left hand well conveys his tense grip on the bird's pinions. The position of thumb and fingers of the right hand seems to suggest a twisting motion, and the melancholy expression of the King's face adds to an impression of grim tension in the ritual of wringing the bird's neck. The likeness is certainly that of Akhenaten (cf. No. 121), and the cartouches of the Aten on the bezels of his armlets seem to show the late form of the Aten's name.

Bibliography: Hoffmann 1964a, no. 105, illus.; Hoffmann 1964b, p. 270, fig. 1; Cooney 1965, pp. 17–18, no. 9, illus.; Hamburg 1965, p. 22, no. 28, and fig. 17; Bille-de Mot 1966, fig. 20; Jerusalem 1967, no. 1, illus.; Roeder 1969, p. 404, no. P.C. 13, and pl. 171.

No. 119
PRACTICE PIECE
Late Period
Collection: The Metropolitan Museum of Art, New York 21.9.13 (Gift of Edward S. Harkness, 1921) On a flake of stone a student-sculptor has roughed out the profile of a king. The pupil's skill is evident in the careful execution of the features in raised relief.
Material: Limestone.
Color: No trace.
Measurements: Height 17.8 cm. Width 14 cm. Thickness 3.1 cm.
Condition: Gashes and scratches on background; blemish on left-hand side filled in with modern plaster.
Provenance: Tell el Amarna. Excavated by W. M. F. Petrie in 1891–1892; findspot probably sculptor's workshop north of the Palace. Formerly in the Amherst Collection.

COMMENTARY: The portrait of a king has been cast aside unfinished. Although the features seem clearly to resemble Akhenaten, the rendering is out of proportion. The ear has been incorrectly placed and leaves no space for the parietal bulge of the crown. The eye has been outlined but not hollowed out. The ear too is not quite finished, but the oval hole in the lobe, as well as the rather softened features, permit a date in the Late Period of Amarna art. The model followed by the pupil was evidently similar to No. 121. On the reverse of this trial piece is a faintly sketched hieroglyphic sign representing an owl.

Bibliography: Petrie 1894, p. 30, and pl. I, 8–9; Amherst 1921, p. 76, no. 850; Winlock 1922, p. 171, fig. 1; Lansing 1947, p. 188, illus.; Hayes 1959, p. 282, fig. 171, right.

No. 120
PAINTED RELIEF OF A KING AND QUEEN
Late Period, Year 15 or later
Collection: Ägyptisches Museum, Berlin (West) 15000
Rectangular slab carved in sunk relief and painted, with confronted standing figures of a royal pair. The king, with left leg crossed behind the right, leans on a staff, the top of which is tucked under his right armpit. He wears a short curled wig with ribbed streamers at the back and a uraeus at the forehead, a floral collar, a short pleated kilt belted with a long, ribbed double sash, and an apron fringed with uraei; he is shod with sandals. The queen, barefooted, has her hair hidden under a skullcap provided with double uraei and streamers and wears a long robe open at the front and tied with a sash under the breasts, a shawl, and a floral collar. With one hand she offers a bouquet of two mandrakes and a lotus bud for her husband to smell and in the other she holds two lotus blossoms and a bud.
Material: Limestone.
Color: Ground yellow ocher; wig and cap blue; streamers, apron, and sashes red; garments white; flesh light red; sandals white; collars white and blue with spots of red; staff blue; flowers gray-green, white, and pink.
Measurements: Height 24.7 cm. Width 20.2 cm. Thickness 6.7 cm.

Height of king to crown of wig 19.3 cm. Height of queen to crown of wig 18.5 cm. Height of king's face 1.9 cm. Height of queen's face 1.9 cm.
Condition: Back has been worked smooth; a channel with shallow slots at intervals has been cut along the left-hand edge.
Provenance: Said to have come from a house at Tell el Amarna (R 45) in 1899.
COMMENTARY: That the slab is complete and not part of a larger composition may be indicated by the fact that the back of the queen's gown trails over the rounded lower edge of the relief. The piece may have been made as a decorative panel to be set into the mud-brick wall of a house or palace. Ever since Newberry first made the suggestion, it has been generally accepted that the couple here represented are probably King Smenkhkare and his first consort, Queen Merytaten. The face of the king, with its rounded contours and rather thin lips, lacks the distortion of Akhenaten's physiognomy, and though there is some emphasis upon the chin, the rear contour of the neck is concave and the head not very conspicuously thrust forward. The face is, in fact, an unlined youthful one with none of the marks of aging apparent in portraits of Akhenaten. On the other hand, the evident paunch of the figure, if nothing else, makes an identification with

the boyish Tutankhamen seem unlikely. If the king is Smenkhkare, as he may well be, the queen represented must almost certainly be Merytaten, whose features differ from those of Nefertiti even when the latter wears the skullcap (Davies 1903, pl. XXX, and Berlin East 21263: Aldred 1961b, p. 79, and pls. 124–125). Indeed, the short jutting chin of this queen makes her identification as Merytaten virtually certain. The nonchalant pose of the king with his garments aflutter in the Amarna wind has been justly praised. Although the sculptor was less successful in his portrayal of the queen, her figure with upraised arms forms an effective counterpoise to that of her husband.

Bibliography: Porter and Moss 1934, pp. 233–234 (the ref. given therein as Borchardt, *op. cit.*, should be corrected to Borchardt 1923, p. 26, fig. 22). Add: Spiegelberg 1903, p. 68, fig. 63; Delbrück 1912, pp. xxvi–xxvii, and pl. 6; Borchardt 1917, p. 9, figs. 5–6; Ghalioungui 1947, p. 35, fig. 6; Lange 1951, p. 140, and pl. 43; Basel 1953, p. 45, no. 98, and fig. 15; Wolf 1957, pp. 520–521, and p. 519, fig. 495; Roeder 1958, p. 56, no. DIV 2, and pl. VI, b; Aldred 1961b, p. 80, and pl. 130; Schäfer 1963, pl. 28; Berlin West 1967, p. 72, no. 773, illus.; Aldred 1968, p. 9; Wenig 1969, pp. 50–51, and pl. 67.

189

No. 121
SCULPTOR'S MODEL WITH ROYAL HEADS

Late Period, about Year 12

Collection: The Brooklyn Museum 16.48

The model shows at the left a profile head of a king confronting that of a queen, who looks inward from the right. The king wears the *afnet* headdress with a large uraeus; his earlobe is indented with an oval hole; two creases are shown in his neck just below the chin. The queen, pictured on a smaller scale, wears a cap confined by a diadem with a coiled uraeus; her earlobe also shows an oval perforation; her neck has a single crease. While only the head and neck of the king are represented, the queen's shoulders, with prominent clavicles, are depicted in frontal view.

Material: Limestone.

Color: Traces of red paint on faces and headdresses.

Measurements: Height 15.7 cm. Width 22.1 cm. Thickness 4.2 cm. Height of king's face 6.5 cm. Height of queen's face 4 cm.

Condition: Left-hand portion broken away and missing; prominent scratches (tooling), especially between the heads. The back of the relief has been worked with an adze to a rough finish resembling that of our No. 12. A hole piercing the panel near the top was probably made to hold a cord for convenient storage; it is too small to take a wooden peg or anything other than a slender metal spike.

Provenance: Tell el Amarna.

COMMENTARY: The deep hanging jaw of the king seems to identify him as Akhenaten. The headdress worn by the queen appears on a statue (Berlin East 21263: Aldred 1961b, p. 79, and pls. 124–125) representing Nefertiti. Since both Nefertiti and Merytaten sometimes wear this style of cap (see No. 120; also Davies 1903, pls. XXII, XXX; Davies 1905a, pl. XLI), no conclusions about the identity of the queen can be based solely on that detail. The profile of the queen, however, bears a strong resemblance to that of the famous painted bust (Fig. 1), and thus this writer has no hesitation in identifying the queen of this model as Nefertiti. The authenticity of the Brooklyn relief has been doubted by some who feel that it does not possess the true "Amarna vibrancy." Since Charles Edwin Wilbour purchased the model at Tell el Amarna on December 21, 1881, six years before the discovery of the cuneiform archives had brought notoriety to that site, there is no doubt of the antiquity of the piece. Any lingering skepticism should be dispelled by comparison with works of nineteenth-century forgers, whose conventions are now readily recognized. This relief shows the hand of a master sculptor who produced a pair of

official portraits for the use of lesser artists commissioned for royal work. That master had tamed the excesses of the earlier period and avoided its mannerisms. While such features as the ears have been naturalistically rendered, down to the holes in the lobes, the lines of the faces are less pronounced and the contours softer. In this writer's opinion the relief may be the work of the artist who was responsible for the style of the later period of Akhenaten's reign and whose dominance is to be seen in many of the products of the workshop of Tuthmose at Tell el Amarna.

*Bibliography: Capart 1927, pp. 35–36, and pl. 49; Taggart 1931, p. 106, illus.; Taggart 1933, p. 61, illus.; Taggart 1935, pp. 12–13, illus.; Capart 1936b, pp. 95–96, and pl. opposite p. 104; Capart 1942, pl. 542; Brooklyn 1952, no. 37, illus.; Aldred 1961b, pp. 80–81, and pl. 131; Brooklyn 1967, pp. 70–71, illus.; Brooklyn 1970, pp. 52–53, illus.

No. 122
OFFERING SCENE

Late Period

Collection: The Brooklyn Museum
60.197.1
Slab carved in sunk relief showing
middle portions of the figures of
the King and a princess standing
before two incense burners surmounted by a bouquet of five lotus
flowers and six buds.
Material: Limestone.
Color: Traces of ocher paint over
entire surface are doubtless recent.
Measurements: Height 23.7 cm.
Width 52.2 cm. Thickness 3.1 cm.
Condition: Water-worn channel
across abdomens of figures; blemishes on altar and behind figure of
King. Left side and back cut in
modern times.
Provenance: Tell el Amarna; found
at Hermopolis.
COMMENTARY: Both figures stand
with the left foot advanced. The
King wears a pleated kilt, held in
place below the navel by a sash,
the long ends of which float free.
The woman behind him is dressed
in a long pleated gown and a shawl
knotted under her breast. Her left
hand, with sensitively articulated
fingers (No. 120), hangs at her
side; her right arm is raised, but
only the bent elbow is visible. This
woman is very likely not the Queen
but one of the princesses, for with
one slight exception (Davies 1906,
pl. XV) all the offering scenes
known to the author in which
Nefertiti officiates show her on a
par with her husband and imitat-
ing his action. Since in this relief
neither of the King's arms hangs
free at his side, it is evident that
his pose is not duplicated by that
of the woman following him and
that she is therefore probably not
the Queen but one of the senior
princesses. She may have held a
sistrum in her raised right hand
(No. 116).

Bibliography: Cooney 1965, p. 8,
no. 3, illus.; Roeder 1969, p. 404,
no. P.C. 25, and pl. 173.

No. 123
A LOVING FAMILY

Late Period (?)

Collection: Fitzwilliam Museum,
Cambridge 4606.1943
An unfinished plaque, cut in silhouette and partly carved, shows
the King and Queen kissing. Each
embraces a daughter with one arm.
Material: Carnelian.
Color: Rich, deep red.
Measurements: Height 5.7 cm.
Width 3.8 cm. Thickness 0.6 cm.
Condition: Intact but unfinished.
Provenance: Not known; formerly
in the Gayer–Anderson Collection.
COMMENTARY: Like the five
plaques carved in similar hard
stones for the bracelets of Amenhotep III in The Metropolitan Museum of Art (26.7.1339 ff.: Hayes
1959, pp. 242–243, illus.), the present plaque was probably destined
to be set in gold. Although the outlines have been only roughly cut
and the internal relief carving has
mostly been left unfinished, the
design can be reconstructed with
reasonable certainty. Akhenaten,
wearing the Blue Crown with flying
streamers and a kilt with apron,
stands at the right, facing left.
With one arm he encircles the
shoulders of Nefertiti; with the
other he embraces a daughter who
stands behind (i.e., beside) him.
Confronting him and raising her
face to kiss him is Nefertiti, who
encircles another princess with
one arm. Her short Nubian wig, as
well as the King's crown and the
hair of one of the princesses, has
been hollowed to receive an inlay,
perhaps of colored glass. Other
scenes of the royal pair kissing one
another occur in some of the later
tombs at Tell el Amarna (Davies
1905b, pl. XXXII A, and Davies
1906, pl. XXII). For representations of Akhenaten and Nefertiti
kissing their children, see No. 92.

Bibliography: None.

No. 124
AN OFFERING OF OINTMENT
Late Period

Collection: Museum of Fine Arts, Boston 1971.294

A fragment in sunk relief portrays a princess wearing a short wig and offering a garlanded ointment jar in her upraised hands. Although little remains of the larger figure that precedes her, it doubtless once represented the King.

Material: Limestone.

Color: Traces of red and blue pigment probably modern.

Measurements: Height 23.3 cm. Width 27.1 cm. Thickness 3.7 cm. Height of head 11 cm.

Condition: About half of slab missing from the left; face of princess damaged.

Provenance: Tell el Amarna; found at Hermopolis.

COMMENTARY: Since the royal daughters usually only shake sistra during the family worship of the Aten, it is clear that this princess, with her pot of unguent held high, is playing a principal role in the ritual. The larger figure preceding her is certainly that of the King, who cannot be other than Akhenaten, and the absence of a uraeus on the princess's brow and her prominent chin make it evident that she is Merytaten and suggest a date subsequent to the disappearance of Nefertiti from the Amarna scene. A feature of this relief is the ancient alteration made to the princess's coiffure. Such changes in the wigs and headgear of royal women is a peculiarity of Amarna art, the reason for which can be only conjectural (cf. No. 19; also Cooney 1965, nos. 17, 18b.)

Bibliography: None.

No. 125
A ROYAL FACE
Late Period

Collection: The Brooklyn Museum 60.197.2

Only the lower part of the face and part of the shoulder and right arm with hand grasping stalks of grain are here shown in sunk relief, but the complete portrait must have been nearly life size.

Material: Limestone.

Color: Traces of blue-green paint on grain; pink flesh tones and blue patches on wig apparently modern.

Measurements: Height 23.4 cm. Width 52.9 cm. Thickness 3.9 cm.

Condition: Damage and blemishes before the face and in region of hand; both lower corners broken through, the right-hand one missing. Back cut in modern times.

Provenance: Tell el Amarna; found at Hermopolis.

COMMENTARY: This incomplete portrait has been identified by Cooney (see bibliography) as that of a man and by Roeder (see bibliography) definitely as Akhenaten. To this writer, however, the soft features and short, firm chin suggest a woman, and the wig, evidently of the short Nubian type, confirms this view, for coiffures of this fashion were virtually a monopoly of royal ladies at Tell el Amarna. The life-size scale of the carving and its high quality reflect the importance of the person represented, who possibly was Nefertiti but more likely Merytaten (No. 120). The cutting of the relief is redolent of the traditional style of later Amarna art and is consonant with a date when Merytaten played an important part in the politics of the times. The scene represented is unique for Amarna. Cooney has drawn attention to its possible connection with the harvest rites for the god Min (Cooney 1965, pp. 10–13). If his parallel is valid, the relief may have pictured part of the coronation ceremony of King Smenkhkare and Merytaten.

Bibliography: Cooney 1965, p. 13, no. 6, illus.; Duke 1965, no. 12, illus.; Roeder 1969, p. 404, no. P.C. 26, and pl. 173.

No. 126
FISHING IN THE MARSHES
Late Period

Collection: The Brooklyn Museum 60.197.9

A traditional scene, here carved in raised relief, is dominated at the left by the upper part of a large figure of a woman (?) facing right, who wears a Nubian wig and holds in her two hands the shaft of a fishing spear (?). To the right, against a background of papyrus stalks, are the rudder posts and steering oars of a state barge, the tillers of which are held by two steersmen who face forward.

Material: Limestone.

Color: Traces of pinkish-red pigment on faces and elsewhere and of gray-blue on woman's wig, all probably modern.

Measurements: Height 23.9 cm. Width 53.8 cm. Thickness 3.7 cm.

Condition: Right-hand corner broken and reassembled from fragments; other corners extensively damaged. Back cut in modern times.

Provenance: Tell el Amarna; found at Hermopolis.

COMMENTARY: The low relief in which this block is carved may indicate that it was an inner detail of a larger scene in sunk relief depicting activities upon a lake (Nims 1968, p. 546). The position of the hands of the main figure suggests that the person represented was holding the shaft of a fishing spear, not pulling on a rope. In view of its size, the figure must depict a member of the royal house, doubtless, as Cooney suggests, a senior princess. If this is so, she is perhaps handing the spear to a male companion. Nearly contemporary scenes show Ankhesenamen attending her husband Tutankhamen as he shoots at fish or fowl (British Museum 1972, nos. 21, 25). Thanks to the epicene nature of Amarna dress and portraiture, the large figure of this scene could possibly be that of a man, as is believed by Roeder, who identifies the person as Smenkhkare. The present writer, however, leans toward Cooney's interpretation, for the features of the figure do not conform to those of the few known portraits of Smenkhkare, and most probably are those of a princess. Since the face does not resemble that of Merytaten, it seems likely that it portrays Ankhesenpaaten. The complete scene would have included a man, perhaps the King, back of the princess or standing in a skiff. That the vessel steered by two coxswains to the right of the relief is a state barge is indicated by the panther skin attached to the rudder post (see Schott 1955).

Bibliography: Brooklyn Institute 1961, p. 4, illus.; Cooney 1965, pp. 87–88, no. 52, illus.; Roeder 1969, p. 405, no. P.C. 31, and pl. 175.

No. 128
HEAD OF A YOUNG GIRL
Late Period (?)
Collection: E. Kofler, Lucerne
The girl, with uptilted face, raises her arms toward a now vanished object. Her slightly elongated skull is bare, and her only adornment is a very large round earring.
Material: Limestone.
Color: Traces.
Measurements: Height 23 cm. Width 53 cm. Thickness 3.5 cm.
Condition: Sawed vertically in two and rejoined.
Provenance: Tell el Amarna; found at Hermopolis.
COMMENTARY: When this relief was unearthed at Hermopolis in 1939, it was a complete block; subsequently it was cut down in depth and bisected, but the two halves are happily now reunited. Günther Roeder identified the subject as a Nubian raising his hands in adoration, but H. W. Müller has seen in the representation a princess with the delicate face of a young girl, and with him the present writer is in agreement. The features show none of the grim lines given to Nubians in the Amarna Period (No. 37), and the shocks or tufts of hair characteristic of peoples from the southlands are entirely lacking. Moreover, the obtuse angle of the lifted face and the height of separation of the forearms do not suggest the pose of an offering bearer or that of a suppliant adoring the King. In this writer's opinion, the relief represents one of the daughters of Nefertiti reaching to seize a trinket that her father dangles before her (Fig. 2). She is shown in right profile with shaved head, her side-lock presumably falling down at the left. The virtually complete slab probably came from a scene in which the royal couple, seated on faldstools in a garden pavilion, were represented as playing with their children (cf. No. 16).

* Bibliography: Müller 1964, pp. 74–75, no. A 107, illus.; Roeder 1969, p. 387, no. 459/VII, and pl. 74.

No. 127
PRINCESS WITH SISTRUM
Late Period
Collection: Detroit Institute of Arts 66.8
The figures of a princess and a person in a pleated gown are partially preserved on this fragment of sunk relief. The princess, at the right, wears a wig and a large earring and carries a sistrum. She follows a larger figure, shown from shoulder to waist, whose robe is knotted below the right breast.
Material: Limestone.
Color: Flesh tones and handle of sistrum pale red; wig blue.
Measurements: Height 23.4 cm. Width 27 cm. Thickness 3.5 cm.
Height of princess's face 8.4 cm.
Condition: About half of original block missing; lower left-hand corner lacking. Back cut in modern times.
Provenance: Tell el Amarna; found at Hermopolis.
COMMENTARY: The pleated garment of the figure at the left suggests that the wearer was Nefertiti and that the person following her must have been one of her daughters. There is, however, a possibility that the larger figure was Akhenaten, who is sometimes pictured in a pleated robe, for instance in the tomb of Ramose at Thebes (Fig. 17). In support of this identification, it may be indicated that the princess, with her pointed chin, resembles Merytaten, who in her later years quite often appears attending her father in offering scenes at which her mother was not present. Whoever the figure with the sistrum represents, it cannot be Nefertiti, as Roeder supposes, for the Queen always repeats the gesture of her husband in offering scenes and never is shown rattling a sistrum.

Bibliography: Cooney 1965, pp. 31–32, no. 18, illus.; Detroit 1967, p. 15, illus.; Detroit 1969, p. 16; Roeder 1969, p. 406, no. P.C. 69, and pl. 183; Peck 1970, pp. 269–270, with fig. 4.

No. 129
A PUZZLING SCENE
Late Period
Collection: Mr. and Mrs. Norbert Schimmel, New York

The slab, carved in sunk relief, evidently bears parts of two separate, if adjacent, scenes, divided by an imaginary line immediately behind the hanging arm of the fragmentary large figure to the left. At the right a bowing woman on a smaller scale presents two trays heaped with food; in the background behind her is a composite column hung with a garland.

Material: Limestone.

Color: Red pigment on face, garments, and offerings; blue on wig.

Measurements: Height 23.1 cm. Width 54.3 cm. Thickness 3.7 cm. Height of head 10.2 cm. Height of face 8.1 cm.

Condition: Slab broken into six pieces and reassembled; deep flaw in the garment of the left-hand figure; face of woman at right partly restored in plaster.

Provenance: Tell el Amarna; found at Hermopolis.

COMMENTARY: That the figure at the left must be a woman is shown by the folds of her gown, which run above the hipline; she is probably one of the senior princesses standing behind the King. The fact that she is back to back with the woman at the right indicates that we have here parts of two separate scenes. The latter woman wears a short Nubian wig with sidelock and a large ear stud, and an inscription behind her identifies her as "the nurse of the King's daughter Ankhesenpaaten, Tia." She was presumably one of the women of rank who had the duty of bringing up and educating the royal princesses. Since she is obviously bowing to present her offering, the inscription must be directly over part of her body and trailing gown and thus it cannot apply to another, still smaller figure, such as Cooney suggested might have been standing behind her. Tia appears before what is evidently the garlanded pillar of a kiosk, and the scene of which she was a part probably showed her in a domestic setting, waiting upon one or more of the royal family, including Ankhesenpaaten (cf. Davies 1905a, pl. XXXII; Davies 1905b, pl. XXXIV). Although the royal nurses are sometimes depicted in tombs at Tell el Amarna (Davies 1905b, pls. IX, XIII), it is exceptional for them to be identified by name.

Bibliography: Hoffmann 1964a, no. 109, illus.; Cooney 1965, p. 19, no. 10, illus.; Hamburg 1965, p. 23, no. 32, and fig. 21; Bille-de Mot 1966, fig. 78; Jerusalem 1967, no. 5, illus.; Michalowski 1968, p. 397, figs. 441, 444; Roeder 1969, p. 404, no. P.C. 12, and pl. 170.

No. 130
A NURSE WITH HER ROYAL CHARGE

Late Period

Collection: Mr. and Mrs. Norbert Schimmel, New York

A little princess looks from the lower right of this charming fragment, grasping the elbow of her nurse in affection or importunity.

Material: Limestone.

Color: Bodies and faces red-brown; some black on hair.

Measurements: Height 23.2 cm. Width 29.2 cm. Thickness 2.2 cm. Height of nurse's head 8.3 cm. Height of nurse's face 5.7 cm. Height of girl's face ca. 4.2 cm.

Condition: Broken in several pieces and rejoined; nearly half of the slab missing; some restoration on cheek of larger figure and around face of child.

Provenance: Tell el Amarna; found at Hermopolis.

COMMENTARY: The larger figure wears a pleated gown, knotted under her right breast, and the short Nubian wig with the addition of a sidelock caught in a large clasp. Very exceptionally, this woman's well-developed breasts are shown frontally, a posture usually reserved in Dynasty XVIII for musicians, dancers (Berlin East 21445: Brunner–Traut 1956, pp. 59–60, no. 59, and pl. XXIII) and mourners (Cairo JE 43275d, from the tomb of Maya at Saqqara: Quibell 1912, pl. LXVII, 1). For this reason, this writer identifies her not as a senior princess but as the wet nurse of the child she fondles. Such women were well-born and highly honored in court circles (No. 129). If the writer is correct in identifying the style of this relief as belonging to the later period of the reign, it is not outside the bounds of possibility that the child pictured could be a prince, although a princess seems a more likely choice. That male children were pictured with elongated skulls is shown by the famous head of Tutankhamen on a lotus flower (Cairo T.755: Desroches–Noblecourt 1963, pl. facing title page), and it would seem that there must have been representations of Tutankhamen at Tell el Amarna because he is named in a label found at Hermopolis (Roeder 1969, pl. 106, no. 831/VIII C).

Bibliography: Roeder 1940, p. 292, fig. 3; Roeder 1951, pp. 23, 32, and pl. 4, b; Hoffmann 1964a, p. 110, illus.; Cooney 1965, pp. 28–29, no. 16, illus.; Hamburg 1965, pp. 23–24, no. 33, and fig. 28; Mitten 1965, p. 31, fig. 3; Bille-de Mot 1966, fig. 75; Jerusalem 1967, no. 7, illus.; Staehelin 1967, pp. 58–59, and pl. 15, 2; Aldred 1968, pl. XI; Yoyotte 1968, p. 106, illus.; Roeder 1969, p. 386, no. 218/VII, and pl. 8.

No. 131
SCENE OF JUBILATION
Late Period
Collection: The Brooklyn Museum 60.197.3
Here is shown in sunk relief part of a group of women, some raising their hands in jubilation and others beating tambourines. Two of these women wear long gowns and elaborate wigs. Preceding the group runs or dances a youth in a shirt and a kilt, and with a short wig with lappets, who raises both hands in acclamation. To the right is a bare tree above which a large bird is about to alight or to take wing.
Material: Limestone.

Color: Traces of red pigment on face of foremost woman and on her tambourine; traces of blue paint on branches of tree.
Measurements: Height 21.3 cm. Width 54.4 cm. Thickness 3.5 cm. Height of head of woman on the right 3.7 cm. Height of face of woman on the right 2.5 cm.
Condition: Lower edge and lower right corner chipped. Back cut in modern times.
Provenance: Tell el Amarna; found at Hermopolis.
COMMENTARY: This genre scene belongs to the lower or upper edge of a main scene and, like all such subsidiary borders, is carved in a somewhat less careful and more impressionistic style than that em-

ployed for the central theme; perhaps these borders were turned over to apprentices in the craft of wall decoration. Such details as the leaves of the tree were doubtless carried out in paint, which has now disappeared. Parallels to scenes of jubilation are found in Amarna tombs. In this case, it seems likely that a group outside the temple is joining in a joyous celebration that is taking place within (Davies 1905a, pl. XVIII). Perhaps the noise has disturbed the bird nesting in the tree (Davies 1905b, pl. VII).

Bibliography: Cooney 1965, pp. 78–79, no. 49, illus.; Roeder 1969, p. 405, no. P.C. 34, and pl. 175.

No. 132
HOMAGE TO ROYALTY
Late Period
Collection: The Brooklyn Museum 68.154
A courtier bows to the left, his gaze humbly directed downward. A headcloth covers his hair, and a line at the waist shows that he is kilted. At the right is the profile of another bowing man.
Material: Limestone.
Color: Traces of pale red flesh tones, probably modern.
Measurements: Height 24.1 cm.

Width 54.4 cm. Thickness 3.6 cm. Height of head 8.1 cm. Height of face 5.1 cm.
Condition: Edges chipped; lower right-hand corner missing; minor scars on surface. Back cut in modern times.
Provenance: Tell el Amarna; found at Hermopolis.
COMMENTARY: The position of the body and the direction of the gaze show that we have to do with officials in the royal presence, who bow profoundly with their hands hanging before their knees (Davies

1941, pl. XXXII). The double line across the forehead suggests that the headdress is a cloth that falls in points in front of the shoulders and is gathered into a broad pigtail at the rear. The high quality of the carving may indicate that the two officials represented were in the immediate entourage of the royal family rather than attendant upon the ladies in waiting (Davies 1905a, pl. XVIII; Davies 1905b, pl. IX).

Bibliography: Brooklyn 1969b, p 47, illus., and p. 167.

No. 133
WOMAN WITH FORMAL BOUQUET
Late Period

Collection: Anonymous Loan to The Brooklyn Museum L72.17
The woman wears a Nubian wig with headband and a very large circular ear stud. Only the top of the huge bouquet she carries over one shoulder is preserved.
Material: Limestone.
Color: No trace.
Measurements: Height 23 cm. Width 53.3 cm. Thickness 3.7 cm. Height of head 13 cm. Height of face 9 cm.
Condition: Broken diagonally from above and behind the head of the woman to area below her chin and recently repaired; damage to upper edge and lower right-hand corner. Back cut in modern times.
Provenance: Tell el Amarna; found at Hermopolis.
COMMENTARY: The person represented in this sunk relief might be either a man or a woman, for similar wigs with headbands are sometimes worn by the military in gala scenes (Davies 1933, pl. II), but the large earring and the rather delicate features seem to favor the latter interpretation. The large formal bouquet she carries seems to identify her as a member of the temple staff who greets the arrival of the royal family by bringing forth the offerings. A similar figure appears on a relief in Munich (ÄS 4870: Munich 1972, p. 68, no. 54, and pl. 35).

Bibliography: None.

No. 134
HEAD OF A BLACK MAN
Late Period

Collection: University College London 009
The head, carved in silhouette and apparently unfinished, represents a black man with thick lips and prognathous jaw. He wears the short military wig and a large hooped earring.
Material: Grayish-white limestone.
Color: No trace.
Measurements: Height 7.7 cm. Width across nose 8.1 cm. Thickness 2.2 cm.
Condition: Surface unsmoothed; eye incomplete.
Provenance: Tell el Amarna. Excavated in 1891–1892 by H. Carter and W. M. F. Petrie; exact locality not given.
COMMENTARY: This head unmistakably represents a man of one of the Nilotic tribes which the Egyptians subjugated during the New Kingdom. Although the nostril has been carefully drilled, the head as a whole appears to be merely roughed out, and the finer details and final polish are lacking. The piece has been described as an inlay, but in this writer's opinion it would be contrary to Egyptian instinct to employ a white stone to represent a black person, even with the idea of adding color. It seems more likely that the sculpture, when completed, was intended to serve as a master model from which clay molds could be made for preparing casts in glass or faience. Many baked clay molds have been found at Tell el Amarna, and while these are mostly for casting beads, amulets, the bezels of rings, and other small objects, similar molds must have been made for larger inlays to be used in architectural decoration.

Bibliography: Murray 1949, p. 199, pl. LXXI, 1; Pendlebury 1951, p. 227, and pl. CVI, 4; Samson 1972, p. 70, pl. 41.

No. 135
GIRL AMID FLOWERS
Late Period
Collection: E. Kofler, Lucerne
A fragment of relief depicts a girl with a short wig and a large round earring against a background of lotus, cornflowers, and a single marguerite. She bends forward to pull on a rope, perhaps attached to a trap net.
Material: Limestone.
Color: Traces of red.
Measurements: Height 21 cm. Width 22.5 cm. Thickness 3.3 cm.
Condition: Damage to lower edge. Back cut in modern times.
Provenance: Tell el Amarna; found at Hermopolis.
COMMENTARY: When unearthed at Hermopolis in 1939, the slab of which this relief formed the right-hand end was complete. Since then the rather badly rubbed left-hand portion has been cut away and presumably lost. It contained a large bunch of grapes (cf. No. 83), vine tendrils and leaves, and lotus flowers. The setting is therefore probably a bower, and the

present fragment may be part of a scene in which the royal family, pictured on a larger scale, was engaged in some sporting activity (cf. Nos. 126, 150). A rough parallel to this representation is afforded by a carved ivory relief on the lid of a casket from the tomb of Tutankhamen, in which maidens in bowers pick mandrakes on a frieze below large figures of the King and Queen (Cairo T. 1189: Carter 1933, frontis.). The girl represented here appears to be pulling the rope of a trap net over a pool frequented by waterfowl. This theme may have been suggested by the ceremonial event conducted by the pharaoh depicted on inner temple walls at Deir el Bahri earlier in the Dynasty (Naville 1908, pl. CLXIII). While the relief in its present state gives the impression that the girl is naked, it is probable that her dress and broad collar were originally indicated in paint.

Bibliography: Roeder 1969, p. 389, no. 113/VIII (also on p. 388 as no. 477/VII), and pl. 59.

No. 136
A ROYAL LADY AND HER RETINUE
Late Period
Collection: Mr. and Mrs. Norbert Schimmel, New York
Prostrate fanbearers and ladies of the royal household follow a large figure of a queen or princess, of which only the hips are preserved. She is clad in a diaphanous gown, open at the front.
Material: Limestone.
Color: Faintly yellow in sunk areas throughout; wigs black.
Measurements: Height 23.5 cm. Width 54.6 cm. Thickness 3.7 cm. Height of head 9.3 cm. Height of face 6 cm.

Condition: Surface chipped and deeply scored in places.
Provenance: Tell el Amarna; found at Hermopolis.
COMMENTARY: The relief shows two prostrate fanbearers and, beside them, the lower legs and sandaled feet of ladies in waiting, part of the retinue of a queen or princess who advances to the right. The women cannot, as Cooney claims, be princesses, for protocol was strictly observed at Tell el Amarna and it was not proper for mere attendants to advance, as these fanbearers do, in front of the royal daughters. The prostrate fanbearers each have one hand flat on the ground and clench the

staffs of their fans in the other. It will be noted that the carving of the four hands of the men follows the orthodox Egyptian tradition of nonspatial representation. Two hands are shown flat on the ground and two holding staffs, but their position is reversed, and both hands, as well as the arms to which they belong, are on the same side of the body.

Bibliography: Hoffmann 1964a, no. 111, illus.; Cooney 1965, p. 25, no. 14, illus.; Hamburg 1965, p. 24, no. 34, and fig. 25; Bille-de Mot 1966, fig. 37; Jerusalem 1967, no. 8, illus.; Woldering 1967, p. 146, fig. 75; Roeder 1969, p. 404, no. P.C. 8, and pl. 171.

No. 137
ATTENDANTS AT COURT
Late Period (?)
Collection: Mr. and Mrs. Norbert Schimmel, New York
Two male fanbearers in tunics and voluminous kilts are followed by six court ladies who are also equipped with fans. Two servitors, bowing low, end the procession.
Material: Limestone.
Color: Yellow in sunk areas; some traces of red.
Measurements: Height 23.9 cm. Width 54.5 cm. Thickness 3.9 cm. Height of head 4.4 cm. Height of face 2.9 cm.
Condition: Lower right-hand corner missing; all edges chipped.
Provenance: Tell el Amarna; found at Hermopolis.
COMMENTARY: This scene, depicting a royal retinue, occurs frequently at Tell el Amarna. The men usually carry semicircular fans made of feathers in their right hands, and the women hold long staffs surmounted by a single ostrich plume; both hold scarfs or sashes in their left hands, and the cortege is preceded and followed by bowing servitors. The present slab is almost intact, and the scene would have been completed on adjacent blocks. Here only parts of the hands of the royal retainers are shown; their fans and also their sandaled feet are missing, and of the obsequious servitors only part of the body of one and above his bent back the hand of another are preserved. From complete representations carved in rock-cut tombs, however, the entire scene may be easily reconstructed (Davies 1903, pls. XXIV, XXX).

Bibliography: Hoffmann 1964a, no. 114, illus.; Cooney 1965, pp. 36–37, illus.; Hamburg 1965, pp. 24–25, no. 37, and fig. 29; Bille-de Mot 1966, fig. 35; Jerusalem 1967, no. 11, illus.; Roeder 1969, p. 404, no. P.C. 15, and pl. 172.

No. 138
FOREIGNERS IN THE KING'S
SERVICE

Late Period (?)

Collection: Mr. and Mrs. Norbert Schimmel, New York

The carving of this relief depicting four foreigners shows the impressive mastery that is characteristic of most representations of the royal family and their immediate entourage. Such work was apparently entrusted only to the best artists available.

Material: Limestone.

Color: All carved portions painted light red in modern times, but traces of original darker red still visible.

Measurements: Height 24.3 cm. Width 53.6 cm. Thickness 3.2 cm. Height of faces ca. 10 cm.

Condition: Broken diagonally and rejoined; damage to top corners; eyes of all four faces mutilated.

Provenance: Tell el Amarna; found at Hermopolis.

COMMENTARY: In Dynasty XVIII the bearers of the great flabella that shaded the king and the queen from the burning sun were Negroes, selected for their strength and appearance from among the men captured in slave raids into the upper Sudan (cf. Bologna 1887: Bologna 1961, pl. 32). In the present relief the idea is carried a bit further, and foreigners from the northeast are shown in attendance upon the King, who (at least in theory) was lord of the Nine Nations of the world as well as ruler of the Egyptians. The universality of his power was symbolized by a foreign legion serving as his bodyguard, which shows four distinct ethnic types (Davies 1905b, pl. XXXI). These types are apparently depicted in the present relief. Although it would be rash to attempt a specific identification, at least three of the men represented appear to be northerners. The fourth and last may be a southerner, but the present writer is disposed to think that the entire quartet represents nations of the north—Libyans, Syrians, Palestinians (Säve-Söderbergh 1941, pp. 163–168); doubtless the southerners appeared in a companion piece. What is represented here are evidently four sunshade bearers pictured as walking in front of the King and Queen, although actually on their left, and these would be complementary to another quartet, shown as behind the royal couple but in reality at their right. Such sunshade bearers attend the King and Queen when they are in a carrying chair, and the closest parallel to the present scene is a representation of the royal couple in a palanquin in the tomb of Huya at Tell el Amarna (Davies 1905b, pl. XIII). Here, however, we meet with some difficulty, for what should be the straight carrying poles of a palanquin are replaced by a curved, four-strand border. This makes it seem likely that the scene represents the royal pair in an open barge drawn along a canal. Although no exact parallel for such a scene is at present to be found, a comparable idea is expressed in the tomb of Kheruef, where damaged reliefs show Amenhotep III and his Queen being towed along a waterway, escorted by troups carrying standards on the banks (Fakhry 1943, pl. XL). Another example, also incomplete and damaged, occurs in the temple of Luxor, where the towing of sacred barks during the Feast of Opet is sculptured on the walls of the colonnade (Wolf 1931, pl. II). At some time during the long migrations of this relief the foreigners depicted on it seemed to have been the personification of hostility, and their eyes have been deliberately hacked out.

Bibliography: Hoffmann 1964a, no. 117, illus.; Hoffmann 1964b, p. 272, pl. III; Cooney 1965, pp. 39–41, no. 21, illus.; Hamburg 1965, p. 25, no. 40, and fig. 32; Mitten 1965, p. 32, fig. 4; Bille-de Mot 1966, fig. 92; Jerusalem 1967, illus. on Hebrew cover; Roeder 1969, p. 404, no. P.C. 3, and pl. 170.

Detail

No. 139
FESTIVAL SCENE

Late Period

Collection: Mr. and Mrs. Norbert Schimmel, New York

In what is evidently a scene of festival, a group of ten court ladies raise drinking bowls to their lips. An incomplete figure at the left, with back turned, probably belongs to another scene.

Material: Limestone.

Color: Traces of red on flesh; of black and blue on wigs; eye of woman at top center outlined in black.

Measurements: Height 22.4 cm. Width 54.2 cm. Thickness 3.6 cm. Height of head 8.7–9.8 cm. Height of face 5.8–7 cm.

Condition: Blemish in center of slab; lower left-hand and upper right-hand corners missing.

Provenance: Tell el Amarna; found at Hermopolis.

COMMENTARY: As Cooney justly remarks, it is sometimes difficult to discriminate between men and women as represented at Tell el Amarna, for both frequently wear the same type of wig. The large ear studs (though these are by no means conclusive) and the pleated gowns at the upper right serve to identify the present group as women, however, probably as attendants of the Queen or the princesses. Some are drinking from wine bowls, and the woman at the extreme right holds what may be a portion of duck in her left hand. Apart from several reliefs in tombs at Tell el Amarna which show the royal family at meat (Davies 1905b, pls. IV, XXXIV; Davies 1906, pl. X), there is only a single damaged scene sketched in outline in the tomb of Parennefer (Davies 1908b, pl. VI), which depicts Akhenaten presiding over an impressive spread of viands, and which may, when complete, have shown the royal family feasting with their retinue, perhaps in the Hall of Eating. Such feasting was evidently part of the jubilee celebrations (Aldred 1959a, p. 27). The grouping of heads in the relief under discussion demonstrates a felicity in the management of crowd scenes often achieved by artists of the Amarna Period.

Bibliography: Hoffmann 1964a, no. 118, illus.; Cooney 1965, p. 43, no. 23, illus.; Hamburg 1965, p. 26, no. 41, and fig. 39; Jerusalem 1967, no. 10, illus.; America–Israel Cultural Foundation 1968, pp. 78–79, no. 287, illus.; Roeder 1969, p. 404, no. P.C. 6, and pl. 170.

No. 140
TWO OFFICIALS

Late Period

Collection: Virginia Museum of Fine Arts, Richmond 61.5

The heads and shoulders of two officials are here pictured in sunk relief. They wear large round earrings and wigs differing in cut but both bound with fillets. They are apparently clad in tunics, and each carries a staff, probably the shaft of a fan, in his right hand.

Material: Limestone.

Color: Wigs blue; earrings yellow; bodies and fan stocks red; all paint modern.

Measurements: Height 22.8 cm. Width 49.5 cm. Left attendant's height of head 11.5 cm., height of face 6.7 cm. Right attendant's height of head 10.5 cm., height of face 6.2 cm.

Condition: Some damage to top left-hand corner; a few minor abrasions on surface.

Provenance: Tell el Amarna; found at Hermopolis.

COMMENTARY: The lunging position of the men's bodies and the angle at which their fan stocks are held show that they are running. They thus must represent two of the high officials who accompany the King on foot as he goes to the temple in his chariot. Enough of the fans survives to indicate that they were not the large state flabella but the insignia of "Bearers of the Fan on the Right of the King." Although there were only four men who could claim this distinction among those privileged to have tombs at Tell el Amarna, it would be rash to attempt to identify the two pictured here with any of them. The fillets and earrings they wear indicate that the ceremony in which they are participating is a festive occasion. As a rule, men are not shown wearing earrings after puberty, but in his tomb the Fanbearer Ay, one of the very prominent figures at Tell el Amarna, is pictured in a scene of his investiture by the King as wearing large earrings (Davies 1908b, pl. XXXI). The long hair of the foremost man is unusual, but it is duplicated on the head of a black granite statue in Florence (Museo Archeologico 6316: Fechheimer 1922b, pl. 63).

* *Bibliography:* Bothmer 1962, pp. 27, 29; Cooney 1965, p. 44, no. 24, illus.; Roeder 1969, p. 406, no. P.C. 104, and pl. 187.

No. 141
A HUMBLE BANQUET
Late Period

Collection: Museum of Man, San Diego, California 14881

At the left, two men seated on stools with a footrest are attended by two young women in festal attire who approach from the right, bringing wine for their enjoyment. The men wear short wigs and long white kilts; the women are clad in flowing robes with elbow sleeves and have large cones of ointment on their heads. The man nearest the viewer holds a wine bowl to his lips; the girl opposite him holds a jar to refill it. The other man accepts a similar bowl from his attendant. At the top of the stela are four columns of inscription. The rounded top of the stela is bordered by the *pet* sign, signifying the sky.

Material: Limestone.

Color: Flesh tones light red; stools, hair, rim of footrest, and base line black; staining of ointment on cones and garments pale orange; garments and *pet* sign white; inscription blue.

Measurements: Height 19.7 cm. Width 17.2 cm. Thickness 4.9 cm.

Condition: Ancient correction to name of second man; paint at lower edge rubbed.

Provenance: Tell el Amarna. Excavated in 1924 by the Egypt Exploration Society, outside of the walls of House R. 44. 2, in the area of the Great Temple.

COMMENTARY: Very few private stelae have been found at Tell el Amarna. Such ex-votos as were common in previous and later periods, which showed the donor worshiping a divinity, were discouraged by the monotheistic worship of the abstract Aten, approachable only by the royal family. Nevertheless, a few private stelae have survived, perhaps the most notable among them being one depicting the old deities, Isis and Shed, found in one of a group of tombs near the City (Porter and Moss 1934, p. 209). These tombs were probably made for their own use by workmen employed in the royal necropolis, and the fact that they were dedicated by relatively humble people explains their form and their rarity. They belong to folk art and only vaguely echo Amarna style. Included in this small body of stelae is an example in East Berlin (14122: Schäfer 1931, pl. 53), made for an Asiatic spearman and his wife, and also a series dedicated by the servants of the steward Any, which are now in Cairo (CG 34176–34181: Lacau 1909, pp. 217–222, and pls. LXVI–LXVIII). The colorful stela from San Diego is another example of such lively works. It owes its excellent preservation to the fact that

it was carefully wrapped in a linen cloth before it was buried near the house of Panehsy, Chief Servitor of the Aten at Tell el Amarna. Like most others of its kind, it is entirely secular in subject matter; it shows no god, makes no invocation. Only the names of the men and of the women who serve them are preserved in the inscription. The man at the left was apparently called Yaya (although the name was corrected in antiquity), and his companion is Menna. The two women are respectively Shety and Mery. We are not told their titles or their occupations or their relationships. All that is evident is the theme of "spending a happy day," presumably in the hereafter.

Bibliography: Griffith 1924, p. 302.

No. 142
A TROPHY OF DUCKS
Late Period
Collection: Museum of Fine Arts, Boston 62.320
These ducks, rendered with remarkable plasticity, hang from the top of a column. At the right appear part of the thigh and floating robe of a woman.
Material: Limestone.
Color: Traces of red and blue pigment, probably modern.
Measurements: Height 23 cm. Width 52.6 cm. Thickness 3.7 cm.
Condition: Upper right-hand corner chipped; otherwise a complete slab.
Provenance: Tell el Amarna; found at Hermopolis.
COMMENTARY: The festoon of ducks decorates one of the exotic composite columns that are a feature of Amarna art. Such papyrus columns support the entablatures of light kiosks in which the royal family disport themselves, and the trophy of ducks usually hangs below the capital (Davies 1905a, pl. XXXII; Petrie 1894, pl. VII). Here the fasciculated bundle of papyrus stalks and its lashing are carefully delineated; below them is apparently the beginning of a base. The figure to the right is rather puzzling, for when complete it would have been much too high to fit into the kiosk. It probably belongs, therefore, to an adjacent scene, in which the woman is standing outside the kiosk looking to the right.

Bibliography: Terrace 1962, pp. 134–135, illus.; Boston 1964a, pp. 194–195, illus.; Cooney 1965, p. 108, no. 63, illus.; Boston 1967a, no. 28, illus.; Roeder 1969, p. 405, no. P.C. 36, and pl. 174.

No. 144
DESERT SCENE
Probably Late Period
Collection: The Brooklyn Museum
60.197.5
The heads, necks, and part of the backs of two young bubalis antelopes and a bit of the body of a third are preserved in sunk relief on this slab. The piece once formed part of a larger scene depicting desert life. At the top is an interrupted base line for another register.
Material: Limestone.
Color: Traces of original red-brown pigment are visible in places on the bodies of the animals, but the present prevailing pale red-brown color is apparently not ancient.
Measurements: Height 23.1 cm. Width 52.5 cm. Thickness 3.4 cm.
Condition: Slight damage to head of second animal; many chips at upper edge of slab. Back cut in modern times.
Provenance: Tell el Amarna; found at Hermopolis.
COMMENTARY: The complete scene of which this slab forms a part may once have shown the Pharaoh hunting in the desert, similar to the one depicted on the lid of a painted box from the tomb of Tutankhamen (Cairo T.324: Smith 1958, pls. 142–143) or that on the rear of the First Pylon of the mortuary temple of Ramesses III at Medinet Habu (Nelson 1932, pl. 116). It is also possible, but less probable, that this relief is part of a great scene showing the sovereignty of the Aten over all creation. This latter theme, which had its origin in the sun temples of Dynasty V (Smith 1965, fig. 178a–b), was reinterpreted on two walls of the Royal Tomb at Tell el Amarna (Porter and Moss 1934, p. 236. Cf. also No. 149).

Bibliography: Cooney 1965, pp. 60–61, no. 37, illus.; Roeder 1969, p. 405, no. P.C. 40, and pl. 174.

No. 143
A ROYAL EQUIPAGE
Late Period, about Year 13
Collection: The Brooklyn Museum
54.186
Spirited plumed horses and part of a state chariot are all that remain from a scene of royal progress that was hidden away in the Royal Tomb, high above the City of the Aten.
Material: Gypsum plaster.
Color: Background yellow; bodies of horses red; plumes red and black.
Measurements: Height 21.2 cm. Width 35.4 cm. Thickness 3.7 cm.
Condition: A piece of irregular shape and very fragile; broken at all edges.
Provenance: Tell el Amarna. From the Royal Tomb, Room 2, probably Wall D, bottom register at extreme right.
COMMENTARY: The Royal Tomb was hollowed out of a cliff in an area of poor rock, the naturally occurring blemishes of which had to be filled in with plaster before stonecutters and painters got to work. The present fragment is a substantial filling from a wall in a chamber reserved for the burial of Maketaten, and the relief was partly modeled while still in a plastic state. The motif is a frequent one in Amarna art. Here the details of the equipage are carefully shown: the plumes of the horses, their blinkers, breastband, and girth; the shaft of the chariot ending in the disk of the Aten; even the royal bow case strapped to the chariot. Only the attendant grooms are missing, together with the owner of the chariot.

Bibliography: Bouriant 1903, pl. IV; Brooklyn 1956, pp. 26–27, no. 30 H, and pl. 50.

No. 145
BROWSING CATTLE
                    Late Period (?)
Collection: Staatliche Sammlung
Ägyptischer Kunst, Munich ÄS
5360

Three bovines feeding in the wild
are pictured in sunk relief. To the
right a tree and at the top edge a
leafy plant suggest abundant pas-
turage.
Material: Limestone.
Color: No trace.
Measurements: Height 21.8 cm.
Width 52.4 cm. Thickness 2.9 cm.
Condition: All edges damaged; surface shows signs of salt efflorescence.
Provenance: Tell el Amarna; found
at Hermopolis.
COMMENTARY: Like the cattle pictured in No. 80, those of this relief
are obviously browsing in the
open. The incised branches of the
tree or shrub to the right probably
once bore painted leaves that
would have made them appear
more succulent. The animal in the
middle, with its large curving
horns and prominent dewlap,
seems to be full grown; the other
two are apparently heifers, with
horns barely sprouting. It is difficult to determine whether these
cattle are domesticated or wild. If
the latter, it is possible that this
slab, like No. 80, formed part of
a hunting scene in which animals
were shown browsing in a quiet
part of the field before the chase
caught up with them. On the other
hand, it is pleasant to think that
the relief we have here may illus-
trate a passage in the Great Hymn
to the Aten: "All cattle are at peace
in their pasture." The pattern
formed by the heads of the animals
recalls reliefs of the Old Kingdom
and thus may betray a Memphite
influence.

Bibliography: Munich 1966, no. 54,
ÄS 5360, illus.; Müller 1970b, p.
185; Munich 1970, no. 54, ÄS
5360, and pl. 33; Munich 1972, p.
68, and pl. 36.

No. 147
A ROYAL GESTURE
Late Period (?)

Collection: Mr. and Mrs. Norbert Schimmel, New York

A hand, perhaps of the King, drops a lump of incense (?) upon a table of offerings.

Material: Limestone.

Color: Traces of yellow on hand and offerings.

Measurements: Height 23.8 cm. Width 27.9 cm. Thickness 3.6 cm.

Condition: About half the slab missing from the right; edges chipped.

Provenance: Tell el Amarna; found at Hermopolis.

COMMENTARY: The unusual gesture here depicted makes the fragment rather puzzling, but Cooney's interpretation is doubtless right. The completed arm (perhaps that of the King) was bent at the elbow, so that the forearm was in a vertical position, and the relaxed fingers of the bent hand have just released a drop of incense, which appears on the altar at the lower left. Without some such interpretation the gesture of the hand would be meaningless, and the shape of the slab demands that the forearm be in a vertical position. The lump of incense (?) on the altar has been variously interpreted as the drumstick of a fowl or the flame from a censer, but it actually resembles neither of these things. However the gesture may be interpreted, the elegantly articulated hand with its nervous, elongated fingers is a beautiful example of Amarna art, which can be matched, if rather rarely, in other examples of the period. On the right is the remainder of an eliminated inscription of which only an *ankh* sign can now be read.

Bibliography: Hoffmann 1964a, no. 104, illus.; Hoffmann 1964b, p. 271, fig. 3; Cooney 1965, pp. 6–7, no. 2, illus.; Hamburg 1965, p. 22, no. 27, and fig. 18; Bille-de Mot 1966, fig. 40; Jerusalem 1967, no. 2, illus.; Woldering 1967, p. 154, fig. 74; Michalowski 1968, p. 397, fig. 442; Roeder 1969, p. 404, no. P.C. 2, and pl. 173.

No. 146
AN OLIVE BRANCH FOR THE ATEN
Late Period (?)

Collection: Mr. and Mrs. Norbert Schimmel, New York

A large, sensitively carved hand holds a fruit-laden bough toward the welcoming rays of the god. At the upper right are the remains of an inscription that was deliberately obliterated in ancient times.

Material: Limestone.

Color: Pinkish red on hand and rays of the Aten; blue-green on leaves and fruit; all probably modern.

Measurements: Height 22.9 cm. Width 45.1 cm. Thickness 3.4 cm. Intracolumnar width 5.6–5.8 cm.

Condition: Slab broken across middle and reassembled; about one-fifth missing from left-hand side; inscription at top right erased; some apparently ancient damage (deliberate?) to lower right.

Provenance: Tell el Amarna; found at Hermopolis.

COMMENTARY: This scene, so far unique, substitutes an olive branch for the traditional bouquet that is usually offered to the Aten. The hand that holds the bough, bending under its weight of fruit, to the caressing rays of the Aten is undoubtedly that of the King, who must have stood almost directly under the sun disk. Undoubtedly the Queen also participated in the completed scene. The carving of this slab is of unusually fine quality, but what gives it a special interest is the drawing of the grasping hand. Here the artist, departing from ancient conventions still employed at Tell el Amarna (cf. No. 118), delineates the thumb in relation to the fingers and the branch they hold in a manner as nearly approaching perspective as any Egyptian draftsman ever attained (see No. 83). Perhaps the olive, an exotic tree recently imported into Egypt, inspired the artist to draw the branch and the holding hand from life.

Bibliography: Hoffmann 1964a, no. 107, illus.; Cooney 1965, pp. 5–6, no. 1, illus.; Hamburg 1965, p. 23, no. 30, and fig. 19; Bille-de Mot 1966, fig. 93; Jerusalem 1967, no. 3, illus.; Roeder 1969, p. 403, no. P.C. 1, and pl. 170.

No. 148
GALLOPING HORSES
Late Period (?)
Collection: Mr. and Mrs. Norbert Schimmel, New York
A slab carved in both sunk and raised relief with the legs and parts of the bodies of unharnessed steeds provides little suggestion of the complete scene from which it comes but furnishes a fine example of the skill of the stonecutter.
Material: Limestone.
Color: All worked areas and part of background painted red-brown in modern times.
Measurements: Height 23.3 cm. Width 49.6 cm. Thickness 3.8 cm.
Condition: Top left-hand corner missing; top and left edges damaged; some traces of plaster (?) fill.
Provenance: Tell el Amarna; found at Hermopolis.
COMMENTARY: The animals of this relief seem certainly to be horses, and so far as can be judged they are without harness. The legs of the horse charging from the right tend to dispel any idea that the complete scene could have represented desert animals fleeing before a huntsman, such as appears on the lid of Tutankhamen's painted box (Davies 1962, pl. III). When all the possibilities are weighed, it seems that what we have here is a fragment of a military scene, perhaps a surprise attack upon an encampment where the horses have been unharnessed from their chariots.

Bibliography: Hoffmann 1964a, no. 121, illus.; Cooney 1965, pp. 45–47, no. 25, illus.; Hamburg 1965, p. 26, no. 44, and fig. 35; Jerusalem 1967, no. 19, illus.; Roeder 1969, p. 406, no. P.C. 78, and pl. 216.

No. 150
FISHING IN A POND
Late Period (?)
Collection: Mr. and Mrs. Norbert Schimmel, New York
An admirably carved slab shows part of a fishing scene, with a *bolti* fish and a pintail duck impaled on a spear or arrow pictured in sunk relief at the left, and a second *bolti*, shown in raised relief at the right, swimming amid the lotus plants of a pool.
Material: Limestone.
Color: Traces of blue in waterlines; other worked surfaces red.
Measurements: Height 23.1 cm. Width 53.7 cm. Thickness 3.6 cm.
Condition: Large chip at upper left corner; lower right corner broken away and reassembled.
Provenance: Tell el Amarna; found at Hermopolis.
COMMENTARY: The scene on this slab can be reconstructed with the aid of a carved ivory panel on a box from the tomb of Tutankhamen (Cairo T.1189: British Museum 1972, no. 21). It doubtless once showed the King, seated by an artificial pool, shooting with a bow at fish and waterfowl. A member of his family, the Queen or a princess, may have attended him to hand him arrows or to retrieve his catch. In the Tutankhamen example the retrieving is done by a male attendant, who brings bird and fish on separate arrows, but here a lucky shot has impaled both on a single arrow, and it seems to be a princess who has done the retrieving; the top of her head, with characteristic coiffure and headband, is visible at the lower left.

Bibliography: Hoffmann 1964a, no. 126, illus.; Hoffmann 1964b, p. 272, pl. IV; Cooney 1965, pp. 64–66, no. 41, illus.; Hamburg 1965, p. 28, no. 49, and fig. 50; Jerusalem 1967, illus. on English cover; Roeder 1969, p. 405, no. P.C. 35, and pl. 174.

No. 149
ANTELOPES IN THE DESERT
Late Period (?)

Collection: Mr. and Mrs. Norbert Schimmel, New York

The fleeing bubalis antelopes on this slab may form part of the scene pictured in No. 144. Both slabs perhaps belong to a large composition that showed the King hunting in the desert.

Material: Limestone.

Color: Traces of red on bodies of animals, of blue on plants.

Measurements: Height 23 cm. Width 52.7 cm. Thickness 23.5 cm.

Condition: Top edge damaged.

Provenance: Tell el Amarna; found at Hermopolis.

COMMENTARY: At the left of this slab are the legs and hindquarters of animals fleeing toward the right. A sloping groundline under their hooves indicates either that the terrain is hilly or that they are pursuing a diagonal course. At the lower edge there emerge from a thicket the heads and necks of two other animals also fleeing to the right. The scene most nearly contemporary with this subject is that on the lid of the painted box from the tomb of Tutankhamen (Davies 1962, pl. III), where the King hunts ostriches, gazelles, asses, and antelopes, who also pursue diagonal paths. These ani-

mals, however, are more mature than those of the present fragment, and it seems to be a feature of Amarna art that the fleeing antelopes are pictured as young.

Bibliography: Hoffmann 1964a, no. 125, illus.; Cooney 1965, pp. 64–65, no. 40, illus.; Hamburg 1965, p. 27, no. 48, and fig. 49; Jerusalem 1967, no. 20, illus.; Roeder 1969, p. 404, no. P.C. 11, and pl. 171.

No. 151
MANGER

Late Period (?)

Collection: Toledo Museum of Art 25.744

A fragment of a manger carved in sunk relief retains the upper parts of the figures of two ibexes standing before a pictured manger containing fodder. At the upper right is another bundle of fodder.

Material: Limestone.

Color: Traces of black on backs of animals and on horns of ibex at the left; traces of green on fodder.

Measurements: Height 25.9 cm. Width 52.1 cm. Thickness 12.7 cm.

Condition: Damage to right-hand corner.

Provenance: Tell el Amarna. Excavated in 1923 by the Egypt Exploration Society at the Northern Palace.

COMMENTARY: It has been claimed by the excavators that a palace in the northern region of Tell el Amarna was a sort of zoological garden, with fish ponds, aviaries, and enclosures for cattle, antelopes, and ibexes. One of the compounds excavated contained the remains of fourteen mangers erected against its mud-brick walls. Most of the stonework had been removed in antiquity, but some fragments had been left *in situ*. They all, like the example in Toledo, were boldly carved with figures of oxen, antelopes, and ibexes and, in one case, with that of a keeper. The mannerisms of Amarna art, so evident in portrayals of the royal family and their attendants, do not appear in representations of animals. These follow traditions established in the earlier years of Dynasty XVIII (cf. No. 77), but nevertheless are infused with a certain dash and bravura that belong to the age of Akhenaten.

* *Bibliography:* Porter and Moss 1934, p. 193. Add: Luckner 1971, p. 65, fig. 6.

No. 152
JAR OF MULTICOLORED GLASS

Late Period

Collection: The Brooklyn Museum 37.340E

The oblate body of the vessel has three loop handles at the shoulder and is set on a short stem and spreading foot. The cylindrical neck is tall and wide with everted rim.

Material: Polychrome glass.

Color: Body violet blue, with dragged and marvered threads of white and yellow.

Measurements: Height 8.6 cm. Width 7.2 cm. Thickness at neck 0.1–0.2 cm. Diameter at lip 5.5 cm., at foot ca. 3.5 cm.

Condition: Repair in rim; two fragments missing.

Provenance: Said to be Saqqara.

COMMENTARY: Although this vessel may not have been found at Tell el Amarna, it must have been made at a time very close to the floruit of Akhetaten and may well have been made by an expert from that City. Jars of a similar type were found there in houses of the Northwest Quarter excavated by the Egypt Exploration Society in 1929–1930 (Frankfort and Pendlebury 1933, pls. XXXVIII, 4 and XLII, 2). Techniques of glassmaking reached a pitch of perfection during the Amarna Period, and the remains of a glass factory in the precincts of the Palace suggest that it may have been under royal patronage.

* *Bibliography:* Brooklyn 1968, pp. 20, 96, no. 17, and pl. V.

No. 153
FISH-SHAPED GLASS FLASK
Late Period (?)

Collection: British Museum, London 55193

A core vessel in the form of a *bolti* fish (*Tilapia nilotica*) shows a dragged decoration of yellow and white festoons, simulating scales, on a deep blue ground.

Material: Glass.

Color: Dark blue, yellow, and white, with touches of turquoise and black.

Measurements: Height 7 cm. Length 14.2 cm. Width 3.8 cm.

Condition: Broken into several pieces and mended, but now complete save for chips missing from near left eye and around right side of mouth.

Provenance: Tell el Amarna. Excavated in 1921 by the Egypt Exploration Society under the floor of a room in House 49. 20 in the Main City. Excavation no. 21/475.

COMMENTARY: The flask, already broken when found, formed part of a group consisting of a wine strainer, jug, and elbow pipe of low-grade silver, and two handsome polychrome glass jugs of similar technique. This rather ill-assorted cache may have been hidden away, perhaps by thieves, during the gradual abandonment of the City. The flask was not made by blowing but by coating a fish-shaped core of sandy clay with dark blue molten glass. The scales and lines of the tail were indicated

by threads of white and yellow glass trailed upon and marvered into the dark blue coating while it was still soft, and other details, such as eyes, lips, and fins, were then added by applying similar threads. When the vessel had finally cooled, the sandy core was removed. Although fragments of similar fish-shaped vials have been found at Tell el Amarna and elsewhere, and a complete specimen from Saqqara is preserved in Cairo (JE 32974: Nolte 1968, p. 137, pl. XXIX, 1), the fish from the British Museum is an outstanding example of the glass-

maker's art. A glass *bolti* fish in The Brooklyn Museum (37.316 E: Brooklyn 1968, pp. 30, 98–99, no. 30, pl. VIII), while less spectacular, is a unique specimen probably of about the same period. Made of yellowish clear glass, it has an underglaze decoration of blue spots indicating scales, and a yellow thread outlines the mouth.

* *Bibliography:* Peet and Woolley 1923, p. 24, and pl. XII, 3; British Museum 1964, p. 202, fig. 76; Bille-de Mot 1966, pl. VIII; Nolte 1968, p. 70, no. 5, p. 137, and pl. XXIX; Brooklyn 1968, p. 99.

No. 154
A MAGICAL FISH
Late Period (?)

Collection: The Brooklyn Museum 48.111

This gaily colored pottery model of a familiar fish doubtless served as a talisman for an Egyptian of the time of Akhenaten.

Material: Buff terracotta.

Color: Head, tail, dorsal and anal fins painted light blue; scales outlined in black and colored blue and red in alternate zones; mouth, eyes, and gills outlined with incised lines and painted red.

Measurements: Height 6.3 cm. Length 11 cm. Depth 3.3 cm.

Condition: Tail broken in two places and reattached.

Provenance: Said to be Saqqara, but perhaps Tell el Amarna.

COMMENTARY: The painting on this charming specimen includes that characteristic "Amarna blue" that originated in the decorated domestic pottery found in the Theban palace of Amenhotep III and persisted into the reign of Akhenaten (Hayes 1959, p. 247). Although the Delta fish eaters were anathema to such a purist and Amun worshiper as King Piankhy of Dynasty XXV, no such scruples

were entertained by the followers of the sun cult at Tell el Amarna. The fish, particularly the *bolti* (*Tilapia nilotica*), appears frequently at that City, painted on walls and floors or depicted on the faience tiles and inlays that ornamented the rooms of palaces. A particularly brilliant example in glass, assembled from fragments found in the City, is now in the British Museum (No. 153), and a number of fish-shaped golden ornaments were excavated at the site. These last call to mind the golden fish distributed by Amenhotep III on the occasion of one of his jubilees (Fakhry 1943, p. 491 and pl. XL). A clue to the significance of the fish is furnished by the six pottery pellets found in the hollow body of the Brooklyn specimen. Since the female *bolti* preserves her eggs in her body until they are ready to hatch, she thus became to the Egyptians a symbol of that self-creation which was characteristic of the primordial sun god (Gamer-Wallert 1970, pp. 54, 113).

* *Bibliography:* Cooney 1949, illus.; Roeder 1952, p. 119, fig. 40; Dambach and Wallert 1966, p. 284, note 5; Brooklyn 1968, p. 99.

No. 155
COMPOSITE FRIEZE WITH
URAEI

Late Period (?)
Collection: Ashmolean Museum, Oxford 1922.92

A slab shows three cobras crowned with solar disks, their bodies carved in raised relief and their heads of contrasting stone sculptured in the round.

Material: Slab red quartzite; cobra heads gray granite.

Color: No trace.

Measurements: Height (after restoration) 31.2 cm. Width (after restoration) 24.7 cm. Depth, top to back of ancient break 10.5 cm. Depth at bottom (modern) 13.5 cm.

Condition: About half of slab restored; one cobra head chipped.

Provenance: Tell el Amarna. Excavated in 1921–1922 by the Egypt Exploration Society in the Maru Temple in the Southern City.

COMMENTARY: The uraeus was evidently one protective deity that was not interdicted at Tell el Amarna. Its close connection with royalty and the solar religion presumably preserved it. Disk-crowned cobras decorate the friezes of baldachins, boat cabins, and other architectural elements. Many uraeus heads made of blue glazed faience have been found at Tell el Amarna, where they had evidently been set into wooden or mud-brick entablatures. The present fragment came from the Maru Aten, or Viewing-of-the-Aten Temple, which was situated south of the Main Wadi of the City. It is almost certain that the compartments on the bodies of the cobras were inlaid with colored glass or faience and that their outlines and the sun disks were gilded.

Bibliography: Peet and Woolley 1923, p. 122, and pl. XXXIII, 5 right.

No. 156
CEREMONIAL SAW

Late Period
Collection: The Brooklyn Museum 65.133

The serrated blade of the saw takes the form of the feather of Truth (Maat); the handle is shaped like a horizontally ribbed papyrus shoot surmounted by an umbel bearing a suspension ring.

Material: Bronze.

Color: Green patination.

Measurements: Length 31.7 cm. Width 4.9 cm. Thickness of blade 0.1–0.2 cm. Length of handle 11.3 cm.

Condition: Slight corrosion and discoloration; otherwise sound.

Provenance: Not known.

COMMENTARY: The only other example of this unusual saw-knife is an identical specimen in Cairo (JE 55372), which was excavated in 1930 by the Egypt Exploration Society in House S. 33. 1 of the Northern Suburb of Tell el Amarna (excavation no. 30/457). Since in the same spot were found other bronze knives, including a fleshing knife, and an ostracon mentioning various cuts of meat, it may be inferred that the Brooklyn and Cairo saws were used in preparing meat for sacrifice. Indeed the general design and the ring by which the saw might be attached by a lanyard to a belt, recalls certain knives, pictured in the hands of butchers (Frankfort and Pendlebury 1933, pp. 67–68, and pl. XLVII).

Bibliography: Brooklyn 1966b, p. 119.

No. 157
SNAFFLE BIT
Late Period (?)
Collection: Ashmolean Museum, Oxford 1933.1209
The bit, of "run-out" type, consists of two identical interlocked but swiveling rods, each terminating in a fixed D-shaped ring and threaded with a rotating cheek-piece provided with square holes at the extremities and two burrs.
Material: Bronze.
Measurements: Height 11 cm. Length 20.2 cm.
Condition: Slight patination; otherwise perfect.
Provenance: Tell el Amarna. Excavated in 1932 by the Egypt Exploration Society in an unspecified private house. Excavation no. 32/117.
COMMENTARY: The bit, one of the few to have survived from ancient Egypt, is made with a precision that would do credit to modern technology. Each half of the mouthpiece has been fashioned by forging a rod twisted upon itself to form a spirally grooved bar with a loop at one end, the loops of the two rods interlocking. Upon each half of the resulting hinged rod has been slipped a bar cast in one piece with a collar and two burrs. Slots are provided at the top and bottom of each bar to accommodate the straps of the leather noseband. The bars are held in position by terminal collars furnished with D-rings to take the reins, which were evidently cast together with both ends of the bit. Bars and terminals must have been cast in closed molds and afterward filed and burnished to a fine finish, presumably with abrasive stones. For a discussion of ancient bits, see Littauer 1969.

Bibliography: None.

No. 158
TILE WITH MARGUERITES
Late Period (?)
Collection: The Brooklyn Museum 35.2001
The rectangular tile, inset with eleven scattered roundels in the form of marguerites, once formed part of the decoration of the Great Palace at Tell el Amarna.
Material: Glazed faience.
Color: Field green, painted with a leafy twig in black and three blue leaves, each with two raised yellowish buds (?); inset flowers white with yellow centers.
Measurements: Height 11.4 cm. Width 16.7 cm. Thickness 0.9 cm. Diameter of marguerites ca. 2 cm.
Condition: Lower left-hand corner broken and repaired.
Provenance: Tell el Amarna. Excavated in 1934 by the Egypt Exploration Society in the Hypostyle Hall of the Great Palace. Excavation no. 34/28.
COMMENTARY: Several tiles of this type have been found in the ruins of the Great Palace at Tell el Amarna, particularly near the Hypostyle Hall, which the excavators believed to have been built for the coronation of Smenkhkare. Such tiles probably formed bright decorative borders set into mud-brick walls. This specimen is the only one in which all inlays are intact.

Bibliography: Pendlebury 1935b, p. 131; Pendlebury 1951, pl. LXXII, 1.

No. 159
GLAZED TILE WITH DOUM PALM

Late Period (?)

Collection: The Brooklyn Museum 52.148.1

A fragment originally of semi-circular shape depicts the doum palm, which is still, as in the past, a feature of the Egyptian landscape.

Material: Faience with polychrome glaze.

Color: Green, brown, and yellow on white ground.

Measurements: Height 11 cm. Width 9.2 cm. Thickness 1.1 cm.

Condition: Broken and repaired; substantial portions missing.

Provenance: Tell el Amarna; found at Hermopolis.

COMMENTARY: The techniques of making glass and faience reached an apogee of excellence at Tell el Amarna, where craftsmen perfected a method of making a polychrome glazed quartz frit, which marks a notable step forward in ceramic arts. Among other successes, they produced tiles with multicolored decoration of plant and animal motifs on a white ground. This fragment shows, in addition to the doum palm, fantastic leaves that are not readily identifiable. Tiles of similar semi-circular shape and glazing technique have been excavated on the site of the Great Temple at Tell el Amarna (Pendlebury 1951, pl. LXII, 2–3).

Bibliography: Brooklyn 1956, pp. 34–35, no. 38 B, and pl. 62; Brunner–Traut 1956, p. 119, note 6; Smith 1958, pl. 154 A; Brooklyn 1968, pp. 28 and 98, no. 27, and pl. V.

No. 160
TILE WITH MANDRAGORA

Late Period (?)

Collection: The Brooklyn Museum 52.148.2

This polychrome tile, probably once semicircular in shape, has a decoration of mandragora (mandrake) fruits and large leaves.

Material: Glazed faience.

Color: Green, yellow, and brown on white ground.

Measurements: Height ca. 10 cm. Length ca. 14 cm. Thickness 1.6 cm.

Condition: Incomplete; edges chipped.

Provenance: Tell el Amarna; said to have been acquired at Hermopolis.

COMMENTARY: This tile is another example of the command over the ceramic arts exercised by Egyptian craftsmen. The yellow fruits are in very low relief; the boldly designed green leaves are outlined in red-brown, and their veining is carefully indicated.

Bibliography: Brooklyn 1956, pp. 34–35, no. 38 B, and pl. 62 (incorrectly called 38 A); Brooklyn 1968, pp. 28 and 98, no. 28, and pl. VI.

SHAWABTIS OF AKHENATEN

The mummiform figurines called *shawabtis* (or, in the New Kingdom, *ushabtis*—"answerers"), which were buried with the dead to substitute for him in labors he might be called upon to do in the afterlife, were not discarded in the Amarna Period. Although their significance may have changed somewhat, dozens of them were prepared for the burial of Akhenaten and deposited in the tomb destined for him at Tell el Amarna. Unlike those made for lesser folk, the King's *shawabtis* did not carry the hoe and basket to equip them for work in the fields of eternity, nor were they inscribed with the magical formula that converted them into proxies for the dead in such labor. Instead, the *shawabtis* of Akhenaten carried the crook and flail of kingship (Nos. 165, 167, 174, 175) or sometimes the *ankh*, signifying eternal life (Nos. 169, 170). Such inscriptions as survive are of the tersest, giving merely the King's titles and his two great names, that is his *prenomen*, or throne name, which he assumed on accession, and his *nomen*, or "Son-of-Re" name, which usually was given at birth, but which Akhenaten adopted only in regnal Year 6. Although some of the royal *shawabtis* were carefully finished (No. 175), it is evident that many of them were unfinished at the time of the King's death (No. 173), and all of them were probably broken in antiquity. Not a single complete one has survived. Many dozens of fragments have been found, however, and these, with the exception of some rough, unfinished ones discovered by Petrie in the workshops of Tell el Amarna (Petrie 1894, p. 17, no. 32; Pendlebury 1951, p. 81, pls. LXIII, 1–2; CV, 12), all come from the Royal Tomb. That tomb was first excavated and roughly cleared by Barsanti and Daressy in 1891, but by that time it had already been plundered and the greater part of the broken *shawabtis* it contained had been removed. Of these, more than two hundred fragments in stone and faience are now scattered throughout the world in public and private collections. Nos. 161 to 175 of this catalogue are a selection representing most of the surviving types, the ramifications of which have been discussed more fully on pp. 40–41.

In general, the King appears as mummiform, wearing either the *afnet* or *nemes* headcloth, more rarely a long tripartite wig; he is usually bearded. Exceptionally, No. 164 shows him in the dress of life and wearing some headdress, such as the Blue Crown or the short Nubian wig, that left the nape of his neck exposed. There is, however, some doubt about the findspot of this specimen; also it may not be a fragment of a *shawabti* but a statuette of a different type. A systematic study of Akhenaten's *shawabtis* will shortly be published by Dr. Geoffrey Martin of University College London, in his monograph on the Royal Tomb at Tell el Amarna.

No. 161
SHAWABTI HEAD WITH *NEMES*
Early Period

Collection: The Brooklyn Museum 33.52

The *nemes* headdress is without stripes; the uraeus lacks its coils. The eyes, sharply incised, slant toward the nose; the eyebrows are in relief. The mouth is full, with pendulous lower lip; the earlobe has a round perforation. The face is youthful and unlined.

Material: Yellow limestone.

Color: No trace.

Measurements: Height 6.4 cm. Width 8.6 cm. Depth 7.6 cm.

Condition: Fragmentary. Nose and most of chin, lower edge of *nemes* missing.

Provenance: Tell el Amarna; Royal Tomb.

Bibliography: Taggert 1933, p. 63, illus.; de Wit 1965, pp. 24–25, with fig. 12; Hofstra 1971, no. 6 but with Brooklyn 35.1875 illustrated in its place (fig., left).

No. 162
SHAWABTI HEAD WITH *AFNET*
Early Period
Collection: The Brooklyn Museum 33.53
This head, with heavy-lidded eyes and drooping mouth, has a melancholy expression, although the face is comparatively unlined, with only slight indications of furrows descending from the nostrils and corners of the mouth. The ears are large, with round perforations in the lobes. The mouth is firm, and from the slightly elongated chin depends the remnant of a long wide beard.
Material: Hard white limestone.
Color: No trace.
Measurements: Height 5.6 cm. Width 5.2 cm. Depth 4.9 cm. Height of face 2.7 cm.
Condition: Broken across neck at base of *afnet* headcloth; uraeus slightly chipped and nose considerably damaged; some pitting in stone.
Provenance: Tell el Amarna; Royal Tomb.

Bibliography: de Wit 1965, pp. 22, 24–25, with fig. 9 (incorrectly called 33.53C).

No. 163
SHAWABTI HEAD WITH LINED FACE
Early Period
Collection: The Brooklyn Museum 33.54
The head of the King is covered by the *afnet* headcloth with the usual uraeus on the brow and with traces of the coils of the serpent running toward the crown. The eyes, summarily carved, lend the face a brooding expression which is heightened by furrows running from ears to chin. The mouth is small, the earlobes perforated with round holes.
Material: Hard white limestone.
Color: Traces of red on lips, chin, and beard.
Measurements: Height 5.8 cm. Width 5.2 cm. Depth 4.8 cm. Height of face 2.9 cm.
Condition: Broken through neck to base of wig; only stump of beard remains; nose broken; right-hand side of wig chipped; some pitting in stone.
Provenance: Tell el Amarna; Royal Tomb.

Bibliography: de Wit 1965, pp. 22–24, with fig. 8 (incorrectly called 33.54A).

No. 164
SHAWABTI (?) WITH CARTOUCHES OF THE ATEN
Early Period
Collection: The Brooklyn Museum 35.1883
The present fragment of a figure of Akhenaten, comparable to a *shawabti* in size and pose, has been thought by some to be a miniature statue of the living King as ruler rather than a funerary piece. However that may be, it is the remnant of a fine sculpture in the early style showing Akhenaten with long neck thrust forward, heavy breasts, and well-rounded buttocks. The King carries crook and flail, and his chest, arms, and thighs are ornamented with cartouches of the Aten. Crown or headdress is wanting. There is no trace of a garment, but one may have been indicated in paint.
Material: Alabaster.
Color: Traces of blue in flail and cartouches.
Measurements: Visible height 8.7 cm. Width 7.6 cm. Depth 4.6 cm.
Condition: Fragment assembled from several pieces; some surface chips.
Provenance: Tell el Amarna; perhaps from the Royal Tomb. The piece was purchased in Cairo, at a time when other *shawabti* fragments from the Royal Tomb had passed into the Egyptian art market.

Bibliography: James 1973, no. 309 c.

No. 165
BUST FROM A *SHAWABTI*
Early Period (?)
Collection: Museum of Fine Arts,
Boston 65.466
The King is shown in the *afnet*
headdress, which has a uraeus
with *S*-coils on the brow and a
very narrow ribbed pigtail at the
rear. The eyes, slanting toward
the nose, are well defined, the
upper and lower lids and the tear
ducts being carefully incised. The
medial line of the mouth has a
pronounced double curve, and the

lips are full—the lower lip almost
pendulous. The unpierced ears are
very large. The top of the royal
crook appears on the left shoulder,
that of the flail on the right.
Material: Yellow limestone.
Color: No trace.
Measurements: Height 8.2 cm.
Width 7.1 cm. Depth ca. 4.3 cm.
Height of head ca. 4.9 cm. Height
of face 3 cm.
Condition: Fragmentary; only head
and shoulders preserved; face broken off and rejoined; beard, nose,
lips, and uraeus chipped.
Provenance: Tell el Amarna; Royal
Tomb.

Bibliography: Boston 1965, p. 223,
illus.

No. 166
FACE FROM A SMALL
SCULPTURE
Early Period
Collection: John S. Thacher, Washington, D.C.
Of what was evidently a sculpture
representing Akhenaten only part
of the face remains. The heavy-
lidded eyes and characteristic thick
lips are carefully worked in the
hard stone, and furrows descend
from the corners of the mouth. A
band across the forehead suggests
a *nemes* headdress or crown.
Material: Mottled pink and black
granite.
Color: No trace.
Measurements: Height 11.4 cm.
Width 8.5 cm. Depth 8 cm.
Condition: Partially preserved from
just over the brow to the chin;
back and top of head, left side of
face and nose, part of right ear,
and end of chin missing.
Provenance: Not known; perhaps
Tell el Amarna.
COMMENTARY: The condition of
this face, which does not exhibit
the same kind of injuries that were
inflicted on the hard-stone statuary found in the Great Temple,
probably indicates that the fragment is from a *shawabti* figure.
The latter were simply smashed
and did not suffer desecration by
the bruising and abrading of the
features and the excision of inscriptions. The figure from which
this face came was large, but so
were a number of cubit-high
shawabtis from the tomb of Tutankhamen specially commissioned
by friends of the dead King. The
size of this piece and of No. 175
may indicate that they are from
similar presentation sculptures.

Bibliography: None.

No. 167
SHAWABTI WITH CROOK AND
FLAIL
Early to Middle Period
Collection: The Brooklyn Museum
35.1531
A fragment from a *shawabti* preserved down to the elbows shows
the King in an *afnet* headdress
with uraeus and wide pigtail, holding the *heka* scepter in his left
hand and the flail in his right.
His eyebrows are coarsely carved
in relief, his eyes prominent (probably unfinished), his mouth exag-
geratedly large and full, his ears
large, with round perforations in
the lobes. He wears a long, wide
beard.
Material: Light red sandstone.
Color: No trace.
Measurements: Height 11.2 cm.
Width 8.4 cm. Depth 6.2 cm.
Height of face 3.2 cm.
Condition: Nose, uraeus, and hands
abraded; tip of beard missing; entire front surface weathered.
Provenance: Tell el Amarna; Royal
Tomb.

Bibliography: de Wit 1965, p. 26;
Hofstra 1971, no. 6, illus.

No. 168
GRANITE HEAD FROM A
SHAWABTI
Middle to Late Period
Collection: The Brooklyn Museum
35.1866
The King's head, in *nemes* headdress, is almost complete and
rather carefully modeled in the
hard stone. The eyebrows and eyelids are in relief, and the curve of
the slightly protruding lips is
sharply defined. The chin is not
overlong, but the jaw is deep, and
the earlobes show a round hole.
Only the stub of a beard remains.
Material: Pink and gray mottled
granite.
Color: No trace.
Measurements: Height 8 cm. Width
9 cm. Depth 7.7 cm. Height of
face 4.2 cm.
Condition: Lower edge of headcloth chipped; ends of pigtail and
beard wanting; tip of nose chipped.
Provenance: Tell el Amarna; Royal
Tomb.

Bibliography: Detroit 1963, no. 25;
de Wit 1965, p. 26; Hofstra 1971,
no. 6 but with Brooklyn 35.1870
illustrated in its place.

No. 169
SHAWABTI WITH MASSIVE WIG
Middle to Late Period
Collection: The Metropolitan Museum of Art, New York 47.57.2
(Rogers Fund, 1947)
This *shawabti* of the King wears a
wig with two locks falling over
the shoulders and a broad mass of
hair hanging at the back. A uraeus
is on the brow, and each of the
crossed hands holds an *ankh* by its
looped end. Below the arms is a
vertical inscription with titles and
the beginning of the King's prenomen. The face of the figure is
youthful and unlined; the eyes are
heavy-lidded and otherwise not
defined; the medial line of the lips
turns downward; the ears are very
large, with unpierced lobes.
Material: Light brown fine-grained
quartzite.
Color: Traces of blue on inscription.
Measurements: Height 14.7 cm.
Width at elbows 8.4 cm. Depth ca.
5.5 cm. Height of head 4.8 cm.
Height of face 3.2 cm. Intracolumnar width 2.2 cm.
Condition: Broken at level of chin
and rejoined; lower part of legs
and feet missing; minor chips on
nose, beard, and knuckles of both
hands.
Provenance: Tell el Amarna; Royal
Tomb.

Bibliography: Hayes 1959, p. 289,
fig. 178.

No. 170
FAIENCE *SHAWABTI*
Middle to Late Period
Collection: The Metropolitan Mu-
seum of Art, New York 66.99.37
(Fletcher Fund, 1966, and The
Guide Foundation, Inc., Gift, 1966)
A fragment of a royal *shawabti*
in blue faience is shown in the
afnet headdress with pronounced dia-
dem and long, narrow pigtail. The
King holds an *ankh* by its shaft in
each of his crossed hands.
Material: Glazed faience.
Color: Predominantly blue; *ankh*
signs white.
Measurements: Height 11.3 cm.
Width at elbows 7.6 cm. Depth
5.2 cm. Height of head 4.6 cm.
Height of face 2.2 cm.
Condition: Broken at level of el-
bows and lower part missing;
chipped on beard, nose, right hand,
and elbow.
Provenance: Tell el Amarna; Royal
Tomb. Formerly in the Gallatin
Collection.

Bibliography: Cooney 1953, p. 12,
no. 49.

No. 173
SHAWABTI HEAD WITH LARGE URAEUS
Late Period (?)

Collection: The Brooklyn Museum 35.1882

Head and shoulders of the King are preserved in this fragment of an unfinished royal *shawabti*. The large uraeus on the *afnet* headdress shows no details; the eyes and ears of the King's face are no more than suggested; only the medial line of the lips is sharply defined. All this gives the face a veiled and haunting quality that is purely accidental.

Material: Fine creamy-white limestone.

Color: No trace.

Measurements: Height 8.7 cm. Width 7 cm. Depth 5 cm. Height of face 3 cm.

Condition: Tip of nose and end of pigtail on back of headcloth missing.

Provenance: Tell el Amarna; Royal Tomb.

Bibliography: de Wit 1965, p. 26.

No. 171
SHAWABTI HEAD IN QUARTZITE
Late Period

Collection: The Brooklyn Museum 35.1867

The wide headcloth of the King is boldly carved as a frame for the familiar, rather melancholy features of Akhenaten, with his heavy-lidded eyes, full lips, and deep jaw slightly thrust forward. The prominent ears have oval holes in the lobes.

Material: Red quartzite.

Color: No trace.

Measurements: Height 9.2 cm. Width 9.3 cm. Depth 7.7 cm. Height of face 4.2 cm.

Condition: Head broken from body diagonally from level of lappets in front to base of skull in rear; uraeus and tip of nose chipped; part of chin and most of beard wanting.

Provenance: Tell el Amarna; Royal Tomb.

Bibliography: de Wit 1965, p. 26.

No. 172
SHAWABTI WITH ANKH SIGNS
Late Period (?)

Collection: The Brooklyn Museum 35.1870

This figurine is one of the more complete of the many *shawabtis* that have come from the Royal Tomb. It shows Akhenaten from top of head to hips, wearing the *nemes* headcloth and holding in his crossed hands two *ankh* signs by their loops. Below his arms is a vertical inscription giving the prenomen of the King. The profile of the figure suggests the exaggerated belly and buttocks characteristic of the royal family. The ears have small oval perforations.

Material: Mottled black granite.

Color: Traces of red on lips.

Measurements: Height 18.1 cm. Width 8.4 cm. Depth 5.5 cm. Height of face 3 cm.

Condition: Part of left side of head and left eye considerably damaged; left elbow chipped.

Provenance: Tell el Amarna; Royal Tomb.

Bibliography: de Wit 1965, p. 26; Hofstra 1971, no. 6, illus. (fig., center) in place of Brooklyn 35.1866 mentioned in text; James 1973, no. 405.

No. 175
HEAD AND SHOULDER OF A *SHAWABTI*

Late Period

Collection: Royal Scottish Museum, Edinburgh 1972.94

The King wears the *nemes* headdress, which retains traces of stripes indicated in paint. The uraeus on the brow has S-coils and a long body that disappears toward the crown of the head. The eyes, slanting slightly toward the nose, are fully carved, and the lobes of the prominent ears are pierced with oval holes. The lips are full, and a long, spatulate, ribbed beard descends from the chin. Remains of a flail are incised on the left shoulder.

Material: Red quartzite.

Color: Traces of pale blue stripes on headdress, of red on lips.

Measurements: Height 11.3 cm. Width 8.8 cm. Depth 7.8 cm. Height of head without beard 6.3 cm. Height of face 3.8 cm.

Condition: Broken diagonally from below left shoulder to tip of right ear, and lower part missing; tip of nose abraded.

Provenance: Tell el Amarna; Royal Tomb.

Bibliography: None.

No. 174
SHAWABTI WITH NAME OF KING

Late Period (?)

Collection: The Brooklyn Museum 37.499

A greatly damaged but once fine *shawabti* is of special interest as retaining the titles, nomen, and prenomen of Akhenaten, together with the epithet: "Great in [his lifetime]," in a column running down the front. The King wears a *nemes* headcloth striped in blue, and the carved inscription was also once painted in brilliant blue. He holds crook and flail in his crossed hands.

Material: Hard yellow limestone.

Color: Blue stripes on *nemes* and pigtail; traces of blue in hieroglyphs.

Measurements: Height 27.9 cm. Width 10.9 cm. Depth 7.7 cm.

Condition: Broken above knees and rejoined; face and upper part of head, right elbow, and lower legs and feet all missing; both hands damaged.

Provenance: Tell el Amarna; Royal Tomb.

Bibliography: James 1973, no. 380.

BIBLIOGRAPHY

Bibliographical entries marked with an asterisk (*) are selective. The publications chosen are primarily those that are most easily accessible to the greatest number of readers and/or that contain useful illustrations. Each entry not accompanied by an asterisk is either complete or contains, it is hoped, references to all works in which the piece in question is illustrated.

Aldred, 1953 — Aldred, C. "The Carnarvon Statuette of Amūn." *The Man* 53 (1953), pp. 194–95.

Aldred, 1956 — Aldred, C. "The Carnarvon Statuette of Amūn." *The Journal of Egyptian Archaeology* 42 (1956), pp. 3–7.

Aldred, 1957a — Aldred, C. "The End of the El-'Amārna Period." *The Journal of Egyptian Archaeology* 43 (1957), pp. 30–41.

Aldred, 1957b — Aldred, C. "Hair Styles and History." *The Metropolitan Museum of Art Bulletin* 15, no. 6 (1957), pp. 141–47.

Aldred, 1959a — Aldred, C. "The Beginning of the El-'Amārna Period." *The Journal of Egyptian Archaeology* 45 (1959), pp. 19–33.

Aldred, 1959b — Aldred, C. "The Gayer Anderson Jubilee Relief of Amenophis IV." *The Journal of Egyptian Archaeology* 45 (1959), p. 104.

Aldred, 1959c — Aldred, C. "Two Theban Notables during the Later Reign of Amenophis III." *Journal of Near Eastern Studies* 18 (1959), pp. 113–20.

Aldred, 1961a — Aldred, C. *The Egyptians.* Ancient Peoples and Places, 18. London, 1961.

Aldred, 1961b — Aldred, C. *New Kingdom Art in Ancient Egypt during the Eighteenth Dynasty, 1570 to 1320 B.C.* 2d ed., rev. and enl. London, 1961.

Aldred, 1961c — Aldred, C. "The Tomb of Akhenaten at Thebes." With Appendix by Dr. A. Sandison. *The Journal of Egyptian Archaeology* 47 (1961), pp. 41–65.

Aldred, 1962 — Aldred, C., and Sandison, A. "The Pharaoh Akhenaten; A Problem in Egyptology and Pathology." *Bulletin of the History of Medicine* 36, no. 4 (1962), pp. 293–316.

Aldred, 1968 — Aldred, C. *Akhenaten, Pharaoh of Egypt; A New Study.* London, 1968.

Aldred, 1970 — Aldred, C. "The Foreign Gifts Offered to Pharaoh." *The Journal of Egyptian Archaeology* 56 (1970), pp. 105–116.

Aldred, 1971 — Aldred, C. *Egypt; The Amarna Period and the End of the Eighteenth Dynasty.* Cambridge Ancient History, rev. ed., fasc. 71. Cambridge, 1971.

America–Israel Cultural Foundation, 1968 — New York, America–Israel Cultural Foundation, 1968. *From the Lands of the Bible; Arts and Artifacts. An Archaeological Exhibition in Celebration of Israel's Twentieth Anniversary.* . . . New York, 1968.

Amherst, 1921 — London, Sotheby & Co. *Catalogue of the Amherst Collection of Egyptian & Oriental Antiquities, Which Will Be Sold by Auction . . . on Monday, the 13th of June, 1921, and Four Following Days.* . . . London, 1921.

Anthes, 1952 — Anthes, R. *Die Maat des Echnaton von Amarna.* Supplement to the Journal of the American Oriental Society, 14. Baltimore, 1952.

Anthes, 1954 — Anthes, R. *The Head of Queen Nofretete.* Translated by K. Bauer. Berlin, 1954.

Arab Information Center, 1967 — "Rare Collection [the Gallatin Collection] Portrays Egyptian Ingenuity." *The Arab World* 13, no. 2 (February, 1967), pp. [8]–[9] and cover illus.

Badawy, 1968 — Badawy, A. *A History of Egyptian Architecture.* [Vol. 3] *The Empire (the New Kingdom) from the Eighteenth Dynasty to the End of the Twentieth Dynasty, 1580–1085 B.C.* Berkeley and Los Angeles, 1968.

Barguet, 1962 — Barguet, P. *Le temple d'Amon-Rê à Karnak; essai d'exégèse.* Cairo, Institut Français d'Archéologie Orientale. Recherches d'archéologie, de philologie, et d'histoire, 21. Cairo, 1962.

Barta, 1966 — Barta, W. "Die neuerworbenen Relieffragmente der Ägyptischen Staatssammlung München aus der Zeit des Königs Amenophis IV.–Echnaton." *Pantheon* 24, no. 1 (1966), pp. 1–9.

Basel, 1953 — Basel, Kunsthalle. *Schaetze altaegyptischer Kunst.* [Ausstellung] 27. Juni–13. Sept. 1953. Basel, 1953.

Bennett, 1965 — Bennett, J. "Notes on the 'aten'." *The Journal of Egyptian Archaeology* 51 (1965), pp. 207–209.

Berlin, 1899 — Berlin, Museen. *Ausführliches Verzeichnis der ägyptischen Altertümer und Gipsabgüsse.* 2d ed. Berlin, 1899.

Berlin, 1924 — Berlin, Museen. *Ägyptische Inschriften aus den Staatlichen Museen zu Berlin.* Vol. 2, *Inschriften des Neuen Reichs; Indizes zu Band 1 und 2.* Edited by G. Roeder. Leipzig, 1924.

Berlin East, 1954 — Berlin, Museen. *Ägypten und das Berliner Ägyptische Museum.* Berlin, 1954.

Berlin East, 1961 — Berlin, Museen. *Führer durch das Berliner Ägyptische Museum.* Berlin, 1961.

Berlin West, 1967 — Berlin, Museen. *Ägyptisches Museum Berlin. Östlicher Stülerbau am Schloss Charlottenburg.* Berlin, 1967.

Bille–de Mot, 1937 — Bille–de Mot. E. "Les objets de Tell el Amarnah aux Musées Royaux d'Art et d'Histoire." *Bulletin des Musées Royaux d'Art et d'Histoire,* series 3, 9, no. 4 (1937), pp. [81]–86.

Bille–de Mot, 1966 — Bille–de Mot. E. *The Age of Akhenaten.* New York and Toronto, 1966.

Bissing, 1905–28 — Bissing, W. von. *Das Re-Heiligtum des Königs Ne-Woser-Re (Rathures).* 3 vols. Berlin and Leipzig, 1905–1928.

Bissing and Reach, 1906 — Bissing, W. von, and Reach, M. "Bericht über die malerische Technik der Hawata Fresken im Museum von Kairo." *Annales du Service des Antiquités de l'Egypte* 7 (1906), pp. [64]–70.

Boeser, 1911 — Leiden, Rijksmuseum van Oudheden. *Beschreibung der aegyptischen Sammlung des Niederländischen Reichsmuseums der Altertümer in Leiden.* Compiled by P. Boeser. Vol. 4, *Die Denkmäler des Neuen Reiches.* The Hague, 1911.

Bologna, 1961 — Bologna, Museo Civico. *L'Egitto antico nelle collezioni dell'Italia settentrionale, 31 ottobre–3 dicembre 1961.* 2d ed. Bologna, 1961.

Borchardt, 1911 — Borchardt, L. *Der Porträtkopf der Königin Teje im Besitz von Dr. James Simon in Berlin.* Berlin, Deutsche Orient–Gesellschaft. Ausgrabungen . . . in Tell El-Amarna, 1. Leipzig, 1911.

Borchardt, 1912 — Borchardt, L. "Ausgrabungen in Tell el-Amarna 1911/12." *Mitteilungen der Deutschen Orient–Gesellschaft zu Berlin* 50 (1912), pp. 1–40.

Borchardt, 1917 — Borchardt, L. "Aus der Arbeit an den Funden von Tell el-Amarna." *Mitteilungen der Deutschen Orient–Gesellschaft zu Berlin* 57 (1917), pp. 1–32.

Borchardt, 1923 — Borchardt, L. *Porträts der Königin Nofret-ete aus den Grabungen 1912/13 in Tell el-Amarna.* Berlin, Deutsche Orient–Gesellschaft. Ausgrabungen . . . in Tell el-Amarna, 3. Leipzig, 1923.

Boston, 1956 — Boston, Museum of Fine Arts. *Handbook of the Museum of Fine Arts, Boston.* 31st ed. Boston, 1956.

Boston, 1962 — Boston, Museum of Fine Arts. *Eighty-Seventh Annual Report for the Year 1962.* Boston [1963].

Boston, 1964a — Boston, Museum of Fine Arts. *Illustrated Handbook.* Boston, 1964.

Boston, 1964b — Smith, W. S. "Department of Egyptian Art." In Boston, Museum of Fine Arts, *Eighty-Ninth Annual Report for the Year 1964,* pp. [48]–56. Boston [1965].

Boston, 1965 — Terrace, E. "Some Recent Accessions." *Bulletin of the Museum of Fine Arts, Boston* 63, no. 334 (1965), p. 223.

Boston, 1967a — Boston, Museum of Fine Arts. *Egyptian Art, Museum of Fine Arts, Boston.* Boston, 1967.

Boston, 1967b — Boston, Museum of Fine Arts. *The Museum Year: 1967; The Ninety-Second Annual Report of the Museum of Fine Arts, Boston.* Boston [1968].

Boston, 1972 — Boston, Museum of Fine Arts. *The Rathbone Years; Masterpieces Acquired for the Museum of Fine Arts, Boston, 1955–1972 and for the St. Louis Art Museum, 1940–1955.* Boston, 1972.

Bothmer, 1962 — Bothmer, B. "Living Gifts from the World of the Dead." *Arts in Virginia* 62, 3, no. 1 (Fall, 1962), pp. 22–29.

Bouriant, 1903 — Bouriant, U., et al. *Monuments pour servir à l'étude du culte d'Atenou en Egypte.* Vol. 1, *Les tombes de Khouitatonou.* Cairo, Institut Français d'Archéologie Orientale. Mémoires, 8. Cairo, 1903.

Breasted, 1948 — Breasted, J. *A History of Egypt from the Earliest Times to the Persian Conquest.* 2d ed. London, 1948.

British Museum, 1939 — British Museum, Department of Egyptian and Assyrian Antiquities. *Hieroglyphic Texts from Egyptian Stelae &c., in the British Museum.* Vol. 8. Edited by I. E. S. Edwards. London, 1939.

British Museum, 1964 — *A General Introductory Guide to the Egyptian Collections in the British Museum.* London, 1964.

British Museum, 1972 — British Museum. *Treasures of Tutankhamun.* [Loan Exhibition]. Introduction by I. E. S. Edwards. London, 1972.

Brooklyn, 1952 — *Egyptian Art in The Brooklyn Museum Collection.* Brooklyn, 1952.

Brooklyn, 1956 — The Brooklyn Museum. *Five Years of Collecting Egyptian Art, 1951–1956. Catalogue of an Exhibition Held at The Brooklyn Museum 11 December, 1956 to 17 March, 1957.* Brooklyn, 1956. Reprinted 1969.

Brooklyn, 1962 — *The Brooklyn Museum Annual I, 1959–1960.* Brooklyn, 1962.

Brooklyn, 1963 — *The Brooklyn Museum Annual II–III, 1960–1962.* Brooklyn, 1963.

Brooklyn, 1964 — *The Brooklyn Museum Annual IV, 1962–1963.* Brooklyn, 1964.

Brooklyn, 1966a — *The Brooklyn Museum Annual VI, 1964–1965.* Brooklyn, 1966.

Brooklyn, 1966b — *The Brooklyn Museum Annual VII, 1965–1966.* Brooklyn, 1966.

Brooklyn, 1966c — *The Pomerance Collection of Ancient Art. [Catalogue of an Exhibition Held at The Brooklyn Museum, June 14 to October 2, 1966].* Brooklyn, 1966.

Brooklyn, 1967 — *The Brooklyn Museum Handbook.* Brooklyn, 1967.

Brooklyn, 1968 — *Ancient Egyptian Glass and Glazes in The Brooklyn Museum.* By Elizabeth Riefstahl. Wilbour Monographs —I. Brooklyn, 1968.

Brooklyn, 1969a — *The Brooklyn Museum Annual IX, 1967–1968.* Brooklyn, 1969.

Brooklyn, 1969b — *The Brooklyn Museum Annual X, 1968–1969.* Brooklyn, 1969.

Brooklyn, 1970 — The Brooklyn Museum. *Brief Guide to the Department of Ancient Art.* By B. Bothmer and J. Keith. The Brooklyn Museum Guide, 5. Brooklyn, 1970.

Brooklyn, 1971 — *The Brooklyn Museum Annual XII, 1970–1971.* Brooklyn, 1971.

Brooklyn Institute, 1961 — Brooklyn Institute of Arts and Sciences. *Annual Report, 1960–1961.* Brooklyn, 1961.

Brunner–Traut, 1956 — Brunner–Traut, E. *Die altägyptischen Scherbenbilder (Bildostraka) der deutschen Museen und Sammlungen.* Wiesbaden, 1956.

Brussels, 1934a — Brussels. Musées Royaux d'Art et d'Histoire. *Département égyptien. Album.* Brussels, 1934.

Brussels, 1934b — "Musée." *Chronique d'Égypte* 9, no. 17 (1934), pp. 23–24.

Brussels, 1963a — Brussels, Koninklijke Musea voor Kunst en Geschiedenis. *Oud-Egyptische Kunst in Twintig Beelden*. By C. de Wit. Brussels, 1963.

Brussels, 1963b — Brussels, Musées Royaux d'Art et d'Histoire. *Vingt oeuvres de l'Égypte ancienne*. By P. Gilbert. Brussels, 1963.

Brussels, 1969 — Brussels, Musées Royaux d'Art et d'Histoire. *Présentation de la collection égyptienne*. By P. Gilbert. Brussels, 1969.

Budge, 1923 — Budge, E. *Tutānkhāmen; Amenism, Atenism and Egyptian Monotheism . . .* London, 1923.

Buffalo, 1938 — "Portfolio for February; Sculpture at Buffalo's Albright Gallery." *Magazine of Art* 31, no. 2 (1938), pp. 90–93.

Bull, 1926 — Bull, L. "Two Letters to Akhnaton King of Egypt." *The Bulletin of The Metropolitan Museum of Art* 21 (1926), pp. 169–76.

Burlington, 1922 — London, Burlington Fine Arts Club. *Catalogue of an Exhibition of Ancient Egyptian Art*. London, 1922.

Cairo, 1949 — *Encyclopédie photographique de l'art.* [Vol. 4] *Le Musée du Caire*. Photographs by A. Vigneau. Text by E. Drioton. Paris, 1949.

Cambridge, 1971 — Cambridge University, Fitzwilliam Museum. *Handbook to the Fitzwilliam Museum, Cambridge*. Cambridge, 1971.

Capart, 1908 — Capart, J. "Une importante donation d'antiquités égyptiennes." *Bulletin des Musées Royaux des Arts Décoratifs et Industriels à Bruxelles*, series 2, 1, no. 10 (October, 1908), pp. 85–86.

Capart, 1909 — Capart, J. *L'art égyptien. Choix de documents accompagnés d'indications bibliographiques*. Series 1. Brussels and Paris, 1909.

Capart, 1911 — Capart, J. *Donation d'antiquités égyptiennes aux Musées Royaux de Bruxelles*. Brussels, 1911.

Capart, 1927 — Capart, J. *Documents pour servir à l'étude de l'art égyptien.* Vol. 1. Paris, 1927.

Capart, 1936a — Capart, J. "Les limites de l'art égyptien." *Bulletin de l'Office International des Instituts d'Archéologie et d'Histoire de l'Art* 7 (1936), pp. 3–[20].

Capart, 1936b — Capart, J., ed. *Travels in Egypt (December 1880 to May 1891). Letters of Charles Edwin Wilbour.* Brooklyn, 1936.

Capart, 1942 — Capart, J. *L'art égyptien. Deuxième partie. Choix de documents accompagnés d'indications bibliographiques.* Vol. 3, *Les arts graphiques.* Brussels, 1942.

Capart, 1949 — Capart, J. *Pour faire aimer l'art égyptien.* Brussels, 1949.

Capart, 1957 — Capart, J. "Dans le studio d'un artiste." *Chronique d'Égypte* 32, no. 64 (1957), pp. 199–217.

Carter, 1927 — Carter, H. *The Tomb of Tut.ankh.Amen Discovered by the Late Earl of Carnarvon and Howard Carter.* Vol. 2. London, 1927.

Carter, 1933 — Carter, H. *The Tomb of Tut.ankh.Amen Discovered by the Late Earl of Carnarvon and Howard Carter.* Vol. 3. London, 1933.

Chassinat, 1901 — Chassinat, E. "Une tombe inviolée de la XVIIIe dynastie découverte aux environs de Médinet el-Gorab dans le Fayoûm." *Bulletin de l'Institut Français d'Archéologie Orientale* 1 (1901), pp. [225]–234.

Chassinat, 1922 — Chassinat, E. *Les antiquités égyptiennes de la collection Fouquet.* Paris, 1922.

Clère, 1968 — Clère, J. J. "Nouveaux fragments de scènes du jubilé d'Amenophis IV." *Revue d'Égyptologie* 20 (1968), pp. 51–54.

Cleveland, 1966 — *Handbook. The Cleveland Museum of Art/1966.* Cleveland, 1966.

Comstock, 1941 — Comstock, H. "The Connoisseur in America." *Connoisseur* 108, no. 479 (1941), pp. 28–33.

Cooney, 1938 — Cooney, J. "Accessions to the Egyptian Department." *The Brooklyn Museum Quarterly* 25 (1938), pp. 92–97.

Cooney, 1939 — Cooney, J. "A Relief from Tell el-Amarna." *The Art Quarterly* 2, no. 1 (1939), pp. 67–75.

Cooney, 1949 — Cooney, J. "A Magical Egyptian Fish." *The Brooklyn Museum Bulletin* 11, no. 1 (1949), pp. 1–4, with fig. 1 facing p. 1.

Cooney, 1953 — Cooney, J. "Egyptian Art in the Collection of Albert Gallatin." *Journal of Near Eastern Studies* 12 (1953), pp. 1–19.

Cooney, 1965 — Cooney, J. *Amarna Reliefs from Hermopolis in American Collections.* Brooklyn, 1965.

Cooney, 1968 — Cooney, J. "Amarna Art in the Cleveland Museum." *Bulletin of The Cleveland Museum of Art* 55, no. 1 (1968), pp. 3–17 and cover illus.

Cooney and Simpson, 1951 — Cooney, J., and Simpson, W. "An Architectural Fragment from Amarna." *The Brooklyn Museum Bulletin* 12, no. 4 (1951), pp. 1–12 and cover illus.

Coremans, 1936 — Coremans, P. "Les rayons ultraviolets, leur nature, leurs applications en technique muséographique." *Bulletin des Musées Royaux d'Art et d'Histoire*, series 3, 8, no. 3 (1936), pp. [50]–55.

Dambach and Wallert, 1966 — Dambach, M., and Wallert, I. "Das Tilapia–Motiv in der altägyptischen Kunst." *Chronique d'Égypte* 41 (1966), pp. 273–94.

Davies, 1903–08 — Davies, N. de G. *The Rock Tombs of El Amarna.* 6 vols. Egypt Exploration Society, Archaeological Survey of Egypt. Memoirs, 13–18. London, 1903–1908.

Davies, 1903 — Davies, N. de G. *The Rock Tombs of El Amarna.* Part 1, *The Tomb of Meryra.* Egypt Exploration Society, Archaeological Survey of Egypt. Memoirs, 13. London, 1903.

Davies, 1905a — Davies, N. de G. *The Rock Tombs of El Amarna.* Part 2, *The Tombs of Panehesy and Meryra II.* Egypt Exploration Society, Archaeological Survey of Egypt. Memoirs, 14. London, 1905.

Davies, 1905b — Davies, N. de G. *The Rock Tombs of El Amarna.* Part 3, *The Tombs of Huya and Ahmes.* Egypt Exploration Society, Archaeological Survey of Egypt. Memoirs, 15. London, 1905.

Davies, 1906 — Davies, N. de G. *The Rock Tombs of El Amarna.* Part 4, *Tombs of Penthu, Mahu, and Others.* Egypt Exploration Society, Archaeological Survey of Egypt. Memoirs, 16. London, 1906.

Davies, 1908a — Davies, N. de G. *The Rock Tombs of El Amarna.* Part 5, *Smaller Tombs and Boundary Stelae.* Egypt Exploration Society, Archaeological Survey of Egypt. Memoirs, 17. London, 1908.

Davies, 1908b — Davies, N. de G. *The Rock Tombs of El Amarna.* Part 6. *Tombs of Parennefer, Tutu, and Aÿ.* Egypt Exploration Society, Archaeological Survey of Egypt. Memoirs, 18. London, 1908.

Davies, 1921 — Davies, N. de G. "Mural Paintings in the City of Akhetaten." *The Journal of Egyptian Archaeology* 7 (1921), pp. 1–7.

Davies, 1923a — Davies, N. de G. "Akhenaten at Thebes." *The Journal of Egyptian Archaeology* 9 (1923), pp. 136–45.

Davies, 1923b — Davies, N. de G. "The Graphic Work of the Expedition." *The Bulletin of The Metropolitan Museum of Art. Part 2, The Metropolitan Museum of Art. The Egyptian Expedition 1922–1923* (December, 1923), pp. 40–53.

Davies, 1926 — Davies, N. M. *The Tomb of Huy, Viceroy of Nubia in the Reign of Tut'ankhamūn (No. 40).* With explanatory text by A. Gardiner. Egypt Exploration Society, The Theban Tombs Series. Memoirs, 4. London, 1926.

Davies, 1933 — Davies, N. de G. *The Tomb of Nefer-hotep at Thebes.* Vol. 1. New York, The Metropolitan Museum of Art, Egyptian Expedition. Publications, 9. New York, 1933.

Davies, 1936 — Davies, N. M., and Gardiner, A. *Ancient Egyptian Paintings.* 3 vols. Chicago, 1936.

Davies, 1941 — Davies, N. de G. *The Tomb of the Vizier Ramose.* Mond Excavations at Thebes, 1. London, 1941.

Davies, 1943 — Davies, N. de G. *The Tomb of Rekh-mi-Rē at Thebes.* New York, The Metropolitan Museum of Art, Egyptian Expedition. Publications, 11. New York, 1943.

Davies, 1962 — Davies, N. M. *Tutankhamun's Painted Box. Reproduced in Colour from the Original in the Cairo Museum.* Explanatory text by A. Gardiner. Oxford, 1962.

Davis, 1910 — Davis, T., et al. *The Tomb of Queen Tiyi.* Theodore M. Davis' Excavations: Bibân el Molûk, 6. London, 1910.

Davis, 1912 — Davis, T., et al. *The Tombs of Harmhabi and Touatânkhamanou.* Theodore M. Davis' Excavations: Bibân el Molûk, 7. London, 1912.

Delbrück, 1912 — Delbrück, R. *Antike Porträts.* Bonn, 1912.

Desroches–Noblecourt, 1961 — Desroches–Noblecourt, C. *L'art égyptien.* Paris, 1961.

Desroches–Noblecourt, 1963 — Desroches–Noblecourt, C. *Tutankhamen; Life and Death of a Pharaoh.* New York, 1963.

Desroches–Noblecourt, 1968 — Desroches–Noblecourt, C. "La cueillette du raisin à la fin de l'époque amarnienne; Toutankhamon fut-il portraituré sous l'aspect d'un petit prince?" *The Journal of Egyptian Archaeology* 54 (1968), pp. 82–88.

Detroit, 1963 — Detroit Institute of Arts. *Life and Art in Ancient Egypt . . . July 9 through September 1, 1963.* Detroit, 1963.

Detroit, 1967 — "Appendix VI, Accessions January 1 to December 31, 1966." *Bulletin of The Detroit Institute of Arts* 46, no. 1 (1967), p. 20 and illus. on p. 15.

Detroit, 1969 — Detroit Institute of Arts. *A Check List of Ancient European, American and Canadian Sculpture in The Detroit Institute of Arts,* October, 1969. Detroit, 1969.

de Wit, 1946 — de Wit, C. *Oud-Egyptische Kunst; Een Inleiding.* Antwerp, 1946.

de Wit, 1950 — de Wit, C. *La statuaire de Tell el Amarna.* Brussels, 1950.

de Wit, 1965 — de Wit, C. "Une tête d'oushebti d'Aménophis IV au Musée du Cinquantenaire." *Chronique d'Égypte* 40, no. 79 (1965), pp. 20–27.

Doresse, 1955 — Doresse, M. "Les temples atoniens de la région thébaine." *Orientalia* 24 (1955), pp. 113–35.

Drioton and Du Bourguet, 1965 — Drioton, E., and Du Bourguet, P. *Les pharaons à la conquête de l'art.* Paris, 1965.

Duke, 1965 — Duke University, Durham, North Carolina, Department of Art. *A Survey of Egyptian Sculpture from the Old Kingdom through the Greco–Roman Period; A Loan Exhibition Held in the Gallery, Department of Art, Duke University . . . October 16–November 28, 1965.* Durham, 1965.

Dunham, 1936 — Dunham, D. "Note on Some Recent Acquisitions from Tell-el-Amarna." *Bulletin of the Museum of Fine Arts, Boston* 34, no. 202 (1936), pp. 22–25.

Dunham, 1937 — Dunham, D. "Some New Objects from Tell-el-Amarna." *Bulletin of the Museum of Fine Arts, Boston* 35, no. 207 (1937), pp. 11–14.

Dunham, 1958 — Dunham, D. *The Egyptian Department and Its Excavations.* Boston, 1958.

Engelbach, 1915 — Engelbach, R., et al. *Riqqeh and Memphis.* Vol. 6. British School of Archaeology in Egypt and Egyptian Research Account. Nineteenth Year, 1913. [Publications, 25]. London, 1915.

Engelbach, 1931 — Engelbach, R. "The So-Called Coffin of Akhenaten." *Annales du Service des Antiquités de l'Egypte* 31 (1931), pp. [98]–114.

Erman, 1936 — Erman, A. *Die Welt am Nil; Bilder aus dem alten Ägypten.* Leipzig, 1936.

Essen, 1961 — *5000 Jahre aegyptische Kunst. 15. Mai bis 27. August 1961 in Villa Hügel, Essen.* Essen, 1961.

Evans, 1928   Evans, A. *The Palace of Minos; A Comparative Account of the Successive Stages of the Early Cretan Civilization As Illustrated by the Discoveries at Knossos.* Vol. 2. part 2. *Town-Houses in Knossos of the New Era and Restored West Palace Section, with Its State Approach.* London, 1928.

Fairman, 1951   Fairman, H. "Chapter X, The Inscriptions." In Pendlebury, J. *The City of Akhenaten.* Part 3, *The Central City and the Official Quarters. The Excavations at Tell el-Amarna during the Seasons 1926–1927 and 1931–1936.* Vol. 1, *Text.* Egypt Exploration Society. Memoirs, 44. London, 1951.

Fairman, 1961   Fairman, H. "Once Again the So-Called Coffin of Akhenaten." *The Journal of Egyptian Archaeology* 47 (1961), pp. 25–40.

Fairman, 1972   Fairman, H. "Tutankhamun and the End of the 18th Dynasty." *Antiquity* 46, no. 181 (1972), pp. 15–18.

Fakhry, 1943   Fakhry, A. "A Note on the Tomb of Kheruef at Thebes." *Annales du Service des Antiquités de l'Egypte* 42 (1943), pp. [449]–508.

Fazzini, 1972   Fazzini, R. "Some Egyptian Reliefs in Brooklyn." *Miscellanea Wilbouriana* 1 (1972), pp. 33–70.

Fechheimer, 1922a   Fechheimer, H. *Kleinplastik der Ägypter.* Die Kunst des Ostens, 3. Berlin, 1922.

Fechheimer, 1922b   Fechheimer, H. *Die Plastik der Ägypter.* Die Kunst des Ostens, 1. Berlin, 1922.

Finch, 1971   Finch, C. "The Archaeolophiles: Leon and Harriet Pomerance." *Auction* 4, no. 5 (1971), pp. 35–38.

Firchow, 1959   Firchow, O. *Aegyptische Plastik.* Leipzig, 1959.

Fischer, 1965   Fischer, H. "Anatomy in Egyptian Art." *Apollo* 82, no. 43 (1965), pp. 169–75.

Fischer, 1967   Fischer, H. "The Gallatin Egyptian Collection." *The Metropolitan Museum of Art Bulletin* 25, no. 7 (1967), pp. 253–[263].

Fouquet, 1922a   Fouquet, D. *Les antiquités égyptiennes de la collection Fouquet.* Text by E. Chassinat. Paris, 1922.

Fouquet, 1922b   Paris. Galerie Georges Petit. *Art égyptien et égypto-arabe. Art grec et romain. Très belles sculptures égyptiennes en pierre des XIIe, XVIIIe et XXIe dynasties. Modèles de sculpteur de l'époque saite. Trouvaille de Tell-el-Moqdam (Léontopolis) . . . Composant la première vente de la collection du Docteur Fouquet, du Caire . . . les lundi 12, mardi 13 et mercredi 14 juin 1922. . . .* Paris, 1922.

Frankfort, 1927   Frankfort, H. "Preliminary Report on the Excavations at Tell el'Amarnah, 1926–7." *The Journal of Egyptian Archaeology* 13 (1927), pp. 209–18.

Frankfort, 1929   Frankfort, H., ed. *The Mural Painting of el-'Amarneh.* London, 1929.

Frankfort and Pendlebury, 1933   Frankfort, H., and Pendlebury, J. *The City of Akhenaten.* Part 2, *The North Suburb and the Desert Altars. The Excavations at Tell El Amarna during the Seasons 1926–1932.* Egypt Exploration Society. Memoirs, 40. London, 1933.

Gallatin, 1950   Gallatin, A. *The Pursuit of Happiness; The Abstract and Brief Chronicles of the Time.* New York, 1950.

Gamer–Wallert, 1970   Gamer–Wallert, I. *Fische und Fischkulte im Alten Ägypten.* Ägyptologische Abhandlungen, 21. Wiesbaden, 1970.

Gardiner, 1947   Gardiner, A. *Ancient Egyptian Onomastica.* Text. Vol. 1. Oxford, 1947.

Gardiner, 1953   Gardiner, A. "The Coronation of King Haremhab." *The Journal of Egyptian Archaeology* 39 (1953), pp. 13–31.

Gardiner, 1961   Gardiner, A. *Egypt of the Pharaohs, an Introduction.* Oxford, 1961.

Gauthier, 1912   Gauthier, H. *Le livre des rois d'Égypte.* Vol. 2, *De la XIIIe à la fin de la XVIIIe dynastie.* Cairo, Institut Français d'Archéologie Orientale. Mémoires, 18. Cairo, 1912.

Gerhardt, 1967   Gerhardt, K. "Waren die Köpfchen der Echnaton-Töchter künstlich deformiert?" *Zeitschrift für ägyptische Sprache und Altertumskunde* 94 (1967), pp. 50–62.

Ghalioungui, 1947   Ghalioungui, P. "A Medical Study of Akhenaten." *Annales du Service des Antiquités de l'Egypte* 47 (1947), pp. 29–46.

Gilbert, 1966   Gilbert, P. *Couleurs de l'Egypte ancienne.* 2d ed. Brussels, 1966.

Giles, 1970   Giles, F. *Ikhnaton; Legend and History.* London, 1970.

Griffith, 1918   Griffith, F. "The Jubilee of Akhenaton." *The Journal of Egyptian Archaeology* 5 (1918), pp. 61–63.

Griffith, 1924   Griffith, F. "Excavations at El-'Amarnah, 1923–1924." *The Journal of Egyptian Archaeology* 10 (1924), pp. 299–305.

Griffith, 1931   Griffith, F. "Excavations at Tell el-'Amarneh, 1923–4. A. Statuary." *The Journal of Egyptian Archaeology* 17 (1931), pp. 179–84.

Groenewegen–Frankfort, 1951   Groenewegen–Frankfort, H. *Arrest and Movement; An Essay on Space and Time in the Representational Art of the Ancient Near East.* London, 1951. Reprinted New York, 1951.

Gunn, 1923   Gunn, B. "Notes on the Aten and His Names." *The Journal of Egyptian Archaeology* 9 (1923), pp. 168–76.

Habachi, 1965   Habachi, L. "Varia from the Reign of King Akhenaten." *Mitteilungen des Deutschen Archäologischen Instituts, Abteilung Kairo* 20 (1965), pp. [70]–92.

Hall, 1927   Hall, H. "A 3000-Years-Old Egyptian Portrait Gallery; Casts of the Living and the Dead from 'The House of the Sculptor' at Tell-el-Amarna." *The Illustrated London News* (March 19, 1927), pp. 470–71.

Hall, 1968   Hall, E. "Some Ancient Egyptian Sculpture in American Museums." *Apollo* 88, no. 77 (1968), pp. 4–17.

Hamann, 1944   Hamann, R. *Ägyptische Kunst; Wesen und Geschichte.* Berlin, 1944.

Hamburg, 1965   Hamburg, Museum für Kunst und Gewerbe. *Ägyptische Kunst aus der Zeit des Königs Echnaton.* [Ausstellung vom 14. Mai bis zum 27. Juni 1965]. Hamburg, 1965.

Hamza, 1941   Hamza, M. "The Alabaster Canopic Box of Akhenaton and Royal Alabaster Canopic Boxes of the XVIIIth Dynasty." *Annales du Service des Antiquités de l'Égypte* 40 (1941), pp. [537]–[552].

Harper, 1971   Harper, P., et al. "Origin and Influence. Cultural Contacts: Egypt, the Ancient Near East, and the Classical World." *The Metropolitan Museum of Art Bulletin* 29, no. 7 (1971), pp. [318]–326.

Harris, 1966   Harris, J. R. *Egyptian Art.* London, 1966.

Harrison, 1966   Harrison, R. "An Anatomical Examination of the Pharaonic Remains Purported to Be Akhenaten." *The Journal of Egyptian Archaeology* 52 (1966), pp. 95–119.

Harvard, 1954   Harvard University, William Hayes Fogg Art Museum. *Ancient Art in American Private Collections. A Loan Exhibition at the Fogg Art Museum of Harvard University, December 28, 1954–February 15, 1955. Arranged in Honor of the Seventy-Fifth Anniversary of the Archaeological Institute of America.* Cambridge, Massachusetts, 1954.

Hassan, 1953   Hassan, S. *The Great Sphinx and Its Secrets; Historical Studies in the Light of Recent Excavations.* Excavations at Giza, 8, 1936–37. Cairo, 1953.

Hawkes, 1965   Hawkes, J. *Pharaohs of Egypt.* New York, 1965.

Hayes, 1951   Hayes, W. "Inscriptions from the Palace of Amenhotep III." *Journal of Near Eastern Studies* 10 (1951), pp. 156–83.

Hayes, 1959   Hayes, W. *The Scepter of Egypt; A Background for the Study of the Egyptian Antiquities in The Metropolitan Museum of Art.* Vol. 2, *The Hyksos Period and the New Kingdom (1675–1080 B.C.).* Cambridge, Massachusetts, 1959.

Hayes, 1962   Hayes, W. *Egypt; Internal Affairs from Tuthmosis I to the Death of Amenophis III.* Part 1. Cambridge Ancient History, rev. ed., fasc. 10. Cambridge, 1962.

Hearst, 1939   London, Sotheby & Co. *Catalogue of the Important Collection of Antiquities, the Property of William Randolph Hearst, Esq. . . . , Which Will Be Sold at Auction . . . on Tuesday, July 11th, 1939, and Following Day.* London, 1939.

Helck, 1958   Helck, H. *Zur Verwaltung des Mittleren und Neuen Reichs.* Probleme der Ägyptologie, 3. Leiden, 1958.

Hermann and Schwan, 1940   Hermann, A., and Schwan, W. *Ägyptische Kleinkunst.* Berlin, 1940.

Hoffmann, 1964a   Hoffmann, H., ed. *The Beauty of Ancient Art; Exhibition of the Norbert Schimmel Collection, November 15, 1964, to February 14, 1965. Fogg Art Museum of Harvard University.* Mainz, 1964.

Hoffmann, 1964b   Hoffmann, H. "A Major American Collection of Ancient Art." *Apollo* 80, no. 32 (1964), pp. 270–83.

Hofstra, 1971   Hempstead, New York, Hofstra University, Emily Lowe Gallery. *Art of Ancient Egypt; A Selection from The Brooklyn Museum . . . February 22 through April 6, 1971.* Hempstead, 1971.

Hornemann, 1966   Hornemann, B. *Types of Ancient Egyptian Statuary.* Vols. IV–V. Copenhagen, 1966.

Hornemann, 1969   Hornemann, B. *Types of Ancient Egyptian Statuary.* Vols. 6–7. Copenhagen, 1969.

Hornung, 1971   Hornung, E. *Das Grab des Haremhab im Tal der Könige.* Bern, 1971.

James, 1973   James, T. *Corpus of Hieroglyphic Texts in The Brooklyn Museum; Dynasty I to the End of Dynasty XVIII.* Wilbour Monographs—V. Brooklyn, 1973.

Jerusalem, 1967   Jerusalem, The Israel Museum. *Egyptian Art of the Amarna Period. The Norbert Schimmel Collection.* Jerusalem, 1967.

Kansas City, 1949   William Rockhill Nelson Gallery of Art, Kansas City, Missouri. *The William Rockhill Nelson Collection, Housed in the William Rockhill Nelson Gallery of Art and Mary Atkins Museum of Fine Arts.* 3d ed. Kansas City, Missouri, 1949.

Kansas City, 1959   William Rockhill Nelson Gallery of Art, Kansas City, Missouri. *Handbook of the Collections in the William Rockhill Nelson Gallery of Art and Mary Atkins Museum of Fine Arts, Kansas City, Missouri.* Edited by R. Taggart. 4th ed. Kansas City, Missouri, 1959.

Keimer, 1947   Keimer, L. "Plusieurs antiquités récemment trouvées." *Bulletin de l'Institut d'Egypte* 28 (1947), pp. 117–37.

Kibbutz Hazorea, 1969   Kibbutz Hazorea, Wilfrid Israel House for Oriental Art and Studies. *Treasures of Ancient Egypt in Israeli Collections.* In Hebrew. Kibbutz Hazorea, 1969.

Koefoed–Petersen, 1943   Koefoed–Petersen, O. *Aegyptens Kaetterkonge og Hans Kunst.* Copenhagen, 1943.

Lacau, 1909   Lacau, M. *Stèles du Nouvel Empire.* Cairo, Musée des Antiquités Égyptiennes. Catalogue général, nos. 34001–34064. Cairo, 1909.

Lange, 1951   Lange, K. *König Echnaton und die Amarna-Zeit; Die Geschichte eines Gottkünders.* Munich, 1951.

Lange and Hirmer, 1968   Lange, K., and Hirmer, M. *Egypt; Architecture, Sculpture, Painting in Three Thousand Years.* 4th ed., rev. and enl. London, 1968.

Lansing, 1947   Lansing, A. "Two Egyptian Royal Portraits." *The Bulletin of The Metropolitan Museum of Art* 5, no. 7 (1947), pp. 188–92.

Leclant, 1955   Leclant, J. "Fouilles et travaux en Égypte, 1953–1954." *Orientalia* 24 (1955), pp. 296–317, with plates XVII–XXXVI following p. 344.

Legrain, 1902   Legrain, G. "Notes d'inspection, I. Les stèles d'Aménôthès IV à Zernik et à Gebel Silsileh." *Annales du Service des Antiquités de l'Egypte* 3 (1902), pp. [259]–266.

Legrain, 1906   Legrain, G. *Statues et statuettes de rois et de particuliers.* Vol. 1. Cairo, Musée des Antiquités Égyptiennes. Catalogue général, nos. 42001–42138. Cairo, 1906.

Legrain, 1909   Legrain, G. *Statues et statuettes de rois et de particuliers.* Vol. 2. Cairo, Musée des Antiquités Égyptiennes. Catalogue général, nos. 42139–42191. Cairo, 1909.

Legrain, 1914   Legrain, G. *Statues et statuettes de rois et de particuliers.* Vol. 3. Cairo, Musée des Antiquités Égyptiennes. Catalogue général, nos. 49192–42250. Cairo, 1914.

Leibovitch, 1943   Leibovitch, J. "Quelques éléments de la décoration égyptienne sous le Nouvel Empire, II. La sphinge." *Bulletin de l'Institut d'Égypte* 25 (1943), pp. [245]–267.

Lepsius, 1848–1859a   Lepsius, R. *Denkmaeler aus Aegypten und Aethiopien nach den Zeichnungen der von Seiner Majestaet dem Koenige von Preussen Friedrich Wilhelm IV nach diesen Laendern gesendeten und in den Jahren 1842–1845 ausgefuehrten wissenschaftlichen Expedition . . .* Part 3, *Denkmaeler des Neuen Reichs.* Berlin, 1848–1859.

Lepsius, 1848–1859b   Lepsius, R. *Denkmaeler aus Aegypten und Aethiopien nach den Zeichnungen der von Seiner Majestaet dem Koenige von Preussen Friedrich Wilhelm IV nach diesen Laendern gesendeten und in den Jahren 1842–1845 ausgefuehrten wissenschaftlichen Expedition . . .* Part 4, *Denkmaeler aus der Zeit der griechischen und roemischen Herrschaft.* Berlin, 1848–1859.

Lepsius, 1904   Lepsius, R. *Denkmäler aus Aegypten und Aethiopien.* Text. Vol. 2, *Mittelaegypten mit dem Faijum.* Edited by E. Naville, L. Borchardt and K. Sethe. Leipzig, 1904.

Littauer, 1968   Littauer, M. "The Function of the Yoke Saddle in Ancient Harnessing." *Antiquity* 42, no. 165 (1968), pp. 27–31.

Littauer, 1969   Littauer, M. "Bits and Pieces." *Antiquity* 43, no. 172 (1969), pp. 289–300.

Lloyd, 1933   Lloyd, S. "Model of a Tell el-'Amarnah House." *The Journal of Egyptian Archaeology* 19 (1933), pp. [1]–7.

Luckner, 1971   Luckner, K. "The Art of Egypt, Part 2." The Toledo Museum of Art. *Museum News,* new series 14, no. 3 (1971), pp. 59–82.

Maspero, 1912   Maspero, G. *Égypte.* Paris, 1912.

Mekhitarian, 1954   Mekhitarian, A. *Egyptian Painting.* Translated by S. Gilbert. Great Centuries of Painting. Geneva, 1954.

Michałowski, 1968   Michałowski, K. *L'art de l'ancienne Égypte.* Paris, 1968.

Mitten, 1965   Mitten, D. "Capolavori d'arte antica in una collezione privata a New York." *Antichità viva; rassegna d'arte* 4, no. 3 (1965), pp. 29–44.

Müller, 1963   Müller, H. W. "Berichte der Staatlichen Kunstsammlungen. Neuerwerbungen. Ägyptische Staatssammlung." *Münchner Jahrbuch der bildenden Kunst,* series 3, 14 (1963), pp. 213–22.

Müller, 1964   Müller, H. W. *Ägyptische Kunstwerke, Kleinfunde und Glas in der Sammlung E. und M. Kofler–Truniger, Luzern.* Münchner ägyptologische Studien, 5. Berlin, 1964.

Müller, 1970a   Müller, H. W. *Ägyptische Kunst.* Frankfurt am Main, 1970.

Müller, 1970b   Müller, H. W. "Berichte der Staatlichen Kunstsammlungen. Neuerwerbungen. Staatliche Sammlung ägyptischer Kunst." *Münchner Jahrbruch der bildenden Kunst,* series 3, 21 (1970), pp. 181–86.

Munich, 1966   *Die ägyptische Sammlung des Bayerischen Staates. Ausstellung in den Ausstellungsräumen der Staatlichen Graphischen Sammlung München . . . vom 21. Juli bis 5. Oktober 1966.* Munich, 1966.

Munich, 1970   *Staatliche Sammlung ägyptischer Kunst.* Munich, 1970.

Munich, 1972   *Staatliche Sammlung ägyptischer Kunst.* Munich, 1972.

Murray, 1930   Murray, M. *Egyptian Sculpture.* London, 1930.

Murray, 1934   Murray, M. "Queen Tety-shery." Part 2. *Ancient Egypt* (December, 1934), pp. 65–69.

Murray, 1949   Murray, M. *The Splendour That Was Egypt; A General Survey of Egyptian Culture and Civilisation.* London, 1949.

Naville, 1908   Naville, E. *The Temple of Deir el Bahari.* Part 6, *Plates CLI–CLXXIV. The Lower Terrace, Additions and Plans.* With architectural description by S. Clarke. Egypt Exploration Society. Memoirs, 29. London, 1908.

Nelson, 1932   Chicago, University. Oriental Institute, Epigraphic Survey. *Medinet Habu.* Vol. 2, *Later Historical Records of Ramses III.* By H. Nelson, et al. The University of Chicago, Oriental Institute, Publications, 9. Chicago, 1932.

New York, 1912   "Complete List of Accessions, October 20 to November 20, 1911." *The Bulletin of The Metropolitan Museum of Art* 7 (1912), pp. 14–16.

New York, 1937   New York, The Metropolitan Museum of Art. *Egyptian Statues and Statuettes.* New York, The Metropolitan Museum of Art. Picture Books. New York, 1937.

New York, 1945   New York, The Metropolitan Museum of Art. *Egyptian Statues.* Text by N. Scott. New York, 1945.

New York, 1946   New York, The Metropolitan Museum of Art. *Egyptian Statuettes.* Text by N. Scott. New York, 1946.

New York, 1961   New York, The Metropolitan Museum of Art. *Ancient Art from New York Private Collections; Catalogue of an Exhibition Held at The Metropolitan Museum of Art, December 17, 1959–February 28, 1960.* By Dietrich von Bothmer. New York, 1961.

New York, 1962   New York, The Metropolitan Museum of Art. *Guide to the Collections; Egyptian Art.* New York, 1962.

New York, 1970   New York, The Metropolitan Museum of Art. *Masterpieces of Fifty Centuries; [Exhibition catalogue].* Introduction by Kenneth Clark. New York, 1970.

Newberry, 1928   Newberry, P. "Akhenaten's Eldest Son-in-Law, 'Ankhkheprurē'." *The Journal of Egyptian Archaeology* 14 (1928), pp. 3–9.

Nims, 1968   Nims, C. Review of Cooney, 1965. *Journal of the American Oriental Society* 88, no. 3 (1968), pp. 544–46.

Nolte, 1968   Nolte, B. *Die Glasgefässe im alten Ägypten.* Münchner ägyptologische Studien, 14. Berlin, 1968.

Otto, 1939   Otto, W., ed. *Handbuch der Archäologie im Rahmen des Handbuchs der Altertumswissenschaft.* Plates. Vol. 1. Munich, 1939.

Paris, 1948   Paris, Musée National du Louvre. *Le département des antiquités égyptiennes. Guide sommaire.* By J. Vandier. Paris, 1948.

Paris, 1961   Paris, Musée National du Louvre. *Le département des antiquités égyptiennes. Guide sommaire.* By J. Vandier. Paris, 1961.

Paris, 1967   Paris, Musée de l'Orangerie. *Vingt ans d'acquisitions au Musée du Louvre, 1947–1967.* Paris, 1967.

Parke-Bernet, 1968   New York, Parke-Bernet Galleries, Inc. *Egyptian, Western Asiatic, Greek, Etruscan & Roman Antiquities . . . Public Auction, Wednesday, June 19 . . .* New York, 1968.

Peck, 1970   Peck, W. "The Present State of Egyptian Art in Detroit." *The Connoisseur* 175, no. 706 (1970), pp. 265–73.

Peet and Woolley, 1923   Peet, T., and Woolley, C. *The City of Akhenaten.* Part 1, *Excavations of 1921 and 1922 at el-'Amarneh.* Egypt Exploration Society. Memoirs, 38. London, 1923.

Pendlebury, 1933a   Pendlebury, J. "A 'Monotheistic Utopia' of Ancient Egypt." *The Illustrated London News* (May 6, 1933), pp. 630–33.

Pendlebury, 1933b   Pendlebury, J. "Preliminary Report of the Excavations at Tell El-'Amarnah, 1932–1933." *The Journal of Egyptian Archaeology* 19 (1933), pp. [113]–118.

Pendlebury, 1935a   Pendlebury, J. "The Heretic Pharaoh's Harem." *The Illustrated London News* (October 5, 1935), pp. 564–65.

Pendlebury, 1935b   Pendlebury, J. "Preliminary Report of the Excavations at Tell el-'Amarnah, 1934–1935." *The Journal of Egyptian Archaeology* 21 (1935), pp. [129]–135.

Pendlebury, 1951   Pendlebury, J., et al. *The City of Akhenaten.* Part 3, *The Central City and the Official Quarters. The Excavations at Tell El-Amarna during the Seasons 1926–1927 and 1931–1936.* Vol. 1, Text. Egypt Exploration Society. Memoirs, 44. London, 1951.

Peterson, 1964   Peterson, B. "Two Royal Heads from Amarna; Studies in the Art of the Amarna Age." *Medelhavsmuseet Bulletin* 4 (1964), pp. 13–29.

Petrie, 1894   Petrie, W., et al. *Tell el Amarna.* London, 1894.

Petrie, 1917   Petrie, W. *Scarabs and Cylinders with Names, Illustrated by the Egyptian Collection in University College, London.* British School of Archaeology in Egypt and Egyptian Research Account. Twenty-First Year, 1915. [Publications, 29]. London, 1917.

Philadelphia, 1960   Pennsylvania, University, Museum. *Egypt.* Text by D. Crownover. Philadelphia, 1960.

Phillips, 1948   New York, The Metropolitan Museum of Art. *Ancient Egyptian Animals.* By D. Phillips. 2d, rev. ed. New York, 1948.

Piankoff, 1962   *The Shrines of Tut-ankh-amon.* Texts translated with introductions by A. Piankoff. Edited by N. Rambova. Bollingen Series, 40:2, Egyptian Religious Texts and Representations, 2. Paperback ed. New York, 1962.

Piankoff, 1964   Piankoff, A. "Les grandes compositions religieuses du Nouvel Empire et la réforme d'Amarna." *Bulletin de l'Institut Français d'Archéologie Orientale* 62 (1964), pp. [207]–218.

Pijoán, 1945   Pijoán, J. *Summa Artis; historia general del arte.* Vol. 3, *El arte egipcio hasta la conquista romana.* 2d ed. Madrid, 1945.

Porter and Moss, 1929   Porter, B., and Moss, R. *Topographical Bibliography of Ancient Egyptian Hieroglyphic Texts, Reliefs, and Paintings.* Vol. 2, *Theban Temples.* Oxford, 1929.

Porter and Moss, 1934   Porter, B., and Moss, R. *Topographical Bibliography of Ancient Egyptian Hieroglyphic Texts, Reliefs, and Paintings.* Vol. 4, *Lower and Middle Egypt (Delta and Cairo to Asyût).* Oxford, 1934.

Porter and Moss, 1937   Porter, B., and Moss, R. *Topographical Bibliography of Ancient Egyptian Hieroglyphic Texts, Reliefs, and Paintings.* Vol. 5, *Upper Egypt: Sites. . . .* Oxford, 1937.

Porter and Moss, 1939   Porter, B., and Moss, R. *Topographical Bibliography of Ancient Egyptian Hieroglyphic Texts, Reliefs, and Paintings.* Vol. 6, *Upper Egypt: Chief Temples (Excluding Thebes) . . .* Oxford, 1939.

Porter and Moss, 1951   Porter, B., and Moss, R. *Topographical Bibliography of Ancient Egyptian Hieroglyphic Texts, Reliefs, and Paintings.* Vol. 7, *Nubia, the Deserts, and Outside Egypt.* Oxford, 1951.

Porter and Moss, 1960   Porter, B., Moss, R., and Burney, E. *Topographical Bibliography of Ancient Egyptian Hieroglyphic Texts, Reliefs, and Pantings.* Vol. 1, *The Theban Necropolis.* Part 1, *Private Tombs.* 2d ed. Oxford, 1960.

Porter and Moss, 1964   Porter, B., Moss, R., and Burney, E. *Topographical Bibliography of Ancient Egyptian Hieroglyphic Texts, Reliefs, and Paintings.* Vol. 1, *The Theban Necropolis.* Part 2, *Royal Tombs and Smaller Cemeteries.* 2d ed., rev. and aug. Oxford, 1964.

Porter and Moss, 1972   Porter, B., Moss, R., and Burney, E. *Topographical Bibliography of Ancient Egyptian Hieroglyphic Texts, Reliefs, and Paintings.* Vol. 2, *Theban Temples.* 2d ed., rev. and aug. Oxford, 1972.

Posener, Sauneron and Yoyotte, 1962   Posener, G. *A Dictionary of Egyptian Civilization.* With the assistance of S. Sauneron and J. Yoyotte. Translated by A. Macfarlane. London, 1962.

Pritchard, 1954   Pritchard, J. *The Ancient Near East in Pictures Relating to the Old Testament.* Princeton, 1954.

Quibell, 1908   Quibell, J. *The Tomb of Yuaa and Thuiu.* Cairo, Musée des Antiquités Égyptiennes. Catalogue général, nos. 51001–51191. Cairo, 1908.

Quibell, 1909   Quibell, J., et al. *Excavations at Saqqara (1907–1908).* Égypt, Service des Antiquités. Excavations at Saqqara. Cairo, 1909.

Quibell, 1912   Quibell, J. *The Monastery of Apa Jeremias.* Egypt, Service des Antiquités. Excavations at Saqqara, 1908–1909, 1909–1910. Cairo, 1912.

Quibell and Hayter, 1927   Quibell, J., and Hayter, A. *Teti Pyramid, North Side.* Egypt, Service des Antiquités. Excavations at Saqqara. Cairo, 1927.

Ranke, 1936   Ranke, H. *The Art of Ancient Egypt; Architecture, Sculpture, Painting, Applied Art.* Vienna, 1936.

Ranke, 1950   Ranke, H. "The Egyptian Collections of the University Museum." *University Museum Bulletin* 15, nos. 2–3 (1950), entire issue.

Revillout, 1907   Revillout, E. *L'ancienne Égypte d'après les papyrus et les monuments.* Vol. 1. Paris, 1907.

Roeder, 1938   Roeder, G. "Die Deutsche Hermopolis–Expedition 1938 (Ausgrabung in Ägypten)." *Forschungen und Fortschritte* 14, no. 23/24 (1938), pp. [261]–263.

Roeder, 1939   Roeder, G. "Die Deutsche Hermopolis–Expedition 1939 (7. Grabung in Ägypten)." *Forschungen und Fortschritte* 15, nos. 23/24 (1939), pp. 291–92.

Roeder, 1940   Roeder, G., et al. "Vorläufiger Bericht über die Deutsche Hermopolis–Expedition 1938 und 1939." *Mitteilungen des Deutschen Instituts für ägyptische Altertumskunde in Kairo* 9 (1940), pp. 40–92.

Roeder, 1941   Roeder, G. "Lebensgrosse Tonmodelle aus einer altägyptischen Bildhauerwerkstatt." *Jahrbuch der preussischen Kunstsammlungen* 62 (1941), pp. [145]–170.

Roeder, 1951   Roeder, G. "Ein Jahrzehnt deutscher Ausgrabungen in einer ägyptischen Stadtruine (Deutsche Hermopolis–Expedition 1929–1939)." *Zeitschrift des Museums zu Hildesheim,* new series, no. 3 (1951), pp. 3–[48].

Roeder, 1952   Roeder, G. *Volksglaube im Pharaohnenreich.* Stuttgart, 1952.

Roeder, 1958   Roeder, G. "Thronfolger und König Smench-ka-Rê (Dynastie XVIII)." *Zeitschrift für ägyptische Sprache und Altertumskunde* 83 (1958), pp. 43–74.

Roeder, 1961   Roeder, G. *Der Ausklang der ägyptischen Religion mit Reformation, Zauberei und Jenseitsglauben.* Die Bibliothek der alten Welt. Reihe der alte Orient. Die ägyptische Religion in Text und Bild, 4. Zurich and Stuttgart, 1961.

Roeder, 1969   Roeder, G. *Amarna-Reliefs aus Hermopolis. Ausgrabungen der Deutschen Hermopolis–Expedition in Hermopolis 1929–1939.* Vol. 2. Edited by R. Hanke. Hildesheim, Pelizaeus-Museum. Wissenschaftliche Veröffentlichung, 6. Hildesheim, 1969.

Ross, 1931   Ross, E., ed. *The Art of Egypt through the Ages.* New York and London, 1931.

Royal–Athena, 1964   New York, Parke-Bernet Galleries, Inc. *Egyptian and Classical Antiquities. Siamese and Near Eastern Art. Islamic Pottery, Pre-Columbian Art. Selections from the Stock of Royal-Athena Galleries, New York . . . Public Auction, Wednesday and Thursday, April 29 and 30 . . . New York, 1964.*

Sa'ad, 1970   Sa'ad, R. "Les travaux d'Aménophis IV au IIIe pylône du Temple d'Amon Rê' à Karnak. *Kêmi* 20 (1970), pp. [187]–193.

Säve-Söderbergh, 1941   Säve-Söderbergh, T. *Ägypten und Nubien; Ein Beitrag zur Geschichte altägyptischer Aussenpolitik.* Lund, 1941.

Sambon, 1931   Sambon, A. *Aperçu général de l'évolution de la sculpture depuis l'antiquité jusqu'à la fin du XVIe siècle.* Paris, 1931.

Samson, 1972   Samson, J. *Amarna, City of Akhenaten and Nefertiti. Key Pieces from the Petrie Collection.* London, 1972.

Sandman, 1938   Sandman, M. *Texts from the Time of Akhenaten.* Bibliotheca Aegyptiaca, 8. Brussels, 1938.

Sauneron and Sa'ad, 1969   Sauneron, S., and Sa'ad, R. "Le démontage et l'étude du IXe pylône à Karnak." *Kêmi* 19 (1969), pp. [137]–78.

Scamuzzi, 1963   Scamuzzi, E. *Museo Egizio di Torino.* Turin, 1963.

Schäfer, 1919   Schäfer, H. "Die Anfänge der Reformation Amenophis des IV." *Sitzungsberichte der preussischen Akademie der Wissenschaften,* 1919, XXVI. *Gesamtsitzung vom 15. Mai. Mitteilung aus der Sitzung der phil.–hist. Klasse vom 8. Mai,* pp. [477]–84.

Schäfer, 1928   Schäfer, H. *Ägyptische und heutige Kunst und Weltgebäude der antiken Ägypter.* Berlin and Leipzig, 1928.

Schäfer, 1931   Schäfer, H. *Amarna in Religion und Kunst.* Berlin, Deutsche Orient-Gesellschaft. Sendschriften, 7. Leipzig, 1931.

Schäfer, 1936   Schäfer, H. *Das altägyptische Bildnis.* Leipziger ägyptologische Studien. 5. Glückstadt, 1936.

Schäfer, 1963   Schäfer, H. *Von ägyptischer Kunst; Eine Grundlage.* 4th ed. Corrected and with an Appendix by E. Brunner–Traut. Wiesbaden, 1963.

Schäfer and Andrae, 1942   Schäfer, H., and Andrae, W. *Die Kunst des alten Orients.* 3d ed. Propyläen-Kunstgeschichte, 2. Berlin, 1942.

Schott, 1955   Schott, S. "Ein ungewöhnliches Symbol des Triumphes über Feinde Aegyptens." *Journal of Near Eastern Studies* 14 (1955), pp. [96]–99.

Schulman, 1964   Schulman, A. "Some Observations on the Military Background of the Amarna Period." *Journal of the American Research Center in Egypt* 3 (1964), pp. 51–69.

Scott, 1948   Scott, N. "Memy-Sabu and His Wife." *The Bulletin of The Metropolitan Museum of Art* 7, no. 3 (1948), pp. 95–100.

Scott and   Scott, J., and Scott, L. *Egyptian Hieroglyphs for Every-*

Scott, 1968   *one; An Introduction to the Writing of Ancient Egypt.* New York, 1968.

Seele, 1955   Seele, K. "King Ay and the Close of the Amarna Age." *Journal of Near Eastern Studies* 14 (1955), pp. 168–80.

Sethe, 1921   Sethe, K. "Beiträge zur Geschichte Amenophis' IV." *Nachrichten der K. Gesellschaft der Wissenschaften zu Göttingen, Philologisch–historische Klasse* (1921), pp. [101]–130.

Silverberg, 1964   Silverberg, R. *Akhnaten, the Rebel Pharaoh.* Philadelphia, 1964.

Simpson, 1955   Simpson, W. "The Head of a Statuette of Tut'ankhamūn in The Metropolitan Museum of Art." *The Journal of Egyptian Archaeology* 41 (1955), pp. 112–14.

Smith, 1967   Smith, R. W. "The Akhenaten Temple Project." *Expedition* 10, no. 1 (1967), pp. 24–32.

Smith, 1942   Smith, W. S. *Ancient Egypt as Represented in the Museum of Fine Arts.* Boston, 1942.

Smith, 1958   Smith, W. S. *The Art and Architecture of Ancient Egypt.* The Pelican History of Art, Z14. Baltimore, 1958.

Smith, 1960   Smith, W. S. *Ancient Egypt As Represented in the Museum of Fine Arts, Boston.* 4th, rev. ed. Boston, 1961, c. 1960.

Smith, 1964   Smith, W. S. "Some Recent Accessions." *Bulletin of the Museum of Fine Arts, Boston* 62, no. 330 (1964), p. 144.

Smith, 1965   Smith, W. S. *Interconnections in the Ancient Near East; A Study of the Relationships between the Arts of Egypt, the Aegean, and Western Asia.* New Haven and London, 1965.

Spiegel, 1950   Spiegel, J. *Soziale und weltanschauliche Reformbewegungen im alten Ägypten.* Heidelberg, 1950.

Spiegelberg, 1903   Spiegelberg, W. *Geschichte der ägyptischen Kunst bis zum Hellenismus.* Der alte Orient; Gemeinverständliche Darstellungen herausgegeben vom Vorderasiatischen Gesellschaft, 1. Ergänzungsband. Leipzig, 1903.

Spink, 1964   London. Spink & Son, Ltd. *Autumn 1964.* [Sale catalogue.] London, 1964.

Staehelin, 1967   Staehelin, E. "Amarna-Reliefs in Amerika." *Antike Kunst* 10 (1967), pp. 58–59, and plate 15, fig. 2, facing p. 56.

Steindorff and Hoyningen-Huene, 1945   Steindorff, G. *Egypt.* Photographed by Hoyningen-Huene. 2d, rev. ed. New York, 1945.

Taggart, 1931   Taggart, E. "A Little Princess Returns." *The Brooklyn Museum Quarterly* 18 (1931), pp. 104–109.

Taggart, 1933   Taggart, E. "The New Wilbour Memorial Hall." *The Brooklyn Museum Quarterly* 20 (1933), pp. 57–69.

Taggart, 1935   Taggart, E. " 'A Day under the Aten Disk.' " *The Brooklyn Museum Quarterly* 22 (1935), pp. [10]–21.

Tait, 1963   Tait, G. "The Egyptian Relief Chalice." *The Journal of Egyptian Archaeology* 49 (1963), pp. 93–139.

Terrace, 1962   Terrace, E. "Some Recent Accessions." *Bulletin of the Museum of Fine Arts, Boston* 60, no. 322 (1962), pp. 134–35.

Terrace, 1964   Terrace, E. "Recent Acquisitions in the Department of Egyptian Art." *Bulletin of the Museum of Fine Arts, Boston* 62, no. 328 (1964), pp. 48–64.

Terrace, 1968   Terrace, E. "The Age of Empire and Rebellion; The New Kingdom in Boston." *Connoisseur* 169, no. 679 (1968), pp. 49–56.

Vandier, 1950   Vandier, J. "Musée du Louvre. Acquisitions du département des antiquités égyptiennes." *Musées de France* 15, no. 2 (1950), pp. 25–30.

Vandier, 1951   Vandier, J. *La sculpture égyptienne.* Paris, 1951.

Vandier, 1958   Vandier, J. *Manuel d'archéologie égyptienne.* Vol. 3, *Les grandes époques; la statuaire.* Text and Plates. Paris, 1958.

Vandier, 1967   Vandier, J. "Vingt ans d'acquisitions au Musée du Louvre, 1947–1967. Département des Antiquités égyptiennes." *La revue du Louvre et des musées de France* 17, no. 6 (1967), pp. 302–310.

Vandier, 1969   Vandier, J. "Chronique des musées. Nouvelles acquisitions. Musée du Louvre. Département des antiquités Égyptiennes." *La revue du Louvre et des musées de France* 19, no. 1 (1969), pp. 43–54.

Wallert, 1967   Wallert, I. *Der verzierte Löffel: Seine Formegeschichte und Verwendung im Atlen Ägypten.* Ägyptologische Abhandlungen, 16. Wiesbaden, 1967.

Ward, 1965   Ward, W. *The Spirit of Ancient Egypt.* Beirut, 1965.

Weigall, 1922   Weigall, A. "The Mummy of Akhenaton." With Appendix by F. Griffith. *The Journal of Egyptian Archæology* 8 (1922), pp. 193–200.

Wenig, 1969   Wenig, S. *The Woman in Egyptian Art.* Translated by B. Fischer. Leipzig, 1969.

Westendorf, 1963   Westendorf, W. "Amenophis IV. in Urgottgestalt." *Pantheon* 21, no. 5 (1963), pp. 269–77.

Westendorf, 1966   Westendorf, W. "Ursprung und Wesen der Maat, der altägyptischen Göttin des Rechts, der Gerechtigkeit und der Weltordnung." In *Festgabe für Dr. Walter Will, Ehrensenator der Universität München, zum 70. Geburtstag am 12. November 1966,* pp. 201–225. Cologne, 1966.

Weynants–Ronday, 1940   Weynants–Ronday, M. "L'évolution cyclique du goût et l'art égyptien." *Chronique d'Égypte* 15, no. 29 (1940), pp. 51–64.

Whittemore, 1925   Whittemore, T. "A Statuette of Akhenaten for America." *The Brooklyn Museum Quarterly* 12, no. 2 (1925), pp. 59–65.

Winlock, 1922   Winlock, H. "A Gift of Egyptian Antiquities." *The Bulletin of The Metropolitan Museum of Art* 17 (1922), pp. 170–73.

Winlock, 1947   Winlock, H. *The Rise and Fall of the Middle Kingdom in Thebes.* New York, 1947.

Woldering, 1964
Hanover, Kestner Museum. *Kestner Museum, 1889–1964.* By I. Woldering. Hanoversche Geschichtsblätter, new series 18, no. 2/4. Hanover, 1964.

Woldering, 1967
Woldering, I. *Gods, Men & Pharaohs; The Glory of Egyptian Art.* Translated by A. Keep. New York, 1967.

Wolf, 1931
Wolf, W. *Das schöne Fest von Opet; Die Festzugdarstellung im grossen Säulengange des Tempels von Luksor.* Ernst von Sieglin-Expedition in Ägypten. Veröffentlichungen, 5. Leipzig, 1931.

Wolf, 1957
Wolf, W. *Die Kunst Aegyptens; Gestalt und Geschichte.* Stuttgart, 1957.

Wreszinski, 1923
Wreszinski, W. *Atlas zur altaegyptischen Kulturgeschichte.* Vol. 1. Leipzig, 1923.

Yadin, 1963
Yadin, Y. *The Art of Warfare in Biblical Lands in the Light of Archaeological Study.* 2 vols. Translated by M. Pearlman. New York, 1963.

Young, 1964
Young, E. "Sculptors' Models or Votives? In Defense of a Scholarly Tradition." *The Bulletin of The Metropolitan Museum of Art* 22, no. 7 (1964), pp. [246]–256 and cover illus.

Young, 1967
Young, E. "An Offering to Thoth; A Votive Statue from the Gallatin Collection." *The Metropolitan Museum of Art Bulletin* 25, no. 1 (1967), pp. 273–82.

Yoyotte, 1968
Yoyotte, J. *Treasures of the Pharaohs; The Early Period, the New Kingdom, the Late Period.* Translated by R. Allen. Geneva, 1968.

CONCORDANCE I
OBJECTS LISTED BY CATALOGUE NUMBER

CAT. NO.	LENDER	ACC. NO.	PAGES
1	Berlin, West	21835	90
2	London, The British Museum	13366	90
3	New York, The Metropolitan Museum of Art	26.7.1395	91
4	Brooklyn, The Brooklyn Museum	58.2	92
5	New York, The Metropolitan Museum of Art	21.9.3	93
6	Berlin, West	14512	94
7	Boston, Museum of Fine Arts	67.922	94
8	Buffalo. Albright–Knox Art Gallery	37:6	95
9	Brussels, Musées Royaux d'Art et d'Histoire	E. 3051	96
10	Brussels, Musées Royaux d'Art et d'Histoire	E. 3052	96
11	Cambridge, Fitzwilliam Museum	2300.1943	97
12	Edinburgh, Royal Scottish Museum	1969.377	98
13	Geneva, Collection of Mr. Nicolas Koutoulakis	none	99
14	New York, The Metropolitan Museum of Art	66.99.41	100
15	New York, The Metropolitan Museum of Art	66.99.40	101
16	Berlin West	14145	102
17	Boston, Museum of Fine Arts	67.637	103
18	Brooklyn, The Brooklyn Museum	41.82	104
19	Berlin West	21834	105
20	New York, The Metropolitan Museum of Art	21.9.4	106
21	New York, The Metropolitan Museum of Art	26.7.1396	107
22	Paris, Musée du Louvre	E. 25409	108
23	Cleveland, The Cleveland Museum of Art	59.188	109
24	Boston, Museum of Fine Arts	37.3	110
25	Brooklyn, The Brooklyn Museum (on loan from Mr. Christos G. Bastis)	L69.38.1	111
26	Brooklyn, The Brooklyn Museum	71.89	112
27	Haifa, Collection of Dr. Rëuben Hecht	none	113
28	Kansas City, William Rockhill Nelson Gallery of Art, Atkins Museum of Fine Arts	44–65	114
29	London, University College London	038	115
30	Munich, Staatliche Sammlung Ägyptischer Kunst	ÄS 4231	115
31	Oxford, Ashmolean Museum	1893.1-41(71)	116
32	Weert, Collection of Mr. H. E. Smeets	none	116-117
33	Boston, Museum of Fine Arts	37.1	118
34	Brooklyn, The Brooklyn Museum	35.2000	118
35	Brooklyn, The Brooklyn Museum	37.405	119
36	Brooklyn, The Brooklyn Museum	64.199.1	119
37	Brooklyn, The Brooklyn Museum	67.175.1	120
38	Brussels, Musées Royaux d'Art et d'Histoire	E. 7232	120
39	Cambridge, Fitzwilliam Museum	4514.1943	121
40	Cambridge, Fitzwilliam Museum	4529.1943	121
41	Cleveland, The Cleveland Museum of Art	59.187	122
42	Edinburgh, Royal Scottish Museum	1963.240	122
43	Edinburgh, Royal Scottish Museum	1960.906	123
44	Munich, Staatliche Sammlung Ägyptischer Kunst	ÄS 4863	124
45	New York, Collection of Mr. Milton Lowenthal	none	124
46	New York, The Metropolitan Museum of Art	68.134	125
47	Berlin, West	2045	126
48	Brooklyn, The Brooklyn Museum	35.1999	126
49	Oxford, Ashmolean Museum	1893.1-41(75)	127
50	Oxford, Ashmolean Museum	1893.1-41(171)	128
51	Brooklyn, The Brooklyn Museum	60.28	128
52	Brussels, Musées Royaux d'Art et d'Histoire	E. 6730	130
53	Kansas City, William Rockhill Nelson Gallery of Art, Atkins Museum of Art	47–13	131
54	Berlin, East	22265	132
55	New York, Collection of Mr. and Mrs. Norbert Schimmel	none	133
56	Paris, Musée du Louvre	E. 11624	134

CAT. NO.	LENDER	ACC. NO.	PAGES
57	Boston, Museum of Fine Arts	64.521 and 63.260	135
58	Brooklyn, The Brooklyn Museum	60.197.7	136
59	London, University College London	011	136
60	Boston, Museum of Fine Arts	36.96	137
61	Basel, Collection of Mr. Elie Borowski	none	138
62	Boston, Museum of Fine Arts	62.1168	138
63	Boston, Museum of Fine Arts	63.427	139
64	Boston, Museum of Fine Arts	63.962	140
65	Boston, Museum of Fine Arts	67.921	141
66	Boston, Museum of Fine Arts	1971.295	142
67	Brooklyn, The Brooklyn Museum	60.197.4	143
68	Brooklyn, The Brooklyn Museum	61.195.1	143
69	Brooklyn, The Brooklyn Museum	62.149	144
70	Brooklyn, The Brooklyn Museum	64.148.3	145
71	Brooklyn, The Brooklyn Museum	65.16	146
72	Brooklyn, The Brooklyn Museum	L71.8.1	147
73	New York, Collection of Mr. and Mrs. Norbert Schimmel	none	148
74	New York, Collection of Mr. and Mrs. Norbert Schimmel	none	149
75	New York, Collection of Mr. and Mrs. Norbert Schimmel	none	150
76	New York, The Metropolitan Museum of Art	27.6.1	151
77	New York, Collection of Mr. Leon Pomerance	none	152
78	New York, Collection of Mr. and Mrs. Norbert Schimmel	none	153
79	New York, Collection of Mr. and Mrs. Norbert Schimmel	none	154
80	Paris, Galerie Maspero	none	154
81	Boston, Museum of Fine Arts	63.961	155
82	Brooklyn, The Brooklyn Museum	61.195.3	156
83	New York, Collection of Mr. and Mrs. Norbert Schimmel	none	156
84	London, The British Museum	58480	157
85	London, The British Museum	59290	157
86	Paris, Musée du Louvre	E. 17357	158
87	Berlin East	20494	159
88	Berlin, East	21223	160
89	Brooklyn, The Brooklyn Museum	16.46	161
90	London, University College London	002	162-163
91	Brooklyn, The Brooklyn Museum	33.685	164
92	Brooklyn, The Brooklyn Museum	60.197.8	165
93	New York, Collection of Mr. and Mrs. Norbert Schimmel	none	165
94	Berlin West	21340	166
95	Berlin West	21351	167
96	Brooklyn, The Brooklyn Museum	29.34	168
97	New York, The Metropolitan Museum of Art	66.99.34	168-169
98	Brooklyn, The Brooklyn Museum	L67.26.1	168
99	Berlin East	21220	171
100	Berlin East	21352	172
101	New York, The Metropolitan Museum of Art	11.150.26	174
102	Berlin East	14113	175
103	Berlin West	21245	176
104	London, Collection of Dr. K. J. Stern	none	177
105	New York, The Metropolitan Museum of Art	31.114.1	177
106	Philadelphia, University Museum of the University of Pennsylvania	E 14349	178
107	Berlin East	21228	179
108	Berlin West	21350	179
109	Berlin West	21356	180
110	New York, The Metropolitan Museum of Art	11.150.21	181
111	Berlin East	21341	182
112	Berlin West	21239	182
113	London, University College London	006	183
114	Berlin East	17813	184
115	Berlin East	21683	185
116	Brooklyn, The Brooklyn Museum	60.197.6	185
117	New York, Collection of Mr. and Mrs. Norbert Schimmel	none	186
118	New York, Collection of Mr. and Mrs. Norbert Schimmel	none	187
119	New York, The Metropolitan Museum of Art	21.9.13	188
120	Berlin West	15000	188
121	Brooklyn, The Brooklyn Museum	16.48	190-191
122	Brooklyn, The Brooklyn Museum	60.197.1	192
123	Cambridge, Fitzwilliam Museum	4606.1943	192
124	Boston, Museum of Fine Arts	1971.294	193
125	Brooklyn, The Brooklyn Museum	60.197.2	193
126	Brooklyn, The Brooklyn Museum	60.197.9	194
127	Detroit, Detroit Institute of Arts	66.8	195
128	Lucerne, Collection of Mr. Ernst Kofler	A 107	195
129	New York, Collection of Mr. and Mrs. Norbert Schimmel	none	196
130	New York, Collection of Mr. and Mrs. Norbert Schimmel	none	196-197
131	Brooklyn, The Brooklyn Museum	60.197.3	198
132	Brooklyn, The Brooklyn Museum	68.154	198
133	Brooklyn, The Brooklyn Museum	L72.17	199
134	London, University College London	009	199
135	Lucerne, Collection of Mr. Ernst Kofler	none	200
136	New York, Collection of Mr. and Mrs. Norbert Schimmel	none	200
137	New York, Collection of Mr. and Mrs. Norbert Schimmel	none	201
138	New York, Collection of Mr. and Mrs. Norbert Schimmel	none	202
139	New York, Collection of Mr. and Mrs. Norbert Schimmel	none	203
140	Richmond, Virginia Museum of Fine Arts	61.5	204
141	San Diego, Museum of Man	14881	204-205
142	Boston, Museum of Fine Arts	62.320	206
143	Brooklyn, The Brooklyn Museum	54.186	207
144	Brooklyn, The Brooklyn Museum	60.197.5	207
145	Munich, Staatliche Sammlung Ägyptischer Kunst	ÄS 5360	208
146	New York, Collection of Mr. and Mrs. Norbert Schimmel	none	209
147	New York, Collection of Mr. and Mrs. Norbert Schimmel	none	209
148	New York, Collection of Mr. and Mrs. Norbert Schimmel	none	210
149	New York, Collection of Mr. and Mrs. Norbert Schimmel	none	211
150	New York, Collection of Mr. and Mrs. Norbert Schimmel	none	210
151	Toledo, Toledo Museum of Art	25.774	212
152	Brooklyn, The Brooklyn Museum	37.340E	212
153	London, The British Museum	55193	213
154	Brooklyn, The Brooklyn Museum	48.111	213
155	Oxford, Ashmolean Museum	1922.92	214
156	Brooklyn, The Brooklyn Museum	65.133	214
157	Oxford, Ashmolean Museum	1933.1209	215
158	Brooklyn, The Brooklyn Museum	35.2001	215
159	Brooklyn, The Brooklyn Museum	52.148.1	216
160	Brooklyn, The Brooklyn Museum	52.148.2	216
161	Brooklyn, The Brooklyn Museum	33.52	217
162	Brooklyn, The Brooklyn Museum	33.53	218
163	Brooklyn, The Brooklyn Museum	33.54	218
164	Brooklyn, The Brooklyn Museum	35.1883	218
165	Boston, Museum of Fine Arts	65.466	219
166	Washington, D.C., Collection of Mr. John S. Thacher	none	219
167	Brooklyn, The Brooklyn Museum	35.1531	219
168	Brooklyn, The Brooklyn Museum	35.1866	220
169	New York, The Metropolitan Museum of Art	47.57.2	220
170	New York, The Metropolitan Museum of Art	66.99.37	220
171	Brooklyn, The Brooklyn Museum	35.1867	221
172	Brooklyn, The Brooklyn Museum	35.1870	221
173	Brooklyn, The Brooklyn Museum	35.1882	221
174	Brooklyn, The Brooklyn Museum	37.499	222
175	Edinburgh, Royal Scottish Museum	1972.94	222

LENDER	ACC. NO.	CAT. NO.	PAGES
Basel, Collection of Mr. Elie Borowski	none	61	138
Berlin, East (Ägyptisches Museum, Berlin, Deutsche Demokratische Republik)	14113	102	175
	17813	114	184
	20494	87	159
	21220	99	171
	21223	88	160
	21228	107	179
	21341	111	182
	21352	100	172
	21683	115	185
	22265	54	132
Berlin, West (Ägyptisches Museum der Staatlichen Museen, Preussischer Kulturbesitz)	2045	47	126
	14145	16	102
	14512	6	94
	15000	120	188
	21239	112	182
	21245	103	176
	21340	94	166
	21350	108	179
	21351	95	167
	21356	109	180
	21834	19	105
	21835	1	90
Boston, Museum of Fine Arts	36.96	60	137
	37.1	33	118
	37.3	24	110
	62.320	142	206
	62.1168	62	138
	63.260	57	135
	63.427	63	139
	63.961	81	155
	63.962	64	140
	64.521	57	135
	65.466	165	219
	67.637	17	103
	67.921	65	141
	67.922	7	94
	1971.294	124	193
	1971.295	66	142
Brooklyn, The Brooklyn Museum	16.46	89	161
	16.48	121	190-191
	29.34	96	168
	33.52	161	217
	33.53	162	218
	33.54	163	218
	33.685	91	164
	35.1531	167	219
	35.1866	168	220
	35.1867	171	221
	35.1870	172	221
	35.1882	173	221
	35.1883	164	218
	35.1999	48	126
	35.2000	34	118
	35.2001	158	215
	37.405	35	119
	37.499	174	222
	37.340E	152	212
	41.82	18	104
	48.111	154	213
	52.148.1	159	216
	52.148.2	160	216
	54.186	143	207
	58.2	4	92
	60.28	51	128
	60.197.1	122	192
	60.197.2	125	193
	60.197.3	131	198
	60.197.4	67	143
	60.197.5	144	207
	60.197.6	116	185
	60.197.7	58	136
	60.197.8	92	165
	60.197.9	126	194
	61.195.1	68	143
	61.195.3	82	156
	62.149	69	144
	64.148.3	70	145
	64.199.1	36	119
	65.16	71	146
	65.133	156	214
	67.175.1	37	120
	L67.26.1	98	168
	68.154	132	198
	L69.38.1	25	111
	71.89	26	112
	L71.8.1	72	147
	L72.17	133	199
Brussels, Musées Royaux d'Art et d'Histoire	E. 3051	9	96
	E. 3052	10	96
	E. 6730	52	130
	E. 7232	38	120
Buffalo, Albright-Knox Art Gallery	37:6	8	95
Cambridge, Fitzwilliam Museum	2300.1943	11	97
	4514.1943	39	121
	4529.1943	40	121
	4606.1943	123	192

LENDER	ACC. NO.	CAT. NO.	PAGES
Cleveland, The Cleveland Museum of Art	59.187	41	122
	59.188	23	109
Detroit, The Detroit Institute of Arts	66.8	127	195
Edinburgh, The Royal Scottish Museum	1960.906	43	123
	1963.240	42	122
	1969.377	12	98
	1972.94	175	222
Geneva, Collection of Mr. Nicolas Koutoulakis	none	13	99
Haifa, Collection of Dr. Rëuben R. Hecht	none	27	113
Kansas City, William Rockhill Nelson Gallery of Art and Atkins Museum of Fine Arts	44-65	28	114
	47-13	53	131
London, Collection of Dr. K. J. Stern	none	104	177
London, The British Museum	13366	2	90
	55193	153	213
	58480	84	157
	59290	85	157
London, University College London	002	90	162-163
	006	113	183
	009	134	199
	011	59	136
	038	29	115
Lucerne, Collection of Mr. Ernst Kofler	A 107	128	195
	none	135	200
Munich, Staatliche Sammlung Ägyptischer Kunst	ÄS 4231	30	115
	ÄS 4863	44	124
	ÄS 5360	145	208
New York, Collection of Mr. Christos G. Bastis	none	25	111
New York, Collection of Mr. Milton Lowenthal	none	45	124
New York, Collection of Mr. Leon Pomerance	none	77	152
New York, Collection of Mr. and Mrs. Norbert Schimmel	none	55	133
		73	148
		74	149
		75	150
		78	153
		79	154
		83	156
		93	165
		117	186
		118	187
		129	196
		130	196-197
		136	200
		137	201
		138	202
		139	203
		146	209
		147	209
		148	210
		149	211
		150	210
New York, The Metropolitan Museum of Art	11.150.21	110	181
	11.150.26	101	174
	21.9.3	5	93
	21.9.4	20	106
	21.9.13	119	188
	26.7.1395	3	91
	26.7.1396	21	107
	27.6.1	76	151
	31.114.1	105	177
	47.57.2	169	220
	66.99.34	97	168-169
	66.99.37	170	220
	66.99.40	15	101
	66.99.41	14	100
	68.134	46	125
Oxford, Ashmolean Museum	1893.1-41(71)	31	116
	1893.1-41(75)	49	127
	1893.1-41(171)	50	128
	1922.92	155	214
	1933.1209	157	215
Paris, Galerie Maspero	none	80	154
Paris, Musée du Louvre	E. 11624	56	134
	E. 17357	86	158
	E. 25409	22	108
Philadelphia, The University Museum, University of Pennsylvania	E 14349	106	178
Richmond, The Virginia Museum of Fine Arts	61.5	140	204
San Diego, San Diego Museum of Man	14881	141	204-205
Toledo, The Toledo Museum of Art	25.744	151	212
Washington, D.C., Collection of Mr. J. S. Thacher	none	166	219
Weert, Collection of Mr. H. E. Smeets	none	32	116-117

LIST OF FIGURES

ADDENDA and CORRIGENDA

INDEX

The publishers take the opportunity of a second printing to include these lists and the index, which were prepared after the book first appeared on the occasion of the jubilee exhibition held at the Brooklyn Museum.

LIST OF FIGURES

Fig. 1 (p. 2). Bust of Queen Nefertiti excavated at Tell el Amarna. Painted limestone. Agyptisches Museum, Berlin (West) 21300.

Fig. 2 (p. 11). Stela showing Akhenaten, Nefertiti, and three daughters, excavated at Tell el Amarna. Painted limestone. Egyptian Museum, Cairo JE 44865.

Fig. 3 (p. 10). Stela with representation of King Amenhotep III and Queen Tiye, excavated at Tell el Amarna. Painted limestone. British Museum, London 57399.

Fig. 4 (p. 19). Detail of a relief showing King Amenhotep III and a smaller figure, almost certainly Amenhotep IV. Karnak, Great Temple of Amun, Third Pylon, east face of northern tower.

Fig. 5 (p. 21). Sunk relief representation of Ay and Tiy being rewarded by the royal family. Limestone. Egyptian Museum, Cairo 10/11/26/1. Detail of Fig. 38 (p. 62).

Fig. 6 (p. 22). Stela with figures, half in the round, of Bek and his wife, Tahery. Yellow-brown quartzite. Agyptisches Museum, Berlin (West) 1/63.

Fig. 7 (p. 23). Plan of Tell el Amarna. From Smith 1958, p. 187, fig. 63.

Fig. 8 (p. 24). Akhenaten and Queen Tiye entering the latter's "sunshade" temple. Drawing of a relief in the tomb of Huya at Tell el Amarna. From Davies 1905b, pl. IX.

Fig. 9 (p. 29). Colossal statue of King Akhenaten excavated at Karnak. Sandstone. Egyptian Museum, Cairo JE 55938.

Fig. 10 (p. 30). Colossal statue of King Amenhotep IV excavated at Karnak, and detail view of head prior to its reattachment to the body. Sandstone. Egyptian Museum, Cairo JE 49529.

Fig. 11 (p. 31). Upper part of a colossal statue of King Amenhotep IV excavated at Karnak. Sandstone. Egyptian Museum, Cairo JE 49528.

Fig. 12 (pp. 6 and 31). Detail of the upper part of a colossal statue of King Amenhotep IV excavated at Karnak. Sandstone. Egyptian Museum, Cairo 29/5/49/1.

Fig. 13 (p. 33). Ninth Pylon of the Great Temple of Amun at Karnak, western tower seen from the north.

Fig. 14 (p. 32). *Talatat* from a shrine to the Aten reused as fill within the Ninth Pylon of the Great Temple of Amun at Karnak.

Fig. 15 (p. 32). *Talatat* from a shrine to the Aten reused as fill within the Ninth Pylon of the Great Temple of Amun at Karnak.

Fig. 16 (p. 34). Amenhotep IV and the goddess Maat. Drawing of a relief in the tomb of the Vizier Ramose at Thebes. From Davies 1941, pl. XXIX.

Fig. 17 (p. 35). Amenhotep IV and Nefertiti at the Window of Appearances. Drawing of a relief in the tomb of the Vizier Ramose at Thebes. From Davies 1941, pl. XXXIII.

Fig. 18 (p. 35). Double representation of Akhenaten, Nefertiti, and two of their daughters worshiping the Aten. Detail of a drawing of Boundary Stela S at Tell el Amarna. From Davies 1908a, pl. XXVI.

Fig. 19 (p. 36). Plan of the Central Quarter at Tell el Amarna. From Smith 1958, p. 195, fig. 65.

Fig. 20 (p. 39). Detail of a painting (Fig. 21) from Tell el Amarna showing the Princesses Neferneferuaten-tasherit and Neferneferure seated on cushions.

Fig. 21 (p. 39). Reconstruction of the painting at Tell el Amarna of which Fig. 20 once formed part. From Davies 1921, pl. II.

Fig. 22 (p. 42). The house of the Sculptor Tuthmose at Tell el Amarna after excavation in 1912.

Fig. 23 (p. 42). Mask of King Akhenaten excavated at Tell el Amarna. Plaster. Agyptisches Museum Berlin/DDR 21348.

Fig. 24 (p. 43). Mask of a king, probably Smenkhkare, excavated at Tell el Amarna. Plaster. Agyptisches Museum, Berlin (West) 21354.

Fig. 25 (p. 44). Head of Nefertiti excavated at Tell el Amarna. Granite. Agyptisches Museum Berlin/DDR 21358.

Fig. 26 (p. 45). Head of a princess, probably Merytaten, excavated at Tell el Amarna. Yellow-brown quartzite. Egyptian Museum, Cairo JE 44869.

Fig. 27 (p. 46). Mask of a woman, possibly one of the foreign women in the King's *harim*, excavated at Tell el Amarna. Plaster. Agyptisches Museum Berlin/DDR 21261.

Fig. 28 (p. 47). Statuette of a king, possibly Akhenaten. Painted wood. Agyptisches Museum, Berlin (West) 21836.

Fig. 29 (p. 48). Seated statue of Akhenaten. Yellow stone. Musée du Louvre, Paris N. 831.

Fig. 30 (pp. 50-51). Relief representation of Re-Herakhty and Amenhotep IV found in the Tenth Pylon of the Great Temple of Amun at Karnak. Sandstone. Agyptisches Museum Berlin/DDR 2072.

Fig. 31 (p. 53). Sunk relief representation of Akhenaten offering to the Aten, excavated at Tell el Amarna. Egyptian Museum, Cairo 26/6/28/8.

Fig. 32 (p. 55). Head of a princess excavated at Tell el Amarna. Yellow-brown quartzite. Egyptian Museum, Cairo JE 44870.

Fig. 33 (p. 56). Sunk relief representation of Akhenaten and Nefertiti offering to the Aten, and Merytaten shaking a sistrum for the Aten. Excavated at Tell el Amarna. Alabaster. Egyptian Museum, Cairo 30/10/26/12.

Fig. 34 (p. 57). Sunk relief representation, found in the Royal Tomb at Tell el Amarna, of Akhenaten, Nefertiti, and two of their daughters worshiping the Aten. Limestone. Egyptian Museum, Cairo 10/11/26/4.

Fig. 35 (p. 58). Slab, with hollows for inlays of glass or faience, bearing a representation of Akhenaten and one of his daughters offering to the Aten. Reddish-brown quartzite. University Museum, Philadelphia E 16230.

Fig. 36 (p. 59). Unfinished head of a queen, probably Nefertiti, excavated at Tell el Amarna. Brown quartzite. Egyptian Museum, Cairo JE 59286.

Fig. 37 (p. 60). Head of Queen Nefertiti excavated at Memphis. Yellow quartzite. Egyptian Museum, Cairo JE 45547.

Fig. 38 (p. 62). Akhenaten and Nefertiti rewarding Ay and Tiy with collars of gold (cf. Fig. 5). Drawing of a relief from the tomb of Ay at Tell el Amarna. From Davies 1908b, pl. XXIX.

Figs. 39-40 (p. 63). Front and rear views of a pair statuette of Akhenaten and Nefertiti. Painted limestone. Musée du Louvre, Paris E. 15593.

Fig. 41 (p. 64). Statuette of Akhenaten, Nefertiti, and a princess, excavated at Tell el Amarna. Limestone. University College London 004.

Fig. 42 (p. 65). Detail of a statue of Akhenaten holding an offering table, excavated at Tell el Amarna. Painted limestone. Egyptian Museum, Cairo JE 43580.

Fig. 43 (p. 65). Bust of King Akhenaten. Limestone. Musée du Louvre, Paris E. 11076.

Fig. 44 (p. 66). Detail of a statuette of Nefertiti excavated at Tell el Amarna. Limestone. Agyptisches Museum Berlin/DDR 21263.

Fig. 45 (p. 69). Fragment of a stela from Tell el Amarna showing Nefertiti placing a collar around the neck of Akhenaten. Painted limestone. Agyptisches Museum Berlin/DDR 14511.

Fig. 46 (pp. 74-75). Officials in a ceremony connected with the first jubilee of Amenhotep III. Relief in the tomb of Khaemhet at Thebes.

Fig. 47 (p. 78). The royal family offering to the Aten. Drawing of a relief in the tomb of Ipy at Tell el Amarna. From Davies 1906, pl. XXXI.

Fig. 48 (p. 95). Squeeze made in 1843-1845 of Boundary Stela N at Tell el Amarna.

Fig. 49 (p. 98). Sculptor's model, excavated at Tell el Amarna, with heads of Akhenaten and Smenkhkare. Limestone. Egyptian Museum, Cairo JE 59294.

Fig. 50 (p. 118). Bust of a girl, possibly Ankhesenpaaten. Painted limestone. Musée du Louvre, Paris E. 14715.

Fig. 51 (p. 131). Statuette of a princess excavated at Tell el Amarna. Red-brown quartzite. Egyptian Museum, Cairo JE 44873.

Fig. 52 (p. 132). Akhenaten, Nefertiti, and Merytaten offering to the Aten. Sunk relief representation on the façade of a shrine excavated at Tell el Amarna. Painted limestone. Egyptian Museum, Cairo JE 65041.

Fig. 53 (p. 134). Suggested restoration of the design on Cat. No. 56. After a line drawing by Norman de Garis Davies, in Davies 1923b, p. 42, fig. 4.

Fig. 54 (p. 165). Unfinished statue of Akhenaten kissing one of his daughters. Excavated at Tell el Amarna. Limestone. Egyptian Museum, Cairo JE 44866.

Fig. 55 (p. 169). Bust of a king, probably Smenkhkare, excavated at Tell el Amarna. Limestone. Agyptisches Museum Berlin/DDR 20496.

p. 11, Fig. 2. The photograph of this stela has been reversed.

p. 12, line 2. For "(No. 57)" read "(No. 55)".

p. 17, line 35. For a recent discussion of the history of the Aten, see Tawfik, S., "Aton Studies" *Mitteilungen des Deutschen Archäologischen Instituts Abteilung Kairo* 29 no. 1 (1973), pp. 77-86.

p. 20, line 18. To this paragraph should be added: "It is possible that this eroticism was religiously inspired. The Aten as the heavenly father had assimilated all the sun-gods and masculine principles in the Egyptian pantheon. The great female divinity who had existed from earliest times and who had manifested herself as the primordial mother-wife-lover, in such aspects as Nut, Isis, Hathor, and Sekhmet, was notably lacking in the new sun-cult. It is perhaps as something instinctive and subconscious, therefore, that Nefertiti takes on the role of the divine female counterpart, a sort of Hathor incarnate."

For a discussion of Nefertiti as a goddess, which appeared after this book went to press, see Wilson, J. "Akh-en-Aton and Nefert-iti" *Journal of Near Eastern Studies* 32 nos. 1-2 (January-April, 1973), pp. 235-241.

p. 27, lines 28-29. For "One by one the vassal states transferred" read "One by one the vassal states on the northern border transferred".

p. 39, Fig. 21. The scale indicated (2/7) is no longer accurate, as the drawing has been reduced in size.

p. 43, line 33. For "(Nos. 95, 108)" read "(Nos. 108, 109)".

p. 48, line 21 (and p. 80). Delete footnote 85; insert instead "(Figs. 16-17)."

p. 49, caption for Fig. 29. The material of Louvre N. 831, given as steatite (?), is actually a mixture of gypsum ($CaSO_4,2H_2O$) and calcite ($CaCO_3$) with a few traces of quartz (SiO_2). This information was kindly provided by the Laboratoire de Recherche des Musées de France, through Mlle. Letellier, of the Egyptian Department of the Louvre.

p. 53, caption for Fig. 31. For "alabaster" read "indurated limestone". For "Cairo 26/6/28/8." read "Cairo 20.6.28. 8."

p. 62, line 28. For "(Fig. 34)" read "(Fig. 33)".

pp. 66, line 4, and 80. Delete Footnote 130.

p. 72, line 43. For "(British Museum 37894)" read "(British Museum 37896)".

p. 72, line 46. For "tomb at Thebes" read "tombs at Thebes."

p. 76, line 34. For "(Nos. 35, 130)" read "(Nos. 35, 53)".

p. 76, line 51. For "(No. 139)" read "(No. 137)".

p. 79, lines 17-18. For "(Nos. 74, 118, 137, 139)" read "(Nos. 74, 118, 120, 137, 139, 146)".

p. 80, Footnote 17. Add: "but see now Nims, C. F., "The Transition from the Traditional to the New Style of Wall Relief under Amenhotep IV" *Journal of Near Eastern Studies* 32 nos. 1-2 (January-April, 1973), p. 185."

p. 80, Footnote 97. Add: "See also, Nims, C. F., "The Transition from the Traditional to the New Style of Wall Relief under Amenhotep IV" *Journal of Near Eastern Studies* 32 nos. 1-2 (January-April, 1973), p. 185."

p. 94. To the bibliography for No. 6 add: "Hoeppli, R., "Morphological Changes in Human Schistosomiasis and Certain Analogies in Ancient Egyptian Sculpture" *Acta Tropica* 30 no. 1-2 (1973), p. 9, fig. 3".

p. 104, No. 18, col. 3, line 21. Add: "(M.M.A. 21.9.469, 573, 597, 604)."

p. 105, No. 19. This head is illustrated in color on p. 81.

p. 106, No. 20, col. 1, lines 14-15. Delete "leaving that breast and shoulder bare." The right breast is covered by an unpleated garment the upper edge of which is represented as a diagonal line running from the left shoulder down to the upper right arm.

p. 108, No. 22. This piece is illustrated on p. 82 in color which is too purple.

p. 111, No. 25. A detail is illustrated in color on p. 83.

p. 113. To the bibliography for No. 27 add: "*Haggada. From Darkness to Light* (Jerusalem and Haifa, 1973), p. 30, illus."

p. 114. To the bibliography for No. 28 add: "Cooney, J. D., "Art of the Ancient World" *Apollo* 96 (December, 1972), p. 477, fig. 4."

p. 116, No. 31, line 54. For "(No. 55)" read "(No. 57)".

p. 116, No. 31, line 59. For "(JE 13415)." read "(see Fig. 31)."

p. 126, No. 47, lines 27-28. Add after "London": "(University College London 2233),".

p. 129. This illustration of No. 51 is a detail; the entire slab shows a large undecorated surface to the left of the scene illustrated.

p. 142, No. 66, bibliography. Add: "Roeder 1969, pl. 189, no. P.C. 111; W. K. Simpson, "Century Two: Collecting Egyptian and Ancient Near Eastern Art for the Boston Museum" *Apollo* 98 (October, 1973), pp. 252-253, with fig. 3."

p. 147, No. 72. A detail is illustrated in color on p. 84.

p. 159, No. 87, col. 3, line 4. For "(Fig. 41)" read "(Fig. 39)".

p. 160, No. 88. This piece is illustrated in color on p. 85.

p. 166, No. 94, lines 2-3. For "LIFE-SIZE HEAD OF AKHENATEN" read "HEAD OF A KING".

p. 166, No. 94, line 52. For "no. 770" read "no. 768".

p. 167, No. 95, line 2. For "HEAD OF A KING" read "LIFE-SIZE HEAD OF AKHENATEN".

p. 171, No. 99. This piece is illustrated in color on p. 87.

p. 180, No. 109, lines 26-27. For "in the same mold" read "from the same model".

p. 181, No. 110, line 32. For "(No. 96)" read "(No. 29.1310: Brooklyn 1952, no. 35, illus.)".

p. 183. The swimming girl (No. 113) should have been illustrated horizontally.

p. 184, No. 114, col. 1, line 37. For "drilled by" read "made by".

p. 185, No. 115, col. 2, line 6. After "Cairo JE 59294" add ", Fig. 49:".

p. 185, No. 116. A detail of this relief appears in color both on the cover and on p. 88.

p. 188, No. 120, col. 3, line 9. After "Berlin East 21263" add ", Fig. 44:".

p. 190, No. 121, line 49. After "Berlin East 21263" add, ", Fig. 44:".

p. 195, No. 127, col. 3, line 12. For "and never is shown rattling a sistrum." read "and only exceptionally is shown rattling a sistrum (Nefertiti is shown shaking one rattle on Roeder 1969, pl. 2. On an unpublished *talatat* from Karnak she plays two such instruments.)"

p. 199, No. 133. The illustration shows only a detail of the relief.

p. 204. To the bibliography for No. 140 add: "*Ancient Art in the Virginia Museum* (Richmond, 1973), p. 34, no. 29."

p. 207, No. 143, col. 1, line 10. For "high above the City" read "in a wady east of the City".

p. 207, No. 143, col. 2, line 1. For "hollowed out of a cliff" read "hewn in a cliff".

pp. 208-209, No. 146. A detail of this relief is illustrated in color on p. 86.

p. 213, No. 153, col. 3, line 4. Add after "pl. VIII:" "Riefstahl, E., "A Unique Fish-Shaped Glass Vial in The Brooklyn Museum" *Journal of Glass Studies* 14 (1972), pp. 10-14),".

pp. 222-223, No. 175. This is illustrated in color on p. 87.

p. 224, Bibliography. Aldred, 1953. The entry should read: "Cranial Deformation in Ancient Egypt?" *Man* 53 (1953), pp. 194-95."

THE ROYAL FAMILY AT THE END OF DYNASTY XVIII

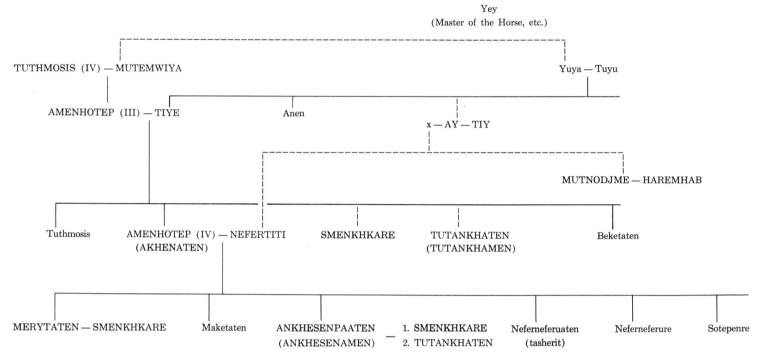

Ruling kings and queens in capital letters

_ _ _ _ — conjectural line of descent

INDEX

This index serves also as an expansion of Concordance II. Under the names of collections or owners it contains references to all pages in the text on which specific objects (including those not in the Catalogue) are mentioned.

In the case of collections, the objects in which are not numbered, the designation NN has been used.

Museums and collections are found under the city or town of their location, not under their names or the names of their owners.

Abu Ghurab, 37
Abydos, 16, 18; temple of Sety I, 73
Administration, 14
Afnet headdress, Akhenaten, 90, 92, 93, 98, 101, 120, 126, 185, 187, 190, 217, 218, 219, 220, 221; Tiye, 105
Afterlife, 76, 205
Age, representation of, 150
Ahmose, King, 13
Ahmose, Queen, 134
Akhenaten, 22, 24, 49, 50, 51, 53, 69; colossal statues, 29, 53, 54, 55, 56, 61, 64; death and burial, 27, 41; divine status, 18, 97; marriage, 18, 25, 26; names, 22, 24, 49, 217, 222; pathology, 53, 56; portrait characteristics, 53, 54, 63, 90, 92, 94, 98, 113, 167, 169, 185; representations of, 34, 46, 49, 62, 67; Nos. 1, 2, 3, 4, 5, 6, 7, 8, 9, 10 (?), 11, 12, 13, 14, 15, 16, 17, 18, 26, 27, 38 (?), 47, 49, 52, 54, 94, 95, 96 (?), 97 (?), 101 (?), 114, 115, 116, 117, 118, 119, 121, 122, 123, 125 (?), 127 (?), 161-175
Akhetaten, 22, 95, 99
Akhmin, 12; provenance, 161; No. 89
Alabastron, name for Tell el Amarna, 90
Amada, 70
"Amarna blue," 213
Amarna style, 20, 40, 43; at Karnak, 48, 61; dating criteria, 48, 49; Early Period, 51, 95, 98; individuality, 76, 150; innovation, 55, 64, 71, 73, 77; Late Period, 63, 64, 191; mannerism, 52, 55, 57, 63, 96, 118; material, influence of, 29, 58, 97; Middle Period, 61, 62; perspective, 79, 120, 133, 209; realism, 12, 53; role of Akhenaten, 53, 55, 62; spatial concept, 72, 73, 156; subsidiary motifs, 58, 122, 124, 198, 212; survival into later periods, 15, 64, 68, 70, 79; traditional features, 55, 64, 212. *See also* Forgeries; Frontality, painting and relief; Groups, representations of
Amenemhet called Surer, tomb of, 72
Amenhotep III, 13, 16, 17, 18, 28, 49, 50, 52, 54, 56, 69, 72; bracelets of, 192; cattle hunt, 158; representations of, 46, 202; No. 109 (?)
Amenhotep IV, 16, 18, 19, 28, 49; epithets, 18; name changed to Akhenaten, 22, 97
Amenhotep (High Steward), 16
Amenhotep, Prince, later Amenhotep IV, 16, 17
Amenhotep-son-of-Hapu, 16
Amherst, Lord, 92
Amherst Collection, 91, 93, 101, 120, 134, 188
Amherst fragments, 90

Amun, 12, 26, 134, 213; desecration, 26; priesthood, 12, 17
Amun-Re, 28
Anen, 17
Animals, representations of, 71, 212; bubalis, 207, 211; cattle, 71, 143, 152, 154, 158, 208; crane, 133; duck, 187, 206, 210; fish, *bolti,* 210, 213; goats, 71, 147. *See also* Horses
Ankh sign, 20, 97, 102, 104, 110, 111, 114, 127, 165, 209, 217, 220, 221
Ankhesenamen, 69, 194
Ankhesenpaaten, 20, 26, 55, 131, 196; representations of, 48, 77; Nos. 16, 102 (?), 105 (?), 126 (?)
Antiquarianism, 18, 73
Any (steward), stela of servants, 205
Apuia, tomb of, 61
Army, 11, 51
Art, folk, 205; post-Amarna, 62, 73, 168, 182; pre-Amarna: conservatism, 14; innovation, 53; popular, 52, 53; style of Amenhotep III, 48, 50, 62, 73, 105. *See also* Amarna style
Asiatic, influence, 13, 14; representations of, 128, 202; stela of, 205
Aswan, 57
Atef crown, 100, 135; No. 14
Aten, 11, 12, 17, 22, 24, 25, 26, 27, 69; chief prophet of, 12; name, 17, 20, 24, 27, 49, 50, 62, 64, 92, 93, 99, 100, 102, 104, 106, 117, 126, 132, 187; pre-Amarna, 17; private worship of, 63. *See also* Cartouche, Aten; Family, royal; Monotheism
Atum, 69
Axes, 139
Ay, 19, 62; family, 17; representation of, 179; No. 108 (?); tomb of, 40, 61, 62
Ay (fanbearer), tomb of, 204

Baal, 13
Barsanti, A., 56, 217
Battle-axe, 121
Battle scene, 12, 210; Ramesside, 79
Beard, royal, 217, 218, 219, 220, 222
Bek (chief sculptor), 53, 55, 56, 57, 58, 61, 63, 64
Beketaten, 25
Bellows, 144, 145
Ben-ben, 28, 29, 37
Berlin, East (Ägyptisches Museum, Berlin, Deutsche Demokratische Republik), no. 2072 (Fig. 30), 29, 50, 51; no. 14113 (Cat No. 102), 64, 175; no. 14122, 205; no. 14511 (Fig. 45), 69; no. 17813 (Cat. No. 11), 12, 184; no. 20494 (Cat. No. 87), 58, 159; no. 20495, 159; no. 20496 (Fig. 55), 168,

169; no. 21220 (Cat. No. 99), 43, 63, 64, 87, 170, 171; no. 21223 (Cat. No. 88), 43, 56, 63, 85, 160, 175; no. 21228 (Cat. No. 107), 179, 180; no. 21261 (Fig. 27), 43, 46; no, 21263 (Fig. 44), 66, 175, 188, 190; no. 21341 (Cat. No. 111), 43, 182; no. 21348 (Fig. 23), 42, 43; no. 21352 (Cat. No. 100), 172, 173; no. 21358 (Fig. 25), 43, 44; no. 21445, 197; no. 21683 (Cat. No. 115), 63, 98, 185; no. 22265 (Cat. No. 54), 47, 132
Berlin, West (Ägyptisches Museum der Staatlichen Museen, Preussischer Kulturbesitz), no. 1/63, 22, 56; no. 2045 (Cat. No. 47), 126; no. 14145 (Cat. No. 16), 11, 20, 38, 47, 49, 56, 66, 68, 72, 73, 76, 77, 102, 116, 134, 165, 195; no. 14512 (Cat. No. 6), 20, 53, 94; no. 15000 (Cat. No. 120), 79, 136, 188, 189, 190, 192, 193; no. 21239 (Cat. No. 112), 43, 46, 182; no. 21245 (Cat. No. 103), 43, 63, 176; no. 21300 (Fig. 1), 2, 4, 11, 20, 40, 43, 54, 173, 182, 190; no. 21340 (Cat. No. 94), 43, 166; no. 21350 (Cat. No. 108), 43, 179; no. 21351 (Cat. No. 95), 43, 167; no. 21354 (Fig. 24), 43; no. 21356 (Cat. No. 109), 43, 63, 179, 180; no. 21834 (Cat. No. 19), 81, 105, 193; no. 21835 (Cat. No. 1), 34, 64, 90, 117; no. 21836 (Fig. 28), 47
Bit, horse, No. 157
Blacks, representations of, 143, 199; No. 134
Blue Crown, 18, 43, 55, 90, 95, 98, 102, 104, 112, 132, 166, 167, 168, 184, 185, 192, 217
Boat, 146; royal barges, 67, 135, 194; sacred bark, 69; shape for military standard, 120; warship, 133
Bologna, Museo, Civico, no. 1887, 202
Bolti. See Fish
Borchardt, L., 180
Boston, Museum of Fine Arts, no. 36.96 (Cat. No. 60), 137; no. 37.1 (Cat. No. 33), 38, 118; no. 37.3 (Cat. No. 24), 110; no. 62.320 (Cat. No. 142), 68, 206; no. 62.1168 (Cat. No. 62), 138, 181; no. 63.260 (Cat. No. 57), 38, 67, 116, 133, 135; no. 63.427 (Cat. No. 63), 70, 139; no. 63.961 (Cat. No. 81), 38, 70, 155; no. 63.962 (Cat. No. 64), 58, 140; no. 64.521 (Cat. No. 57), 38, 67, 116, 133, 135; no. 64.1944, 99; no. 65.466 (Cat. No. 165), 41, 217, 219; no. 67.637 (Cat. No. 17), 70, 103, 112, 118; no. 67.921 (Cat. No. 65), 71, 73, 141, 145; no. 67.922 (Cat. No. 7), 61, 70, 94, 95, 97, 115; no. 1971.294 (Cat. No. 124), 63, 105, 177, 193; no. 1971.295 (Cat. No. 66), 70, 142
Boundary stela. *See* Stela, family; Tell el

Amarna
Bouquet, 50, 116, 132, 150, 155, 185, 192,
   199, 209
Bow, composite, 13
Bow case, 207
Bronze, 13, 14, 214, 215
Brooklyn, The Brooklyn Museum, no. 16.46
   (Cat. No. 89), 117, 161, 163; no. 16.48
   (Cat. No. 121), 63, 98, 126, 185, 186, 187,
   188, 190, 191; no. 29.34 (Cat. No. 96), 47,
   64, 130, 168; no. 29.1310, 181; no. 33.51,
   41; no. 33.52 (Cat. No. 161), 41, 217; no.
   33.53 (Cat. No. 162), 41, 217, 218; no.
   33.54 (Cat. No. 163), 41, 217, 218; no.
   33.685 (Cat. No. 91), 54, 58, 164; no.
   35.1531 (Cat. No. 167), 41, 217, 219;
   no. 35.1866 (Cat. No. 168), 41, 217, 220;
   no. 35.1867 (Cat. No. 171), 41, 217,
   221; no. 35.1870 (Cat. No. 172), 41, 217,
   222; no. 35.1882 (Cat. No. 173), 41, 217,
   221; no. 35.1883 (Cat. No. 164), 41,
   217, 218; no. 35.1999 (Cat. No. 48), 38, 54,
   109, 126, 128; no. 35.2000 (Cat. No. 34),
   55, 103, 118; no. 35.2001 (Cat. No. 158),
   58, 215; no. 37.405 (Cat. No. 35), 55, 76,
   79, 119; no. 37.499 (Cat. No. 174), 41, 217,
   222; no. 37.316E, 213; no. 37.340E (Cat.
   No. 152), 212; no. 41.82 (Cat. No. 18), 38,
   56, 79, 104, 109, 110, 115; no. 48.111 (Cat.
   No. 154), 213; no. 52.148.1 (Cat. No. 159),
   58, 216; no. 52.148.2 (Cat. No. 160), 216;
   no. 54.186 (Cat. No. 143), 40, 207; no.
   58.2 (Cat. No. 4), 37, 57, 64, 90, 92, 93,
   106, 117, 125; no. 60.28 (Cat. No. 51), 70,
   128, 129; no. 60.197.1 (Cat. No. 122), 58,
   63, 185, 192; no. 60.197.2 (Cat. No. 125),
   165, 193; no. 60.197.3 (Cat. No. 131), 70,
   198; no. 60.197.4 (Cat. No. 67), 143, 154;
   no. 60.197.5 (Cat. No. 144), 154, 207, 211;
   no. 60.197.6 (Cat. No. 116), cover, 37, 63,
   70, 88, 192; no. 60.197.7 (Cat. No. 58), 73,
   136; no. 60.197.8 (Cat. No. 92), 58, 77,
   165, 192; no. 60.197.9 (Cat. No. 126), 68,
   135, 194, 200; no. 61.195.1 (Cat. No. 68),
   70, 143; no. 61.195.3 (Cat. No. 82), 70,
   156; no. 62.149 (Cat. No. 69), 144; no.
   64.148.3 (Cat. No. 70), 71, 73, 141, 144,
   145; no. 64.199.1 (Cat. No. 36), 34, 70,
   119; no. 65.16 (Cat. No. 71), 58, 122, 146;
   no. 65.133 (Cat. No. 156), 214; no. 66.175,
   18; no. 67.175.1 (Cat. No. 37), 34, 70, 120,
   195; no. L67.26.1 (Cat. No. 98), 168, 175;
   no. 68.154 (Cat. No. 132), 198; no. L69.38.1
   (Cat. No. 25), 34, 66, 83, 109, 111, 113;
   no. 71.89 (Cat. No. 26), 54, 103, 112; no.
   L71.8.1 (Cat. No. 72), 71, 77, 84, 147;
   no. L72.17 (Cat. No. 133), 182, 199
Brussels, Musées Royaux d'Art et d'Histoire,
   no. E. 3051 (Cat. No. 9), 96, 98, 120; no.
   E. 3052 (Cat. No. 10), 96, 98, 120; no. E.
   6730 (Cat. No. 52), 47, 64, 90, 130; no.
   E. 7232 (Cat. No. 38), 120
Bubastis, 16
Buffalo, Albright-Knox Art Gallery, no. 37:6
   (Cat. No. 8), 34, 94, 95, 114, 117, 120, 162
   (including refs. to Cat. No. 28 and
   Boundary Stela N)

Cairo, 41, 97, 100, 102, 174, 175, 181, 218
Cairo, Egyptian Museum, no. 10/12/24/6, 43,
   180; no. 30/10/26/12 (Fig. 33), 56, 62;
   no. 10/11/26/1 (Fig. 5, cf. Fig. 38), 20, 21,
   40, 61, 62, 179; no. 10/11/26/4 (Fig. 34),
   56, 57, 61, 63, 73, 128; no. 20.6.28.8 (Fig.
   31), 53, 56, 61, 116; no. 29/5/49/1 (Fig. 12,
   illus. also on p. 6), 29, 31, 53, 54, 56;
   no. JE 32974, 213; no. JE 38257, 105, 174;
   no. JE 43275d, 197; no. JE 43580 (Fig. 42),
   64, 65, 125; no. JE 44865 (Fig. 2), 11, 47,
   102, 134, 195; no. JE 44866 (Fig. 54), 165;
   no. JE 44869 (Fig. 26), 43, 44, 45; no.
   JE 44870 (Fig. 32), 55; no. JE 44873 (Fig.
   51), 131; no. JE 45547 (Fig. 37), 60, 61;
   no. JE 49528 (Fig. 11), 29, 31, 53, 54, 56;
   no. JE 49529 (Fig. 10), 29, 30, 53, 54, 56;
   no. JE 55372, 214; no. JE 55938 (Fig. 9,
   28, 29, 53, 54, 55, 56; no. JE 59286
   (Fig. 36), 58, 59, 60; no. JE 59294 (Fig.
   49), 98, 99, 185; no. JE 65041 (Fig. 52),
   132; no. JE 65926, 99; no. JE 91723, 135;
   no. CG 34176-34181, 205; no. CG 42091,
   160, 168, 182; no. CG 42097, 160; no. T. 1,
   177; no. T. 223, 104; no. T. 324, 207, 210,
   211; no. T. 755, 197; no. T. 1189, 200, 210
Cambridge, Fitzwilliam Museum, no.
   2300.1943 (Cat. No. 11), 12, 18, 29, 61,
   70, 94, 97, 115; no. 4514.1943 (Cat. No.
   39), 121; no. 4529.1943 (Cat. No. 40), 34,
   121; no. 4606.1943 (Cat. No. 123), 165, 192
Carnarvon Collection, 91, 107
Carter, Howard, 37, 57, 90
Cartouche, 184; Akhenaten, 95, 138; Aten,
   17, 20, 50, 92, 93, 95, 100, 104, 106, 111,
   113, 114, 126, 132, 185, 187, 218; Nefertiti,
   56; Re, 24
Chapman, S., 135
Chariot, 13, 67, 71, 123, 128, 138, 142, 148,
   151, 153, 204, 207
Children, representations of, 55, 76, 131;
   No. 53
Cleveland, The Cleveland Museum of Art,
   no. 59.186, 111; no. 59.187 (Cat. No. 41),
   122; no. 59.188 (Cat. No. 23), 109, 111, 113
Colossus of Memnon, 16
Columns, composite, 196, 206
Composite statues, 43, 58; Nos. 19, 21, 87 (?),
   88, 99, 100, 101, 103, 104
Cooney, John D., 104, 135, 136, 140, 149,
   150, 152, 155, 156, 187, 193, 194, 196, 200,
   203, 209
Copper, 14
Co-regency, Akhenaten and Smenkhkare, 25,
   26, 184; Amenhotep III and Amenhotep IV,
   18, 49, 50, 61
Costume, Akhenaten, 54, 97, 127, 195;
   non-royal, 122, 124, 181
Crete, 72
Curtis group, 63

Daressy, G., 217
Davies, Norman de Garis, 40, 95
Deir el Bahri, Temple of Hatshepsut, 119,
   134, 200
Deir el Medineh, 140
Desecration, modern, 38, 117; monuments
   of Amun, 26; reliefs, 37, 202; sculpture,
   37, 41, 92, 219
Detroit, The Detroit Institute of Arts,
   no. 66.8 (Cat. No. 127), 195
Didactic name of Aten. See Aten, name
Disk, rayed, 20, 48, 50, 51, 53, 67, 69, 102
Djed sign, 104
Djeserkaresonb, tomb of, 53
Djoser, 18
Double Crown, 135, 184
Dynasties, III, 18; V, 37, 53, 207; VI, 180;
   XII, 147; XVIII, passim; XIX, 27; XXI,
   108; XXV, 108, 213

Ear, representations of, 64, 160, 171
Earlobe, pierced, 57, 63, 64, 94, 98, 101, 112,
   115, 120, 127, 160, 167, 175, 185, 186, 188,
   190, 217, 218, 219, 220, 221, 222;
   unpierced, 219, 220
Earring, 102, 105, 182, 195, 199, 200, 204
Earstud, 102, 111, 116, 137, 165, 182, 196,
   199, 203
Edinburgh, The Royal Scottish Museum,
   no. 1960.906 (Cat. No. 43), 123; no.
   1963.240 (Cat. No. 42), 122; no. 1969.377
   (Cat. No. 12), 63, 98, 190; no. 1972.94
   (Cat. No. 175), 41, 87, 217, 219, 222, 223
Egypt Exploration Society, 38, 112, 125, 155,
   158, 212, 214

Eisenberg, J., 116
Elephantine, 16
Emotion, representation of, 77
Erotic symbolism, 20, 54, 108, 116, 131
Esna, 28, 68
Ex-votos, 43, 126, 205
Eye, representations of, 63, 64, 98, 115, 168,
   175, 179, 180, 182, 217, 218, 219, 220
Eyes, inlaid, Nos. 19, 88, 94, 101

Face, representations of, 66, 136, 179, 180,
   218. See also Akhenaten, portrait
   characteristics; Ear, Eye; Mouth
Faience, 14, 41, 58, 157, 158, 164, 199, 214,
   215, 216, 220
Falcon, symbol of Re-Harakhty, 20, 24, 50, 67
Family, royal: religious role, 68, 69, 70, 76,
   102, 134, 205; representation of, 73, 77
Fanbearer, 120, 142, 200, 201, 204
Figure, representations of, 55, 64, 92, 95,
   108, 122, 163, 178, 183. See also
   Akhenaten, portrait characteristics; Neck
Fish, bolti, 210, 213
Fishing and fowling scene, 68, 194, 210
Florence, Museo Archeologico, no. 6316, 204
Flowers. See Bouquet
Flute, 149, 151
"Fly-whisk" scepter, 115
Foot, representations of, 72, 102, 134, 136,
   177
Forgeries, 56, 95, 190
Fouquet Collection, 178
Frankfort, H., 77, 79
Frontality, painting and relief, 53, 128, 197
Gallatin Collection, 100, 101, 169, 220
Gayer-Anderson Collection, 97, 121, 192
Gebel el Silsila, 20, 29, 37; stela, 28, 51
Gebelein, provenance, No. 110 (?)
Geneva, Collection of Mr. Nicolas
   Koutoulakis, NN. (Cat. No. 13), 25, 67,
   99, 137
Genre scenes, 58, 70; Nos. 41, 63, 64, 70, 71,
   72, 131
Glass, 14, 58; Nos. 152, 153
Glassmaking, 212, 213
Groups, representations of, 64, 76, 77, 149,
   203

Hagg Qandil, provenance, No. 104 (?)
Haifa, Collection of Dr. Rëuben R. Hecht,
   NN. (Cat. No. 27), 20, 34, 62, 109, 113
Hands, representations of, 72, 79, 120, 125,
   132, 159, 181, 187, 200, 209
Hanover, Kestner-Museum, no. 1964.3, 99
Haremheb, sarcophagus, 73; tomb at
   Memphis, 73
Harim, 18, 38
Harp, 149
Hathor, 119
Hatnub, quarries, 90
Hatshepsut, 119
Head, representations of, 54, 55, 62, 76,
   160, 197
Headdress, female, alteration, 105, 193;
   male, 198, 204. See also Nemes headdress;
   Nubian wig
Heb sign, 104
Heh sign, 118
Heka scepter, 97, 219
Heliopolis, 12, 14, 17, 22, 29, 37
Herdsman, 147
Hermopolis, 27, 38, 58, 63, 68, 69, 70, 71, 92,
   150, 151; Provenance, Nos. 17, 26, 51, 55,
   57, 58, 61, 63, 64, 65, 66, 67, 68, 69, 71, 73,
   74, 75, 77, 78, 79, 81, 82, 83, 92, 93, 116 (?),
   117, 118, 122, 124, 125, 126, 127, 128, 129,
   130, 131, 132, 133, 135, 136, 137, 138, 139,
   140, 142, 144, 145, 146, 147, 148, 149, 150,
   159, 160 (?). See also Tell el Amarna,
   provenance
Hierakonpolis, 12
Hittites, 27

Horses, 13, 128, 138, 142, 148, 151, 153, 154, 207, 210
Hunting scene, 67, 68, 71, 154, 207, 208, 211
Huy, tomb of, 62
Huya, tomb of, 25, 62, 73, 105, 147, 165, 174, 202
Hyksos, 13
Hymn to Aten, 11, 71, 145, 208

Ibes crown, 116
Iconoclasm, 26
Imy khent, 97
Inlay, 58, 157, 159, 160, 164, 177, 179, 192, 199, 214, 215. *See also* Eyes, inlaid
Ished tree, 69
Isis, 205

Javelin, 13. *See also* Spears
Jubilee, 24, 61, 68, 203; Amenhotep III, 18, 213; Aten, 20, 24, 29, 51, 70, 94, 97, 100, 115

Kann Collection, 158
Kansas City, William Rockhill Nelson Gallery of Art and Atkins Museum of Fine Arts, no. 44-65 (Cat. No. 28), 34, 94, 95, 114, 117, 120, 162 (including refs. to Cat. No. 8 and Amarna, Boundary Stela N); no. 47-13 (Cat. No. 53), 54, 76, 131, 178
Karnak: Colossi. *See* Akhenaten, Colossal statues
Karnak, East, 53; Provenance, Nos. 7, 23, 25, 27, 30, 36, 37, 40 (?), 41, 42, 43, 44, 45 (?) Pylons: II, 29; III, 18, 19, 49, 50, 66, 67; VII, 67; VIII, 67; IX, 29, 32, 33 and *passim;* X, 29; block, 50, 51 temples of Aten, 20, 28, 29, 51, 97, 119, 128
Kennard Collection, 116, 127
Khaemhet, tomb of, 72, 74, 75
Kherep baton, 127
Kheruef, tomb of, 72, 135, 202
Khonsu, 150
Kiosk. *See* "Sunshade" kiosks
Kissing, representations of, 165, 192
Kitchen, representations of, 144
Knife, ceremonial, 214
Kush, 11, 24, 62, 124

Landscape, 58, 73
Lector priest, 97
Lepsius, Carl Richard, 95, 114
Lepsius Collection, 126
Libyan, representation of, 202
London, The British Museum, no. 12, 162; no. 13366 (Cat. No. 2), 37, 90; no. 37869, 72; no. 55193 (Cat. No. 153), 213; no. 57399 (Fig. 3), 10, 11, 102, 134; no. 58480 (Cat. No. 84), 157; no. 59290 (Cat. No. 85), 157
London, Collection of Dr. K.J. Stern, NN. (Cat. No. 104), 58, 159, 177
London, University College London, no. 002 (Cat. No. 90), 55, 108, 162, 163, 178; no. 004 (Fig. 41), 64; no. 006 (Cat. No. 113), 183; no. 009 (Cat. No. 134), 58, 199; no. 011 (Cat. No. 59), 120, 136; no. 038 (Cat. No. 29), 115; no. 2233, 126
Lucerne, Collection of Mr. Ernst Kofler, no. A 107 (Cat. No. 128), 195; NN. (Cat. No. 135), 200
Lustration scene, 69
Lute, 149, 151
Luxor, 29, 52, 97; temple of Amenhotep III, 28, 69, 134, 202
Lyre, 149

Maat, 12, 104, 214
Mahu, tomb of, 145
Maketaten, 20, 37, 117, 131, 207; death and burial, 25, 40; representations of, 48, 114; Nos. 16, 89
Malqata palace, 158

Manger, 212
Martin, Geoffrey T., 217
Maru, 22
Maryannu, 13
Masks, coffin, 43; death, 43, 180; mummy, 43; portrait, 43, 46; Nos. 108, 109, 111, 112
May, tomb of, 135, 146
Maya, tomb of, 197
Medamud, 29
Median line, 92
Medinet Ghurab, 55; provenance, No. 19 (?)
Medinet Habu, 29, 67, 139, 154, 207
Memphis, 12, 16, 17, 25, 61, 67, 97; influence of, 61, 208; provenance, Nos. 11 (?), 39 (?)
Menna, stela of, 205; tomb of, 53, 77
Mery, stela of, 205
Meryre, tomb of, 48, 128
Merytaten, 20, 22, 25, 26, 34, 72, 111, 114, 116, 117, 118, 127, 161, 194; representations of, 46, 48, 67; Nos. 16, 17, 33 (?), 34 (?), 49, 58 (?), 60 (?), 88 (?), 92 (?), 97 (?), 99 (?), 103 (?), 116 (?), 120, 124, 125 (?), 127 (?)
Middle Kingdom influence, 14
Min, 193; priesthood, 12
Mitanni, 27
Monotheism, 11, 17, 24
Montu, 13
Mourning scenes, 25, 40, 76
Mouth, representations of, 64, 168, 171, 180, 182
Müller, H. W., 195
Müller-Reinhardt Collection, 177
Munich, Staatliche Sammlung Ägyptischer Kunst, no. ÄS 4231 (Cat. No. 30), 115; no. ÄS 4863 (Cat. No. 44), 123, 124; no. ÄS 4870, 199; no. ÄS 5360 (Cat. No. 145), 71, 154, 208
Musical instruments. *See* individual names, Flute, Lyre, etc.
Musicians, 149, 151, 197
Mut, 150
Mutemwiya, 134
Mutnodjme, 20, No. 106 (?)

Nakht, tomb of, 53
Nebamun, tomb of, 53
Neck, representations of, 57, 63, 64, 90, 93, 98, 102, 106, 107, 109, 113, 127, 160, 166, 173
Nectanebo I, 29
Neferkheprure-waenre, prenomen of Amenhotep IV, 18, 138
Neferneferuaten, used by Nefertiti, 24, 49; used by Smenkhkare, 25
Neferneferuaten-tasherit, 20, 165
Neferneferure, 20
Nefertiti, burial, 41; crown, 20, 54, 102, 103, 112, 114, 116, 127, 128, 135, 136, 171; disappearance, 25; divine status, 20; epithets, 20, 49, 104; equality with Akhenaten, 20, 70, 102, 116, 192; family, 13, 17, 19; portrait characteristics, 54, 62, 108, 109, 111, 112, 164; representations, 34, 46, 54, 61, 62, 64; Nos. 3 (?), 16, 17, 18, 20, 22, 23 (?), 24, 25, 26, 28, 29, 31, 38 (?), 48 (?), 49, 50, 58 (?), 59 (?), 91 (?), 92, 99, 100, 121, 125 (?), 127 (?)
Nemes headdress, 217, 219, 220, 221, 222
New York, Collection of Mr. Christos G. Bastis, NN. (Cat. No. 25), 34, 66, 83, 109, 111, 113
New York, Collection of Mr. Milton Lowenthal, NN. (Cat. No. 45), 124
New York, Collection of Mr. Leon Pomerance, NN. (Cat. No. 77), 152, 212
New York, Collection of Mr. and Mrs. Norbert Schimmel (A new catalogue of the Schimmel Collection is being prepared and the numbers of the objects in that collection are being changed. The old Schimmel

numbers are not, therefore, used below, but they are provided in the bibliography for each object mentioned in this catalogue; i.e., the number following "Hoffmann 1964a"), NN. (Cat. No. 55), 12, 67, 133; NN. (Cat. No. 73), 61, 70, 148; NN. (Cat. No. 74), 76, 79, 149; NN. (Cat. No. 75), 63, 77, 150; NN. (Cat. No. 78), 153; NN. (Cat. No. 79), 154; NN. (Cat. No. 83), 156, 200, 209; NN. (Cat. No. 93), 76, 165; NN. (Cat. No. 117), 58, 98, 186; NN. (Cat. No. 118), 79, 187, 209; NN. (Cat. No. 129), 196, 197; NN. (Cat. No. 130), 11, 55, 76, 79, 197; NN. (Cat. No. 136), 18, 200; NN. (Cat. No. 137), 76, 79, 124, 152, 181, 201; NN. (Cat. No. 138), 69, 79, 202; NN. (Cat. No. 139), 76, 79, 149, 203; NN. (Cat. No. 146), 79, 86, 208, 209; NN. (Cat. No. 147), 79, 120, 209; NN. (Cat. No. 148), 68, 210; NN. (Cat. No. 149), 68, 154, 207, 211; NN. (Cat. No. 150), 68, 200, 210, 211
New York, The Metropolitan Museum of Art, no. 11.150.21 (Cat. No. 110), 131, 159, 181; no. 11.150.26 (Cat. No. 101), 107, 174; no. 21.9.3 (Cat. No. 5), 54, 57, 92, 93; no. 21.9.4 (Cat. No. 20), 54, 57, 90, 92, 106, 117; no. 21.9.13 (Cat. No. 119), 98, 120, 188; no. 21.9.469, 21.9.573, 21.9.597, and 21.9.604 (all part of Cat. No. 18), 38, 56, 79, 104, 109, 110, 115; no. 23.3.33, 153; no. 26.2.47, 183; no. 26.7.1339-43, 192; no. 26.7.1395 (Cat. No. 3), 53, 64, 91; no. 26.7.1396 (Cat. No. 21), 58, 107; no. 27.6.1 (Cat. No. 76), 37, 151; no. 31.114.1 (Cat. No. 105), 177; no. 47.57.2 (Cat. No. 169), 41, 217, 220; no. 50.6, 168; no. 66.99.34 (Cat. No. 97), 64, 169; no. 66.99.37 (Cat. No. 170), 41, 217, 220; no. 66.99.40 (Cat. No. 15), 53, 63, 101; no. 66.99.41 (Cat. No. 14), 77, 100; no. 68.134 (Cat. No. 46), 125
Newberry, P., 184, 188
Nims, C., 135, 143
Nubia, 16
Nubians, representations of, 120, 124, 141, 142, 143, 195
Nubian wig, 54, 109, 120, 182; Akhenaten, 96, 103, 113, 217; commoner, 143, 199; Nefertiti, 104, 109, 110, 120, 126, 192; princess, 177, 193, 194; with sidelock, 196, 197
Nursing scene, 119
Nyuserre, 37

Obelisks, 14, 37
Officials, 11, 14, 18, 40, 198, 204
Ointment, cone, 119, 205; spoon, 183
Old Kingdom influence, 181, 208
Opet, feast of, 202
Osirian rites, 25, 26
Osiris, 76, 100; tomb of, 18
Oxford, Ashmolean Museum, no. 1893.1-41(71) (Cat. No. 31), 20, 54, 77, 116, 127, 163; no. 1893.1-41(75) (Cat. No. 49), 38, 70, 127; no. 1893.1-41(171) (Cat. No. 50), 128; no. 1893.1-41(260), 163; no. 1893.1-41(267) (Fig. 20), 38, 39, 49, 55; no. 1922.92 (Cat. No. 155), 139, 214; no. 1924.162, 130; no. 1933.1209 (Cat. No. 157), 215

Painting, 38, 48, 49, 52, 55, 73
Panehsy, house of, 132, 158, 205; tomb of, 127, 128
Panther skin, on boat, 135, 194
Parapets, alabaster, 56, 61, 72
Parennefer, tomb of, 34, 40, 62, 72, 203
Paris, Galerie Maspero, NN. (Cat. No. 80), 71, 154, 208
Paris, Musée du Louvre, no. A.F. 6757-6758, 97; no. E. 11076 (Fig. 43), 64, 65; no. E. 11624 (Cat. No. 56), 38, 47, 49, 68,

76, 77, 134, 165; no. E. 14373, 156;
no. E. 14715 (Fig. 50), 118, 178;
no. E. 15593 (Figs. 39-40), 63, 64, 102, 159;
no. E. 17357 (Cat. No. 86), 58, 158;
no. E. 25409 (Cat. No. 22), 54, 64, 82, 90,
108; no. E. 26103-26104, no; no. N. 831
(Fig. 29), 48, 49, 63, 64, 66
Pasi, inscription of, 184
Pastoral scene, 71
Perring, J. S., 37
Pet sign, 99, 205
Petrie, W.M.F., 37, 38, 56, 57, 90, 91, 105, 115,
116, 174, 217
Philadelphia, The University Museum,
University of Pennsylvania, no. E 14349
(Cat. No. 106), 64, 108, 123, 178;
no. E 16230 (Fig. 35), 57, 58
Piankhy, 213
Plants, representation of, 165; doum palm,
216; grain, 165; grape vine, 156, 200;
mandragora, 216; marguerite, 215; olive
branch, 209; pomegranate, 131
Plectrums, 149
Portraiture, 43, 46. *See also* Masks
Pottery, 213
Priesthood, 12, 16, 17. *See also* Min; Re;
Re-Atum
Princesses, portrait characteristics, 54, 55;
representations of, 49, 56, 63; Nos. 16, 32,
53, 90, 106 (?), 122, 123, 128, 129, 130 (?)
Private sculpture, 181
Ptah, 61; high priest of, 16, 61
Pylon. *See* Karnak

Quibell, J., 180
Ramesses II, 27, 37, 38
Ramesses III, 67, 154, 207
Ramesseum, 28, 139
Ramose, 16; not at Tell el Amarna, 48;
representation of, 54; tomb of, 29, 34, 35,
40, 48, 50, 51, 72, 76, 109, 195
Re, 14, 17, 18, 24; priesthood, 17
Re-Atum, priesthood, 12, 17
Red Crown, 94
Re-Herakhty, 17, 18, 22, 28, 99; as falcon, 20,
24, 50, 67; priest of, 97
Rekhmire, 14
Reshep, 13
Richmond, The Virginia Museum of Fine
Arts, no. 61.5 (Cat. No. 140), 70, 204
Roeder, Günther, 46, 193, 194, 195

San Diego, San Diego Museum of Man,
no. 14881 (Cat. No. 141), 205
Saqqara, 43, 46, 61, 197, 213; provenance,
Nos. 152 (?), 154 (?)
Saw, ceremonial, 214; No. 156
Scarab, Amenhotep III, 67; Amenhotep IV,
126
Sculptor's models, 43, 56, 63; Nos. 12, 115,
121
Serabit el Khadim, 174
Sesebi, 22
Seshat, 69
Sety I, 73
Shawabtis, Akhenaten, 40, 41, 217; Nos.
161-175; Nefertiti, 41; Smenkhkare, 41;
Tutankhamen, 41, 219
Shed, 205
Sheduf, 133
Shety, stela of, 205
Shields, 121, 133, 139
Ship. *See* Boat
Shu, 24
Shuppiluliumash, 27
Sidelock, princesses, 72, 102, 103, 117, 118,
131, 137, 165, 178, 185; Syrian, 135;
with Nubian wig, 196, 197; with short
wig, 118, 123, 124
Simpson, W. K., 104
Sinai, 105, 174
Sistrum, 34, 70, 76, 103, 114, 116, 118, 127,

137, 161, 178, 185, 192, 193, 195
Sitamun, 16
Skin color of women, 105, 177
Sleep, representations of, 71, 73, 141, 145
Smenkhkare, 25, 26, 54, 61, 126, 193, 215;
representations of, Nos. 98 (?), 101 (?),
114, 120, 126 (?); tomb of, 41, 62
Smiting scenes, 12, 49, 67, 133, 135; queen,
135
Sobekhotep, tomb of, 53
Solar cult, 12, 14, 17
Soldiers, 12, 55, 121, 141
Soleb, 16; temple of Amenhotep III, 12
Sotepenre, 20
Spears, 121, 139, 194
Sphinx, 67; No. 13; female, 54; Great, 18
Statues. *See* Composite statues
Statues represented in relief, 55, 97, 155, 174
Stela, family, 38, 47, 49, 56, 68, 72, 76;
Nos. 16, 56; private, 205; No. 141.
See also Tell el Amarna, Boundary stela
Sudan, 22, 202
Sun temples, 37, 53, 207
Sunshade bearers, 124, 202
"Sunshade" kiosks, 22, 24, 25, 67, 69, 99,
137, 174
Sword, 13
Syria, 11, 16, 24

Talatat, 28, 29, 37, 38, 48, 50, 51, 52, 62, 67,
97, 111, 124
Tambourines, 198
Technique, relief, 29, 40, 52, 58, 70, 79;
sculpture, 40, 46, 58, 117
Tell el Amarna, 11, 22, 25, 27, 28, 34, 37, 48,
57, 58, 76, 79, 97
Boundary stela: 40, 41, 49, 55, 56, 64, 72,
98, 104
Stela A, 34, 48, 116, 131, 162; Stela B,
34, 48, 117; Stela K, 22, 34, 48; Stela
M, 22, 34, 48; Stela N, 34, 94, 95, 114,
117, 120, 162. *See also* under Cat. 8
(Buffalo 37:6) and Cat. 28 (Kansas
City 44-65); Stela P, 117; Stela Q, 34,
117; Stela S, 34, 35, 61, 117; Stela U,
34, 117; Stela X, 20, 34, 48. *See also*
Stela, family
Dump, 37, 90, 92, 125; Great Palace, 22,
37, 38, 56, 112, 115, 126, 128, 144, 155,
215; Great Temple, 22, 76
Houses:
no. 49,20, 213; no. N48,15, 90;
no. O47,15, 185; no. P47,1, 160;
no. P47,2, 160, 166, 167, 171, 176, 179,
180, 182; no. P47,1-3, 43, 61, 173, 182;
no. P49,1, 132; no. P49,6, 159;
no. Q44,1, 168; no. R44,2, 205;
no. R45, 188; no. S33,1, 214; no. T.68,
177; no. U36,20, 157; no. U36,37, 157;
no. U37,22, 157
Maru Temple, 22, 137, 214; private shrines,
47, 76, 102, 132; private tombs, 12, 40,
63, 70, 73, 121, 139, 148, 149, 198, 203,
205; Provenance, Nos. 1, 2, 3, 4, 5, 8,
9 (?), 10 (?), 12, 14 (?), 15, 16 (?), 18,
20, 21 (?), 24, 28, 29, 31, 32, 33, 34, 35,
38, 46 (?), 48, 49, 50, 52, 53 (?), 54, 56,
59, 60, 62 (?), 70 (?), 72 (?), 76, 80 (?),
84, 85, 86 (?), 87, 88, 89 (?), 90, 91, 94,
95, 96, 99, 100, 101 (?), 102 (?), 103,
104 (?), 105, 106 (?), 107, 108, 109, 111,
112, 113, 115, 119, 120 (?), 121, 134, 141,
143, 151, 153, 154 (?), 155, 157, 158, 161,
162, 163, 164, 165, 166 (?), 167, 168, 169,
170, 171, 172, 173, 174, 175. *See also*
Hermopolis, provenance
Royal tomb, 24, 40, 56, 71, 73, 207, 217;
sculptor's workshops, 43; zoological
garden, 212
Temples, foundation of, 70; represented in
relief, 70, 142, 155, 156
Tety, 180

Texts, phonetic spelling, 24, 27; vernacular,
14
Thebes, 12, 16, 26, 28, 40, 48, 52, 61, 67, 72,
109, 158; temples of Aten, 17, 28; Valley of
the Kings, 62. *See also* Karnak; Luxor
Thoth, 69
Tia (royal nurse), 196
Tilapia nilotica (*bolti* fish), 213
Tiy (wife of Ay), 62
Tiye, 16, 40, 48, 135; at Amarna, 24, 174;
family, 17; portrait characteristics, 107,
174; representations of, 62, 107, 135, 174;
Nos. 19, 21 (?), 30 (?), 101; sarcophagus,
25; shrine, 25, 62; tomb of, 40
Toledo, The Toledo Museum of Art, no. 25.744
(Cat. No. 151), 212
Trial piece, 98; Nos. 9, 10, 38, 59, 119
Tribute bearers, 24, 77
Trinity, divine, 68, 102, 134
Tutankhamen, 20, 26, 27, 54, 55, 67, 68, 69,
76, 194; at Karnak, 67; at Tell el Amarna,
197; representations of, 168, 182, 197;
Nos. 96 (?), 98 (?), 120 (?); sarcophagus,
73; tomb of, 62, 104, 200
Tutankhaten, later Tutankhamen, 26, 27
Tuthmose (chief sculptor), 43, 46, 56, 63,
66, 191
Tuthmosis III, 162
Tuthmosis IV, 17, 18
Tuthmosis, Prince, brother of Amenhotep IV,
16
Tutu, representation of, 97; tomb of, 62
Tuyere, 141, 145
Tuyu, 16

Uraeus, 20, 64, 69, 96, 101, 102, 104, 105, 110,
111, 113, 115, 116, 126, 132, 135, 136, 165,
168, 184, 185, 188, 190, 193, 214, 217, 218,
219, 220; changed from single to double,
105
User-Seth, No. 62
Ushabits. See Shawabtis

Was sign, 97, 104
Washington, D.C., Collection of Mr. J. S.
Thacher, NN. (Cat. No. 166), 41, 217, 219
Weben Aten (chapel), 112, 118
Weert, Collection of Mr. H. E. Smeets,
NN. (Cat. No. 32), 34, 116, 117
White Crown, 28, 94, 97
Wig. *See* Nubian wig
Wilbour, Charles Edwin, 190
Wilkinson, Gardner, 40
Window of Appearances, 51, 70, 76, 77, 109;
No. 63

Yaya, No. 141
Yuti (chief sculptor of Tiye), 105
Yuya, 16, 17, 19, 54

Zarnikh, 28